Experimental

HSM Hopkins Studies in Modernism
Douglas Mao, *Series Editor*

Experimental

American Literature and the Aesthetics of Knowledge

Natalia Cecire

Johns Hopkins University Press
Baltimore

Printed in the United States of America on acid-free paper
9 8 7 6 5 4 3 2 1

Johns Hopkins University Press
2715 North Charles Street
Baltimore, Maryland 21218-4363
www.press.jhu.edu

Cataloging-in-Publication Data is available from the Library of Congress.

A catalog record for this book is available from the British Library.

ISBN-13: 978-1-4214-3376-9 (hardcover)
ISBN-13: 978-1-4214-3377-6 (paperback)
ISBN-13: 978-1-4214-3378-3 (ebook)

Johns Hopkins University Press uses environmentally friendly book materials, including recycled text paper that is composed of at least 30 percent post-consumer waste, whenever possible.

Contents

Preface

There is no such thing as experimental writing, and this is a book about it.[1] When I began this project as a graduate student in the San Francisco Bay Area, several years ago, I quite understandably believed that experimental writing was A Thing, with an intellectual genealogy crossing the sciences and the arts that I could, with enough pluck, trace. I thought I could historicize American experimentalism by picking up the trail that Language writers, including a beloved advisor, had left me: Pound, Stein, Williams, Zukofsky, Olson, Creeley, Coolidge, okay. I assumed that this would involve a forward-moving trajectory and a single, contiguous historical period, albeit with isolated antecedents further in the past. What I learned was: yes and no.

"Experimental" is a word that still has enormous power and meaning; it does work. In that sense, it's A Thing. The argument of this book, though, is that the work "experimental" does is bound up in a series of ideologies about writing, language, aesthetics, politics, knowledge, science, and above all, modernity, many of which have been seriously thrown into question by the people who think about each of these things for a living. As a consequence, this book on one hand maps the ideologies that gave experimentalism its power and, on the other hand, argues that, in fact, much of the work that "experimental" does is not tenable, or shouldn't be.

Let's take science, just for starters—a contentious, emotionally charged concept that carries twin connotations of virtue and danger. The consensus among historians of science is that science is, well, historical. That means, in particular, that it's not autonomous, not isolated from the material conditions under which it's conducted, the politics of who is allowed to do it or whose observations are counted as legitimate and whose are not, or the social conditions that shape what does and does not look like verification in a particular place and time. Bruno Latour's pithy formulation of this principle is that "we have never been modern"—by which he means that nature has never been separable from culture.[2] That's easy enough to accept in the abstract, but the implications are slightly more challenging: that there is no scientific result that is not at least in part a result of the historical conditions that made it; that we can hope for goodness in the sciences but never purity, never autonomy. This doesn't square with the formalist account of "the" scientific method that many of us were taught in school or the earnest belief that (Western, modern) science "carv[es] nature at its joints" (usually because it "works," as evidenced in consumer technologies—never mind that many other things also "work").[3] So when, in literature, "experimental" is used to mean "scientific" (in whatever sense), often what is happening is that aesthetic autonomy is being snuck in through the back door in the form of scientific autonomy—an autonomy that never really existed. And more: our belief in scientific autonomy is a historical product of several processes, including nineteenth- and twentieth-century pro-science advocacy that aimed to formalize and institutionalize these knowledge practices as authoritative. I am not saying anything new to even a casual reader of history of science by pointing this out; I am only considering its logical consequences for literary history. Insofar as it operates as a proxy for aesthetic autonomy, we can therefore understand the making of scientific autonomy as part of the history of literary experimentalism.

My aim in this book, then, is not so much to offer an account of what experimentalism "really" means as to examine where we get the idea that it means anything in the first place—or why we would want literature to do epistemological work at all. The question that I most wish to unfold across these chapters is why "experimental" means "good," when it does mean good (which it often does). When does "experimental" mean aesthetically good, epistemologically good, politically good—and when does it mean making one kind of goodness a proxy for, or guarantee of, another?

My method is more or less to take Language writing and the "experimental" discourse around it at its word when it claims that certain early twentieth-century writers were experimental, to ask what that means, and to ask what made that writing available to such a reading—without, however, endorsing the implications of calling these works experimental, with an analytical (indeed, critical) eye toward the virtues of experimentalism. I focus almost entirely on early twentieth-century writers (sometimes dipping back into the Gilded Age) who have come to be canonized as "experimental," with a few edge cases. Ezra Pound, Gertrude Stein, and William Carlos

Williams, who appear in chapters 2, 3, and 5, are central figures in the standard story of who is an experimental American writer. A few others are edge cases or typically appear in different discourses: Stephen Crane and Jacob Riis, considered alongside Pound; Gottlob Frege, considered alongside Stein; Marianne Moore, readily admitted to the "experimental" canon when named but almost never considered central, whom I examine alongside the choreographer Busby Berkeley and a few others in chapter 4. In this way, I take three pillars of a retrospective genealogy created in the 1970s and 1980s and fill around them with contemporaries who seem to me to be part of the same pattern.

It is important to note that none of these writers called themselves experimental with any regularity. Instead, something about their writing, thinking, and historical milieu made them a usable past for later writers who were very much invested in the idea of being experimental. My approach, then, understands these writers' experimentalism palimpsestically, as belonging in part to their moment and in part to the way that they were later read (and misread). In this, I build on Leif Sorensen's insightful exploration of the ways that literary "recovery" produces objects that are of two periods at once—the period of their making and that of their recovery. I understand the experimental "lineage" as a recovery project, parallel to but distinct (often excruciatingly distinct) from feminist, Black, Chicano, and other recovery projects. I thus read this early twentieth-century writing in relation to the epistemic virtues that it performs, which are, I argue, the key to understanding how the idea of experimental writing came to function in such contradictory ways. In particular, epistemic virtues explain why experimentalism so often succeeds in confusing varieties of goodness, such that the "politics of form" could, for a time, come to be associated more with the writers I study here—writers whose politics generally range from muddled to terrible—than, say, more overtly political writers such as Lucille Clifton or Adrienne Rich.

Epistemic virtues organize this book and help to unfold the bases on which experimental writing has been valorized. I borrow the term "epistemic virtue" from the historians of science Lorraine Daston and Peter Galison, who in their 2007 monograph on objectivity explain it as a value containing ethical as well as epistemological valences. The performance of epistemic virtue works to bring specific practices under the sign of science (that is, knowledge with a privileged purchase on reality). "Objectivity," for example, is never neutral; in the production of scientific knowledge, objectivity is usually seen as an abstract good, but its manifestations in methods, practices, equipment design, bodily postures, attitudes, and feelings may vary widely in ways that reflect on the person (or persons or actor-networks) in whom objectivity is invested. There are always slippages, Daston and Galison argue, between "objectivity" in the abstract and the objective scientist, who is rendered a certain kind of *good person* by way of being a good scientist. Epistemic virtues merge epistemology with ethics, thus giving an appearance of consistency to the messy, overlapping, sometimes contradictory practices and values through which scientific knowledge is made. Moreover, epistemic virtues can radically conflict with one another—indeed, even different versions of objectivity can conflict with one another. For example, in one scenario of scientific practice, epistemic virtue may take the form of adherence to a standardized model, allowing the isolation of particular variables, and in another, it may take the form of sensitivity to individual cases. Such practices are very differently "scientific." Yet such disparate practices are given consistency by their abstraction into epistemic virtue. Practices that are good for generating knowledge about specific phenomena in specific settings and disciplinary discourses, when perceived as evidence of epistemic virtue, come to appear as portable and free-floating indices of epistemological rigor in entirely different contexts. Thus when the synthetic virtue of flash, as exemplified in Gilded Age social-scientific population thinking, is deracinated from the intellectual and material challenges that give rise to it, it comes to appear as if it were of a piece with the nearly antithetical analytical virtue of precision. Both are "experimental."

The point I am making about epistemic virtues looks like a banal one when we widen the frame: the trappings of Western scientific modernity, of which the epistemic virtues that guarantee scientific knowledge are only a part, have often been represented as unexceptionable sites of virtue, an elevation that depends on abjecting the unmodern (natural, religious, animistic, magical, "traditional," "folk," amateur, craft) in predictably racialized, gendered, sexualized, and imperialist ways.[4] Grasping this point is essential for understanding this book, but it is not *the* point of this book. Rather, I aim to explain how epistemic virtues in action enable this move, why experimental writing is so deeply indebted to epistemic virtue's abstracting function, and how we might begin to discuss specific experimental works' epistemological commitments in more nuanced terms, while also acknowledging the broader uses to which they have been put.

Epistemic virtue's ability to abstract diverse specific practices into seemingly commensurate "scientific" ideals explains why US literary experimentalism can appear to constitute a semi-unified genealogy and, at the same time, be so difficult to pin down in light of its sheer heterogeneity. Epistemic virtue can create slippages, I argue, across not only epistemology and ethics but also politics and aesthetics. For epistemic virtues must manifest in material practices, and they therefore have aesthetic qualities and political effects, even if they are then enclosed in values most legible as epistemology and ethics. The material practices through which objectivity is performed, for example, may differ aesthetically from those that perform precision. Literary experimentalism is not science (and it is not, as some critics have tendentiously claimed, an "alternative" science either); rather, it has retrospectively used some of the same coherency-making tactics, drawing on epistemic virtues to make wildly varying practices theoretically consistent. We can locate epistemic virtues in the writing of early twentieth-century writers who have been retrospectively made into the experimental "canon"; as an entire cottage industry in modernist studies has successfully shown, there was no shortage of engagement with the sciences in early twentieth-century American writing, and indeed, much of this book is devoted to elaborating that engagement, which I see as much more crucially located in the social and biological sciences than in the more canonical physical sciences. But as I argue in chapter 1, "Experimental," the epistemic virtues that I examine in this book did not take on their coherency-making function *for literature* until writers in the later twentieth century started telling a story of experimental writing in the United States, one that is related to, but distinct from, ideas of experimentalism in film, theater, music, or the plastic arts.

This book is organized around epistemic virtues, then, yet epistemic virtues cannot exist on their own. Rather, they manifest materially and ramify affectively. To put it another way, epistemic virtues work through aesthetics, linking sensory experience with feeling under the sign of epistemological guarantee. Consequently, two further threads run across each chapter: mediation and affect. Each epistemic virtue that I examine, within the period on which I focus, correlates to privileged modes of mediation and representation that act as the material trace of those virtues' performance, whether the chiaroscuro of Pound's flash, the resolute anti-visuality of Stein's objectivity, the top-down ("aerial" or "lapidary") views of Moore's precision, or the serial logic of Williams's contact. Especially in writing that is "experimental" but in no meaningful way an instance of (scientific) "experiment," epistemic virtue is performed not through some punctual authorial act at the writing's imagined moment of genesis but rather via forms whose histories make them legible markers of epistemological stability—the "luminous detail," so-called broken grammar, Moore's intensified hypotaxis; in short, the range of forms that have, despite their extreme diversity, historically come to constitute the "look" of literary experimentalism. That epistemic virtues can conflict accounts for the wide and at times conflicting formal qualities that take on "experimental" associations. And while epistemic virtues secure knowledge, their status as virtues and their mediation by material forms means that they also have affective resonances. For example, flash can engender epiphanic rapture, while precision is a virtue that easily slips into pathology, looking just this side of neurotic—tense, yet not exciting. Moreover, such affects may "leak": the anxiety that is precision's concomitant is thus often attributed to its efficient cause, the "precise" author. I would resist any schematic taxonomy of epistemic virtues' aesthetic faces—I have examined some and not others in this book. But it is crucial, I think, to acknowledge that experimental writing, though often conversant with knowledge practices that we currently think of as "scientific" (whether institutionalized or not) *is not science* (whether institutionalized or not). Its purchase on knowledge is often abstract and more bound up in knowledge practices' affective and representational norms than in their specific methods or knowledge claims. This is not to diminish the epistemological aspirations of experimental writing, however—after all, affective and representational norms are as integral to knowledge practices as methods and claims. Attending to mediation and affect allows me to track the ways that epistemological security can be invoked without necessarily being in any literal sense achieved.

Chapter 1, "Experimental," analyzes the many meanings of "experimental" writing in our present moment, separating its broad resonances and affinities with other arts from the more specific actor networks that have led (for example) to what Wai Chee Dimock has called the "puzzling" "presence of Amiri Baraka but not Rita Dove, Lyn Hejinian but not Robert Hass, Samuel Delany but not Derek Walcott" on the avowedly experimental-oriented online poetry audio archive PennSound.[5] These are not, of course, puzzling patterns to anyone familiar with contemporary US poetry, even if they are not patterns upon which we can universally agree. The difference between the capaciousness almost to emptiness of the many definitions of experimental writing and the predictability of its realization in canons, anthologies, archives, and citations—names that are either on the list or not on the list—gives rise to a tacit contest over whether "experimental" is really some combination of epistemological, political, and formal, on one side, or whether it is social (depending on friendship networks, on coteries, on small press and publishing infrastructures, etc.), on the other.

Chapter 1 explains why it is both: the epistemological, political, and formal are themselves social. To take seriously the epistemological and political concerns of experimental writing, then, is to take seriously their embeddedness in social structures across multiple historical moments. This chapter historicizes experimentalism through the kind of double period that characterizes literary recovery. I revisit the historical period that was made the locus classicus of experimentalism (the early twentieth century) by writers of a later period (the 1970s and 1980s). It is easy to see why the epistemological concerns of the early twentieth century might be of interest to writers seeking to frame an "experimental" trajectory, but that designation—and the specificities of who is on the list and who is not—came later. The real and complex epistemological concerns of select early twentieth-century writers was reread by Language writers (and fellow travelers) through the concerns of a post-Vietnam skepticism of a state-dominated account of scientific modernity that had been badly compromised by its complicity with, and facilitation of, violent atrocity. In critiquing Cold War state ideology, late twentieth-century experimental writers aimed to challenge the very foundations of what was widely posited to be legible and true. Experimental writing's challenge to state knowledge privileged language and communication as a mode of world making and thus took on resonances in the language arts, poetry in particular, that were less salient in other artistic domains. Yet that challenge relied, ultimately, on a fantasy of scientific autonomy that was itself historical, arising from the early twentieth century's actual epistemological volatility, especially as the social and biological sciences found ways to become "experimental" without necessarily doing what, in some of the physical sciences, looked like canonical "experiments." The social power of epistemic virtues aided in making these diverse practices legible as coherent guarantees of knowledge.

In chapter 2, I describe an epistemic virtue so rarely named (despite its ubiquity) that I have had to come up with a name for it, "flash." Flash is the ability to partially yet absolutely sufficiently metonymize a data sublime. It is an epistemic virtue because it combines an epistemological desideratum—a comprehensive and accurate view of the whole—with an ethico-political desideratum, the ability to see the "big picture." To master flash is to "have vision." Data visualizations that promise to show you why the American health-care system is the way it is "in one chart" exhibit flash; what has come to be called the gross domestic product (GDP), always an approximation of a vast thing in motion appearing as a single number, also exhibits flash.[6] Flash delimits space and freezes time, just for an instant, giving a picture of the whole while simultaneously signaling that the whole cannot be pictured (remains sublime). It is the epistemic virtue of biopolitics, in effect, rendering populations tractable without relinquishing their intractability, and it took on cultural currency over the course of the nineteenth century as social science transformed itself and professionalized. And thus, too, it is an epistemic virtue of the mass, always epistemologically suspect for both its spectacularity and its associations with the crowd.

Yet flash need not be quantitative: it is evident, too, in the rendering of the individual human face as a metonym for a body and the tacit population (a family tree, a sequence of environments, a history of racial origins and diseases and traits) that every body represents in late nineteenth-century social science. "Flash" thus resituates what we know about Ezra Pound's poetics—its "luminous detail," its ideogrammic method, its "Dichten = condensare"—in the ways that flash, as an epistemic virtue, was performed in Gilded Age American writing and social thinking, especially in Stephen Crane's hyper-condensed short fiction and poetry and the social reformer Jacob Riis's "flashes from the slums" of New York. Pound's immediate references may have included engineers like Enrico Marconi, but his population thinking and his sense of how—and why—to capture the uncapturable had much more in common with eugenicists like Francis Galton and Karl Pearson. The slippage that epistemic virtue always contains means that, in securing knowledge, Pound's poetics also acquired a patina of ethical and political virtue (as, indeed, did eugenics proper in its moment). The case of Pound illustrates just how powerful epistemic virtues can be in conflating different registers of virtue, as well as the urgency of disarticulating those registers when analyzing the politics of literary form.

In chapter 3, "Objectivity," I take up the virtue most widely addressed and problematized in feminist science studies in relation to the writer most frequently named as an experimental progenitrix, Gertrude Stein. Stein had the good and bad fortune to have studied with some of the leading scientific minds of her day, including William James at Harvard and the eminent eugenicist physician and anatomist Lewellys Barker at the Johns Hopkins Medical School. Stein did a summer at Woods Hole and was a beneficiary of a boom in (elite white) women's education near the end of the nineteenth century. For this reason, Stein has often been read in relation to the sciences, with critics awkwardly establishing her scientific bona fides through her proximity to institutional authority and the men who held it. (Indeed, in *The Autobiography of Alice B. Toklas*, Stein did the same.)

I am not interested in establishing Stein as a "real" scientist, however; in many ways she was a bad one, although what it meant to be a good scientist in psychology and neuroanatomy was very much contestable in the 1890s. Rather, I examine Stein's laboratory and literary practices in relation to objectivity, a profoundly gendered epistemic virtue, focusing especially on early fictions like "Melanctha." Objectivity seeks to create independence from a knowing subject; in its aspiration toward portability, it is crucially concerned with communication yet also profoundly distrusts conventional forms of communication through natural language and heuristics. For Stein, I argue, a fascination with the possibility of objectivity ultimately exceeded its practicability in any empirical setting, making her turn to grammatical systems a better site for working through objectivity's gendered, embodied, and ambivalent implications. Stein's writing and its gravitation toward systems of formal logic shows how situationally objectivity operates as a virtue.

In chapter 4, "Precision," I think across the aesthetics of precision dancing (for example, in the Ziegfeld Follies and the choreography of Busby Berkeley), natural history, and Marianne Moore's poetry. Precision is as much an edge case for experimentalism as Moore is: it is an epistemic virtue, yet its guarantees are too local to stand on their own, and precision for its own sake risks reversing figure and ground. In this sense, it can be seen as flash's opposite number, guaranteeing not the sufficiency of the part but the infinite etiolation of the whole. Catherine Gallagher notes how "form as structure comes into view only from a distance; form as style requires unusually close proximity"; flash and precision thus each engage what we might call the form of life via distinct understandings of "form."[7] If flash can look culpably popular, precision can look culpably recondite, culpably elite; yet both perform what Michael Taussig has called the "labor of the negative," managing the ways that some things must be known and other things must just as surely and publicly not be known.[8] If flash is a face, precision is a pussy. Precision, I argue, takes a bomb's-eye view, analyzing by morcellizing its (as it were) target. Murdering to dissect, precision is thus a virtue that easily develops into a vice, threatening to exceed nature's demands and instead impose an unnatural law that must be adequated—a normativity so narrow as to become pathological. In that sense, precision runs toward the ancillary, irrelevant, and above all *technical*, adducing detail that is both a guarantee and a sign of its own irrelevance.

This quality of relying on its own irrelevancies as epistemic guarantee renders precision a virtue marked by disturbing aporias of feeling or erotism: precision fails to titillate, as disclosure and even violence turn out to be not revealing but tedious, pedantic. As Edmund Wilson complained in the *Dial* (to which Moore was then a contributor and which she would soon edit) in 1923, "The ballet at the Ziegfeld Follies is becoming more and more like a military drill: to see a row of girls descend a flight of stairs in a deliberate and rigid goose-step is not my idea of what ballet ought to be; it is like watching setting-up exercises."[9] Precision hints at, and sometimes literally produces, a capacity for violence (the military drill, the goose step) that is nonetheless not only unsexy but somehow even self-disqualifying, as the actual performance takes on the boring quality of the kind of calisthenic exercise that one does as preparation for the real thing. In that sense, precision also operates as a queer virtue, a deviant normativity whose epistemology of the closet constantly discloses all the technical details and yet seems to withhold satisfaction all the same.

Chapter 5, "Contact," examines a virtue of immediacy, the virtue that, for William Carlos Williams, enabled a sense of indigeneity that produced an "American language" and an American style and the virtue that, in the same period, underwrote anthropology's turn to participant observation and fieldwork. Contact is a virtue of intimacy and involvement, and just as flash and precision each take up problematics of privacy and revelation, contact operates in a dyad with objectivity, infusing the same questions of communicability with the very metaphysics of presence that objectivity aims to eschew. With its investment in touching and bodily involvement and its ability to produce fantasies of nation and culture arising from "soil," contact also speaks to Language writing's hopes, near the end of the twentieth century, for the "materiality of language" and its ability to pierce state ideology, not least through personal contact with Russian writers. Contact evokes simplicity, immediacy, and organic continuity between location and language. Yet, in its seeming neutrality, "contact" elides important power relations, echoing early twentieth-century anthropology's attempts, with mixed success, to efface and correct earlier, epistemologically and ethically inadequate scenes of "first contact" that were compromised by the interests of church, empire, and profit.

I thus situate Williams's recurrence to "contact" in a longer trajectory of palimpsestic attempts to rewrite and replace earlier scenes of violent occupation through new scenes of contact that nonetheless derive their charge from the trace of violences that came before. Thus, in *Spring and All* (1923), "THE WORLD IS NEW" only because it has been destroyed and begun over again. Contact is the epistemic virtue most closely held in common between "experimental" writing and a much different, often politically opposed strand of twentieth-century US literature, science fiction. I compare such gestures to Cold War science fiction's continual rewriting of scenes of benevolent or quasi-benevolent first contact, particularly in Ursula K. Le Guin's *Left Hand of Darkness* (1969) and in the Star Trek franchise (1966–present), and to Michael Davidson, Lyn Hejinian, Ron Silliman, and Barrett Watten's *Leningrad* (1990), which disjunctively chronicles four Language poets' mission of peace at a writers' conference in the USSR. These works reveal contact as far more complex and ambivalent than its claims to organic simplicity would suggest. If experimental writing and science fiction diverge both formally and politically, they often hold in common a belief in a scientific autonomy that is, if not currently possible, the hoped-for logical end point of scientific modernity. A fully realized language of the future, these works hope, will enable difference without violence—epistemic virtues that are fully virtuous, politically and ethically as well as epistemically. Yet the structure of contact shows how indebted epistemic virtues often are to the violences that they disavow. When epistemic virtues act as proxies for political virtue, too often important distinctions are elided.

Finally, a coda, "Future Texts," takes a step back from the aspirations for scientific modernity embedded in experimental writing and considers other paths. Experimental writing as a "white recovery project," as I describe it in chapter 1, accepts the gambit of scientific modernity (or, to put it another way, of racial capitalism) and aims to remake poetics as fully modern. In that sense, it is a strategy that acknowledges the devastating possibilities that result from being consigned to the unmodern: becoming associated with precarious life, surplus, ab-usable or waste life, in the global necropolitical calculus.[10] Experimentalism takes on the strategy that has more recently characterized institutional reactions to the loss of Cold War–era university funding, such as digital humanities: we will concede that the arts of resemblance are, *on the whole*, unmodern and disposable, but *this* version is not; *we* are modern and empirical, and we wear it as a virtue. We renounce superstition and Romanticism as ruses. We are making the world better through the purity of our commitment to secular reality.[11] This is a caricature, but one that captures an underlying, if not always avowed, logic.

Few "experimental" writers, including many Language writers themselves, still find the promise of such a politics of form realizable, or the trade-offs of epistemic virtue tenable, today. If the George W. Bush administration did not sufficiently expose the limits of a poetics of epistemic virtue, increasing pressure within contemporary poetry has brought experimentalism to confront its history of whiteness (or, alternatively, to retroactively include writers of color in histories of experimentalism on the basis of form, even though they were often peripheral to the social coteries and the networks of patronage that benefited many white experimental writers).[12] This confrontation is less a demand for liberal inclusion, however, than a demand to rethink the founding gesture by which literary writers have claimed modernity at the expense of the unmodern. It is not a surprise that nonwhite writers have found it difficult to be read as "experimental," but the quick fix of selecting a few "diverse" faces to sit among the elect misses the more fundamental problem with the way that scientific modernity insists on marking off the elect from the damned, the future-bound from the lagging and "primitive." In that sense, this is a book that comes to bury experimentalism as well as (in some degree) to praise it. Building on Fred Moten and Stefano Harney's notion of unscientific "experiment[s] of hold" and Christina Sharpe's description of "the wake," the coda examines works from Sun Ra's *Space Is the Place* (1974) to Dawn Lundy Martin's *Life in a Box Is a Pretty Life* (2015) to show how some artists have imagined a loosened grasp on secular time and a refusal of liberation insofar as "liberation" means "exception."[13] These writers explore ways toward a future without modernity. As Ishmael Reed wrote in his fantasia of epistemological insecurity, *Mumbo Jumbo*, "We will make our own future Text."[14]

Acknowledgments

The defining condition of this book is the extended period of my search for stable academic employment from 2008-9 to 2013-14. It was an important part of my formation as a scholar, lasting, as it did, nearly as long as my actual PhD, and it materially shaped the ways I could and could not work on this book. I don't wish to recuperate what was basically a horrible experience of instability, endurance, and overwork (and I had it *much* better than most) as some sort of valuable learning opportunity. It was mostly bullshit, and there are a lot of things I would rather not have had to learn. I am also still mad about all the books I lost in the Berkeley-Atlanta move. It has made me very grateful, however, for the many people who have helped me get here. Above all, Lyn Hejinian, Dan Blanton, and Mark Goble, my PhD committee at Berkeley, somehow never seemed to lose faith. They have shaped my thinking and my scholarly practice from the ground up, all the while letting me think that I was shaping myself. Lyn's generous thinking and total integrity have been a model for me. Dan's insightful feedback, endless patience, and unwavering support continue to sustain my scholarship. And Mark's supportive presence and practical attitude have been invaluable. Colleen Lye's brilliance, kindness, and uncannily always correct advice, from my first day of grad school, is one of the things I most value in my life. I am so lucky to have learned from her. Katie Snyder, Ian Duncan, and Oliver Arnold, in their serial capacities as placement directors and well after, all tried to help me get a damn job, often going far above and beyond the call of duty, and I am grateful to all of them for their generosity and persistence. And several senior scholars have offered kindness, opportunities, feedback, and real support—invitations to speak, phone calls, letters of recommendation, intel, and coffee: Deepika Bahri, Robin Bernstein, Joe Cleary, Anna Mae Duane, Jed Esty, Anne Fernald, Jennifer Fleissner, Jackie Goldsby, David Golumbia, Sean X. Goudie, Inderpal Grewal, Dorothy Hale, Noel Jackson, Dan Katz, Jeffrey Knapp, Brian Lennon, Marilee Lindemann, Alan Liu, Meredith McGill, Mark McGurl, Philip Nel, Liesl Olsen, Anthony Reed, Martha Nell Smith, Katie Trumpener, Priscilla Wald, Ken Warren, Karin Westman, and Laura Wexler. Trip Kirkpatrick also deserves special mention not only for his friendship, intellectual prodding, and straight-up tech help but also for the many times he bailed me out when my car got towed in New Haven (*through no fault of my own, I should add*), usually at great inconvenience to him.

Kimberly Q. Andrews, Lindsey Andrews, Tyler Bickford, Julia Bloch, Bart Brinkman, Nihad Farooq, Harris Feinsod, Rachel Galvin, Nicholas Gaskill, Andrew Goldstone, Hillary Gravendyk, Angie Heo, Benjy Kahan (Team Ficus), Lauren F. Klein, Lee Konstantinou, Andrea Lankin, Charles Légère, Miriam Posner, Jenny Rhee, Scott Selisker, Leif Sorensen, Rachel Watson, and Mia You have included me in their intellectual lives, at conferences and virtually, and most of the time, for many of them, while we were up for the exact same jobs. (I still think all the former candidates for that one UCSB job should form a research group, or possibly a journal.) They have read my drafty chapters, heard out both my smartest and my dumbest ideas—usually hopelessly mixed together—and told me which were which, shared their work, and have, through it all, been complete nerds in the best possible way. I am endlessly grateful for their intellectual generosity and personal kindness.

My work on this book has been supported, over the years, by the UC Berkeley Graduate Division, a Roberta C. Holloway Postdoctoral Fellowship in Poetry and Poetics at Berkeley, a postdoctoral fellowship with the Bill and Carol Fox Center for Humanistic Inquiry at Emory University, an American Council of Learned Societies New Faculty Fellowship held in the Department of English at Yale University, the NEH Making Modernism summer seminar at the Newberry Library in Chicago, the First Book Institute at the Center for American Literary Studies at Pennsylvania State University, and the University of Sussex School of English. I am grateful to all of them for the financial and intellectual support that contributed to this book. My labor unions, UAW at Berkeley and UCU at Sussex, have been indispensable sources of support in a career marked by significant instability. I also owe a debt of gratitude to my many colleagues in insecure academic positions, without whom the university would not run and to whom I owe my semester's research leave at the University of Sussex in 2017, which enabled me to complete this book. I am grateful for the work and help of librarians at the Beinecke Library at Yale and Elizabeth Fuller at the Rosenbach Library of the Free Library of Philadelphia, both of which I visited in the course of doing research for this book. Catherine Goldstead and Doug Mao at Johns Hopkins University Press have been unfailingly patient, supportive, and brilliant editors, and I thank them for the many ways that they have made this book better. Carrie Watterson was a brilliant and chill copy editor. Portions of chapters 1 and 5 appeared in an earlier form in "Experimentalism by Contact," *diacritics* 43, no. 1 (Autumn 2015): 6–35. A previous version of portions of chapter 3 appeared in "Marianne Moore's Precision," *Arizona Quarterly* 67, no. 4 (Winter 2011): 83–110. Thanks to those journals for permission to republish that work. Portions of "The Death of the Ball Turret Gunner" by Randall Jarrell are reprinted with the permission of Faber and Faber. Poems from *Life in a Box Is a Pretty Life* are copyright © 2015 by Dawn Lundy Martin and are reprinted with the permission of Nightboat Books. Portions of "An Egyptian Pulled Glass Bottle in the Shape of a Fish," "Marriage," "An Octopus," "Poetry," and "To a Snail" by Marianne Moore and portions of Ketjak by Ron Silliman are reprinted with the permission of University of California Press. Portions of "In Distrust of Merits" and "What Are Years?" are from *The Collected Poems of Marianne Moore* by Marianne Moore. Copyright © 1941, 1944 by Marianne Moore. Copyright renewed 1969, 1972 by Marianne Moore. Reprinted with the permission of Scribner, a division of Simon & Schuster. All rights reserved. A line from Tjanting by Ron Silliman is reprinted with the permission of Salt Publishing. Portions of Leningrad are reprinted with the permission of Mercury House Press.

I am deeply grateful to the units that ultimately gave me an institutional home, the School of English and the Centre for American Studies at the University of Sussex. The academic support staff here, especially Sarah Ayliff, Rebecca Bowe, Emma Carlyle, Anne Crawford, Ahmed Koyes, Grace Ryan, Laura Vellacott, and Liz Walker, have helped me enormously in so many ways. I am also grateful to my academic colleagues in and around Sussex, Caroline Bassett, Sara Crangle, Martin Dines, Beatrice Fazi, Hannah Field, Seb Franklin, Honor Gavin, Andrea Haslanger, Annabel Haynes, Doug Haynes, Michael Jonik, Joe Luna, Chloe Porter, J.D. Rhodes, Katharina Rietzler, Kirsty Rolfe, Arabella Stanger, Keston Sutherland, Helen Tyson, Francesco Ventrella, and Hope Wolf, for their intellectual engagement, support, and friendship. Daniel Kane, Sue Currell, and Maria Lauret, my senior colleagues in American Studies, have been especially helpful, supportive, and insightful. Keston Sutherland and Jenny Greenshields also deserve special thanks for housing me for a solid month after my abrupt move to the UK at a moment when

Brighton flats were thin on the ground. Anne-Marie Angelo has been a supportive and generous friend since we met on the day of my interview, and a great source of UK life tips, laughter, feminist solidarity, and pub quiz outings. Pam Thurschwell, fellow member of the Order of the Sacred Flowchart, has read my chapters and provided me with valued mentorship and free apples; she is also, objectively speaking, the coolest person I know. Rachel O'Connell's genius, wisdom, and personal excellence are inexpressible, and I am grateful to know her every day. Sam Solomon's brain is the Trill slug that gives me life; my debt to him goes well beyond any particular idea, chapter, joke, mycological turn, Lorine Niedecker reading group, *30 Rock* clip, dip, sauce, or curd snack. My Sussex colleagues have given me a place to think and grow.

Special thanks are due to my family, especially Bud and Sylvia Cecire, who have always supported me and, among other things, housed me while I waited for my Tier 2 visa to be processed. My parents, Ken and Veronica Cecire, taught me to read and let me nerd out in a relatively unrestricted fashion from that point on. Maria Traversa is one of the loveliest people on this planet and has helped me in a thousand ways. Maria Cecire is a brilliant colleague as well as an amazing sister and luminous human being. Please read her incredible book, *Re-enchanted*, out now with University of Minnesota Press. This book is for my siblings—Maria, Michael, Joseph, and Bernard.

How do I name everything else that has gone into this book? Bird thoughts from Charlie, Arcadia helping me move (I think multiple times), Hove life with Daniel and Jenny, fruit support from Martin, veg support from J.D., Andrea H., and Tom S., life coaching from Bramble, film criticism from Willa, sneak attacks from my cat nemesis—I'm missing so many people in this list. You know who you are. Thank you.

OK, that's it!

Experimental

Experimental

A screaming comes across the sky. Not a weapon, and yet a weapon: in this film, the scream is an animal cry, redolent with communicative significance yet uninterpretable, and destructive precisely in its signifying potency. It's the inquisitive call of an alien space probe that speaks only the language of the humpback whale. It is never explained why, in *Star Trek IV: The Voyage Home* (1986)—a deeply silly science fiction movie about time-traveling space whales and an oddly trenchant allegory of the linguistic turn—the space probe's version of this message of peace destroys everything it comes near, incapacitating nearby spaceships and apocalyptically boiling Earth's ocean. All we know is that language, when alien enough, has the power to radically, even violently, alter the physical world.[1]

This is not at all coincidentally the aspiration of what has come to be called "experimental writing," and the San Francisco Bay Area in the 1980s—the primary setting of *Star Trek IV*—is also one of the primary junctures at which this particular codification of what it meant to be "experimental" took on currency. "Experimental," in contemporary writing, has long been recognized as a contentious, difficult-to-define, problematic, often openly invidious term, fraught with ethical judgment and strangely resistant to historicization. As Robert Mitchell points out, it often serves, simply, as a term of approval, a sign that a work is interesting or worth reading.[2] Attempts to render the term more specific often look primarily to form, and those that look to history tend to be concerned primarily with notions of chronological priority that can again be routed back to form: newness, innovation, invention—revealing how profoundly "experimental" has come to signify the *formalization*—and dehistoricization—of temporal qualities.[3] I wish to offer an account of US literary experimentalism that registers and explains these tendencies, without altogether accepting their logic. While experimentalism may manifest formally, it only signifies historically.

Though little is agreed about "experimental writing," the term as it has been used for the past few decades has come to name a loose but meaningful set of expectations: political "oppositionality" or ethical stakes, a claim to a kind of "realism" that supersedes the realism of the nineteenth-century literary category that usually goes by that name, the refusal of a "lyric subject," and a special concern with form.[4] It oscillates between a specific canon, sometimes narrow to the point of rigidity, that runs from Pound and Stein through the Objectivists, the New American Poetry, and Language, and a capaciousness unto meaninglessness. "Experimental" also suggests some historical assumptions: its canonical center lies in the early twentieth century, but it is the term to which we turn when we do not wish to limit ourselves to that moment (in contrast with "avant-garde" or "modernist"): "experimental" resists periodization. Tacitly, too, although this has become increasingly contested, "experimental" suggests a white authorship, a feature that I will take seriously and discuss further below. This is the "experimental writing" for which this book seeks to account, not an essence or (still less) a form, I will argue, but rather a historical formation with specific contexts and stakes. The stakes lie in, roughly, the paradox of a world infused by language yet dangerously—life-threateningly—unable to communicate. To put it another way: What do we do when an alien space probe is destroying the Earth itself with the foreign language of whale song?

The Double Period of Experimental Writing

The nuclear aircraft carrier CVN-65, better known as the USS *Enterprise*, was launched from Newport News Shipbuilding in 1960 and was finally retired in 2012. Newport News Shipbuilding, the largest "private" employer in the state of Virginia, naturally relied heavily on military contracts and was (and is) located just across Hampton Roads from Norfolk Naval Base. The *Enterprise* was the US Navy's first wholly nuclear-powered vessel and was deployed to Vietnam in 1965, reportedly launching 151 tons of ordnance on the first day alone.[5] During that deployment, its home base was the naval base at Alameda, California, an island in San Francisco Bay just by the Port of Oakland, where, in 1986, it would play a starring role in *Star Trek IV: The Voyage Home*.[6] The *Enterprise* is an example of a highly successful Cold War technology, drawing on private industry to harness nuclear science for US military power. It would not have been possible without what came to be known as "big science." Big science entailed research conducted on a massive scale by large collaborative teams of scientists from multiple institutions, often at large equipment-intensive facilitators (e.g., particle accelerator facilities), often funded by the Department of Defense, and moved across the military-industrial complex just as ships moved across Hampton Roads between Newport News Shipbuilding and Norfolk Naval Base. As James Capshew and Karen Rader observe, "In addition to the basic ingredients of money, manpower, and machines the media and the military were often seen as essential to the pursuit of Big Science."[7] Big science became the dominant model of scientific research in the United States in the 1940s, with large national laboratories such as Los Alamos and Fermilab established throughout the twentieth century, and it remains so today.[8] The Cold War was a period of particularly close collaboration between US state power and the knowledge-producing fields, not only in the physical sciences or in the production of military force embodied in craft like the *Enterprise*, but also in the social sciences, arts, and humanities.[9]

The emergence of a US "experimental tradition" in the late twentieth century borrows the language, and frequently the epistemic virtues, of the sciences because it seeks to respond to what Jean-François Lyotard called a "crisis of legitimation" in the production of knowledge, especially the sciences. In outlining this emergence, I mean to make a fairly polemical argument, namely that "experimental writing" as it is typically used in contemporary discourse is periodizable; in other words, it should be understood as a historical phenomenon prior to being understood as a set of formal phenomena. I am thus explicitly opposing all readings of the experimental as definable by formal "invention," "discovery," or the "new," much less as punctual "experiments" that conjure forth imagined scenes of composition.[10] These are expressions of the ideology of modernism that should be examined and contextualized, not accepted at face value.[11] That this narrative of ex nihilo formal creation has become so central to the language around experimental writing is indeed a reassertion of a fantasy of scientific knowledge production as in principle independent of the political sphere in the face of its increasing untenability during the Cold War period. Literary experimentalism's resistance to periodization, in other words, is the product of an ideology of scientific autonomy that was consolidated in the twentieth century, precisely under the conditions of science's most direct control by the state. Scientific research not only became more directly and substantially funded by the state, both from civilian and military sources, but also moved to a new, collaborative scale, with hundreds of scientists from multiple institutions working on a given project. Big science, by its very nature, could not sustain fantasies of autonomy or Romantic genius: the scientist became by definition a social and, indeed, political creature.

Further complicating matters, experimentalism's period is a double one. Experimentalism is rooted in the early twentieth century *as reinterpreted by the late twentieth century*, produced by the overlaying of what was present in the early twentieth century with what certain writer-critics of the later twentieth century were ready to see.[12] My point is not to dismiss late twentieth-century accounts of experimentalism as mere projection. Rather, I understand that experimentalism as real in the way that the US border is real: historical, made, not inevitable, continuously contested, and nonetheless extremely consequential. As I discuss in a later section, experimentalism's double period rests on a "recovery" structure. In arguing this, I am in sympathy with nonlinear historical projects proposed by scholars like James Chandler and Ian Baucom, which emphasize repetitive and cumulative historical structures. Carrying forward a Benjaminian sense of history, Baucom identifies the ways in which the "present time" can "inheri[t] its nonimmediate past by intensifying it."[13] To be clear, I do not aspire to assimilate this account of literary experimentalism to the economic *longue durée* that both Baucom and Chandler, in their distinct ways, map out. As I see it, literary experimentalism belongs to a shorter and more modest pattern. Baucom's Benjaminian insistence on the resurgence of "nonimmediate pasts," however, offers a model for thinking through the centrality of early twentieth-century epistemic virtues to a late twentieth-century formation as not merely a formalist aesthetic atavism (as Joshua Clover has provocatively described the "genealogical avant-garde") but as an "intensification."[14]

This is not, of course, to gloss over Clover's incisive critique of the ways in which the recovery structure of experimental writing has promoted reductive diachronic narratives that masquerade as history. As Clover puts it, the "genealogical avant-garde" "*has no choice but to affirm the very cultural continuity which it must also claim to oppose.* Its existence is premised on the continuity of an avant-garde with identifiable generic character"; thus, it must maintain a working theory of its own transhistoricity alongside its avowed commitment to historical change (hence the persistence of the abstractly "oppositional" in experimental discourses). Clover's account comports well with the ways in which experimentalism has often been either treated as purely formal in scope or shoehorned into a sketchy Whig history of "innovations." Indeed, Baucom and Chandler's nonlinear histories bring some insight into the dilemma that Clover diagnoses: both argue that the typicalizing and "case"-weighing imagination embedded in the novel (among other forms) is the sine qua non of historicism.[15] If, as Baucom argues, "historicism's fundamental task is . . . to place objects within their situations *and to invent situations and periods of time in which to place objects*," then to produce situations, characters, and settings *as* typical, as the novel does, is to make historicism possible.[16] Thus the novel (almost always, implicitly or explicitly, the realist novel or historical romance), Chandler and Baucom argue, announces its historical status in part by making available the sense of a period or *status quo*—the sense of *typicality*—on which historicizing gestures must rest. In other words, we historicize the novel because the novel is one of the cultural forms that makes historicization itself possible and, indeed, desirable.

If the novel, as classically theorized, both announces its historicity and produces the cognitive tools with which to historicize itself, however, experimentalism as it is usually understood (including experimental novels) does the reverse, often explicitly dispelling the typical and the "traditional" as its primary self-defining move.[17] In what is nearly always a normative gesture, experimentalism repeatedly produces naive realisms against which it can be framed as atypical, oppositional, and (especially) new, producing its own terms for legibility *as* experimental.

A potted history of American experimental writing—the one I once thought this book would be—might begin with Edgar Allan Poe (whom Paul Grimstad takes up in his *Experience and Experimental Writing*, and whom William Carlos Williams repeatedly identifies as an antecedent), detour through Émile Zola's 1879 essay "The Experimental Novel," and dwell extensively on certain modernists (Pound, Stein, Williams) before heading into Objectivism, Black Mountain College, and the New York School.[18] It would hang together through suspicion of a unitary lyric subject and a commitment to "formal innovation" on the model imagined by Ezra Pound in his "How to Read": literary history as "a twelve-volume anthology in which each poem was chosen . . . because it contained an invention."[19] There is a great deal of use to this history, and there is probably a plausible version of it to be written in the form of "stuff James Laughlin liked." As the founder of New Directions Press, Laughlin—also a poet and a student of Pound (and, later, an active participant in State Department-backed cultural diplomacy)—attempted something like Pound's proposed anthology with his 1936 *New*

Directions in Prose and Poetry and often used "experimental" to describe the work he promoted through his press. Much of the New Directions list, including work by Pound, Williams, H.D., and Zukofsky, remains understood as experimental today. Magazines including the *Egoist* and *Poetry* sometimes advertised themselves as containing "experimental poetry," and the prominent critic Yvor Winters, in his condemnatory *Primitivism and Decadence: A Study of American Experimental Poetry* (1937), uses it to describe a modernism ranging from Pound, Williams, and H.D. to Robinson Jeffers, Hart Crane, T. S. Eliot, and Kenneth Burke.[20] "Experimental" is not an unknown term in the early twentieth century, and its uses are in some ways compatible with later ones. Yet its canonizing function, and the connotations of resistance to a "lyric I" (cf. the *Egoist*!) and commitment to formal and political radicalism that the term would take on, are only diffusely present in the early twentieth century. If later accounts of experimentalism take little notice of Laughlin or Winters, it is perhaps not out of a lack of concern with the early twentieth century (which, as I discuss below, is central to how experimentalism has been understood) but because such figures have played little role in what experimentalism became, and aspired to become. For example, as Greg Barnhisel argues, Laughlin's Ford Foundation–backed journal *Perspectives USA* played "a small but key role in identifying a characteristic American modernism; in directing modernism away from its radical origins toward bourgeois individualism; [and] in transforming modernism from an avant-garde, oppositional movement to a style"—hardly an attractive turn for an experimental forebear.[21] To borrow Marianne Moore's phrase, "Omissions are not accidents"; rather, these omissions instruct us that what is now meant by "experimental" is a retrospective genealogy whose very idiosyncrasies are essential to its force. To amend our contemporary sense of the experimental by insisting on its continuity with earlier, rejected versions would be, in my view, to miss its main sources of rhetorical power, which have rarely if ever been located in Yvor Winters or *Perspectives USA*. A discontinuous history helps to uncover the often dissonant layers that have constituted the power and promise of experimental writing toward the close of the twentieth century.

As Paul Stephens has pointed out, "experimental" only begins to be used frequently to describe in literature in the 1980s, in contrast with experimental music, theater and performance, and film.[22] Out of the 1970s, a concerted and largely successful rewriting of twentieth-century literary history emerged, effected by usually white experimental writers, especially those associated with Language writing, such as Ron Silliman, Barrett Watten, Bob Perelman, Lyn Hejinian, Rae Armantrout, Carla Harryman, and Michael Davidson. Their critical project constructed something like the potted history I have given above: a continuous "experimental tradition" running from Ezra Pound, Gertrude Stein, and imagism through Objectivism and into certain clusters associated with Donald Allen's *New American Poetry* anthology, especially Black Mountain and the New York School.[23] While aesthetic affinities certainly shaped these micropublishing infrastructures, however, they need not have been primary. Daniel Kane, in his archival history of social crossings between punk and New York School poetry, has traced the "messy and fascinating" little magazine ecosystem of 1960s and 1970s New York, demonstrating how central "personal networks" were to the making of a "trajectory from early-modernist magazines . . . to [Harry] Mathew[s] and [John] Ashbery's *Locus Solus*," over and above specific aesthetic or political commitments.[24] Yet by the 1980s, a narrative of "experimental" continuity had emerged. As Charles Bernstein acknowledged in a 2002 interview with Marjorie Perloff, "The radical [read: experimental] modernism I was putting forward in [1983]—poets and poetics—has received much greater acknowledgment since that time, both inside and outside the academy, as the result of the advocacy of many poets, scholars, and editors."[25]

Many of the Language writers, in other words, were (and are) also *critics* whose critical enterprise, concertedly and intentionally revising early twentieth-century American literary history, was integral to the creative one. This project is clearly outlined through the Language writers' voluminous critical writings; for example, in their collaborative 1988 essay "Aesthetic Tendency and the Politics of Poetry: A Manifesto," published in the academic journal *Social Text*, Ron Silliman, Carla Harryman, Lyn Hejinian, Steve Benson, Bob Perelman, and Barrett Watten assert that "beginning with Stein and Zukofsky, and significantly reinforced by the examples of the abstract poems of Frank O'Hara and John Ashbery and the aleatorical texts of Jackson MacLow [*sic*] in the fifties, there has been a continuity of experimental work that foregrounds its status as written language." The work being done here is not only that of naming a canon but also that of producing it as a "continuity" across the twentieth century. Indeed, as Perelman would later put it in *The Marginalization of Poetry*, Language writers were united primarily by their "opposition to the prevailing institutions of American poetry," which were characterized first and foremost by what Perelman describes as a grave literary-critical error: a misreading of the legacy of modernism. "In this situation," he argues,

> modernism was no longer especially important. The discursive tone of later Eliot, the incantatory vaticism of Yeats, the kaleidoscopic novelty of Surrealism minus Marx and Freud, the authoritative common sense and rural cast of Frost (often translated to the suburbs), and an attenuated version of Williams as poet of the quotidian—these echoes might be read everywhere, but the more basic facts of modernism were shunned. The poet as engaged, oppositional intellectual, and poetic form and syntax as sites of experiment for political and social purposes—these would not be found.[26]

Language's critical project was to restore what it saw as modernism's true legacy, whose stakes were simultaneously political and epistemological. Language's modernism—what it sought to reestablish as the more important modernism—produced a poet who was intellectual, and a poem that was experimental. Perloff, an advocate of Language writing, would frame the "two modernisms" theory as "Pound/Stevens: Whose Era?," arguing that "the split goes deep, and . . . raises what I take to be central questions about the meaning of Modernism—indeed about the meaning of poetry itself in current literary history and theory."[27] In *The Poetics of Indeterminacy*, Perloff elaborates one side of this "split" as "the new literalism," comprising a list of what are by now many of the usual suspects: Pound, Stein, Williams, Cage, and others.[28] As Jerome McGann put it in an early and influential account of the political stakes of experimental writing, "As Frost, Yeats, Auden, and Stevens are the 'precursors' of the poets of accommodation, Pound, Stein, and especially Zukofsky stand behind the L=A=N=G=U=A=G=E writers."[29] This is why "experimental" writing overlaps with and finds its center of gravity in modernism and yet is not identical to it: Language's modernism—"experimental" modernism—is a recovery canon constructed concertedly from the 1970s through the turn of the millennium, which sought out the features of modernism best suited to serve as antecedents to post-Vietnam concerns.[30] Although the "recovered" authors cannot reasonably be said to have been obscure in their own moment, understanding them as "experimental" nonetheless means that they share in what Leif Sorensen has identified as the "untimeliness" of recovery, a process in which "the desire that drives recovery fragments the recovered figure."[31] My point is not that experimental writers misread the modernist canon or approached it in an ahistorical, inappropriately desiring way, as if a neutral relation to the past were either possible or a good idea, but rather that such desiring—in this case, the desire for a linguistic practice that would be *good for knowledge*—is built into what it now means to be "experimental." As I will discuss later in this chapter, this amounted to a desire for an *epistemically virtuous* language.

Language: Representing and Intervening

What was the creative project that motivated the critical rewriting of literary modernism? For Language writers, it included an attempt to decenter the authorial voice and the Western subject as such, a resistance to capitalist empire in general and to the legacy of the Vietnam War in particular, and a turn to deconstruction. But why might the rubric of the "experimental" link those concerns? In this section, I outline how the linguistic turn created conditions for valorizing an "experimental" approach to literary language defined by a new understanding of language as able not only to "represent" reality but also to "intervene" in it. While the concerns through which Language aimed to reenvision the history of twentieth-century US literature were patently ethical, political, and aesthetic, they are ultimately traceable to epistemological grounds, or what Lyotard, in 1979, called the "postmodern condition," in response to the rise of a postindustrial knowledge economy.[32]

The long and violent career of the USS *Enterprise* is only an extreme example of the way in which, as Lyotard puts it, "science seem[ed] more completely subordinated to the prevailing powers than ever before," revealing what he calls "a strict interlinkage between the kind of language called science and the kind called ethics and politics."[33] Within that semiotic moment, wherein, as Lyotard points out, "the 'leading' sciences and technologies have had to do with language," the subordination of knowledge production to state violence appeared to be a problem of language, requiring a response in and through language.[34] Language therefore emerged as an active force through which knowledge could be made to facilitate—or oppose—state violence.

For example, in a classic ethnographic essay describing a year (1984–85) spent embedded in a defense strategy center, Carol Cohn corroborates this sense of language's centrality to scientific mastery in the register of nuclear strategy.[35] "When you speak it [defense strategy's specialized language]," she writes, "you feel in control. . . . Learning the language gives a sense of what I would call cognitive mastery; the feeling of mastery of technology that is finally *not* controllable but is instead powerful beyond human comprehension, powerful in a way that stretches and even thrills the imagination."[36] Indeed, linguistic mastery, Cohn argues, became centralized as the proxy and substitute for what was sublimely unknowable: "The 'reality' of which they speak is itself a world of abstractions . . . invented to hold together abstractly, its validity judged by its internal logic."[37] Such a science—one that could speak authoritatively of reality yet was constructed with war as its founding premise—was conducted in and through a *language*. As McGann perceptively put it in 1983:

> The "languages" within which these [experimental] writers live and move and have their being are quite specifically the "languages" of the cold war West after the debacles of the Korean and the Vietnam Wars. . . . In them poetry appears at a crisis of its traditional modes of expression. So false and self-conflicted seem the ordinary public forms of discourse—in the media, the policy organs of government, and the academic clerisy—that the artistic representation of such discourse must either be subjected to their one-dimensionality or it must activate a critical engagement.[38]

Reconstituting modernism's legacy in the terms of an oppositional, knowledge-oriented poetics—as, in other words, a continuous experimental literary trajectory—was a political project that met "the postmodern condition" on its own ground.

In short, the "turn to language" in writing of the late Cold War period responded to a crisis in knowledge that was playing out in explicitly linguistic terms—and not just in the fond imaginations of poets but also in the sciences and in US global policy, whether through the "cultural Cold War" or through the clear imbrications of state power and scientific knowledge inaugurated by big science.[39] The emergence of "experimental" as a privileged term for describing politically engaged poetry results from a widespread interpretation of problems of scientific knowledge as problems of politics, an interpretation that was amply supported by explicit US state policy. As Steven Shapin and Simon Schaffer put it in *Leviathan and the Air-Pump*, their landmark study of Robert Boyle and seventeenth-century experimentalism—first published in 1985 and itself very much an artifact of its moment—"solutions to the problem of knowledge are solutions to the problem of social order."[40] The emerging subdiscipline of sociology of scientific knowledge, in which Shapin and Schaffer played a key role, powerfully delineated the tight mutual relations between social consensus and knowledge production.

Language's politico-epistemological efficacy was powerfully conceptualized through Ludwig Wittgenstein's idea of the "language game," which plays a key role in both *Leviathan and the Air-Pump* and *The Postmodern Condition*. The "language game" is borrowed from Wittgenstein's posthumously published *Philosophical Investigations*: language, by this account, is less a system of representation than a system of actions. Consequently, it should be understood not in terms of "meaning" but rather in terms of *use*: "Think of the tools in a tool-box: there is a hammer, pliers, a saw, a screw-driver, a rule, a glue-pot, glue, nails, and screws.—The functions of words are as diverse as the functions of these objects."[41] The language-game model has the advantage of accounting for nonlexical words such as articles, prepositions, and conjunctions, which have functions rather than referents. Crucially, moreover, this model conceives of language and sociality together, so that, as Wittgenstein puts it, "to imagine a language is to imagine a life-form"—a statement so powerful for those invested in the uses of language and literature in the late Cold War period that it served as the first epigraph to Fredric Jameson's 1981 monograph *The Political Unconscious*.[42] Carol Cohn's "rational world of defense intellectuals" likewise operates through a language game—one that permits a "form of life" frighteningly unmoored from that of the everyday.[43]

This translatability between language and action—utterance and social form—proved enormously enabling for analyzing the operations of language, power, and knowledge in the later twentieth century. If, as Shapin and Schaffer argued, "solutions to the problem of knowledge are solutions to the problem of social order," and language-games are the medium through which those epistemo-political problems are enacted, then language—now conceptualized as active and agential, not ("merely") representational—is also the medium through which political violence can be opposed. As Lyn Hejinian would later frame it in her essay "Barbarism," "The emphasis on language in our writing can be explained by our sense of urgency of the need to address and, if possible, to redress social fraud . . . [since] fraud produces atrocity."[44] By speaking of "fraud" here, Hejinian uses a term with both epistemological and ethical stakes: fraud is an unethical misrepresentation of reality, simultaneously morally and factually wrong. The chain of reasoning that Hejinian deploys—from political "urgency," to a problem of ethics that is indistinguishably also a problem of knowledge, to a renewed attention to language as such—is subtended by a theory of language that was enormously influential in the second half of the twentieth century, far beyond the sphere of Language writers. Sianne Ngai's observation that Language's temporality of simultaneity has a "paranoid" valence clarifies the language-oriented nature of resistance.[45] After all, as Timothy Melley has argued, Cold War paranoia centers not on sinister agents but on paths of communication; knowledge itself emerges as essentially linguistic and, often, hermetically formalist.[46] Hejinian extends this line of thinking in "Barbarism," aiming through language to reintroduce contact with the outside world—empiricism—to what historians of science have called "Cold War rationality."[47] "The pervasive hypocrisy of the 1950s and 1960s was operating in several strategic forms," Hejinian specifies: "as outright lies (e.g., 'Everybody is happy in Alabama'), as deceptive metaphors (as in that depicting Vietnam as an upended domino liable to fall to Communism . . .), and, finally, in the more subtle form of a complete failure to examine political language and indeed any language at all, thus establishing the pretense that language is 'natural.'"[48] All these "strategic forms" are linguistic. But Hejinian's choice of words—"strategic forms"—points toward the Cold War context in which this language is embedded (despite the essay's 1996 publication date), for strategic forms are the substance not only of the language that conduces to atrocity but also the language-game of Cold War rationality. This is one reason that Language writing so heavily preoccupied itself with knowledge and knowledge production in its dual poetic and critical projects.[49] It sought to produce an "experimental" writing that was genuinely productive of knowledge yet "alien" to the state-sanctioned knowledge-producing language, and language-game, of defense strategy.

The turn to understanding language as active rather than representational, whether by way of Wittgensteinian language-games or, as was more common among Language writers, by way of deconstruction, drew new attention to language's performativity and provided one of the bases on which Language writers would recanonize modernism. In McGann's words, "In poetry . . . knowledge will appear *as a form of activity* rather than as a content, a possession, or an idea."[50] Newly valorized were writers like Gertrude Stein and Louis Zukofsky, whose emphasis on function words (conjunctions, prepositions, articles, etc.) and deemphasis of representation seemed to anticipate Cold War–era concerns with what language can *do*.

A pair of terms supplied by another theorist of scientific knowledge in the 1980s, Ian Hacking, summarizes the logic that experimental writers and cultural theorists alike applied to language: "representing" and "intervening." In *Representing and Intervening* (1983), Hacking outlines a theory of scientific realism—here meant in the philosophical sense that, for example, the concept we call "electron" corresponds not just to an intellectual model of physical phenomena but to a real physical entity in the world. Philosophical realism, Hacking argues, is the correct scientific philosophy because those theories that conduce to nominalist accounts of scientific knowledge erroneously concern themselves with matters of representation. Realism, in contrast, is supported by acts of *intervening* in nature through *experiments*: if we spray an object with electrons, it will take on a negative electrical charge. In a rhetorical gesture of bullshit-cutting, Hacking avers, "*So far as I'm concerned, if you can spray them then they are real.*"[51] Hacking's true interests are nowhere near as simple as this framing may suggest—he goes on to acknowledge that "unfortunately the issues cannot be so glibly dismissed"—but the terms "representing" and "intervening" usefully set up the hierarchical opposition between saying and doing that tacitly structure late twentieth-century approaches to language, especially to experimental writing.[52] (Needless to say, in this schema, doing is privileged over saying.) What Hacking calls "intervening" in the sciences is precisely the domain of experiment, and the same ability to intervene is claimed for experimental writing.[53]

Experimental writers of the 1980s thus rightly saw themselves embedded in a society in which the production of knowledge, especially physical and social-scientific knowledge, and state violence were deeply mutually implicated, and they saw language as the medium within which both occurred. Moreover, experimental writers saw this mutual implication occurring primarily by way of language-games and other agential theories of language, and they sought to implement different and oppositional language-games that were, like the language-games underwriting state violence, simultaneously epistemological and political in scope. As Ron Silliman put it in a 1988 essay, "language, since the structuralist movement of the 1950s, has served as a model and impetus for much of the academy's theoretical renaissance. From semiotics, which analyzes the world by treating its data as though it were a system of signs, to Foucault's concept of disciplines as discourses, the medium of language has been intimately involved with the elaboration of contemporary social theory."[54] Silliman's centralization of language as the material substrate of knowledge production was not only typical of Language writers but also resonated with Lyotard's citation of "phonology and theories of linguistics, problems of communication and cybernetics, modern theories of algebra and informatics, computers and their languages, problems of translation," and so on as the "'leading' sciences" of the postmodern moment.[55] This is why the language of the "experimental" became so appealing for describing this poetic project: as historians of science including Geoffrey Cantor, Lorraine Daston, Peter Galison, and Shapin and Schaffer have outlined, the notion of experiment already embeds a history of ethical and political connotations.[56] And part of the writers' project was a critical one, to recenter the version of modernism that could be understood as "experimental," which is to say, the version with the capacity to mount this oppositional epistemological language-game. Language writing and its recanonization efforts responded to an urgent geopolitical situation whose terms were already remarkably suited to a poetic response: language was not a matter of representing but of intervening. Or as an unnamed Starfleet officer would declare of a space probe's whale song: "It's impacting all our systems."[57]

Epistemic Virtues and the Abstraction of Knowledge

I've argued so far that "experimental" writing, as it is currently understood, is doubly periodizable, as a trajectory emerging from the early twentieth century as reread by writers of the late twentieth century. Experimental writing poses a paradox for historicization: it is both strongly associated with the early twentieth century and highly resistant to periodization. Thus the literary critic Alan Marshall owns a preference for "experimental" precisely for its tendency to spread, even if only to eventually point back to the early twentieth century: "It gives me the scope to reach back beyond the modernist, the innovative, the news that stays news, to America's two greatest nineteenth-century poets, Whitman and Dickinson, and then to reach forward again to the modernism of Ezra Pound and William Carlos Williams and beyond."[58] As Bob Perelman has argued in a similar context, "this promiscuity is useful . . . not merely a sign of theoretical weakness," bespeaking something that seems to be "sequential and transhistorical in equal measure."[59]

What, then, makes the beginning of the twentieth century such a rich resource for writers retrospectively constructing an experimental canon? And what, in turn, explains experimentalism's resistance to being bound to the period? Most of this book is devoted to answering these questions by turning to the early part of the "experimental tradition" as it has come to be constructed through the work of Ezra Pound, Gertrude Stein, Marianne Moore, and William Carlos Williams, attending to these writers' explicit purchase on an epistemological aesthetics. That these writers, like many other modernists, were interested in questions of knowledge, and of scientific knowledge production in particular, is well documented, and this book does not devote much space to reproducing that scholarship.[60] Rather, I wish to illuminate these writers' roles in scientific discourses of the period—not as importing ready-made scientific concepts or techniques, nor as projecting "alternative" scientific practices, but rather as participants in an ongoing renegotiation of what counted as good knowledge-making. In this section I explain what made good knowledge-making such a focus of concern at the turn of the twentieth century and introduce a concept that will help me organize those concerns, the "epistemic virtue." The turn of the twentieth century was a period in which the idea of being "experimental" in the sciences grew both more powerful and significantly more abstract. Attention to a few key examples will help to illuminate why the version of experimentalism that means "out there" or "weird" and the version that means "rigorous scientific engagement with reality" are different facets of the same phenomenon. Experimentalism became legible as a ratifying disposition or attitude rather than a concrete set of practices, a process of abstracting method. Epistemic virtues are certainly not unique to this period, but they help us to make sense of that abstraction.

While discourses about experimental writing often circulate around formalist appeals to "method," such accounts quickly break down because they misleadingly suggest that there *is* a unified scientific method that is portable out of specific disciplinary and historical circumstances and into literature. As I discuss below, the notion of a "scientific method" is essentially nineteenth-century propaganda. Yet the discourse of portable method also points us in a useful direction, for the dehistoricization of method is itself historicizable. At the turn of the twentieth century, new scientific domains emerged, consolidated, and professionalized, requiring new reconfigurations of "method." As Steven Shapin has put it in another context, "Faith in Method grew even as incompatible versions of what such a Method might be proliferated."[61] A new popular understanding of the nature of science—as an animating force abstractable from its articulation in particular acts or social settings—underwrote a conviction that all domains of experience could be improved by a renewed commitment to knowledge and that "scientific" methods (whatever that meant) were the best way to enact that commitment. The unification of the sciences, one of the great projects of the nineteenth century, produced an *abstraction* of method—method's re-rendering as a mindset, intellectual disposition, or even spiritual orientation. In the process, *experimentalism* came to be disarticulated from specific *experiments* (situated, material, and historical). The abstraction of scientific method was a historical phenomenon that made it possible to construe new specific acts and discourses as "experimental." Some of these practices, like psychology, would maintain a strong association with the "experimental" over the decades, while others, like Montessori education, would do so only in vague and attenuated ways. In fact, Montessori education is a good example of a practice that has, for many, become associated with the version of "experimental" that connotes "out there hippie stuff." Maria Montessori herself, however, was very literal about forwarding her pedagogy as an experimental science. That it has lost its legibility as "science" yet retained its status as "experimental education" can be attributed to the decentralized nature of social-scientific experimental norms at the turn of the twentieth century. In none of the new domains of the late nineteenth century's science boom was a single, standard "method" applied; rather, the abstraction of method—sometimes a radical abstraction to an experimental "spirit" or "sentiment"—opened "experimentalism" up to multifarious instantiation.

"Scientific method," then, is an invention that can be traced. Though the notion of an abstractable method has (much-claimed) roots in Francis Bacon's *Novum Organum*, its rise to popularity can be located in the nineteenth century, the period in which "science" came to be understood as a consolidated intellectual formation united by an abstracted notion of method.[62] Aggressive efforts to promote and popularize science in the nineteenth century relied significantly on a rhetoric of "method." As Richard Yeo, writing of British popularizers such as John Herschel, William Whewell, and the British Association for the Advancement of Science, has observed, "The distinction between the content and method of science"—that is to say, between materials, objects, and practices, on one hand, and an animating method, spirit, or intellectual discipline, on the other—"has been a significant element in the cultural legitimation of the scientific enterprise."[63] The centrality of "method" as a defining feature of scientificity, and of experimentalism in particular, is a historical and quite intentional phenomenon. "At various levels of debate," Yeo continues, "scientific method was represented as *accessible*, *single*, and *transferable*. These three characterizations respectively claimed that the method of science could be understood and practised by a large number of people; that there was a single method common to all branches of science; and that this method could be extrapolated from natural science to other subjects."[64] Accordingly, specific techniques were rendered as what Montessori, proposing her "experimental pedagogy," called a "scientific spirit" residing in the "mind and heart."[65] Thus the biologist Stephen Forbes argued in 1904 that "scientific method" was "not the mere use of tools of any sort, however complicated and valuable; not the manipulation of apparatus, or any form of mechanical operation on anything," but rather a "*mental method*, and the study of this method is a study of the action of the scientific mind while engaged in the pursuit of scientific truth."[66] This popular understanding of "the scientific method" came to be codified in and widely propagated by the philosopher and educator John Dewey's description of a five-step scientific reasoning process in his 1910 textbook for teachers *How We Think*.[67] As Rudolph argues, Dewey's five-step account won widespread popularity in pedagogy in large part because it was portable and promised to teach a genuinely experimental science without the encumbrances of specialized laboratory equipment and tightly controlled exercises. Moreover, it "allowed educators to embrace the rhetoric of science and, thus, take advantage of the cultural authority science possessed following the wave of late nineteenth-century popularization."[68] By 1918 the five-step "scientific method" was being used retroactively to describe the work of scientific luminaries like Galileo, Newton, and Darwin, and its popular dominance as an account of scientificity was secured.[69]

The abstraction of method rendered science's terrain—whatever "science" was—infinite, in principle. Thus in his widely read 1892 treatise *The Grammar of Science*—a title that already reconstitutes science less as a set of practices or even a method than as a language—the influential statistician and eugenicist (and student of Francis Galton) Karl Pearson asserted that "the field of science is unlimited; its material is endless, every group of natural phenomena, every phase of social life, every stage of past or present development is material for science."[70] Moreover, "every phase," for Pearson, included aesthetic domains: aesthetic experience rested upon epistemological satisfaction. "Does not the beauty of the artist's work lie for us in the accuracy with which his symbols resume innumerable facts of our past emotional experience? . . . If this account of the aesthetic judgment be at all a true one, the reader will have remarked how exactly parallel it is to the scientific judgment."[71] Pearson argued, in other words, for an aesthetics of knowledge: knowledge was aesthetically satisfying, and aesthetic satisfaction depended on a work's reliability as knowledge.

One does not have to look far to find examples in this period of attempts to generalize "scientific" and "experimental" thought in ways that could meaningfully extend its purview into areas hitherto typically dominated by arts and letters. This period is hardly the first to see such claims, of course. Firstness is less important for my purposes, however, than the development and institutionalization of new sciences that explicitly saw those domains as their purview but, in order to take them on, also had to respecify what it meant to be "scientific." Sigmund Freud, for example, outlined revised expectations of what constituted a "scientific" study in his new science of the mind, psychoanalysis. "In medical training you are accustomed to *see* things. . . . Even in psychiatry the demonstration of patients with their altered facial expressions, their mode of speech and their behaviour, affords you plenty of observations which leave a deep impression upon you," he writes. "In psycho-analysis, alas, everything is different. Nothing takes place in a psycho-analytic treatment but an interchange of words between the patient and the analyst."[72] Evidence is no longer visible but rather discursive —"hearsay," as Freud provocatively names it—and symptoms are no longer necessarily organic but rather rooted in "psychical life."[73] "You have grown accustomed to regarding [psychological and discursive explanations] with suspicion, denying them the attribute of being scientific," Freud concedes.[74] Yet in the absence of any existing science that is "in a position to tell you anything serviceable of the relation between body and mind," he continues, a new science is needed, even if its proofs, because of the nature of the material investigated, must remain disappointingly invisible.[75] That being a "science" is the epistemological gold standard is not in question for Freud, but if there is to be a science of psychic life, then science must be conceived more capaciously.

Montessori, whose experimental schools enjoyed US coverage in a 1911 *McClure's* magazine series and whose book *The Montessori Method* was translated into English in 1912, likewise sought to construct a "scientific pedagogy." Montessori urged the elevation of "pedagogy from the inferior position it has occupied as a secondary branch of philosophy, to the dignity of a definite science."[76] Yet even in taking for granted the higher epistemological status of the sciences, Montessori, like so many others seeking to expand experimental domains, also sought to redefine the core of what experimentalism might mean in order to accommodate her new objects of study—here, "the intimate relationship between the observer and the individual to be observed [i.e., between the teacher and the student]; a relationship which does not exist between the student of zoology or botany and that form of nature which he studies."[77] Importing methods and techniques directly from other disciplines, Montessori insists, would deny the specificity of the new science, for what works for a botanist will not do for an experimental pedagogue. In formulating her "scientific pedagogy," Montessori therefore rejects the rationalization of the child body—a false scientism that she excoriates—in favor of a "scientific spirit." "To prepare teachers in the method of the experimental sciences is not an easy matter," she writes.

> When we shall have instructed them in anthropometry and psychometry in the most minute manner possible, we shall have only created machines, whose usefulness will be most doubtful. . . . It is my belief that the thing which we should cultivate in our teachers is more the *spirit* than the mechanical skill of the scientist. . . . In other words, we wish to awaken in the mind and heart of the educator an *interest in natural phenomena* to such an extent that, loving nature, he shall understand the anxious and expectant attitude of one who has prepared an experiment and who awaits a revelation from it.[78]

To be made portable to new domains, "experimentalism" had to be abstracted from the materiality and situatedness of particular *experiments* and, at least in Montessori's view, be reconfigured in philosophical and even affective terms—as something residing in the "mind and heart" of the new experimental pedagogue. Pearson, Freud, and Montessori, exponents of new "human" fields, offer prominent turn-of-the-century examples of the way in which *experimentalism* was produced as abstractable from any particular *experiments*.[79] To put it another way: experimental*ism* was already a site of marginal knowledge practices, albeit ones grasping toward the center.

With experimentalism newly available to a wider domain, a variety of rhetorics gave experimental writing an air of desirability and, indeed, inevitability. This is the rhetorical tack that Zola took in his polemical 1879 essay "The Experimental Novel," which embraced experimental science as the key to all mythologies.[80] Borrowing from and adapting an 1865 work by the physiologist Claude Bernard—somewhat beyond Bernard's own expectations or intentions—Zola represented the advent of an experimental literature as the natural extension of a progression, based on a Comtean hierarchy that was already present in the sciences, beginning with the canonically experimental sciences (the physical sciences) and extending thereafter to the sciences of life (such as Bernard's experimental medicine), the new social sciences, and finally—triumphantly—the experimental novel.[81] "From that point, we move into the domain that, until now, belonged to philosophy and literature; it will be the sciences' decisive conquest of the hypotheses of the philosophers and writers," Zola wrote. "We have experimental chemistry and physics; we will have [Bernard's] experimental physiology; still further on, we will have the experimental novel."[82] Obviously!

As both Zola and Pearson indicate, the spread of the sciences was explicitly thought of as an encroachment on the terrain of—and a wresting of authority from—the arts, letters, and philosophy. Indeed, Gertrude Stein's transcripts from Harvard-Radcliffe show that the psychology courses she so famously took with William James were at that time (the 1890s) still classified under the college's bureaucracy as philosophy.[83] The growth of the sciences meant a new way of constituting expertise in the human and cultural domains. "If I have put the case of science at all correctly, the reader will have recognised that modern science does much more than demand that it shall be left in undisturbed possession of what the theologian and metaphysician please to term its 'legitimate field,'" Pearson writes. "It claims the whole range of phenomena, mental as well as physical—the entire universe—is its field. It asserts that the scientific method is the sole gateway to the whole region of knowledge."[84] Knowledge itself, Pearson argues, is defined by this (increasingly abstracted) method, or it is not knowledge at all.

The new yet uncertain reach of scientific authority made experimentalism a status to which any knowledge-producing enterprise might aspire. Yet for precisely that reason, existing scientific practices were challenged to accommodate recalcitrant objects of study in new ways. Such objects might be alive (children), dynamic (ecosystems), invisible (human consciousness), difficult to define (culture), logistically difficult to count or keep track of (populations), and in various ways resistant to existing practices. Whereas, by the eighteenth century, a certain stability had developed around experimental practices in subdomains of what would come to be called the physical sciences, it was far from clear what an experimental medicine—much less an experimental novel—might look like in the decades when both came to seem profoundly desirable.[85] Indeed, Bernard's *Introduction to the Study of Experimental Medicine*, the text that Zola closely adapted for his polemic, is at great pains to establish that an experimental medicine is even possible, devoting several sections to questioning and readapting reigning notions of the "experiment." Breaking with Georges Cuvier's widely adopted (and in many places still tacitly or explicitly current) suggestion that observation is "passive" while experiment is "active"—a premise of Hacking's representing/intervening distinction—Bernard undertook to place "observational" sciences on a continuum with "experimental" sciences, different in degree rather than in kind. "Experiment [*l'expérience*] being in effect nothing but a judgment, it necessarily entails comparison between two things, and what is intentional or active in the experiment is really the comparison that the mind [*esprit*] wishes to make."[86] Bernard's text is thus as notable for its insistence on revising the terms of the "experimental" as for any specific proposal. In particular, like Montessori, Forbes, and Dewey after him, Bernard removes the onus of experimentalism from the site of any particular experiment, placing it instead on modes of reasoning and of feeling and, in particular, proposing critical comparison as a marker of experimentalism. In other words, the shifting stakes of calling a practice "experimental" prompted shifting uses of the term.

The abstraction of "method" into something residing in what Montessori identified as the "heart and mind," what Bernard called "*raisonnement expérimental*," and what Forbes called a "*mental method*" was thus both an *effect* and an *agent* of science popularization. It is important to understand *effect* and *agency* as twinned: it would not be accurate to suppose that official, professional science disseminated theories and methods that then became watered down by an enthusiastic but corrupting public.[87] For at the end of the nineteenth century, "official, professional science" did not always exist; and where it did exist, it frequently only became canonized as official and professional retrospectively. Professionalization and popularization were and are complexly related concomitants, not opponents.[88] Thus the new pedagogical, public-facing mission of the natural history museum in the early twentieth century was the flip side of professional zoologists' and botanists' desires to protect their working specimens from exposure to a common and ostensibly unappreciating public; "outreach" in many cases helped create the "out" to which a newly professionalizing discipline could reach.[89] Defending against the authority of mere technique (which Bernard would go so far as to claim could be carried out by a completely ignorant servant), proponents of new domains of scientific inquiry—only some of which would go on to achieve canonical scientific status—affirmed science's epistemological authority while proliferating the ways in which it could manifest.[90]

This book examines the ways that early twentieth-century literature that has retrospectively been canonized as "experimental" participated in the refashioning of the "experimental" and the "scientific" at the turn of the twentieth century, not transplanting a portable, fully formed "scientific method" onto existing literary practices (as if either the "method" or writing were stable), but rather entering into the space of engagement that was in the process of constituting innumerable new ways—of varying longevity—of being "experimental." This engagement took place on the very grounds of science's new authority: the "spirit" that animated its various practices, or what Lorraine Daston and Peter Galison have usefully theorized as "epistemic virtues." Epistemic virtues are a crucial, structuring concept for this book, supplying a means of organizing the ways in which "experimentalism" was conceived and enacted in the late nineteenth and early twentieth centuries. Arguing that the concept of scientific "objectivity" is best understood as a part of the history of the scientific self, Daston and Galison identify "epistemic virtues" as the desiderata according to which a scientific self is constructed. An epistemic virtue, in brief, is a virtue whose chief advantage lies in its ability to secure knowledge. That ability to secure knowledge, however, is always also readable as a moral virtue, allowing *good for knowledge* to stand in for *good* (in general). "Intertwined" as they are with the construction of the scientific self, "epistemic virtues . . . turn out to be literal, not just metaphorical virtues," a feature that explains the moralizing exhortations that recur in scientific literature—and in late twentieth-century discourses about experimental writing.[91] "The language of these exhortations," Daston and Galison observe, "are often frankly religious, albeit in different registers—the humility of the seeker, the wonder of the psalmist who praises creation, the asceticism of the saint. . . . [E]ven if religious overtones are absent or dismissed as so much window-dressing, there remains a core of ethical imperative in the literature on how to do science and become a scientist."[92] Epistemic virtues tether ethical values to the production of knowledge; thus good knowledge production is also understood as ethically good.[93] Yet epistemic virtues are not universal, transhistorical, or necessarily consistent with one another; as Daston and Galison argue, "New epistemic virtues come into being; old ones do not necessarily pass away," and "older ones are inevitably modified by the very existence of the newer ones, even if they are not replaced outright."[94] Moreover, epistemic virtues may actively compete; thus "practices judged laudable by the measure of truth-to-nature—such as pruning experimental data to eliminate outliers and other dubious values—may strike proponents of objectivity as dishonest."[95]

Consequently, the legibility of epistemic virtues as inherently "good" (tacitly ethically and politically as well as epistemologically) often obscures the tensions between distinct epistemic virtues as well as between the different practices through which they may be performed. Daston and Galison offer loose periodizations for the dominance of particular virtues, associating truth-to-nature with the eighteenth century, mechanical objectivity with the nineteenth, and structural objectivity with the beginning of the twentieth, but they are at pains to underscore the provisionality of any such periodization and the complexity of the ways in which those virtues were manifested. Epistemic virtues are not methods, but they act as effective proxies for method: they are not acts but principles for acting (or for suppressing acts).

A major premise of this book is that experimental writing as we now understand it does not *do experiments* (follow a method) but rather *performs epistemic virtues*. The epistemic virtues that I explore here are flash, objectivity, precision, and contact—virtues associated respectively with population sciences, neuroanatomy, natural history and toolmaking, and anthropology. Flash and precision constitute inversions of one another, operating through similar part-whole logics but in different directions, with flash valorizing comprehensiveness and precision valorizing the technical and by definition minor. Similarly, objectivity and contact are each concerned with distance as a measure of epistemic security—one requiring distance as a safeguard against projection and distortion, the other requiring proximity and touch. Experimental texts, I argue, aim to embody epistemic virtues. Yet *which* virtues take precedence may vary widely and conflict markedly, as may the literary forms through which they manifest.

This is the historical substrate of the many attempts to link experimental writing to experimental science—not a set of acts or methods, in the end, but a set of epistemic virtues—what are ultimately aspirations. It is a situational, historical, and cultural link, not a philosophical or formal one. In a way, this means that insisting on the experimentalism of experimental writing is nonsense—if we assign the only authoritative experimentalism to the sciences and do not consider as equally historically important the uses to which literary "experimentalism" has been put. But if we take seriously this historical link, many of the confusions and contradictions that beset experimental writing come into better focus. It explains why, in an age of very publicly compromised scientific practices, an appeal to a version of knowledge-making rooted in a virtuously self-denying ("poethical," as Joan Retallack puts it) scientific subject would offer a way toward a politically efficacious poetics that might jam the kind of language-game of big science that sent nuclear aircraft carriers from Alameda to Vietnam.

At the same time, epistemic virtues make possible many of the slippages and inconsistencies that attend experimental writing's claims, especially the way that form can masquerade as or substitute for a politics. Epistemic virtues inseparably guarantee knowledge by guaranteeing virtue, and vice versa. That epistemic virtues can conflict with one another, sometimes sharply—as the contrasts between flash and precision, objectivity and contact demonstrate—is covered over by their status, each, as good for making knowledge, even as the kinds of knowledge that they can guarantee vary widely. Moreover, the abstraction of method and epistemic virtues' power to act as method's proxy also explains the frequent accusations of elitist formalism that have often been leveled at contemporary experimental writing, despite experimental writing's often explicitly anti-capitalist orientation. For epistemic virtues call forth a fantasy of autonomous, pre- or nonpolitical knowledge production that contrasts with the dominance of the postwar military-industrial complex. Experimental writers can disavow the autonomy of the literary text, the author, or the lyric voice without, however, relinquishing a different autonomy located in a more-true, disinterested version of the sciences. Where aesthetic autonomy is delegitimized, it can nonetheless reenter as a fully affirmable aspiration toward scientific autonomy.

Romantic and Other Precedents

Over the years that I've been working on experimental writing, perhaps the question that has most often been posed to me is "What about Romanticism?" The question refers to the observation that in the 1801 preface, William Wordsworth called his *Lyrical Ballads* "an experiment"; tacitly, it is also a question about whether the Romantics weren't just as punk rock as the twentieth-century writers I discuss.[96] There is, certainly, a way in which *Lyrical Ballads* seems to fit the experimental bill: it claims to attempt something new, that attempt is rooted in an appeal to language's purchase on reality ("the real language of men"), and Wordsworth and other Romantics are genuinely interested in the sciences. Throughout the book, I will make moves similar to the one Mary Poovey makes when she points out that Romantic poets like Wordsworth, Coleridge, and Shelley, in offering poetic purchase on the problem of induction, already concede that this scientific problem requires addressing by poets.[97] Is Romantic poetry experimental? Should this book begin in 1800?

The short answer is no. When contemporary critics say "experimental writing"—when Charles Altieri writes about "poets trained in the experimental or 'innovative' tradition," or when Laura Hinton and Cynthia Hogue allude to "experimental women's writing," for example—they mean something, and that something is not Romanticism.[98] In fact, it is something closer to what Joan Retallack has called "antiromantic modernisms" (on which more anon): while we can surely find similarities between the writing usually called "experimental" and Romantic poetry, historically speaking, Romanticism has never been a touchstone of the postwar poetics called "experimental," whereas a certain version of modernism—one imagined to oppose Romanticism—has been the object of a concerted critical project.[99] In fact, notwithstanding the occasional local exception (for instance, Barrett Watten's discussion of Coleridge in *The Constructivist Moment*), "experimentalism" as it is used today usually means almost anything *but* Romanticism: it, and especially (one version of) the Romantic lyric subject, is often what experimental writers explicitly claim to be writing *against*.[100] As Perloff has put it, "It was . . . opposition to this romantic paradigm that prompted the theoretical discourse of Language manifestos in the first place."[101] Gillian White has powerfully read this gesture as symptomatic of an abstract "lyric shame"—"shame attributed to, projected onto, and produced by readings that anthropomorphize poems as 'lyric'"—that has conventionally, if often unfairly, been tethered to Romantic lyric.[102] It would be reasonable to argue that the bifurcation between experimentalism and Romanticism is a false one, resting on a misinterpretation or reduction of Romantic poetics. Certainly, many reductive things have been said about Romanticism in the name of experimentalism. Yet these reductive statements are a historical fact: to say that experimental writers in the 1970s and 1980s positioned themselves against Romanticism *wrongly* does not obviate the fact that they *did it*, usually precisely in the name of experimentalism.[103]

I do not wish to prescribe "correct" uses for the term "experimental"—it is its uses, after all. Moreover, appeals to Romantic and other precedents for the narrower twentieth-century experimental canon that concerns me in this book tell us something about why "experimental" is an appealing and useful category. I therefore briefly outline the ways that the definitions on which such appeals rely are literary-historical dead ends, even as they are fruitful in other ways.

The first version of the "experimental" that underpins the question "What about Romanticism?" is basically a synonym for goodness or critical interest—an experimentalism defined in the very capacious sense of trying something out or of taking a risk. It is a model to which post-Vietnam US experimental writers themselves recur from time to time, and its rhetorical power as an evaluation that can masquerade as a description is undeniable.[104] The availability and wide use of this dimension of the "experimental" speaks to the utility—even necessity—of an "experimentalism" that can address a truly broad variety of forms.[105] Yet because it is covertly an evaluation, its descriptive affordances are limited; to designate a work "experimental" on these grounds is to say very little about what it actually does.

The second version of experimentalism that underpins "What about Romanticism?" is what I'll shorthand as "scienciness." In this version, a literary text is experimental if it engages deeply with knowledge practices that we would now call scientific. It is certainly the case, as numerous scholars have documented, that scienciness is a feature of Romantic literature—even if "science," as a unified conceptual category, emerged thereafter.[106] Yet this, too, is, in its way, an evaluation masquerading as a description, only the evaluative component has been deferred to deciding what counts as "scientific." The scienciness criterion presumes that we know what it means for literature to be "scientific," yet this category remains powerfully contested even for more explicit knowledge-making practices. Historians of science have called the study of this contestation "boundary studies"; historians and philosophers have been (understandably) powerfully motivated to develop a definitive formal rule to delimit legitimate scientific inquiry from pseudoscience and compromised knowledge practices, especially in light of pressing political crises of epistemological authority, like that posed by climate change.[107] It is not for want of searching that no such rule has yet been found that holds up.[108] It follows a fortiori that no such rule exists for the delimitation of a "sciency" literature either. Moreover, such a definition makes experimental literature parasitic on a presumably prior and established scientific practice, precluding the possibility that experimental writing and other knowledge-making practices might be more fundamentally codetermined.[109] And finally, it includes enormous amounts of literature (apart from Romanticism, of course) that would rarely if ever be associated with the "experimental" label—Victorian realist novels, on whose close engagement with the sciences there is a substantial critical literature, are a prime example.[110] (Zola's use of the term "experimental," mentioned above, also falls into this category, although perhaps differently.)[111] Because of this, the scienciness criterion on its own holds no explanatory power for understanding experimentalism's uses or what is at stake in calling a work experimental during its peak usage to describe literature. To put it another way, to call a literary work experimental is a polemical gesture that clearly means something more than to note that it engages with natural philosophy; this book aims not to reduce that gesture.

Like the more explicitly evaluative version of "experimentalism" discussed above, the scienciness criterion teaches us something useful about how the term is used: importing a sense of transhistorical epistemological soundness from the sciences has been a much-valued (albeit, to my mind, suspect) affordance of the term. What it loses in descriptive or historical specificity, the scienciness criterion gains in normative force, a force, moreover, whose very normativity is obscured by its location in an ostensibly neutral domain, what we now call science.

The final version of experimentalism that animates turns to Romantic and other precedents equates experimentalism to "formal innovation," which is to say its claims to a privileged literary purchase on the real via literary form. This version captures something important about how experimentalism is used: as way of conjoining time and form. I will revisit this phenomenon at the end of this chapter. The notion of "formal innovation" places forms in time in a particular way, arguing for *firstness*: the first use of a given form (its "innovation"). The argument that would classify *Lyrical Ballads* as "experimental" on these grounds would situate it in literary history as introducing new forms and, perhaps, newly asserting the value of newness, a double firstness that embeds an orientation toward time in the form itself. The centralization of "firstness" in this version of experimentalism matches Pound's above-mentioned dream of a twelve-volume history of literature containing only innovations, an idea modeled on a teleological history of science and technology.[112] To care about firstness is to, very reasonably, wonder why this book does not address any number of texts that either introduced new literary forms or were received as if they had done so.

This version, too, is tacitly normative, and it, too, teaches us something about how experimentalism is used. Here, the move is to invest a work with value by investing it with newness. That newness, moreover, can be attributed to form and need not have any particular literary-historical content; it is the formalization of a (notional) temporal relation. This is evident, for example, in the way that Laughlin, the publisher of New Directions, introduced *Spearhead: 10 Years' Experimental Writing in America* (1947). There, he defines "experimental" in the negative, against those writers who are "content to work within the technical limits current as conventional tradition."[113] This is a newness that requires the production of some static foil, in the familiar way that modernist rhetorics have often produced nineteenth-century literature as homogeneously static.

These versions of "experimental" trade descriptive power for normative force; to put it another way, many of the attributes that make "experimental" such a useful and appealing term actively work against our ability to describe it. This book is not about disciplining critics' uses of the term but about explaining it, and there is no reason not to continue to call *Lyrical Ballads* or anything else "experimental," as long as we also remember that what is at stake in calling a text "experimental," or in aligning it with epistemic virtue, is much different in 1800 than in 1980, partly because experiment's transhistorical connotations are themselves historical. I take experimentalism as a set of uses and affordances (and, as I will discuss below, of limitations as well). During and after the late Cold War period, the term "experimental" has been *useful* for describing certain kinds of literature. There is no clear rule as to what that literature is, but there is something like what musicians call a *tessitura*, the part of an instrument's or a voice's range that is its "sweet spot." Experimentalism has a period because the scope of its significance does; experimentalism is a made thing, though it is not made out of nothing.

To parallel to my comments about periodization, I wish to make a final note about nationality. As early twentieth-century uses of "experimental" reveal, a key feature of experimentalism as it has been constituted in the late twentieth century is a disavowed Americanization. American experimental writers and experimentalism-advocating critics have often claimed continuities with European and Russian avant-gardes, and experimentalism's rendering as "formal innovation" makes it in principle as geographically portable as it is historically portable. Just as "experimental" is often the term that is used in order to avoid naming a specific period, it is also often the term that is used to avoid naming a "national" literature. Yet the version of experimentalism that emerges when names get named is tacitly US-centric, as reflected in the importance of Allen's *New American Poetry* anthology—emphasis on "American"—in back-of-the-envelope genealogies.[114] It is important, I think, to recognize the twentieth-century cosmopolitanism-as-Americanism that informs the inclusion of European, and especially French, writing in experimental genealogies. The French group Oulipo has taken a particularly prominent place in some accounts of literary experimentalism, especially those that see contemporary "conceptual" writing as its endpoint.[115] The intellectual currents contributing to the social-scientific "French theory" of the twentieth century and to the Oulipo alike, however, cannot easily be separated from the complex workings of US imperialism in Europe after World War II, as Kristin Ross and others have pointed out.[116] Demonstrating American artistic cosmopolitanism was a key aim of Cold War cultural diplomacy; thus there is no contradiction between James Laughlin's energetic efforts to publish a wide range of foreign literature (including by Raymond Queneau) with New Directions and his promotion of "10 Years' Experimental Writing in America."[117] My aim in pointing this out is not to limit the use of "experimental" as a label but rather to contextualize experimentalism's claims to cosmopolitanism during a period of widespread US cultural imperialism and to indicate the tacit US-centrism that the concept nearly always entails.

Experimental Writing Is a White Recovery Project

Any account of experimental writing that hopes to make sense of its uses and affordances must attempt to explain its ongoing, and recently much debated, centering of racial whiteness.[118] To explain this, it is helpful to revisit the recovery structure of experimental writing. As I discussed earlier in the chapter, Language writers and sympathetic academics saw themselves as retrieving and championing a suppressed radical literary tradition, a recovery project in a literal sense that was contemporaneous with, yet strangely insulated from, a wave of feminist, LGBTQ, and anti-racist recovery projects in the United States. This meant shaping a past legacy as well as producing contexts within which new work could be understood and appreciated—"overthrowing and entering literary history," as Perelman puts it in *The Marginalization of Poetry*.[119] But the grounds of experimental modernist works' marginalization (and the degree to which particular works were marginalized is certainly contestable) and the terms on which they were newly valued were very different from those taken up by the recovery projects that came to be understood (fairly or not) as driven by "identity politics."

In this context, it is important to understand the entry of experimental poets into the academy and the creation of institutional structures spanning the small-press and academic worlds as not only part of a wider economic trend but also as a key component of the recovery project that made the narrative of a literary experimentalism "from Gertrude Stein to L=A=N=G=U=A=G=E poetry" possible.[120] (Needless to say, other recovery projects also gained institutional footholds in the form of departments of ethnic studies, women's and gender studies, LGBTQ studies, Black and Africana studies, and so forth, albeit on very different terms.)[121] What is at stake in experimental writers' entry into academia is not whether they thereby "lost all indie credibility," as Andrew Epstein humorously puts it, but rather what academic institutions contributed to a recovery project.[122] Epstein notes that "probably fewer than a dozen Language poets have found permanent employment in universities, and most of them were hired to teach literature rather than poetry writing, leaving creative writing programs still largely staffed by poets less amenable to the avant-garde."[123] But what Language and other "experimental" writers were able to do *as critics* was perhaps more consequential, from a literary-historical perspective, than what they might have done as teachers of poetry workshops.[124] Teaching "literature rather than poetry writing" and writing literary history in academic publications performed some of the fundamental functions of recovery, producing contexts for understanding past and present writing as "experimental" and creating book markets, PhD dissertations (including my own), and hiring fields.

Academic institutions' role in experimental writing has often been oriented toward recovery, then, as when Bernstein proposes that "William Carlos Williams mee[t] the MLA."[125] Perelman, for one, aims to dispel the charge that Language writing is (culpably) academic by framing its engagement with poststructuralism as incidental to a more foundational historical legacy: "Language writers have used structuralist and poststructuralist theory at times to furnish ad hoc support for negative assertions about the problematic status of description, self, and narrative in writing and positive ones about wider possibilities for meaning if more ambitious sets of reading practices are recognized; but these positions have come out of writing practices closely informed by the modernists, especially Stein, and the Objectivists, especially Zukofsky, and by Black Mountain, Beat, and New York School poetry."[126] If we were to substitute different names for Stein, Zukofsky, and so forth, we might read Perelman's account as an uncannily close description of what Henry Louis Gates Jr.'s *The Signifying Monkey* accomplished—at once affirming a preexisting African American literary history, making it legible as a history, and rendering it in the terms of the most prestigious academic discourses of the moment.[127] Like in other recovery projects, institutions that straddled academic and nonacademic spheres and made the latter available to the former were key in the recovery—that is, the retrospective construction—of experimental writing.[128]

Among these institutions, I will briefly mention just a few. The National Poetry Foundation, which was founded in 1971 by the Pound scholar Carroll F. Terrell at the University of Maine, Orono, became an effective institution for integrating poetry and scholarship through publishing and conferences. The foundation published books of creative writing and criticism that contributed to canon formation across the two (so, for example, it published both *The Collected Prose of Carl Rakosi* and *Carl Rakosi: Man and Poet*), as well as what is perhaps the foremost anthology of Language poetry and poetics, *In the American Tree*.[129] Similarly, the foundation's Person and Poet book series maps a trajectory running from a Pound-centered modernism (though, interestingly, the series includes a two-volume *T. S. Eliot: Man and Poet*) through the Objectivists, Black Mountain, the San Francisco Renaissance, and on to Language. Its conferences—focusing entirely on individual modernists in the 1980s and subsequently branching out into explorations of groups and decades, such as 2000's "The Opening of the Field: North American Poetry in the 1960s"—likewise suggest canonization.[130]

Other institutionalizing nodes cropped up as well, enabling poet-critics to produce the critical context for both the recovery of an experimental modernism and their own work. *Sagetrieb*, a journal published by the National Poetry Foundation and sister to the Pound-focused *Paideuma*, is particularly notable.[131] Founded in 1982, *Sagetrieb* was initially dedicated to "poets in the Pound-Williams tradition," which was later amended to the "Pound-H.D.-Williams tradition" and later still to the "imagist/Objectivist tradition." Its mission was nearly explicitly to construct the very traditions that its masthead so cheerfully named, running special issues on Robert Creeley, Robert Duncan, Marianne Moore, Charles Reznikoff, and multiple special issues on H.D. and William Carlos Williams, among others.[132] As Kaplan Harris put it in a review of the journal's history, "*Sagetrieb* set out to reach diverse constituencies by placing one foot in academia and one in the avant-garde," drawing editors and contributors from among academics like Marjorie Perloff, Hugh Kenner, and Paul Mariani, as well as from among poets including Robert Creeley, Carl Rakosi, and Denise Levertov.[133] Yet in doing so, *Sagetrieb* and other pro-experimental journals also helped to create the critical conditions for rendering what Harris calls "the avant-garde" of that moment legible as the (early twentieth-century) historical avant-garde's rightful successors and, moreover, to recast that trajectory as a continuity understandable through the lens of contemporary concerns.[134]

Book series at university presses created lists that supported this recovery as well. Three series are particularly notable for the way that they categorized literary trajectories and for the opportunities that they created for crossover between creative writing, "poetics" writing, and professional literary criticism. They are Avant-Garde & Modernism Studies at Northwestern University Press, edited by Rainer Rumold and Marjorie Perloff; Modern and Contemporary Poetics at the University of Alabama Press, edited by Charles Bernstein and Hank Lazer; and Contemporary North American Poets at the University of Iowa Press, edited by Alan Golding, Lynn Keller, and Adalaide Morris. The author lists and advisory boards of these three series overlap significantly and include numerous prominent contemporary experimental writers. Book series are often essential instruments in the work of literary recovery, with all the difficulties that they introduce. Oxford University Press's Schomburg Library of Nineteenth-Century Black Women Writers, edited by Gates, for example, made paperback editions of now-canonical authors such as Frances E. W. Harper, Anna Julia Cooper, Harriet Jacobs, and Pauline Hopkins available for the classroom. But the question of who needed to be recovered, how, and on what terms was notably different when it came to experimental writing, and, in particular, with few exceptions, the texts and authors recovered by and for experimental writing were conspicuously white. Understanding experimental writing's recovery structure and comparing it with other recovery projects of the same period brings into relief how problematic and strange experimentalism's claims to political priority really were.

By now the mutually exclusive definition of "experimental" and "minority" literatures has been denounced as often as it has been proposed, including by white experimentalists themselves. As Lyn Hejinian has recently put it in a retrospective account of Language's track record of engaging with race (or rather, not doing so), "This failure—and I do think it is such—was, in part, a matter of bad faith: a failure to face what's going on. In this sense, color-blindness is an exercise in bad faith. It may be well-meaning, but that's irrelevant."[135] Harryette Mullen is just one of many prominent writers who has pointedly addressed "the sense of a mutual exclusiveness separating practices of innovative writing from identity or the politics of identity, the prevailing assumption that 'codes of oppressed peoples' or writing that was oppositional in a politically, socially, or racially conscious way was somehow incompatible with writing that might be described as experimental, avant garde, innovative, or formally oppositional to 'official verse culture.'"[136] This "sense of a mutual exclusiveness" is well known and frequently decried, but persistent all the same. As Dorothy Wang has argued, experimentalist discourses have had a distinct and singular allergy to writers of color (whereas white feminism, for example, has become highly integrated into experimentalist canon-making and criticism, though not without struggle): "race alone," she argues, "seems unspeakable."[137] Wang has offered a thorough and cogent critique of this tendency, identifying not only the either/or logic defining the relation between experimental and minority discourses but also the dynamics through which exceptions are made. Especially insofar as experimentalism has been theorized as a repudiation of the subject (the model centering on and projecting outward from Language), any discussion of race is held in suspicion as a form of "identity politics"; consequently, Wang argues, minority writers have often been identifiable as "experimental" precisely insofar as they are *not* identifiable as nonwhite.[138] Thus, she writes, "good minority poetry is set against bad minority poetry, which focuses on 'identity' (that hated concept, again), and to be experimental in the 'best and broadest sense of the term' is, implicitly, not to discuss race or ethnic identity."[139] Supposed repudiations of identity thus simply reinscribe whiteness as the "unmarked" identity.[140]

The quiet violences built into the discourse of the "experimental" are well established at this point, thanks largely to the work of writers and critics of color, including Nathaniel Mackey, Fred Moten, Sonya Posmentier, Anthony Reed, Evie Shockley, Dorothy Wang, and Timothy Yu.[141] I wish here to probe a little further into the forms taken by the persistent bifurcation between contemporary "experimental" and "minority" literatures. This bifurcation runs deeper than what Wang has described as "exclusion"; indeed, it will be part of the work of this book, in theorizing experimentalism, not simply to decry its racial politics but to explain them. A perspective inflected by history of science discloses that, while there are certainly aspects of experimentalism to value, including politically, there is a fundamentally racist strain to experimentalism—again, understood as a historical discourse rather than a set of formal traits—that can be traced to its epistemological aspirations. As Anthony Reed has observed, critics such as Perloff have drawn attention to the way in which Language poetry has become "more inclusive with respect to gender, race, and ethnic diversity" since the 1990s. Yet such statements, Reed points out, represent such gestures as "largesse," "without questioning why nonwhite, nonmale writers had not been more involved in the first place."[142] Notwithstanding what Tyler Bradway identifies as a hopeful recent "excavation of hidden, degraded, and ignored experimentalisms developed among marginalized writers and communities," there remains a default assumption that experimentalism is rooted in a white poetics.[143] I argue that, indeed, experimentalism's whiteness is not simply a matter of a cluster of now-canonical white writers' avoidances, as Hejinian suggests, but rather a structural consequence of the very frame of experimentalism.[144] This helps to explain not only the canonization of contemporary experimentalism but also the carefully monitored boundaries of retrospective modernist literary history, especially defensiveness around Gertrude Stein's wartime politics.[145] It also explains why, more than a decade after Mullen's compelling diagnosis of an "aesthetic apartheid," such diagnoses seem to require constant renewal, as Stefania Heim points out in her introduction to a 2015 *Boston Review* roundtable on the subject, coedited with Wang.[146] Where performative language serves as a *proxy for* radical politics—and I wish to stress that there is also something enabling and powerful in this poetics—the contradiction of a generally "oppositional" "radical politics" without anti-racism is already all too available.[147] We have already seen how experimental poetics, especially as practiced by Language writers, worked in tandem with a concerted reconstitution of modernism to foreground an "oppositional" experimental dimension, a critical project contemporaneous with the "recovery" of women's and minority literatures, but focused almost entirely on white writers. Experimental writing is a white recovery project not by accident or by happenstance exclusions but foundationally, based on an understanding of oppositionality whose center was always white.[148] By creating an impression of consistency across aesthetic, epistemological, ethical, and political domains, epistemic virtue, the very feature of experimental writing that is thought to guarantee its political edge, has usually operated to obfuscate the political liabilities that different knowledge practices may harbor.

Such obfuscation is evident across the recovered trajectory of US experimental writing. There is something exceptionally cringeworthy about a poem like Ezra Pound's "Commission" that—published in 1919, easily within a generation's memory of Emancipation—announces its allegiance to "the enslaved-by-convention" and clearly imagines "their oppressors" not as actual oppressors but as people who too complacently enjoy Palgrave's *Golden Treasury*.[149] In 1919, lynching continued to claim the lives of Black men and women, and the successful antiblack, pro-lynching film *The Birth of a Nation*, directed by another modernist "formal innovator," was only four years old. But there is nothing surprising about Ezra Pound's oppositional modernist gesture in "Commission," a poem that appeared in the same issue of *Poetry* as "In a Station of the Metro," nor about his proposal that, in changing the use of language, one might change the political course of the nation: this is already part of a conventional account of early twentieth-century poetics.[150] Such claims, when framed as a desire to maintain "cleanliness" and "the health of the very matter of thought itself"—and, not coincidentally, as a simultaneous turn toward a "scientific" "method," as in Pound's *ABC of Reading*—take on a frankly racist valence.[151] The late twentieth-century experimental hope is that the "oppositional" and "political" quality of such a use of language can be preserved without the opposition quite so directly targeting people of color and Jews. My point is not that experimental writing is tainted by association with any experimental writer with problematic politics—that would be quite a stupid claim. Rather, my point is that an abstract political "oppositionality" rooted in epistemic virtues, especially insofar as those epistemic virtues are imagined as scientific, was always doomed to default to centering whiteness. Experimental writing, as it came to be codified in the later twentieth century, actively sought an oppositional politics through an epistemological clarity that was to manifest in language, and often this meant appropriating a minority position, however egregiously ("enslaved-by-convention").

This tendency has most famously manifested in what Timothy Yu has called the "ethnicization of the avant-garde." It is the claim, variously taken up by Language and post-Language writers, that the inherently politically oppositional quality of "innovative" forms implicitly draws on ethnic forms, is politically aligned with the ends of racial justice, or—most tendentiously and controversially—subjects the writers of such works to the kinds of marginalization experienced by racial minorities in the United States.[152] Ron Silliman's claim (much repudiated, notably by Hejinian and Bernstein) in a letter to Peter Glassgold of "the comparability of the phrase 'language poetry' to epithets such as n——, c——, k—— or f——" reveals the potential end point of such logics.[153] But we do not have to look to Language's least flattering moments to see how experimental writers of the late twentieth century have self-identified as politically marginalized.[154] Yu has pointed out a late twentieth-century "sense among many white radicals that the language of resistance and revolution truly belongs to oppressed minorities and that white activists could only hope to borrow it."[155] Borrow it they did, as Grace Hale has documented in *A Nation of Outsiders*, an account of postwar white appropriations of minority positioning from Norman Mailer's essay "The

White Negro" (1957) to white co-optations of Black Power.[156] White experimental writers frequently positioned their work as politically oppositional through alignments with racially marginalized groups. As Yu points out, there are distinct moments in which white male writers have staked Language's claim to "an authentic social position of dissent, comparable to the positions of women and minorities."[157] Such claims are staked on formal grounds, as in Charles Bernstein's labeling of an "official verse culture" to which Language is opposed, in ways that parallel Pound's invocation of the "enslaved-by-convention."[158]

Needless to say, such intellectual alignments did not lead to a meaningful desegregation of experimental writing. Moreover, as Yu observes, later moves toward "inclusion" in the 1990s took the form of counterfactual histories, ruefully aware that "ethnic" and "experimental" literatures have often taken parallel and mutually exclusive trajectories.[159] But I am less concerned to point out this failure—a task already admirably and repeatedly undertaken by the critics and poets cited—than to attempt to explain the logic that underwrote it. That logic, as I have already suggested, lies in the terms on which experimental writing understood itself as politically "oppositional." Wang has rightly identified the experimental resistance to "identity" and "expression" as central to its race problem; certainly, "expression" characterizes the poetics that Barrett Watten names as the (somehow) ultimately less efficacious outgrowth of 1960s political resistance in his essay "The Turn to Language and the 1960s." "The confirmation of a politics" in the 1970s, he suggests, was only made possible by "the failure of poetic subjectivity in its confrontation with the historical present."[160] But the repudiation of "expression" and "identity" is an epiphenomenon of a more foundational, let us call it "scientific," epistemological commitment, evident, for example, in Joan Retallack's framing of what she calls the "poethical wager." Retallack discloses the aesthetic, epistemological, and ethical (potentially political) dimensions of the "swerve" (clinamen) that she associates with "experimental thought" when she argues that "swerves (like antiromantic modernisms, the civil rights movement, feminism, postcolonial critiques) are necessary to dislodge us from reactionary allegiances and nostalgias."[161] A series of political alignments—"the civil rights movement, feminism, postcolonial critiques"—are placed in parallel with the aesthetic orientation of "antiromantic modernisms," each having its part to play in "dislodg[ing] us from reactionary allegiances and nostalgias."[162] The tendentiousness of Retallack's parallel, in claiming comparable political stakes for "antiromantic modernisms" and (e.g.)

postcolonial critique, echoes Pound's tendentious cry against the "oppressors" of the "enslaved-by-convention." Moreover, like Pound, Retallack locates "the courage of the swerve" in an orientation toward "the sciences."[163] My point here is not to castigate Retallack in particular but rather to point out the *kind* of political efficacy being claimed for experimental writing, an oppositionality *as such* locatable in an orientation to language and literary form, following in the very "experimental" tradition that post-Vietnam writers worked so hard to canonize. Likewise, Jerome McGann's 1987 essay "Contemporary Poetry: Alternate Routes," an early articulation of the poetic "two cultures" thesis, argues that the key distinction in then-contemporary poetics is political, repeatedly labeling the two strains "accommodationist" and "oppositional," respectively.[164] Oppositional to what? "To all that means to appear authoritative, fixed, and determined," McGann proposes, an opposition that occurs "within the world of language because language is taken as the representative social form per se" in this moment.[165] McGann is, I think, largely correct about the logic underwriting Language's political claims. I wish here to outline why it attaches to a scientific orientation (McGann, too, uses the language of the "experimental") and can understand itself as somehow more, because more *foundationally*, politically "oppositional" than self-identified Black, feminist, Chicano, and other writing of the same moment.

Experimentalism presumes a distinction between representing and intervening, as I have already discussed, with intervening operating as the valorized, "experimental" term of the binary. If, as Wittgenstein frames it, "to imagine a language is to imagine a life-form," or, as Shapin and Schaffer put it, "solutions to the problem of knowledge are solutions to the problem of social order," then it is easy to see why language that subordinates "representing" to "intervening" could be understood as inherently political: some language merely represents (mimetically), but experimental writing, it is suggested, actually acts in the world.[166] Thus, for example, in a 1983 talk at the Modern Language Association convention on the occasion of the one hundredth anniversary of William Carlos Williams's birth, Charles Bernstein attempts to rescue a radical Williams from what he calls "the officially sanctioned verse of our time . . . neutral and univocal . . . in the guise of voice or persona," or what Barnhisel has identified as the "banal and unremarkable" middlebrow modernism of Cold War cultural diplomacy: unchallenging, "just a style," and "what middle-class audiences like because they *should*—because it is prestigious and good for them."[167] Against this, Bernstein posits a Williams whose "work is an *intervention* within the culture against static forms of knowledge, against schooled conceptions and traditional formulations."[168] Bernstein imputes experimental epistemic virtue, here indicated by "intervention," to Williams and construes this as political virtue.[169] Meanwhile, "voice" and "persona," for Bernstein, are evidence of writing being "*used* to convey emotions or ideas rather than allowed to enact them"—of showing, not doing; of representing, not intervening.[170] Where "identity" is the deprecated term that renders much nonwhite-authored writing illegible as experimental, as Wang argues, it is because the appearance of "identity" is framed as a kind of representing, an acceptance of the terms on which language normally operates and therefore a fundamental concession to dominant linguistic models. The "aesthetic apartheid" that Mullen names is thus subtended by a founding premise of experimentalism, namely that representing and intervening are actually opposed and mutually exclusive processes. To represent, within this framework, is to *not intervene*, because intervening means disrupting the very (ideological) premises of linguistic representation.

Reading experimentalism as a white recovery project means sympathetically attending to the reasons such recovery seemed urgent in the post-Vietnam moment. It also allows us to draw on the intellectual tools of critical ethnic studies to understand its "untimely" dynamics. As Sorensen notes, the critical projects of recovery create the conditions for making texts recoverable, notably through "institutional changes that create audiences for texts that previously struggled to find them."[171] The critical work of post-Vietnam experimental writer-critics—a somewhat famously "academic" cohort of writers appointed at Buffalo, UC Berkeley, UC San Diego, Penn, and elsewhere—recentered a particular version of "experimental" modernism at a time when depictions of modernism as an outgrowth of capitalist liberal democracy were literally state policy, and spoke back to official discourses of knowledge on those discourses' own terms. That those terms had always privileged a tacitly white and masculine decoupling from "identity" and "representation" was implicitly more of a feature than a bug, insofar as this logic responded to a specific epistemological field operating in and through language—one whose regimes of knowledge production upheld a global war machine. Experimentalism's white recovery project was a specific tactic aimed at a specific problem, whose purchase was gained at the cost of other, at least equally pressing political desiderata. Since then, the ground has shifted yet again, and it has become increasingly evident that, as Mimi

Thi Nguyen has succinctly put it, "liberal peace is not distinct from liberal war."[172] Under these circumstances, it becomes more difficult to imagine that there are winning moves in the language game of technological modernity. The new political baseline suggested by the persistence of a "peace" indistinguishable from war (e.g., military drones over Somalia and Yemen, with which the United States is ostensibly not at war) throws experimentalism's project into ever greater question, even as growing historical distance makes its investments and situatedness more available to analysis.

Epistemic virtues, in other words, have the morally suasive force of other kinds of virtue—religious, political, ethical—but they are not identical to other virtues, nor are they always consistent with one another. The centrality of epistemic virtues to experimental writing explains why "experimental" has sometimes served as a proxy for "politically radical." At the same time, as my discussions of flash, objectivity, precision, and contact show, privileging any given epistemic virtue does not necessarily mean that political virtues follow, and indeed, on the contrary, it sometimes means that they are foreclosed.

The Language of the Future

Literature has been declared dead more times than a Norwegian Blue parrot, and not just dead but *over*. Literature, as we continually see from contemporary university politics, is perpetually temporalized as past and *of* the past, however counterfactually.[173] Such claims are evident both within the university and in the persistent media claims that the jobs "of today" (or sometimes "of the future") are all in STEM fields. This is as ideological as the pastness attributed to women, "primitives," and geopolitical others (for instance, popular media characterizing contemporary Middle Eastern Islam as "medieval").[174] Meanwhile, science, technology, and commerce are temporalized as belonging to the future, often in breathlessly paradoxical language ("the future is now").[175] Thus it seems overdetermined that the *Routledge Companion to Experimental Literature* (2012) concludes with electronic literature—labeled "the digital age," as if it had arisen in the recent past.[176] The volume's structure represents electronic literature as a historical end point, even though, as Lori Emerson has argued, the peak moment of creativity in electronic literature may well have been concurrent with early personal computing, in the 1970s and 80s, before the "openness" that characterized early interfaces transitioned to the preeminence of "user-friendliness" inaugurated by the Apple Macintosh.[177] Even among experimentalisms, the newest newness is tacitly conferred on the most obviously technology-bound forms, whether actually new or not.[178]

Such temporalizations have characterized even defenses of literature. Philip Sidney, in his 1595 *Defence of Poesie*, ties literature both to the past and to infancy, pleading that its detractors "go very near to ungratefulness, to seek to deface that which, in the noblest nations and languages that are known, hath been the first light-giver to ignorance, and first nurse, whose milk by little and little enabled them to feed afterward of tougher knowledges."[179] Poetry, for Sidney, is to be valued precisely for being tethered to temporal earliness, tellingly figured through the maternal labor of breastfeeding. Thus, "truly neither philosopher nor historiographer could at the first have entered into the gates of popular judgments, if they had not taken a great passport of poetry, which in all nations at this day, where learning flourisheth not, is plain to be seen; in all which they have some feeling of poetry. . . . Even among the most barbarous and simple Indians, where no writing is, yet have they their poets, who make and sing songs."[180] This is an apology that concedes poetry's status as primitive—"barbarous and simple"—the opposite of modern. Thomas Love Peacock's satirical *Four Ages of Poetry* (1820), against which Shelley wrote the better-known *Defence*, echoes Sidney's themes of primitivism and infancy, now in a mocking vein: "While the historian and the philosopher are advancing in, and accelerating, the progress of knowledge, the poet is wallowing in the rubbish of departed ignorance, raking up the ashes of dead savages to find gewgaws and rattles for the grown babies of the age."[181] Literature's status as an atavism has historically been treated not so much as a point to be argued as a natural phenomenon to be explained. Thus Michel Foucault's influential account of modernity's decisive turn to a semiotics of representation understands the literary as such as an anachronistic vestige of an earlier, "magical" order of resemblances, wherein language and meaning were consubstantial.[182] "There is nothing now, either in our knowledge or in our reflection, that still recalls even the memory of that being. Nothing, except perhaps literature," which, in restoring to language the primacy of form, "[*finds*] *its way back* from the representative or signifying function of language to this *raw being*."[183] Literature, in this reading, is a path backward in time.[184]

The literary avant-gardes of the early twentieth century, and those who styled themselves as their successors, went on the offensive against this temporalization, appropriating scientific modernity as their own. Perhaps some art—and moonlight—belonged to a moribund past, but not these linguistic arts of the future: modernism, futurism, the avant-garde, and later the post-avant-garde, "innovative writing," and of course "experimental writing." Thus Bob Perelman has argued that "the goal of any ambitious, innovative writing is to catch up with the present," while Lyn Hejinian has averred that "what matters must be concerned with what will come to matter: the future."[185]

Rejecting nostalgia and aligning themselves with technological futurity, these writers accepted the premise of scientific modernity—with all its contradictions—and sought to craft languages of the future. And for a moment, in the late twentieth century, linguistic futurism converged with the sciences' linguistic turn. In "Barbarism," Hejinian took up a defense of Language poetry's purchase on the political by reappropriating the word "barbarism" to signify an attempt to use language against, instead of for, the military-industrial complex and its logics. "The word 'barbarism,' as it comes to us from the Greek *barbaros*," she writes, "means 'foreign'—that is, 'not speaking the same language' . . . —and such is precisely the task of poetry: *not to speak the same language as Auschwitz*. Poetry after Auschwitz must indeed be barbarian; it must be foreign to the cultures that produce atrocities."[186] Citing and reinterpreting Adorno, Hejinian justifies experimental writing's faith in the political efficacy of language using a term with a long history in Marxist thought but with no reference to the word's temporal, specifically primitivist connotations. Those connotations, moreover, are very much present in Marxist uses, especially Rosa Luxemburg's famous formulation "either an advance to Socialism or a reversion to barbarism": Luxemburg explicitly frames barbarism as a regression, in keeping with Marxist developmentalism.[187] Hejinian's turn to etymology itself performs all the contradictions of experimentalism's grasp of a language of the future. Hejinian uses a primitivist term, "barbarism," but does so as if in isolation from its primitivist connotations, in an apparent attempt to shed troubling social connotations in favor of an implicitly truer one—as if performing her own "barbaric" foreignness to a violent sociolinguistic order. This Poundian cleansing of language is at once utopian and itself primitivist in its privileging of etymological origins, hopeful of language's power to disrupt violent forms of life and yet also perpetuating them. Hejinian's reinterpretation of barbarism identifies it with a temporally modern experimentalism, in a gesture that "makes it new" precisely by recurring to the very old, and sweeping away all the history in between. In this sense, the redeployment of "barbarism" exemplifies the self-negating position of what Paul de Man, identifying an impulse to futurity unmoored from any particular historical moment, called "literary modernity," which "exists in the form of a desire to wipe out whatever came earlier, in the hope of reaching at last a point that could be called a true present, a point of origin that marks a true departure."[188]

This literary purchase on futurity is conventionally associated with "experimental" or "post-avant" writing, in no small part due to experimental writers' own insistence on the politics of form. This is an association that this book will be concerned to explain. Yet the lesson of *Star Trek IV: The Voyage Home* is startlingly similar—that the language of the future may turn out to be the voice of an extinct past. Time travel literalizes the predicament posed by scientific modernity, that the concept of the "modern" engenders a self-different temporality within which the forward-looking and the retrograde must coexist. *Star Trek*'s solution is to bifurcate these times, projecting a future peaceful scientific modernity in which knowledge production is relatively untainted by political interests. In this sense it enacts the fantasy that Sandra Harding has identified in "Northern philosophies of science and technology," wherein "scientific rationality and technical expertise are presented . . . as the one-way time machines that supposedly enable elite Westerners and men around the globe to escape the bonds of tradition."[189] Time travel, here, is not just a fanciful metaphor; it is also the mechanism for representing relations between present compromised (political) knowledge production and an imagined, more autonomous, more scientific science. We can see in this framing not only the hopes of Cold War–era big science but also the experimental literary alternative to it—not to mention the hopes of science fiction, a genre whose own conflicts around race and gender have paralleled those in experimental writing in recent years. In *Star Trek IV*, the difference between the future and the present is staged as the difference between a true scientific modernity and a compromised, "primitive" one. In the better, more scientific future modernity, the hyper-logical Vulcan Spock (Leonard Nimoy, who also directs) can instantaneously review enormous amounts of apparently neutral, autonomous information, enabling him to correctly identify the dangerous space probe's message as the song of the extinct humpback whale.[190] In contrast, Admiral Kirk comically warns his crew that the past to which they are traveling—the film audience's present, 1986—is "terra incognita . . . an extremely primitive and paranoid culture," an assessment that will be reaffirmed by the film's portrayal of 1980s science as dangerously tainted by political, especially Cold War, concerns.

The future is thus a mechanism for holding out hope for a truer, because truly autonomous, science, in contrast with the undeniably compromised science of the 1980s. The film's sole sympathetic scientist of the 1980s is a marine biologist named Gillian, who is genuinely and disinterestedly dedicated to saving George and Gracie, two whales due to be released into the wild and in grave danger from whale hunters. These are the whales that the crew must bring to the twenty-third century to communicate with the space probe whose radically alter language is destroying the Earth. (It is blithely assumed, in the film, that the Earth's oceans of the twenty-third century will still be able to support cetacean life.) Soon to be betrayed even by her colleagues at the Cetacean Institute, who will release George and Gracie "without even letting [her] say goodbye," Gillian is understandably suspicious of Kirk and Spock's interest in the whales. Recalling tales of government plots to weaponize marine biology, such as the US Navy's Marine Mammal Program and the 1973 thriller *The Day of the Dolphin*, she demands of Kirk, "You're not one of those guys from the military, are you? Trying to teach whales to retrieve torpedoes or some dipshit stuff like that?"[191] It is fitting that at the end of the film she opts to accompany the crew of the *Enterprise* back to the twenty-third century not to be with the whales so much as to join a science crew. "You're going to your ship; I'm going to mine," she tells Kirk elatedly at the end of the film. "I've got three hundred years of catch-up learning to do." The epistemically virtuous scientist is a scientist of the future, held away "from any traces of contamination by history," as Bruno Latour puts it, while science that is compromised by politics and military power is attached to a tainted present diegetically imagined as past.[192] In this way, the film models assumptions about epistemic virtue that startlingly resonate with the work of the Language writers who were just offscreen.

Meanwhile, the comical translation problems the crew will encounter in visiting San Francisco in 1986 reprise in a lighter vein the film's founding anxiety about language and translatability, embodied at first in the destructive whale song of the alien probe. The biggest of these gags revolves around the need for a large energy source after time travel has depleted the rickety repurposed Klingon vessel that the crew of the *Enterprise* has borrowed. Spock, ever a source of historical facts, points out that such a source could be found on a nuclear aircraft carrier, such as the one docked at Alameda—the real USS *Enterprise*, of course, made available for filming by cooperation with the US Navy.[193] The fictional and futuristic *Enterprise* ("its [deeply newness-invested] five-year mission: to explore strange new worlds; to seek out new life and new civilizations; to boldly go where no man has gone before") meets its double in the real and decidedly contemporary US naval vessel of the same name, than which there is hardly a more apt embodiment of the scientific military-industrial complex in action. Nostalgic for the wrecked ship that they once crewed, Commander Chekhov radios to Kirk: "Admiral, we have found the nuclear wessel! . . . And Admiral—it is the *Enterprise*." The two ships—one scientific and futuristic, one military and present—are thus brought into confrontation: they are heroically the same yet also radically different, as if the path from one *Enterprise*, compromised and war bound, to the other, exploratory and knowledge bound, is just a matter of time.

In the decidedly post-Cold War "present" of the film, it does not occur to Admiral Kirk that sending Commanders Uhura and Chekhov—the latter a Russian with a pronounced accent—to wander around San Francisco asking after the "nuclear wessels" (as Chekhov calls them) will raise suspicions. The climax of this subplot occurs when Uhura and Chekhov actually break into the ship to apply a device to the reactor to drain energy for their own use. Caught by American military officers, Chekhov is interrogated in a comical Who's-On-First-style sequence:

> OFFICER 1 (smiling cynically): All right. Take it from the top.
> CHEKHOV: The top of what?
> OFFICER 1: Name.
> CHEKHOV: My name?
> OFFICER 1 (sarcastically): No, *my* name.
> CHEKHOV (dismayed): I do not know your name!
> OFFICER 1: You play games with me, mister, and you're through!
> CHEKHOV: I am? . . . May I go now?[194]

The dialogue eventually culminates in a chase sequence whose soundtrack clearly marks the genre as comic. Here, Cold War tensions are rendered as a comedy sketch that turns on the discrepancy between the language-games that Chekhov and his military interrogator think they are playing. Despite framing the Soviets as the enemy, and therefore deeply culturally alter, this scene proposes that American and Soviet counterparts in the Cold War would in fact essentially speak the same language of suspicion and antagonism, whereas poor Chekhov is the real stranger not because he is Russian but because he is from the future. His cleanly literal language, epistemically virtuous, is what Hejinian might call "not . . . the same language as Auschwitz," where Auschwitz is a metonym for precisely the kinds of state atrocities committed by military power, and the USS *Enterprise* in particular. Chekhov is from *an Enterprise* but not this one, and he doesn't speak its language.

Star Trek IV thus proposes a vision of linguistic power that is surprisingly consonant with the poetics emerging in the San Francisco Bay Area of the same moment. Playing the right language game—or failing or refusing to—can have enormous political and physical consequences. And in this particular rendering of time- and space-travel tropes, we can see how mass-cultural Cold War science fiction attempts to access, from a different angle, meaningful purchase on scientific modernity.[195] In seeking this purchase, however, *Star Trek IV*, as much as Language writing, assents to the temporal and racial ideologies that scientific modernity tacitly presupposes. The starship *Enterprise*'s technological modernity is predicated on the contrast between its own autonomous, neutral science and the political, "primitive" uses to which the nuclear aircraft carrier *Enterprise* puts its vast energy-producing power.

Experimental writing likewise constructs its own modernity by way of contrast with what is nonmodern, which is to say, literature in general—the "conventional tradition" that James Laughlin, like so many others in the twentieth century, set against the experimental.[196] Experimentalism's wager is to take the part of scientific modernity, to argue that there can be a language of the future by tacitly accepting scientific modernity's premise that language, along with many other things, is ordinarily to be understood as a thing of the past. Language writing's besetting tendency to regard writers of color as insufficiently "innovative" thus comes into relief as a logical consequence of having already accepted the terms of scientific modernity, in which some places, practices, and people are scientific and temporally forward, and others are not.

Perelman crystallizes the dilemma that this acceptance poses when he examines the productively "promiscu[ous]" periodization of the avant-garde in the anthology *Poems for the Millennium*, volume 3, edited by Jeffrey Robinson and Jerome Rothenberg.[197] "Robinson and Rothenberg do not share Pound's political baggage," Perelman writes, "but they do share his conception of poetic history," in which "a sense of advance does not always entail chronological advance."[198] In their literary history as in Pound's, "innovation" appears as a formal property that only strategically reduces to chronological firstness. The faulty (if appealing) premise of Perelman's statement is that Pound's "conception of poetic history" isn't the political baggage itself. Within this schema of formal modernities, racially identifiable poetics come to be read as pathological attachments to the past—what Anne Cheng, building on the Freudian concept of a lost object unhealthily retained out of time, has theorized as "racial melancholia." Sara Ahmed has further elaborated how, especially in a (post)colonial context, "racism becomes readable as what the [racialized subject] is attached *to*. . . . The moral task is thus 'to get over it,' as if when you are over it, it is gone."[199] The temporal dimension of this alleged or real melancholia is crucial to the ways that it operates as a disqualification to participation in avant-gardism.[200] Language's white recovery project, experimentalism, recovers a language of the future precisely by recuperating those elements of literary history that were already consonant with scientific modernity's developmental imperatives.

Nguyen has argued that, after World War II, what Johannes Fabian called the "denial of coevalness" that underwrote empire was retheorized as what she calls "the gift of freedom," something that is liberal empire's to bestow and that, following Derrida's concept of the gift, always incurs an extended and unpayable debt.[201] Importantly, the gift of freedom is typically bestowed through war, avowed or otherwise—for example, through the *Enterprise*'s deployment to Vietnam. If succeeding iterations of empire produce the other as temporally past, then the gift of freedom marks liberal empire's right "to set and speed up the timetable," as Nguyen puts it. Thus, she argues, "the invitation to coevality also imposes violence . . . through the intervention (a war, or development) that rescues history for those peoples stalled or suspended in time."[202] This is one reason that the Mexican poet Octavio Paz casts a cold eye on the rhetoric of avant-gardism and certain national literatures' alleged failure to get with the program: "Underdevelopment is a United Nations euphemism for backwards nations."[203]

Experimentalism's anti-imperialist language-game, explicitly developed in reaction against the atrocities of the Vietnam War and drawing on a massive intellectual edifice of language theory and literary history, thus ironically comes full circle, perpetually made complicit by the very epistemic virtues that it hoped to use to propel a politically engaged language of the future—a language built on the autonomous, genuinely disinterested knowledge production that can only be imagined as *of* the future. The early twentieth-century epistemic virtues that I will investigate in the chapters that follow—flash, objectivity, precision, and contact—all reveal something of this complicity, even as they also open up thrilling vistas of knowledge. I aim to describe their epistemological power and the aesthetics of knowledge that they enabled. Taking for granted the provisionality and slipperiness of experimentalism's radical and, by some lights, nearly ridiculous claim—that literature can make knowledge claims and, by doing so well enough, can act politically in the world—I look for the duct tape and chewing gum that holds it together, that has made "experimental" a meaningful term for so many people.

2 Flash

"The wild effects of the light enchained me to an examination of individual faces; and although the rapidity with which the world of light flitted before the window, prevented me from casting more than a glance upon each visage, still it seemed that, in my then peculiar mental state, I could frequently read, even in that brief interval of a glance, the history of long years."[1] After nightfall, under gaslight's chiaroscuro, faces in the crowd become oddly individuated, and though each face gets but "a glance," that glance is sufficient to reveal "the history of long years." Walter Benjamin, reading by way of Charles Baudelaire, saw in the narrator of Poe's "The Man of the Crowd" (1840) an avatar of modernity, exposed, in the crowd, to continual shocks.[2] Certainly, as Benjamin and many others have traced, the crowd was an object of close literary attention in the nineteenth century. Certainly, too, it was—powerfully and consequentially—the object and shaper of a variety of practices that would come to be called the social sciences, as well as some that would come to be called other things: literature, journalism, reform, philanthropy, documentary, social work, policing, pseudoscience. Each aimed to know and represent the social body, or what would come to be known as "population."

Within these notionally crowd-oriented knowledge projects, what is remarkable is the sufficiency and informational superabundance of the illuminated individual face. Although Poe's narrator begins with sociological pronouncements about various social types—businessmen, clerks, gamblers—reminiscent of what Benjamin called the "panoramic literature" of the period, eventually the narrator's observation of the crowd will give way to fixation on a single figure, that of "the man of the crowd," whose striking face—"a countenance which at once arrested and absorbed my whole attention"—is that of the crowd itself.[3] After a nightlong chase, the story climaxes with the

Figure 1. Henry Bowditch Pickering, *A Group of Saxon Soldiers and Their Composite*, circa 1892. Countway Library of Medicine, Harvard University.

narrator "gaz[ing] at him steadfastly in the face," to no avail: unlike the earlier faces merely glanced at, "er lasst sich nicht lesen"; it will not be read.[4] The face *in* the crowd is maximally legible, revealing sociological knowledge at a glance; but the infinitely pathological face *of* the crowd, or what we might otherwise call *the crowd in the face*, is considerably blurrier (figure 1). Poe's story, written during the very early days of disciplinary sociology, stages the crowd's resistance to legibility in the aggregate, even when the whole crowd has somehow been embodied in a single figure.

The crowd in the face was also visualized in the many popular imitations of Francis Galton's composites, which attempt to work around the crowd's illegibility; Allan Sekula has influentially called these composites an effort "to embed the archive in the photograph."[5] Like Poe's narrator, such composites attempt to give the crowd a single face and thereby visualize social pathology; if there is any way to approach knowledge of the social body, these gestures suggest, it will be through its *figure*, a face in, and somehow of, the crowd. Faces are not the only illuminated, self-sufficient, self-distinguishing figures; they are a privileged form of synecdoche, thought to encapsulate the whole body—indeed, as in physiognomy, the whole self—and perhaps, as here, the whole social body, and all in a glance. This aspiration, which crosses a variety of attempts to know the social body, is what I am calling "flash." Elsewhere it is called a glance, *Blick*, or *coup d'oeil*. I trace it, however, especially from the final decades of the nineteenth century, where we will see how closely implicated flash is not only with vision but with effects of light and dark. It is an epistemological, even scientific, aspiration that always has something to say in advance about aesthetics. When I talk about flash as an epistemic virtue, then, I am not talking about *a* flash (of light, of insight, the literary "moment"), although flash as a virtue is often (not always) embodied in such flashes. Epistemic virtues are desiderata for securing knowledge; thus "flash" names the virtue that secures population knowledge. It therefore often comes bound up in the virtues of public-mindedness, investigative or journalistic integrity ("sunshine is the best disinfectant"), and concern for the health of the social body.

Flash is not a method; rather, it is a set of values aimed at the management of information, and especially of too much information. Like the face in the crowd, flash delivers the important elements; it is always reductive yet somehow also self-sufficient, and, in its reductiveness, all the more comprehensible. So, for example, in an 1897 letter to Joseph Conrad, Stephen Crane praises the suggestive simplicity of a single detail in Conrad's *The Nigger of the Narcissus*: "By such small means does the real writer suddenly flash out in the sky above those who are always doing rather well."[6] In Crane's appealing image of Conrad beaming in the sky like the Bat-Signal, flash reveals the "real writer"; the flash is an instrument of discernment that separates the genuine article from the merely plausible. In Crane's reading, a single, small detail carries "the weight of a real and present death"; partial yet sufficient, flash marks out what is real, and, in doing so, it dislodges the sense of reality from *verisimilitude* or *resemblance*, resituating it instead in the encoding of detail in an intuitable glance.[7] Flash thus undertakes the characteristic experimental gesture of embracing a *nonverisimilar real*. The gesture of claiming a superior realism by way of superseding an inadequate, too-basic baseline realism is something that late nineteenth-century naturalisms and "experimental" modernisms hold in common.[8] Against any sharp distinction across these literary-historical categories (and in sympathy with critics like Mark Seltzer, Bill Brown, Dana Seitler, and Jennifer Fleissner), I aim, here, to explain uses of flash across literary, social-scientific, and visual registers by contextualizing them in a specific historical epistemological framework—roughly, what Emily Steinlight calls the "biopolitical imagination"—and within a broader understanding of experimental writing.[9] Although I will take writing by Stephen Crane and Ezra Pound as key points of reference in this chapter, it will soon become clear that, in the main period of my interest, flash—despite clear roots in Romantic aesthetics—does not derive its powers from singular authorial personae or from privileged forms of singularity like aura or indexicality, but rather from a performance of communicative transparency between the many and the many—a transparency all the more remarkable for taking place unmistakably and self-consciously *in code*. Like contemporary literary experimentalism, the aesthetics of flash is both wary of mass culture and deeply committed to the mass—committed to the mass's unmanageability, that is, as well as the possibility of apprehending it, if only provisionally, as a clarity grounded in obscurity. Pound—attributing to it the status of a science—would call this "the method of the Luminous Detail."[10] Flash is not an obviously "scientific" virtue in the way that, for instance, objectivity is; yet it animates the fin-de-siècle attempt to develop methods of "representing and intervening" adequate to difficulties of counting and accounting for the social body.[11]

A Momentary Gleam of Light: Flash's Time

Jacob Riis's 1888 woodcut-illustrated newspaper essay "Flashes from the Slums: Pictures Taken in Dark Places by the Lightning Process" makes the photographic flash the protagonist of its investigation. Flash (or "flashlight") photography was a new invention of the late nineteenth century, a magnesium strip or powder ignited in the moment of taking the picture, sometimes dangerously.[12] Although Riis's story is illustrated using woodcuts taken from the photos, Riis is at pains to foreground the use of this technology as a guarantor of what it reveals; indeed, the essay opens with a dramatic narration not of what the investigator sees but of what the investigated must have seen—little, that is, but the photographic flash:

> With their way illuminated by spasmodic flashes, as bright and sharp and brief as those of the lightning itself, a mysterious party has lately been startling the town o' nights. Somnolent policemen on the street, denizens of the dives in their dens,

> tramps and bummers in their so-called lodgings, and all the people of the wild and wonderful variety of New York night life have in their turn marvelled at and been frightened by the phenomenon. What they saw was three or four figures in the gloom, a ghostly tripod, some weird and uncanny movements, the blinding flash, and then they heard the patter of retreating footsteps, and the mysterious visitors were gone before they could collect their scattered thoughts and try to find out what it was all about.[13]

The mysteriousness of the nearly spectral photographers, who are "gone before" their subjects can apprehend them, turns on their swiftness. Time is of the essence: the flash is "spasmodic" and "brief as . . . the lightning itself." Its instantaneity is its advantage.

The photographic flash as Riis uses it helps to explain the temporal dimension of the broader concept of "flash" that I wish to describe in this chapter. Flash assumes that instantaneity is an epistemological good.[14] The discourse around contemporary writing by Stephen Crane offers an adjacent case: Crane's writing has frequently been compared to photography, and it is sometimes assumed that the imputation of "photographic realism" rests primarily on the photograph's authority as a faithful, mechanically (therefore supposedly disinterestedly) produced representation or, alternatively, on indexical theories of the photograph. But contemporary reception suggests that Crane's photographic quality and the realism it entailed were, in the end, a matter of style—indeed, of a *stylization* that invoked the epistemological qualities of the flash, instantaneity chief among them. Consider, for example, an unsigned 1896 review of *Maggie* in the *Wave*:

> In *Maggie, a Girl of the Streets*, Stephen Crane has written a story something on the plan of the episode of Nana in [Émile Zola's] *L'Assommoir*, the dialect and local color being that of the Bowery. Mr. Crane strikes no new note in his picture of the other half. Most of his characters are old acquaintances in the world of fiction and we know all about—or at least certain novelists have pretended to tell us all about the life of the mean streets of a great city. In ordinary hands the tale of *Maggie* would be "twice told." But Mr. Crane is, of course, out of the ordinary. I think that the charm of his style lies chiefly in his habit and aptitude for making phrases—short, terse epigrams struck off in the heat of composition, sparks merely, that cast a momentary gleam of light upon whole phases of life. There are hundreds of them throughout this tale of *Maggie*. Indeed, it is the way Mr. Crane tells his story. The picture he makes is not a single carefully composed painting, seri-

ous, finished, scrupulously studied, but rather scores and scores of tiny flashlight photographs, instantaneous, caught, as it were, on the run.[15]

Told straight away that the "plan" of the novel is lifted from that ur-naturalist, Émile Zola, that we "know all about" the scene of "local color" that Crane chooses, and that the author "strikes no new note," we are ready to hear *Maggie* panned. *Maggie* is unoriginal in the way that the naturalist novel is always unoriginal: mean streets, great city, stock characters, an "other half" whose way of living Jacob Riis has already described.[16] And yet the critic turns: this very tawdry conventionality becomes the grounds for praising Crane's distinctive style, and, in a surprising reversal, the naturalist novel, so often accused of being all plot and no style, emerges as virtually *all* style.[17] That style is that of flash: Crane's "terse epigrams" are reminiscent of the magnesium flash photograph, less because of the flash photograph's mimetic powers than insofar as it offers an *epistemological* flash: it is "instantaneous" and thus provides a picture that is worth a thousand words—but is more likely to be found captioned in a daily paper by just a choice few.[18] Like Riis's "patter of retreating footsteps," Crane's style creates the sensation of being "caught . . . on the run," and that very sensation of the artist's speed—above accuracy, clarity, or detail—seems to guarantee *Maggie*'s purchase on reality.

"Some of the words illuminate like flashes of light," Hamlin Garland wrote of *Maggie*.[19] What kind of illumination does a flash of light give? To understand instantaneity as an epistemological good is to understand one's object of study as temporally specific, changeable and likely to change over time. Riis certainly understood the urban poor in this way. As Cindy Weinstein observes, Riis seems to turn to the photograph in *How the Other Half Lives* (1890) as a way of compensating for a statistical project that seems hopelessly inadequate to the ever-teeming, always-changing tenements.[20] Indeed, for Riis, the problem of social knowledge seems to foist itself on a happily ignorant public not by protest or political engagement but by the way that the sheer physical crowding and overflow of bodies inside the city increase over time, in a fashion almost geological in its inexorability. "To-day three-fourths of [New York's] people live in the tenements," he writes, "and the nineteenth-century drift of the population to the cities is sending ever-increasing multitudes to crowd them."[21] Time and movement are serious problems for developing a reliable account of the slums, and, therefore, although "statistics and censuses . . . appear throughout *How the Other Half*

Lives," as Weinstein observes, "each attempt at authenticity is accompanied by acknowledgment of likely error."[22]

Given the epistemological challenges posed by movement over time, instantaneous capture allowed an observer to see things that were in motion, and therefore otherwise unseeable or uncountable, much in the way that Eadweard Muybridge's serial photographs of moving animal and human bodies made it possible to track the shape of motion. (Muybridge made a number of zoetrope strips from these photographic series.) "I tried to count the children that swarmed there, but could not," Riis writes.[23] As Weinstein suggests, for Riis, flash photography precisely corrects for the problem of "continual motion" that too often renders statistical accounts inaccurate and instantly obsolete.[24] Flash, then, responds to something known or believed to be known in advance about the thing it seeks to know: that the object of study is not static but, on the contrary, elusive and in perpetual motion in time, and apprehensible only through a swiftness that freezes time, however provisional the instantaneous image may be (but then, you can take scores and scores of them, on the run).

Flash's instantaneity also counters a distinguishing feature of living, and especially human, objects of study—their agency. Riis explicitly names the element of surprise as a guarantor of the flash photograph's reliability; writing of the investigative party in "Flashes from the Slums," he assures readers that "their night pictures were faithful and characteristic, being mostly snap shots and surprises." It is in the nighttime that the flash is needed to illuminate the tenements and in which the darkness renders these photographs a surprise. "In the daytime," in contrast, the investigators "could not altogether avoid having their object known, and, struggle as they might against it, they could not altogether prevent the natural instinct of fixing up for a picture from being followed. When a view was of interest and value as they found it, they were sometimes unable to stop the preparation and posing from almost destroying the interest in it."[25] These are, in short, people. They can run, hide, talk back, and dissemble, and are—or are perceived as—perfectly likely to do so. The tenement dwellers' insistence on controlling their self-presentation "almost destroy[s]" the epistemological value of the photograph, even after their agency has been discursively demoted to a "natural instinct." The nighttime flash, with its element of surprise, neutralizes that agency by allowing the photographers to "avoid having their object known" (figures 2 and 3).

In the same period, flash's instantaneity similarly helped to neutralize

Figure 2. *Waked Up by the Flashlight.* Woodcut illustration for "Flashes from the Slums: Pictures Taken in Dark Places by the Lightning Process," *Sun* (New York), February 12, 1888.

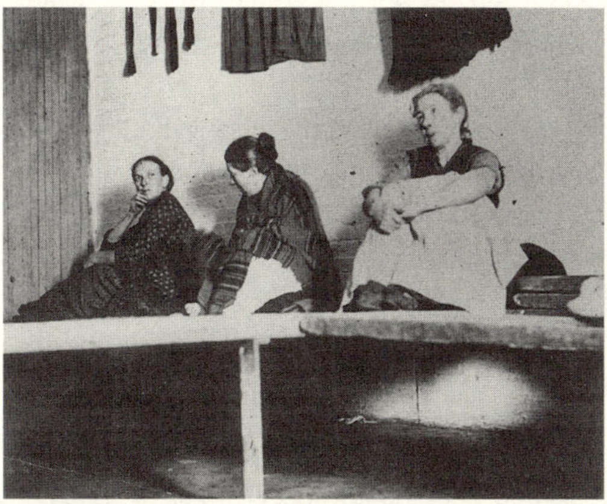

Figure 3. *Waked Up by the Flashlight*, the lodging room (for women) of the Thirtieth Street Police Station. Photograph by Richard Hoe Lawrence, 1887, PR 032, #12, New-York Historical Society.

agency at Jean-Martin Charcot's hospital for hysterics at the Salpêtrière. As Ulrich Baer has observed, "Hysteria had always been associated with masking, histrionics, deception, and imitation," and "the photograph was meant to exteriorize, make visible, and arrest the hysterical symptom in a way that would allow for a clean separation between this symptom and the patient's alleged intention."[26] This was particularly important, Baer argues, in establishing the legitimacy of Charcot's diagnoses, which were continually accused of having been staged; thus, "as part of his strategy to diagnose symptoms that could not have been rehearsed, Charcot began to put the surprise factor of the flash to work" by leading a hysterical patient into a darkened room and flash-photographing her.[27] Three such images appear in the *Iconographie photographique de la Salpêtrière*.[28] For Charcot as for Riis, knowing the people in question means not being known by them, a circumstance that the flash enables by setting up a temporary but crucial asymmetry of vision. "The blinding flash," as Riis calls it, ever so briefly produces person and person as investigator and investigated, seer and seen. This gesture is, in an important sense, objectifying. Yet it also constructs human objects of study as agential and functionally uncontainable except by surprise, in the briefest of instants. Despite a naturalizing language that construes human actions as "symptoms" or "natural instincts," the use of the flash responds to a problem of human intention. Instantaneity is an epistemological good, then, when one's objects are active and human and one needs for them to stay that way, and yet also be, however momentarily, as available to scrutiny as if they were not.

While photographic flash is literally (relatively) instantaneous, flash's instantaneity (say, in the literary register) may be performed or otherwise signaled aesthetically, as Crane's writing helps us to see. Instantaneity inheres in the mode that Edwin Cady calls Crane's "métier," the sketch, with even Crane's longer works consisting of "montages of sketches" (a tellingly cinematic metaphor).[29] I wish to highlight two features of the sketch that especially characterize its congeniality flash epistemology: first, the sensation of rapidity that it imparts and, second, its nonverisimilitude, suggesting comprehensiveness through partialness and selection.[30] Jacqueline Goldsby notes that the sketch is "best appreciated for its swift, penetrating observations," marking, with the word "swift," the element of speed implicit in the genre, regardless of how long it actually took to write any given sketch.[31] Yet while the sketch suggests speed, it does not, for that, sacrifice "penetrating observations." The sketch operates through a sensation of speedy motion and through partial glimpses. Such sketches—what Wertheim and Sorrentino, reverting again to a visual metaphor, call Crane's "graphically realistic pen portraits"—are in this sense openly illusionistic yet somehow superlatively communicative.[32]

Swiftness offers epistemological ballast to flash because it catches life in motion, then, but also because it serves as a mechanism for encoding—not a direct transmission of reality but rather its rendering as something less instantaneously created than instantaneously apprehensible. Thus, in "Flashes from the Slums," Riis carefully enumerates the panorama of the "wild and wonderful variety of New York night life," the spectacle of the mass being presented to a mass public via newspaper, only to briefly reverse the view: this mass is an audience too, and, whether tenement dweller or newspaper reader, what you are treated to is the mass spectacle of the flash itself. The "uncanny," blurry, and spectral spectacle of picture taking thus briefly stands in nonverisimilar proxy for the variety of life it is meant to reveal. "Flashes from the Slums" thus act as a point of translation, a way of transmuting human life into something readable and back again. There is, in other words, an informatic quality in flash, an epistemological confidence in the sufficiency and transparency of partial and nonverisimilar representation, to the degree that the representation exceeds the reality effect of the thing it represents.[33]

An Abstract of the World: Flash's Condensation

In its instantaneity, flash offers brevity. Yet this is not a brevity of spareness or withholding. Rather, flash's brevity is one of sufficiency, even plenitude, suggesting condensation or contraction. Certainly Crane's writing has been treated in this way, as in the *Wave* reviewer's praise of Crane's "short, terse epigrams" or, later, in Pizer's description of the "inherently compact" poetic devices in *Maggie*. Pound made it an entire poetic principle: "Dichten = condensare."[34] A flash, however partial, always means more than it shows. And while flash always rests its authority on a sense of instantaneity, that sense may be produced by the condensation of information gathered slowly, laboriously, and tediously into a single *coup d'oeil*, rather than the scene of instantaneous production on which, for instance, the flash photograph relies. Instantaneous apprehension, the *coup d'oeil* suggests, is in itself an epistemological good. Whereas flash's instantaneity suggests the management of an object's agency and propensity to change over time, its condensation affirms an object's variety and potentially vast extension across time and space. Flash is thus congenial to what Theodore Porter, following Ernst Mayr, calls "population thinking," the way of understanding variance in a sample not as erroneous deviation from an ideal (as in work by earlier statisticians such as Adolphe Quetelet) but rather as the genuine and necessary variability within any given population.[35] Broadly, then, instantaneity presumes an epistemological problem of individual variation—a tenement dweller's ability to be asleep one moment and composing herself for the camera the next, for instance—whereas condensation presumes an epistemological problem of population, geographic, or historical variation.

Most data visualization partakes in some degree of the values of flash, in probably the most direct instance of flash's epistemological, and specifically *informational*, orientation. Like the faces in the crowd, data visualizations aim to offer an intuitive sense of the whole at a glance. Data visualization is so common in contemporary media that it does not strike us as unusual that there is nothing about the image that mimetically *resembles* the thing it describes; in fact, the image is intuitable and informative insofar as irrelevant particulars have been stripped away. Data visualization is usually thought to have emerged in the late eighteenth century, and it is often given an origin story in the work of the eighteenth-century political economist William Playfair. The German naturalist Alexander von Humboldt is likewise famous for diagrams that draw a vast, even quintessentially sublime, whole into a single contained, manageable view. As Charlotte Bigg has demonstrated, the panorama—the cylindrical paintings that their inventor, Robert Barker, called "*la nature à coup d'oeil*"—shares an aesthetic with Romantic-era scientific and professional attempts to render environments comprehensible, notably in geography and military topography. The principles that underwrote the panoramic view manifested in the methods by which panoramas were constructed, relying on trained judgment to produce "a true picture of the scene, topographically exact but also faithful in rendering the impressions experienced on-site."[36] The horizontal projections of these circular views developed in the early nineteenth century demonstrate the hierarchy of values implicit in the *coup d'oeil*: an elevated, comprehensive view of the scene was achieved through smooth and carefully rendered distortions in the landscape, such that distortions actually enabled what was understood as the most accurate possible view (figure 4). As Lorraine Daston argues, the production of a "single bright flare of insight" or (to use Humboldt's term) *Totaleindruck* from "the condensation of laborious, step-by-step procedures" has a history not merely of re-presenting data but also of creating the terms on which scientific objects might be understood as existing in the first place.[37]

Condensation, as Daston's description hints, is one of the nonverisimilar ways in which flash achieves its reality effect. As we see in the foregoing examples, many kinds of information can be and have been treated in this way, and the continuities between Playfair's line graphs and Saussure's distorted maps reveal that data visualization need not be fundamentally quan-

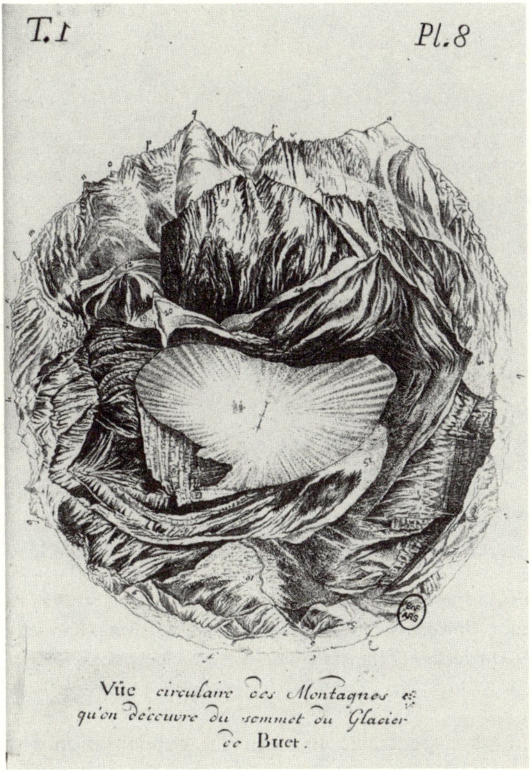

Figure 4. Horace-Bénédict de Saussure, *Vûe circulaire des Montagnes qu'on découvre du sommet du Glacier de Buet. Voyages dans les Alpes*, vol. 1 (Geneva: Barde, Manget et Compagnie, 1786), plate 8 (opposite p. 512). Gallica, Bibliothèque nationale de France.

titative. What they hold in common is an aesthetic strategy for controlling the sublime scale of information and rendering it communicable, without, however, reducing the sublimity of the underlying data.[38] Indeed, as Michelle Murphy has incisively pointed out in another context, flash may just as easily be said to produce populations and data sets *as* sublime: as she puts it, "The sublime of the economy is glimpsed . . . in the flash of advertising."[39] While the aesthetics of flash would come to be regarded with suspicion in some fields (such as comparative anatomy, which valued flash's opposite number, precision, more highly), the condensing powers of flash remained compelling in the versions of scientific representation that kept faith with

Figure 5. Lewis Lindsay Dyche, Kansas Panorama, 1893. University of Kansas Natural History Museum, University of Kansas Biodiversity Institute. Kenneth Spencer Research Library, University of Kansas Libraries.

their roots in mass spectacles. In particular, condensation was a frequent convention in turn-of-the-century museum dioramas, which are often seen as direct descendants of the panorama.[40] As Frederic Lucas put it in a 1921 pamphlet for the American Museum of Natural History in New York, many dioramas "brin[g] together in one composite picture a number of animals that probably would not be found in so small an area at any one moment of the season depicted, but might all be found there at some moment of the season. . . . In this, the day of moving pictures, we may say that as the moving picture condenses into five minutes' time the events of days or weeks, so these groups depict in a few square feet of space the life and happenings of a much larger area."[41] A panorama from the Kansas pavilion at the 1893 Chicago World's Fair, for example, encapsulates a variety of terrains and their native fauna in a single display (figure 5). Much like the mountain and forest landscapes drawn together in this diorama, the stuffed animals are obviously displayed in much greater density than in the wild, so that a viewer can take the variety in all at once. What would in reality be spread out over both time and space is here condensed in a single view.

Flash's condensation also pertains in a literary register; for example, the godlike perspective of the abandoned child on the mountaintop near the end of Crane's short story "Death and the Child" (1898) seems almost a direct citation of the panoramic *coup d'oeil* tradition, with its military subject and its positioning from above.[42] Like a magnification of the zoetrope-like fistfight in Crane's celebrated short story "The Blue Hotel," the "whirl[ing]" battle is apprehensible as a flash, from above, and is distinguished by what flashes out of it: "Part of the battle had whirled very near to the base of his hill, and the noise was great. Sometimes he could see fantastic smoky shapes which resembled the curious figures in foam which one sees on the slant of a rough sea. The plain, indeed, was etched in white circles and whirligigs like the slope of a colossal wave. . . . Lines of flame flashed out here and there. It was a mystery."[43] Mystery and optical illusion, Crane's rendering of the battle as "shapes," "circles," and "lines"—as abstraction, as code—also makes of that view at once a direct image and a schematic; distorted and unreadable as they are, the figures "etched" into the plain below are not a representation but rather what the child literally sees of the battle from above, condensed and projected onto two dimensions. The diagram of the battle is identical to the battle itself. And in this, the cipher-like battle performs the experimental tension of a realism without resemblance: the optimally real *coup d'oeil* appears precisely in the form of an unreadable schematic, seen from above, panoramically, encoded in the abstraction of battle lines and flanks. The flash is thus, as Bigg describes the panorama's *coup d'oeil*, "both comprehensive and absolutely exact in all its details"—both "pitilessly real," as one contemporary described *Maggie*, and "impressionist."[44]

"Death and the Child" is a story of the misperception of proportions and quantities engendered by the Greco-Turkish War, in which a young journalist, Peza, foolishly overeager for battle, becomes implicated. Indeed, distorted topography is the reason the child is abandoned in the first place: "Terror had operated on these runaway people in its sinister fashion, elevating details to enormous heights, causing a man to remember a button while he forgot a coat, overpowering every one with recollections of a broken coffee-cup, deluging them with fears for the safety of an old pipe, and causing them to forget their first-born. Meanwhile the child played soberly with his trinkets."[45] The confusion of fear is described as an inability to judge quantities and measures, "elevating details to enormous heights"; likewise, as the story opens, it is asserted that "the peasants who were streaming down the mountain trail had in their sharp terror evidently lost their ability to count," while, in contrast, "the sea, the sky, and the hills combined in their grandeur to term this misery inconsequent." Peza, too, struck with excitement by the peasants' being struck with excitement, foists his services as a soldier onto an amused lieutenant, whereupon "things immediately assum[e] new and extraordinary proportions" for him.[46] The story closes when Peza, horrified and chastened by the fray of battle, scrambles up the hill and comes face-to-face with the child, who asks him, as if to mark the difference in their statures, "Are you a man?" The final tableau offers spatial distortions that render up the real lay of the land: "Peza gasped in the manner of a fish. Palsied, windless, and abject, he confronted the primitive courage, the sovereign child, the brother of the mountains, the sky and the sea, and he knew that the definition of his misery could be written on a wee grass-blade."[47] Both Peza and the child are transformed into topography, or rather a topographical diagram, in which the small abandoned child deservedly takes up vastly more space—of mountain, sky, and sea proportions—than do Peza's small, inscribed woes. Finally, Peza has, as it were, some perspective.

In its account of flight and battle, "Death and the Child" does not particularly privilege individual or aggregate acts (the tension that Weinstein reads in Riis's *How the Other Half Lives*, for instance); rather, its apprehension of the social depends on flash: the rendering of a distended yet right topography that both schematizes the human terrain and insists on that schema's superior adequacy to the real. These visualizations in "Death and the Child," like those of military topography and the panorama in a previous century, thus exemplify what Mark Seltzer has called the fin de siècle's "merger between the desire to quantify and the desire to see"—with the understanding that "to see" means to see in a particular way: all at once, in an instantaneous but fully sufficient flash, glance, or *coup d'oeil*, comprehending yet also superseding the slow accumulations of statistical and demographic methods that, as Riis so anxiously attests, seem almost preemptively defeated by time's passing.[48] Flash's affinity for condensation thus helps to account for what Michael Fried has identified as "two opposing tendencies, one toward miniaturization and the other toward a certain monstrosity, [that] coinhabit Crane's prose."[49] Flash discloses the means by which, pace Fried, the miniature and the monstrous are not, in the end, opposed at all; rather, Crane's nonverisimilar realism consists in his repeated demonstration of how it is possible to contain the latter in the former.

While instantaneity and condensation can notionally be disarticulated, I wish to insist on flash's formal and conceptual entanglement with both principles. Early cinematic devices such as the zoetrope, which produces the illusion of a moving image by whirling its successive frames in a cylinder, offer a convenient metaphor: at any given moment, the zoetrope offers at once a static, partial, instantaneous component image and an aggregated moving image persisting, and changing, through time. Flash's multifarious engagements with scale offer it special purchase on the social, a domain in which the epistemological challenges of both agency and variation obtain. Flash manages the mass *for* the mass, condensing the crowd as a flash and offering the flash back to the crowd; in this sense it is explicitly "popular" and "simple," less despite its nonversimilitude than because of it. Pound, too, will lay a claim to this simplicity in nonverisimilitude. Flash is, in a meaningful sense, a kind of abstraction.

Criticism of recent decades has emphasized the social-scientific authority of approaches that privilege aggregate behavior, smoothing away the problem of agency.[50] Yet the archive of what counts as social knowledge in the first place is shaped in part by retrospective disciplinary taxonomies that may not include the broader domain of social knowledge within which flash operated.[51] Flash is thus important precisely for the ways that it crosses knowledge domains of varying degrees and forms of authority—from the statistical atlas to journalism to still more ambiguous popular forms like Riis's *How the Other Half Lives*. Attending to flash reveals that the convenient shorthanding of "individuals" and "aggregates" in the production of social knowledge might be better understood in the terms of managing the breadth of epistemological challenges posed by living human populations bound in time. Condensation translates sprawling temporal and spatial variations into a flash that is apprehensible, if not producible, instantaneously.

The visual interarticulation of instantaneity and condensation in flash are exemplified in the demographic work of the geographer Henry Gannett, an eventual founding member of the National Geographic Society, whose major works include the statistical atlases of the US Censuses for 1880, 1890, and 1900 (the US Census Bureau published such atlases for each census from 1870 to 1920). These large folio volumes offer page after page of *coup d'oeil* color visualizations and statistical tables of US demographics, and they demonstrate that, like Riis, Gannett was cognizant of the challenges that time and human agency posed to the construction of statistical knowledge. Gannett's atlases depict a society in motion, with several data visualizations explicitly recording not an instantaneous single state but rather an instantaneous *rate of change*. A whole section of the 1880 atlas (which was co-compiled with

Fletcher Hewes) is labeled "Progress," beginning with a brief essay chronicling the changes to US territories since 1780 and concluding with a series of visualizations such as "Growth of States in Population" and "Rank of the Most Populous Cities at Each United States Census," depicting and juxtaposing multiple rates of demographic change corresponding to different localities.[52] Despite the graphical tightness of the visualizations, they also offer a sense of almost overwhelming plenitude, proposing multiple comparisons within each visualization. In the "Growth of States" image, for example, each state is represented by its own bar graph representing population growth, with each bar graph stacked one over the other for further comparison; additionally, each of these graphs is captioned with a small bar graph comparing the state's physical area to that of the state of Ohio, which, Hewes and Gannett write, "being centrally located and symmetrical in form, has been chosen as a unit of comparison."[53] Thus the atlas proposes both enormous variation and the essential comparability of those variations, down to the translatability of each state into some quantity of Ohios. Gannett's 1890 atlas likewise condenses the measurement of an ever-changing population in numerous plates depicting, for example, "Inter-state Migration" and "Proportion of the Foreign-Born to the Aggregate Population."[54]

Gannett's 1907 *Statistical Abstract of the World*—incongruously physically small and slender for its scope and in comparison to the folio atlases—perhaps sums up the flash impulse that the US government itself, in issuing census atlases from 1870 to 1920, adopted as a way of knowing the (national, settler colonial) social body. Decrying the "widely scattered" state of information on people and commerce, Gannett affirms the necessity of "bring[ing] these statistics together in compact form," which here take the form of tables.[55] Here, too, instantaneity and compactness serve as guarantees against time's vicissitudes: "Statistics of the most recent single year are given in preference to the mean of several years, as being on the whole nearest to the truth. Population, production, and commerce are increasing year by year, so that the mean of the five years 1900 to 1905 would be farther from the facts in 1906 than would be the figures of the single year 1905."[56] Like that of Riis, Gannett's flash serves to briefly and provisionally contain phenomena that multiply uncontrollably, not only increasingly but at an increasing rate. The provisionality is as important as the containment: flash's temporal limitation (that is, its instantaneity) signals the *Statistical Abstract*'s responsiveness to change over time. Yet that instantaneity comes with an informational plenitude that Gannett seems to regard as indispensable, and that relies on a temporal composite effect of aggregating recent data from different years. "The figures given are the latest obtainable," Gannet specifies. "The dates of those in different tables differ in many cases, and even those relating to different countries in the same table may differ. This is unavoidable; otherwise the tables would be much less complete than they are."[57] In Gannett's view, comparing data from different years is a feature, not a bug: it affords his tiny *Statistical Abstract of the World* a condensed comprehensiveness without which it would be neither an abstract nor of the world.

Black Riders: Flash's Chiaroscuro

The epistemological impulse exemplified by the Gannett atlas, the museum cyclorama, the Riis photograph, and the Crane sketch privileged "a single bright flare of insight" that made the temporally and spatially variable social body available to apprehension.[58] The "bright flare of insight" found its correspondence in the late nineteenth century in a material culture in which visual contrasts between light and dark characterized a variety of technologies of social knowledge, both popular and professional, including the gaslight, the magic lantern, and the magnesium-powder photographic flash (sometimes, as if in battle, discharged with a gun). As I have discussed above, Riis pointed to the flash's instantaneity as a guarantor of reality in "Flashes from the Slums," as well as in an article of the same year, "Visible Darkness, New York's Underside Flashed on the Camera."[59] Riis's photographic images were backed by their instantaneity (which was frequently purely nominal, as photos often required several seconds of stillness) and by their ability to condense his descriptive narratives into exemplary visual scenarios.[60] But how were those values rendered visible in the image?

One way is via contrasts between light and dark, whether described or enacted visually. For flash photography, a high-contrast and relatively nonverisimilar chiaroscuro was a hallmark; as the article on flash photography in *Cassell's Cyclopædia of Photography* (1912) observes, "The generality of flashlight photographs . . . are distinguished by the glaring whites of the eyes and the harsh blacks and whites" produced by the flare of magnesium powder.[61] Moreover, as Kate Flint points out, far from de-aestheticizing the scene, flash's chiaroscuro often manifested in "great pools of contrastive and visually impenetrable darkness at the sides of images, almost approximating a painterly frame."[62] Thus when contemporaries praised Crane's writing as "photographic," the authorizing force of that description does not lie in the evocation of an indexical "ontology of the photographic image," as in André Bazin's classic essay.[63] The flash photograph circa 1890 very openly signaled its status as a made object and the means of its production, and indeed it was that signaling—its style—that served as its guarantee.[64]

The form of flash photography thus points up the broader practices of which it was a part—practices that were simultaneously investigative and a form of amusement, which were no less modest in their epistemological claims for their sensational mode. The contrasting lights and darks that characterized flash photography formed a part of a broader visual rhetoric of the real, one that circulated especially around popular urban sociology and the forms of journalism to which it was indebted. The possibility of surprising one's subjects and seeing them as they "really are" was conventionally described in the terms of contrasting light and gloom in a genre known as "lights and shadows" literature. "Their formulaic character," John F. Kasson observes, "is clear in titles such as: *The Miseries of New York*; *The Mysteries and Miseries of New York*; *The Mysteries and Miseries of New Orleans*; *New York by Gaslight: With Here and There a Streak of Sunshine*; *Sunshine and Shadow in New York*; *New York by Sunlight and Gaslight*; *Lights and Shadows of New York Life*; *Lights and Shadows in San Francisco*; *Chicago by Gaslight*; and *Boston Inside Out! Sins of a Great City!*"[65] Such publications rendered up safe versions of the "gaslight tour"; as Kasson notes, "For those who wished to know [the city's secrets], such guidebooks insisted, the pathway they provided in their pages offered the only safe mode of conduct."[66]

"Lights and shadows" literature made a claim to knowledge of the social, and its chiaroscuro rhetoric resonated with immersive flash-oriented media like the panorama, the magic lantern, and the museum group, which produced the sensations of actually investigating for oneself, often directly through strategic use of light and dark. The panorama, for example, disoriented the viewer in a dark corridor below the painting before allowing the viewer to emerge, as if transported, completely surrounded by a panoramic painting lit from above. In its preoccupation with chiaroscuro, "light and shadows" literature thus evokes in language the light effects of these immersive media. The genre's sensationalism does not, I wish to emphasize, cleanly delimit it from the experimental domain that I explore here; indeed, the close contiguity of "light and shadows" literature with more explicitly sociological investigations usefully disallows the fantasy of an autonomous, ideologically neutral social science uninflected by its popular manifestations. The chiaroscuro of lights and shadows signified the real precisely by pointing to the conditions under which problematic scenes of social encounter could be rendered up as social knowledge—the interarticulated condensation and instantaneity of flash. Consequently, while chiaroscuro is a formal quality, here it also functions as an index of epistemic processes, not quite a method but rather adhering to an epistemic virtue.

More recently, David Trotter has pointed out the ways in which "flash scenes" in early Hollywood cinema generated what would come to be understood as the distinctive Hollywood style, focusing on an image for just a few seconds as a proxy for more explicit narrative development.[67] The "flash scene" was a shot of just a few seconds, and it was a term often used by censorship boards that, recognizing that certain visual information had to be conveyed, insisted that it be conveyed briefly and by suggestion rather than explicitly. So, for example, the Kansas Board of Review determined that D. W. Griffith's film *The Birth of a Nation* could only be screened in Kansas contingent on certain eliminations, including "Reel 2: Reduce to flash mulatto woman on floor with bare shoulders."[68] Here information is not captured instantaneously but rather transmitted; like other instances of flash, however, the flash scene is a partial representation that stands as sufficient, transmitting the substance without transmitting the whole. And as with "lights and shadows" literature or Riis's lantern slides, the flash scene gave access to taboo or (sometimes literally) forbidden social knowledge from which a mass audience requires protection, yet which that audience also presumably already knows. Knowledge of the mass is given to the mass, but in code. It is significant that the kind of encoding of social knowledge that flash performs is often knowledge at its limits: the fleeting, the taboo, the violent, that which reveals racial and sexual difference, that which both must and must not be known. In this sense, the epistemic virtue of flash carries the connotation of transmitting an occulted knowledge, in the way that the 1840s genre known as the "flash press"—short-lived weeklies like the *Flash*, the *Whip*, and the *Libertine*—circulated news of a scandalous urban demimonde, another kind of "other half."[69]

Chiaroscuro's social and technological coding as a signifier of nonverisimilar realism perhaps helps to explain the literary evocation of chiaroscuro that runs throughout naturalist fiction, and through Crane's work in particular. In *Maggie*, for instance, scenes of casual violence are punctuated by chiaroscuro tableaux that briefly suspend time, supplanting narrative motion with visual contrasts. After the initial introduction of the mother's violent drunkenness, to give just one example, the boy Jimmie runs out into the hallway of the tenement building, where he "flounder[s] about in darkness" until an old woman opens the next door and "a light behind her thr[ows] a flare on the urchin's quivering face."[70] Similarly, in a key moment after she is "ruined," Maggie faces her neighbors' disapproval "before open doors framing more eyes strangely microscopic, and sending broad beams of inquisitive light into the darkness of her path" (66). Light and dark here do not simply draw on symbolic associations with knowledge and ignorance, morality and depravity; rather, they reproduce the material technologies of social investigation in the 1890s. As Flint puts it, highlighting the biopolitical ends of such technologies, "The apparatus of urban surveillance had long shone unwelcome light on destitute people."[71] Maggie's moment of examination reenacts the social reformer's contrast between lights and shadows, mapping literal light from the doorways onto the "inquisitive light" of reformers' investigations, gaslight tours, and flash photographs. That the eyes that examine Maggie are "strangely microscopic" suggests the degree to which the scrutiny is unidirectional and clinical in quality; the eyes that examine Maggie are small (microscopic) and therefore not subject to examination. Perhaps even more importantly, "microscopic" also suggests that the eyes are microscope-*like*, magnifying the disgraced and illuminated girl. The beams of light that bar Maggie's way create a distorted, high-contrast space that shrinks the examiner to a set of eyes and enlarges the examinee. Crucially, the distortions imposed by flash do not undermine the scene's coding as "real" and revelatory of knowledge; indeed, they constitute it.

Yet the scene has a visual point of view—Maggie's—and while the contrast of lights and shadows clearly makes Maggie the spectacle, it also produces a scopic encounter with her spectators, or rather her spectators' eyes, which recede in the darkness yet are "framed." If Maggie is a type ("a girl of the streets") in the way that Riis's growler gangs and boarding-house lodgers are types and her "ruin" is an exemplary ruin consumable by anonymous spectators, the act of spectation is also given back to us, through Maggie's focalized perspective. The one of the flash—the ruined "girl of the streets" illuminated in this brief moment—is counterbalanced by the many of the tenement whom Maggie exemplifies, as we see Maggie being seen. The chiaroscuro tableau of Maggie's disgrace is a flash that represents the tenement dwellers in the scene to themselves.

Crane's association with photography, especially with the new photographic techniques of the instant, pervades the criticism, including that of Crane's contemporaries, perhaps by now to the point of cliché. In an 1896

New York Times review of *The Red Badge of Courage*, for example, an effusive Harold Fredric calls Crane "a Muybridge, with his instantaneous camera."[72] As Bill Brown points out in a brief reading of Fredric's review, such a comparison goes beyond "either Zola's faith in the primacy of photographic perception or the typical equation of photography and literary realism," resting on what Fredric calls the "effect of a photographic revelation." "What the novel begins to register," Brown concludes, "is the technology that made 'photographic revelation' a novelistic possibility."[73] In other words, the material practices of photography, and the contexts in which it was used, require that we understand the "photographic" quality so widely attributed to Crane's writing in more than metaphorical terms. The initially Romantic epistemic virtue of flash thus intersects with material and intellectual cultures at the turn of the twentieth century with consequences for all three, as the ideals of a nonverisimilar yet maximally communicative aesthetics come to signal to the masses knowledge, above all, about itself. As Steinlight, following Eric Santner, argues, the biopolitical imagination that seeks to narrate population does so in the service of the (notional) sovereignty of the "popular body."[74] Flash is thus a "popular" virtue, to the point of spectacularity.

Faces in the Crowd: Figuration, Redemption, Information

What to do with the "popular"? While I have argued that flash is an epistemic virtue for and of the social masses, there is no denying that there is something problematic, even contradictory, about this relation. After all, the crowd is conventionally what undoes knowledge and virtue alike. The crowd's status as both seer and seen thus renders flash a deeply (though not uniquely, as I discuss in the chapter on precision) problematic epistemic virtue, standing as it does in ambiguous relation to the implicitly moral virtues that more obviously attend epistemic virtues like objectivity. Poe's "man of the crowd" is thus both inscrutable and "the type and genius of deep crime."[75] If anything, flash is the epistemic virtue of immorality negotiated, all the more potently communicated for its coding: the obscene sight of bare skin that must be reduced to a flash, a photograph of a Bowery alley, or the face of a ruined girl of the streets. Moreover, it is not altogether easy to distinguish flash's moral dubiousness from its epistemic dubiousness; its ultimate concern with legibility opens it to charges of ideological investment, while its embeddedness in often exploitative or sensationalist depictions of the mass open it to both ethical and epistemological suspicion.

Michelle Murphy's study of the "economization of life," moreover, powerfully shows how deeply population thinking and the flash experimentalism that supports it—what Murphy, following anthropologists of medicine, calls "experimentality"—are invested in the constitutively racist biopolitical and necropolitical management of populations.[76] "Race is the grammar and ghost of populations," as Murphy puts it and as Galton's body of work confirms.[77]

The locations of flash that I have discussed so far also put pressure on the literary experimentalism with which I have aimed to affiliate it. Sensationalist popular sociology, stunt journalism, magic lantern shows, naturalist fiction, even Hollywood narrative cinema: these are genres and media that are—justly—little likely to suggest "experimental writing," or to suggest "experimental science," for that matter. Popular, sensationalistic, often openly ideological, and imprecise, their purchase on the representation of the social body is not currently held in high esteem. Even when undertaken in conjunction with practices now associated with "rigor"—demographics, data visualization, statistics—there is something fundamentally not only popular but populist in the valorization of flash: the idea that one can simply *look* and *see*. An aspiration toward the easily transmissible, low-fidelity yet somehow perfectly sufficient representative suggests a belief in communicability apparently at odds with the ferocious critique of clarity leveled by late twentieth-century experimental writers like Ron Silliman, who called "the increasing transparency of language" across the history of capitalism a "social aphasia" whose native genres were "fictional realism" and "the presumed objectivity of daily journalism."[78] Flash is *informational*, with all the Benjaminian resonances of "information," and in that sense there would seem to be something deeply perverse about proposing it as an epistemic virtue on which an experimentalism might rest.[79]

Yet if flash proposes a faith in transparency, and an uncritical relation to the mass that would give many an experimentalist pause, it also proposes that transmissibility as already encoded, already nonverisimilar. Portability comes at the cost of mimetic fidelity, and, in that sense, flash is deeply consonant with the claim to be more real than realism that is embedded in much experimental difficulty. Flash's transparency always depends upon a concealment, even an occultism, or, as in the Hays Code, in effect during most of the golden age of Hollywood, censorship. And while the mathematical theory of information concerns itself with *loss* (for instance, in the mp3 audio file format, so famously inferior to vinyl), flash's occulting—its chiaroscuro, its dark as well as light—is not a liability but rather the very condition of its virtue, the source of its claim to a more real realism. Flash is apprehensible precisely insofar as it is a *figure*—and as Erich Auerbach explains, *figura* is also *umbra*, a (fore)shadow or concealment that makes way for revelation.[80]

To put it another way, there is a persistent *badness* about flash that is, in fact, its condition of possibility. Leo Bersani illustrates this remarkable invertability in a comment on Benjamin, to whom I will return shortly, and his "great popularity" among literary critics: "He was a brilliant man, and his writing has many insightful flashes, which we might just as accurately call flashy insights."[81] Flashy, trashy: this is epistemic virtue as epistemic vice, brilliance as *Schein*. I am not arguing that the transmissibility that flash presumes is never ideological, then (far from it!), nor am I making the separate and distinct suggestion that every inhabitation of flash's values should now be considered "experimental" (as if that would be useful). Rather, I am suggesting that flash's figures demand a reckoning with the complex part that the "popular" has to play in the production and validation of knowledge, which, furthermore, has consequences for a literary discourse (viz. experimentalism) that claims purchase on knowledge production.

While expertise is classically conceptualized as by definition elite, with the people serving primarily as the ground against which the figure of the scientist stands, historians of science have attended to the much more multidirectional traffic between popular and professional domains.[82] As Andreas Daum points out, the "trickle down" model of knowledge, as if it were created ex nihilo by experts and only then made contact with "culture" at large, has never held up well.[83] In particular, in the period with which I am primarily concerned, Katherine Pandora and Karen Rader, following scholars such as Susan Scott Parrish, Neil Harris, and James W. Cook, have pointed out that popular spectacles like P. T. Barnum's "Feejee Mermaid" were not merely sensationalized and distorted natural history but also an exercise in the cultivation of popular verification. Such displays (as well as more conventional ones) "authorized the public to judge for themselves rather than defer to the authority of experts," and thus proposed the very crowd that was so avidly being studied by contemporary social scientists as itself the verifier.[84]

That Barnum's Feejee Mermaid was so famously a hoax perhaps casts some unfortunate doubts on the public's veridical abilities. Yet to use Barnum's reception as a cautionary tale would be to miss the point: not that dubious "popular" genres like the magic lantern slide show, stunt journalism, and the naturalist novel are virtuously "scientific" but rather that their very existence is already predicated on, and propagates, the expectation that popular judgment will matter in the cultivation of knowledge consensus. Indeed, it is precisely a *popular* imperative to know the social body with which the University of Chicago sociologist Albion Small justified the establishment of professional sociology, declaring in the inaugural issue of the *American Journal of Sociology* (1895) that "It is a very callow sociologist who imagines that he and his colaborers are inventing the subject-matter of a new science. They are trying to perfect means of answering obtrusive questions about society which the ordinary man is proposing every hour. They are not creating but merely representing popular curiosity."[85] Small's scientific modesty, here, is as obfuscating as it is legitimating. The claim to merely represent and respond to a popular will to (self-)knowledge glosses over the ways that professional sociology encompassed religious and state efforts at prescriptively managing "population," from a perspective that very much saw the poor as the "other" half. The mass might wish to know itself, but it would be primarily elites who were well positioned to act on that knowledge. As Murphy argues in an analysis of experimental American population control efforts in 1970s Bangladesh, "experimentality," a variant of the Foucauldian concept of governmentality, is "a mass intervention into consciousness and bodily practices" that "relentlessly produces evidence that then legitimates continued interventions as a self-perpetuating relation of rescue."[86] Yet Small's appeal to "popular curiosity" also accords with the way that biopolitics finds its ultimate warrant in the "democratization of sovereignty," as Foucault puts it.[87]

Transmissibility's thorny benefits, especially in relation to mass culture, come particularly to the fore in a use of flash that will be more recognizable as what has been canonized as "experimental," Ezra Pound's poetics of the luminous detail. "Measure, compare—but first of all, *look*, is Pound's injunction," Rebecca Beasley observes in a delicate unfolding of the ways that Pound intertwined notions of visuality and scientificity.[88] I point to Pound in part to link flash more clearly to what came to be understood as the "experimental tradition": Pound is often cited centrally therein, whereas Crane and Riis never are. Indeed, the National Poetry Foundation in Orono, Maine, which has had a powerful institutional role in supporting the cause of US experimental writing in the late twentieth century, placed Pound at the center of its efforts, publishing not only a journal of Pound studies, *Paideuma*, but also *Sagetrieb*, "a journal devoted to poets in the Pound/Williams tradition" whose inaugural (1982) masthead included Pound scholars Hugh Kenner, Carroll F. Terrell, and Marjorie Perloff, this last a "champion of a counter-tradition that has since become required reading," as Kaplan Harris puts it.[89] What Gertrude Stein was to the Language writers, Pound was to the National Poetry Foundation. Further, Pound's poetics offers a new view on flash, in that, in the guise of the "luminous detail," its plenitude is supplied less by a synchronous social body than by a historical past. For Pound and, as I will sketch further below, Benjamin, flash, when applied to history, renders up impossible knowledges, retrieving what has been lost not in an original period integrity but in its meaning for the present.[90] Flash's transmissibility, in other words, is also a commitment to *revelation* and, indeed, redemption.

Pound—himself a fairly prolific, if unloved, writer of popular social science, as Michael Coyle has documented—first advocates what he calls "the method of the luminous detail" in a serialized essay for the British magazine the *New Age*, published in 1911 and 1912, and while he insists repeatedly on calling it a "method," it quickly becomes evident that it is less a method than an epistemic virtue, a set of principles by which knowledge can be secured.[91] The name "luminous detail" already evokes flash's chiaroscuro, and Pound's description likewise accords with the features of flash that I have already described, finding sufficiency in partiality. As Pound writes, "The method of Luminous Detail [is] a method most vigorously hostile to the prevailing mode of to-day—that is, the method of multitudinous detail, and to the method of yesterday, the method of sentiment and generalisation."[92] The luminous detail insists on the concrete and particular over and above the complete; "Go in fear of abstractions," Pound urges in his polemic "A Few Don'ts by an Imagiste," and here we see abstraction consigned to "the method of yesterday."[93] But "multitudinous detail," or comprehensiveness, is equally dismissed in favor of the *luminous* detail, which functions something like Gregory Bateson's perhaps overquoted characterization of information, "the difference that makes a difference."[94] And, like the distinguishing flash of Stephen Crane's description or the Hollywood flash scene, the luminous detail has an explicitly informational quality for Pound: "In the history of the development of civilisation or of literature, we come upon such interpreting detail. A few dozen facts of this nature give us intelligence of a period—a kind of intelligence not to be gathered from a great array of facts of the other sort. These facts are hard to find. They are swift and easy of transmission. They govern knowledge as the switchboard governs an electric circuit."[95] The luminous detail functions like Poe's individual faces in the crowd, carrying whole histories in ways that the aggregate never could, always somehow lifting the relevant out of the mass of irrelevancies, a synecdoche that is also something more than just synecdoche, bearing the relation to the whole that the switchboard bears to the electrical circuit. It doesn't begin to describe the whole, and yet it's all you need to know. And like other instances of flash from the turn of the twentieth century, the flash of the luminous detail is informational, "swift and easy of transmission."

When Pound transmutes the theory of the luminous detail into a poetics of the "ideogrammic method" in his 1934 *ABC of Reading*, he again deliberately pegs this mode of discrimination to the sciences, calling the ideogram "the method of science." As before, the appeal to method here speaks more to a fantasy of an authoritative, unified method than to any specific scientific practices; but even as Pound explicitly attempts to distance himself from what he calls "irrelevant particular connotations tangled with a particular group of young people who were writing in 1912"—that is, imagism—he retains in his appropriation of the Chinese ideograph a belief in an instantaneous communicable transmission that is certainly significantly less than its referent yet is sufficient all the same.[96] For Pound, the ideograph draws its power from being neither directly mimetic nor alphabetic, but rather *stylized*—a figure. As Pound puts it, "In tables showing primitive Chinese characters in one column and the present 'conventionalized' signs in another, anyone can see how the ideogram for man or tree or sunrise developed, or 'was simplified from,' or was reduced to the essentials of the first picture of man, tree or sunrise."[97] As with the schematizing chiaroscuro of the flash photograph, the Hollywood flash scene, or the stylization of the sensationalist literature of the urban underclasses, this stylization is conceived as subtractive, "reduced to the essentials" and all the more potent for it. Yet the reality effect of this subtractive figuration is not mysterious, for instead of faithfully indexing a referent, flash's nonmimetic forms index their own management of the challenges of multitudinous data, and multitudinous data about the social body in particular. Flash supplements the crowd's unreadability by giving the crowd a readable face.

Pound is well known for aphorisms that are as brief and condensed as the poetics that they advocate, such as "Dichten = condensare" and "an 'Image' is that which presents an intellectual and emotional complex in an instant of time."[98] And the poem whose first line supplies the title for this section, the celebrated "In a Station of the Metro" (1913), all too clearly renders "the apparition of these faces in the crowd" in a schematized, and here, orientalized, chiaroscuro: "petals on a wet, black bough"; light on dark. The chiaroscuro tableau of the petals overlays, clarifies, and corrects the at first only diaphanous "apparition" of "faces in the crowd," in a figure neither quite mimetic nor metaphoric. Luminous, and almost self-illuminated, the "apparition of these faces in the crowd" stands in a relation of metonymic sufficiency to the crowd, much in the way that the poem so often stands in for Pound's early work. If Pound's early poems more broadly are dominated by ruminations on the poet's relation to the social whole that will give way to increasingly complex, and increasingly disturbing, social theories, we can see why flash's rendering of epistemic concerns in aesthetic forms would prove so useful. That, as Vincent Sherry has put it, "the technique designed to generate the incandescent image has borne the fruit of obscurity" does not, I would suggest, represent the "defeat" of the luminous detail so much as disclose the grounds of its purchase on the real.[99] Like the flash of social-scientific and para-social-scientific population knowledge, the Poundian flash obeys the logic of what Michael Taussig, following G. W. F. Hegel, calls the "labor of the negative"—the work of maintaining in play the uncanny chiasmus of what is known and what must not be known in and about a social body.[100] As I will explore in chapter 4, flash's counterpart, the "technical" virtue of precision, which prefers the method of multitudinous detail and thereby announces its own irrelevancy to general knowledge, undertakes the same "labor of the negative" from the other direction. For flash, that work is epitomized in the face, which is "the figure of *appearance*, the appearance of appearance, the figure of figuration" in an "endless back-and-forth of revelation and concealment," as Taussig writes.[101] This brings to a point the importance, the *centrality*, of the "popular," not only the face but the face in the crowd, the source of flash's moral and epistemological badness. For these are not disarticulable from flash's status as epistemic *virtue*; rather, they belong to a dialectic of knowledge and agnosis, revelation and concealment that "brings insides outside," with which the early social sciences had constantly to engage.[102] Moreover, as Coyle has argued, Pound's luminous detail itself owed much to a social scientist, the anthropologist Leo Frobenius, who advocated an epistemology of "symbolic events" that could "distinguish 'the significant from the trivial, the expressive from the merely accidental.'"[103] Pound's strangely informatic binarisms thus do not stand in opposition to but rather are a logical concomitant of the complexity of his poetics. If Pound stages "failure," then—say, in *Hugh Selwyn Mauberley*, with its pathetic evocations of artistic strivings in the face of a recalcitrant "age"—this gesture, too, seems to mark out a revelatory chiaroscuro tableau, another instance of what Daniel Tiffany has called Pound's "cryptaesthetic."[104]

Thus while it may be tempting to read flash—especially in its informatic mode—as an apolitical form, insofar as it applies to the social body, the relation of representative partialness that flash proposes is indeed implicitly political, although the content of that politics is ambiguous. (Flash presupposes nothing about how its adequation comes about.) A substantial part of the project of the *ABC of Reading* is to advance a theory and practical study of the luminous detail for literary history, arguing that "a man can learn more about poetry by really knowing and examining a few of the best poems than by meandering about among a great many . . . if a man will really learn Greek he can get nearly 'all of it' in Homer."[105] There is no question that, for Pound, this mode of apprehending knowledge is political; indeed, he says as much, arguing that "a people that grows accustomed to sloppy writing is a people in process of losing grip on its empire and on itself."[106] Pound's faith in the "people" is slippery to say the least, but his faith in the ability of the luminous detail to reassert itself out of the depths of the undistinguished stands almost comically firm: "There is one quality which unites all great and perdurable writers, you don't NEED schools and colleges to keep 'em alive. Put them out of the curriculum, lay them in the dust of libraries, and once in every so often a chance reader, unsubsidized and unbribed, will dig them up again, put them in the light again, without asking favours."[107] Out of time but "in the light again," the artwork winks back up out of the depths, not as a historical artifact but rather at the service of the "people" who need it.

If I am belaboring the theory of literary history that Pound seems to suggest here, it is because I wish to place it in (perhaps perverse) conversation with its more famous counterpart, Benjamin's historical materialism, which aims to access the mass for itself. Benjamin is a connoisseur of verity-bearing flashes, in both the technological form of the camera flash and the intellectual form that Daston, following Humboldt, identifies as a "flare of insight."[108] From the camera, for Benjamin, comes the destruction of aura and the production of a new, distracted relation between art and the mass. "The fact that this new mode of participation first appeared in a disreputable form," he adds, "should not mislead the observer": it is a new relation of politicization, made possible by the reproducible medium's amenability to mass reception.[109] And from historical materialism, there is a "past [that] can be seized only as an image that flashes up at the moment of its recognizability," more time-bound and more provisional than a luminous detail but bearing the same swift, implicitly visual communicative power.[110] As Sigrid Weigel has argued in detail, Benjamin's epistemology of flash is at once visual and cognitive, "a simultaneous cognition (*Erkenntnis*) or in*sight* (*Ein*sicht)" that "favors simultaneity and constellation over continuity, similitude over representation or sign, and the detail or fractionary (*Bruchstück*) over the whole."[111] In Benjamin's account, a flash makes fleetingly available some truth of an overabundant and ever-accumulating history, and it must do so through a provisional and instantaneous "messianic arrest of happening."[112] For Benjamin even more than for Pound, to encounter history in this way is to enter into a relation with the mass, for the flashing up of the historical image is occasioned precisely by "the danger of becoming a tool of the ruling classes"—a danger that is political, certainly, but epistemological as well.[113] The flash of the historical image counters and corrects the "secret heliotropism" toward ruling-class narratives that continually warps the past.[114] What these different but evocatively resonant flashes in Benjamin's theory (or his "flashy insights") disclose is the intimacy between flash's epistemic guarantees and the site of the popular from which it arises and to which it returns.

Pound's luminous detail—imagined as stable and enduring—and Benjamin's historical image—imagined as fleeting and provisional—are of course not exact correlates, especially insofar as Pound holds to a theory of historical progress, however discontinuous, that Benjamin repudiates. In fact, they are something more like doppelgängers, echoing one another formally but to different ends. Both manage an overwhelming historical plenitude, although the politics of that management—Pound's ultimately fascist, Benjamin's explicitly antifascist—weigh against any hope that the installation of epistemic virtues, even an epistemic virtue of the crowd, might confer political sanctity. Yet both, in applying the epistemology of flash to history, propose redemptive models of transhistoricity in which flash's figuration completes and answers the past that it also represents. Singularity stands in fully adequate yet occulted relation to the whole.

In a synchronic register, such, too, is the matter of the face in the crowd, the faces that Poe's narrator first can, then cannot read. The face in the crowd is, as the Pound poem suggests, a privileged form of flash, and for good reason. Tom Gunning has identified facial photography in particular with a "gnostic impulse" that made the face, "a guarantor of meaning and significance, a mode of communication that exceeded any conventional or cultural system of exchange."[115] In another context, Taussig has identified the face as "the figure of figuration, the ur-appearance . . . of secrecy itself as the primordial act of presencing" and, following Levinas, "the evidence that makes evidence possible."[116] Benjamin saw the face as the limit of the photograph's ability to stand as evidence, aura's "last retrenchment."[117] And perhaps the most influential essay ever written on Crane, Fried's "Stephen Crane's Upturned Faces," reads all tableaux of communicative figuration in Crane as variations on a face, an abstracted *figure* that always figures writing—most powerfully in Crane's novella of literal defacement, *The Monster*.[118] Although each of these scholars has a slightly different purchase on the representational power of the face, the recurring tropes of epiphany, illumination, a chiaroscuro interarticulation of secrecy and revelation, and figuration as such disclose how frequently the face stands as a privileged embodiment of flash, transmitting information *insofar as* it seems to withhold it. As Tiffany writes of the Poundian flash, "Opacity and negativity—the power to withhold from the eye the visualization promised by the image—become the salient features of the image."[119]

By letting faces in the crowd stand as partial yet sufficient representations of the social mass, flash literalizes, and thus collapses, the concept of "figuration." Gérard Genette identifies the literary "figure" as the form of the "gap" or "space" "between what the poet has *written* and what he has *thought*"—the shape of the gap between the words used and the so-called literal meaning.[120] The figure thus always points to the "literal" translation that it supplants, enacting the epistemological supersession of an ostensibly ideological zero-degree realism that experimentalisms repeatedly claim to perform.[121] But flash is a kind of figuration whose very departures from mimetic literality—condensation, instantaneity, and chiaroscuro—index their own management of what otherwise, in Poe's phrase, would not permit itself to be read, because of problems of scale, dispersal through time and space, rapid change over time, and the subject's notional tendency to deceive; it is both figure and catachresis—a placeholder for what is otherwise unnameable. In other words, while, as Genette observes, figures are by definition comparative, functioning as figures only insofar as they exceed some ostensibly literal "zero degree," flash is a figure whose zero degree "lasst sich nicht lesen."[122] Flash is therefore *productive of knowledge*, even as it also functions as a figure or nonliteral representation. For example, if, as Pound says, the luminous detail is "swift and easy of transmission," it is also transmitting something that, in the luminous detail's absence, would be unavailable altogether; like a schematic diagram of a battle that is also, literally, the battle, the luminous detail *is* the knowledge that it transmits, collapsing, as Taussig observes, "the distinction, between the representation and that which the representation represents."[123] The knowledge produced by a composite photograph, likewise, is of "typical" features that literally don't exist anywhere *but* in the composite; flash is revelatory at the same time as it is representational and revelatory *of* the thing it represents. Flash's epistemological freight, and its figural complexities, prove enormously fruitful for a poet like Pound, and that epistemological freight is owed not to flash's forms themselves so much as those forms' embeddedness in a historical knowledge-making enterprise.

Flash thus finally operates as both an *informational* and a *redemptive* virtue, a mode of engaging with the mass that tacitly recognizes the interarticulation of secret and revelation—virtue and vice, lights and shadows, ones and zeroes—and thus makes a superior mimesis of nonverisimilitude. To return to Taussig's description, it performs the "labor of the negative," the work that social bodies must do to maintain not only its truths but its public secrets—the "population" as the scene of reproduction, genetic inheritance, and miscegenation. It is this reversibility that explains the constant recurrence to scandal, secret, crime, and (what amounts to the same thing in 1890s America) embodied (e.g., racial and sexual) difference in the discourses of flash—from census visualizations to the faces of ethnic and criminal types in Galton's composites to the orientalism of the Poundian ideogram. Some bodies seemingly belong to an acknowledged "public," while others belong to what Riis would call the "other half." As Michael Warner has argued, "Public and private are learned along with such terms as 'active' and 'passive,' 'front' and 'back,' 'top' and 'bottom.' They can seem quasi-natural, visceral, fraught with perils of abjection and degradation or, alternatively, of cleanliness and self-mastery. They are the very scene of selfhood and scarcely distinguishable from the experience of gender and sexuality."[124] Moreover, flash enacts the dynamic through which embodied difference stands as a figure of the *self*-difference of individual bodies, always part "public" and part "private," with the potential for *unheimlich* reversal that they entail, the revealable secret in every body. Thus Taussig argues that "when it comes to secrecy, the head shares a curious division of labor with the genitals and can even be substituted for them . . . the head being that part of the body generally left naked . . . while the genitalia are that part of the body generally covered."[125] It is no wonder, then, that the physiognomy of

Poe's man of the crowd is also "the type and genius of deep crime"; no wonder, too, that Taussig sees an antecedent to Michel Foucault's repressive hypothesis—"*sex as that secret which has to be spoken so as to preserve it*"—in the evocation of a flash in Foucault's 1963 essay on transgression:

> Transgression, then, is not related to the limit as black to white, the prohibited to the lawful, the outside to the inside, or as the open area of a building to its enclosed spaces. . . . Perhaps it is like a flash of lightning in the night which, from the beginning of time, gives a dense and black intensity to the night it denies, which lights up the night from the inside, from top to bottom, and yet owes to the dark the stark clarity of its manifestation, its harrowing and poised singularity.[126]

Lights and shadows literature like *Boston Inside Out! Sins of a Great City!* thus emerges as the all-too-ordinary manifestation of the labor of the negative, an element of a popular discourse in which the tawdry secrets of an urban society are also the way into social knowledge of even the most naïvely positivistic sort. As Foucault would go on to argue in *The History of Sexuality: An Introduction*, the public secret of sex lay at the center of a variety of economic and political discourses, in particular the "emergence of 'population' as an economic and political problem."[127] The epistemic virtue of flash, so foundationally visual in its conception, discloses the aesthetic dimension embedded in the problem of knowing the face in, and of, the crowd.

3 Objectivity

Early in her posthumously published 1903 novella *Q.E.D.*, while describing the three middle-class white women whose love triangle supplies the plot, Gertrude Stein undercuts the correlation between the visible body and character type: "[It] is one of the peculiarities of American womanhood," the narrator states, "that the body of a coquette often encloses the soul of a prude and the angular form of a spinster is possessed by a nature of the tropics."[1] The confusion of character types ("the soul of a prude"), bodily forms ("of a coquette"), and localities ("of the tropics") seems to both affirm and undo typology, setting up, only to counter, the expectation that character types correspond to the visible body. The materialities of body and environment are determinate, yet vision lies. By abstracting the visible body (into "the body of a coquette" or "the angular form of a spinster"), Stein preserves a coherent typology (there are coquette bodies and there are spinster bodies) while at the same time unmooring them from their supposed referents (the coquette body is actually not a coquette's body). This dynamic of insisting on structures while also revealing them as contentless is typical of Stein's writing, whether at the level of character typology or at the level of language (or, as in "Melanctha," both at once). Although Stein's "experimental" writing is often characterized as "breaking," disrupting, destabilizing, and even digesting preexisting structures, the typological tensions in *Q.E.D.* show that there is much more at work than mere destruction. What is at work, I wish to show in this chapter, is objectivity.

There is hardly a more central figure in the late twentieth-century "experimental" recovery moment than Gertrude Stein, the more so because Stein is an important figure of white feminist recovery as well. For Language and Language-adjacent writers constructing an experimental lineage, Stein has usually been the sine qua non, obligatorily mentioned in contexts in which other writers (e.g., Williams, Oppen, even Pound) might be switched in or out, to the degree that Peter Nicholls could (in an essay about Pound!) identify a "poetics . . . running from Gertrude Stein to the Language writers" —what would come to be known as the "experimental" tradition.[2] "Gertrude Stein to the Language writers" is a trajectory that we are meant to understand based on end points alone. Language and Language-adjacent writers have also been important critical voices in Stein studies, among other things publishing a roundtable on Stein's *Tender Buttons* in a 1978 issue of *L=A=N=G=U=A=G=E*.[3] Later, as Language writers became established in academia, monographs including Bob Perelman's *The Trouble with Genius* (1994) and Michael Davidson's *Ghostlier Demarcations* (1997) contributed further to Stein studies, and Joan Retallack edited a volume of selected writings by Stein for the University of California Press (2008). Some of the same writers were active in defending Stein's politics when (now debunked) hypotheses were floated that Stein was an active Vichy collaborator. The question of Stein's wartime politics blossomed into an outright public controversy in 2011–12, when the legal scholar Alan Dershowitz and then-managing editor of the *New Yorker* Emily Greenhouse, among others, published articles accusing the San Francisco Museum of Modern Art's landmark 2011 show *The Steins Collect* of hiding what had come to be enshrined as public knowledge in Janet Malcolm's 2007 *Two Lives*, a double biography of Stein and Alice B. Toklas, and in Barbara Will's *Unlikely Collaboration: Gertrude Stein, Bernard Faÿ, and the Vichy Dilemma* (2011). Charles Bernstein almost single-handedly rounded up a dossier titled "Setting the Record Straight," publishing it in the Kelly Writers House's house organ, the experimental-aligned poetry and poetics journal *Jacket2*, which included contributions by Edward Burns, Ulla Dydo, Joan Retallack, and Marjorie Perloff.[4]

I am not suggesting that experimental writers and advocates of experimental writing unthinkingly rushed to defend a favorite (most of them acknowledge how mixed and problematic Stein's politics overall were, and Bernstein makes a persuasive case that Stein has been maliciously targeted); my point is rather that Stein is at stake for experimentalism. Indeed, Bernstein argues that the attack on Stein was made reputable by mainstream liberal publications that have "taken a strong ideological stand against the kind of poetic innovation associated with Stein" such as the *New Yorker* and the *New York Review of Books*.[5] In particular, Stein been a key figure in articulating the hinge between the aesthetic and epistemological aims of experimental writing, as Lyn Hejinian showed in her 1981 talk "Language and Realism," which drew a line from Émile Zola's "experimental" naturalism to what she describes as a more fundamental realism in Gertrude Stein's writing. Stein's "realism," as Hejinian describes it, prefigures later twentieth-century experimentalism's "attempt to get at both verisimilitude and veracity"—an epistemic virtue, in short, and one to be realized through "a special way of writing."[6] Although it is rarely stated in quite this way, Stein's formally enacted epistemic virtue has long served as a guarantee, if not of Stein's personal politics, then of the political virtue of her writing—a virtue bound up in "veracity" and a privileged access to reality. Stein's objectivity, which emerges formally in her writing, enables this interpretation. Yet situating it in the longer trajectory of her scientific and artistic practices also discloses its limits: far from allowing her writing to transcend the historical contingencies of scientific practices that were in many ways explicitly racist and misogynistic, objectivity was a way of inhabiting them.

If Stein is at stake for experimental writing, objectivity is equally at stake not only for the sciences but for all claims to knowledge. Of all epistemic virtues, it is perhaps the most canonical, the most central, and any scientific practice that is construed as not objective is bound to be labeled "bad science" or even "not science." It is for this reason that Evelyn Fox Keller's classic 1978 essay "Gender and Science," often seen as a founding document of feminist science and technology studies, attacked objectivity as a desideratum.[7] Moreover, Keller doesn't pick objectivity out of the air—she opens with a quotation from Georg Simmel, repeated in a work by the psychoanalyst Karen Horney: "The requirements of . . . correctness in practical judgements and objectivity in theoretical knowledge . . . belong as it were in their form and their claims to humanity in general, but in their actual historical configuration they are masculine throughout. Supposing that we describe these things, viewed as absolute ideas, by the single word 'objective,' we then find that in the history of our race the equation objective = masculine is a valid one."[8] There are two steps to Simmel's claim, then, on which Keller's analysis rests: first, knowledge per se is guaranteed by objectivity; second, objectivity is masculine. Though feminist science and technology studies has developed significantly since Keller's essay, objectivity and its place within Simmel's formula (knowledge = objectivity = masculine) has remained a key site of contestation for the field. Unlike flash, contact, or even precision, which are relatively rarely theorized, albeit pervasive, concepts, objectivity has a library's worth of work devoted to it in varying guises, in relation to not only the sciences but also history, philosophy, and knowledge in general.

In what does objectivity consist? In their 2007 book *Objectivity*, Lorraine Daston and Peter Galison track the range of uses of the term and the practices through which it has manifested.[9] Across all of them runs an attempt to render knowledge independent of the knower; in other words, they argue, objectivity is best defined in the negative, as the containment of subjectivity and its potential incursions on reality.[10] Once we understand this, objectivity's historicity comes into focus: what it means to be "subjective" depends on what it means to be a "subject." Different versions of objectivity that compete and often coexist, then, control for the excesses of different versions of the subject, whether the too-passive imitator of mere detail (such that objectivity might come into conflict with precision) or the psychologized mind all too easily gripped by fantasy and projection. Bound up in objectivity, then, is—as Keller recognized—the gendered question of what it means to be a subject or an object, and how thereby to render knowledge of objects portable and communicable across different and distinct subjects.

As this account suggests, then, when examined as an epistemological practice of attempting to liberate knowledge from the particularities of individual human knowers, rather than as a general label for epistemic goodness, objectivity raises more questions than it lays to rest. Is it always desirable, and to what degree? What kind of subject is being contained by a practice that is called "objective"? What does objectivity look like in a practitioner who is not by default thought to be much of a subject (as in T. S. Eliot's famous line "only those who have personality and emotions know what it means to want to escape from these things")?[11] To study Stein's objectivity is consequently to undertake to understand how she constructed subjects and, concomitantly, how she contained them, teasing knowledge away from any given, individual subject and allowing that knowledge to mean, even act, independently of any given subject's intention or psychological disposition.

Bad Scientist: The Harvard Psychological Laboratory and Bottom Natures

Stein studied psychology at Harvard-Radcliffe from 1893 to 1897 and then attended the Johns Hopkins Medical School from 1897 to 1901; the game of connecting the canonical modernist writer to the canonical (usually male) eminent scientist, in Stein's case, is not difficult. During this period she published two papers in Harvard's *Psychological Review* and attempted to publish a third paper in the *American Journal of Anatomy* in 1902.[12] The first paper, "Normal Motor Automatism" (1896), was coauthored with William James's student Leon Solomons. Solomons wrote up the findings, and Stein later claimed that she had never agreed with Solomons's conclusions.[13] The second paper, "Cultivated Motor Automatism" (1898), was published by Stein alone. But these years offer something more important than a ratification of Stein's scientific credentials by association with William James, Hugo Munsterberg, and Lewellys Barker: they evince formative engagements with scientific practice that shaped Stein's understanding of what constituted subjectivity.[14] Indeed, especially at Harvard-Radcliffe, what a subject is and how and under what conditions it might be suppressed were the explicit topic of her research.

In her lecture "The Gradual Making of *The Making of Americans*," Gertrude Stein describes her research in college as a kind of unruly or bad science: "One of the things I did was testing reactions of the average college student in a state of normal activity and in the state of fatigue induced by their examinations. I was supposed to be interested in their reactions but soon found that I was not but instead that I was enormously interested in the types of their characters that is what I even then thought of as the bottom nature of them."[15] In the work described—the research for Stein's second paper, "Cultivated Motor Automatisms"—the young Stein's wayward interest veers from individual subject reactions to character typology, the famous "bottom nature" that would drive *Three Lives*, *The Making of Americans*, and the portraits. This ultimately materialist theory of subjectivity posited an embodied selfhood that could to a greater or lesser degree be reined in by the will. Moreover, Stein's meta-reflection on her own interest discloses how consequentially her developing theories about subjectivity shaped her (scientific) experimental practice, for Stein's early experiments brought under scrutiny not only the subjectivity of the research subjects but also that of the experimenters (Stein and her collaborator, Leon Solomons).

"Normal Motor Automatism" was designed as a series of experiments in automatic writing, with Stein and Solomons serving as the experimental subjects as well as the experimenters. Stein and Solomons tried to reproduce in "normal" subjects—themselves—the symptoms of the "second personality" thought to be a feature of hysteria. Writing, usually considered a conscious and even creative activity, was to be shown as something that the body could undertake without the participation of the conscious self. "Normal Motor Automatism" thus intervened in a debate in studies of consciousness about whether a second consciousness could exist.[16] Arguing that automatic movements can be induced in normal subjects that are indistinguishable from phenomena observed in hysterical subjects, Solomons and Stein suggest that there is no "double personality" by, in effect, suggesting that all people have something like a double personality, a tendency toward automatism that emerges from the body rather than from a mysterious unconscious. Solomons and Stein are careful to specify that this automatism is normal and merely rendered observable by distraction.[17] The distinction is more affective than conceptual: rather than suggesting, as Freud does, that even the normal subject has uncanny and perhaps frightening qualities, Solomons and Stein domesticate automatism, making it physiological and (as in the study's title) "normal." To maintain this distinction, Solomons and Stein walk a fine line, maintaining that the subjects are completely normal, and at the same time establishing that the automatism observed is really automatism. Thus Solomons writes of their experimental design, "Above all, we wished to avoid anything like a real production of a second personality. For the experiments to really settle the point at issue it was essential that no suspicion should rest upon the complete 'normality' of the subject throughout the experiments. Our idea was to reproduce rather the essential elements of the 'second personality,' if possible in so far as they consist of definite motor reactions unaccompanied by consciousness."[18] Solomons's anxious, slightly moralistic tone as he sets out these fine distinctions between a second personality and "the essential *elements*" thereof—banishing "suspicion" —only underscores how the "normal subject" of this study emulates, and thus is always in danger of being confused with, a pathological one. Solomons seems aware of steering dangerously close to the realm of hysteria, while needing, for reasons of epistemic virtue, to avoid it absolutely. The scientific imperative is met in the same way as the social imperative: through the exercise of self-control. Indeed, it is the ability to exercise self-control that, for Solomons and Stein, distinguishes the normal subject from the hysteric. "Our trouble [in inducing normal motor automatism]," Solomons argues, "never came from a *failure of reaction*, but from a *functioning of the attention*. It was our inability to take our minds off the experiment that interfered. . . . The hysterique [*sic*] has no trouble here, for he is *unable* to *attend* to the sensation, attention to which bothered us."[19]

The way that Solomons attributes inability, first to the normal subject, then to the hysterical subject, shows how many functions the will is made to perform in upholding these experiments' epistemological integrity. The normal subject, with superior powers of attention, naturally attends to her own movements, responds to the "almost irresistible" "desire to take charge of it," and therefore stops any motor automatism. Solomons at first describes this as an "inability to take our minds off the experiment" but then transfers the label of inability to the hysterical subject's *opposite* tendency, an "[inability] to *attend*." In the context of the experiments, each kind of subject exhibits an insufficiency—in the case of the normal subject, an inability to manifest the desired phenomenon; in the case of the hysterical subject, an inability to control the attention—but only one of these can be remedied. The hysterical subject can never be made to attend, but the normal subject's attention can be turned to suppressing attention, exerting a doubled control where the hysteric can exert none. That the phenomenon theorized as "attention" was in practice conflated with the will—a will that the hysteric lacks—is evident in Solomons's language: "We *would* not, the histerique [*sic*] *can* not, attend to these sensations [of motor automatism]," he writes.[20]

The experimental design of "Normal Motor Automatism" therefore both thematizes and enacts some fundamental quandaries in how to do science. Stein and Solomons had to embody dualities on at least three levels. First, they inhabited dual roles, as both experimenters and experimental subjects. Second, as experimenters, they had to maintain an internal split between willful creativity (as a hypothesizing experimenter) and willful self-suppression (as the objective observer). And finally, as experimental subjects, they had to reproduce the self-splitting of the hysteric, again divided between willful consciousness and the willful suppression of consciousness (to allow motor automatism to manifest). "Normal Motor Automatism" turns on distinctions between investigator and subject, hypothesizer and observer, "normal" and (quasi)hysterical, which are, as Friedrich Kittler points out, gendered positions.[21] Moreover, these distinctions are maintained solely by a heroic self-control, the strenuousness of which task Solomons makes us feel over and over again: "Nothing is more difficult than to allow a movement of which we are conscious to go on of itself. The desire to take charge of it is almost irresistible. But as we shall see later it is a habit that can be overcome, and a trained subject can watch his automatic movements without interfering with their non-voluntariness."[22] The multiple negations in this passage—"nothing is more difficult," "irresistible," "without interfering with their non-voluntariness"—strikingly suggest the complex position of the subject who must constantly self-regulate. Moreover, the nature of the experiments frequently collapsed the roles of investigator and subject, since, as Solomons admits, the phenomena of consciousness can be observed only by being "directly experienced"; thus Stein and Solomons sometimes had to engage in all three dualities *at the same time*—dualities that did not map neatly onto one another, for all their resonances.[23] In this series of experiments, Solomons and Stein both slip in and out of feminized states of quasi-hysteria, automatism, passive observation, and experimental subjecthood. By Solomons's report, tremendous pressure is put on the will: the willpower that sustains objectivity is also the willpower that produces object*hood*—the quasi-hysterical "automatic" state. Thus the experimenter-subject becomes "a machine among machines," as Kittler puts it, neutral, reliable, and finally, the being capable of observing objectively and simultaneously the being worthy of being objectively observed.[24] While Stein's own experimental practices depart significantly from "Normal Motor Automatism," the potential for confusion between objective scientist and object *of* science remains crucial as Stein continues to interrogate (and practice) objectivity.

"Normal Motor Automatism" is a fascinating text, which no doubt accounts for the disproportionate attention that has been paid to it. But its primacy in the literature on Stein's early work is curious, for a few reasons. Stein was not responsible for the final write-up that appeared in the *Psychological Review*, and in *Everybody's Autobiography* she went so far as to attribute the data analysis entirely to Solomons and to disagree with it. More to the point, when Stein wrote up her own experiment two years later, it differed significantly from the first paper in both content and tone. If to lack objectivity is to do bad science, then the quandaries presented by Stein's second, solo study, "Cultivated Motor Automatism" ("CMA"), disclose the limits of epistemic virtue. In it, Stein sorts out the complicated self-divisions that, in "NMA," involve a scientific theory of subjectivity (that is, the lab subjects' embodied, "normal" automatism) with a methodological problem of scientific self-positioning. In "CMA," Stein adopts a much more recognizably standard experimental design, expanding her sample by nearly two orders of magnitude and, crucially, not herself being a member of the sample. Separating the knower from the known by design, "CMA" is by definition the more objective study.

Yet "CMA," because of its "better" and thus more pedestrian design, conducing to conclusions that seem all too embarrassingly typical of the late nineteenth-century disciplinary context in which the study was done, is in many ways the "less interesting" study, as evidenced in the comparatively smaller role it has played in Stein criticism relative to "NMA." Tim Armstrong, for example, focuses on the earlier paper to the near exclusion of the latter, mentioning Stein's single-authored "CMA" only in passing and unequivocally designating the earlier paper "the more important"; Kittler never mentions "CMA" at all.[25] Barbara Will, meanwhile, goes so far as to express dismay at Stein's shift from what she (I think questionably) characterizes as a "radical awareness" that "the subject is by definition fractured" in "NMA" to the "totalizing" and "reductive" typological bent of "CMA."[26] The relative conformity of "CMA" to epistemic virtues of its historical moment, and the biologically deterministic theories of the subject that they underwrite, looks neither radical nor sui generis; rather, in its literal experimentalism and corresponding epistemic virtue, it looks disappointingly of its historical moment—embarrassing and "bad."

Here, too, the gendered dynamics of a procedure of "questionable objectivity," as Will puts it, come into relief, especially considering that that questionable objectivity made it easy for Stein to be reduced—and it is a reduction—from the position of the scientist to that of a quasi-hysteric.[27] Indeed, the terms on which Stein distances herself from "NMA" are telling. "I did not think that either of us had been doing automatic writing," she writes. "We always knew what we were doing how could we not when every minute in the laboratory we were doing what we were watching ourselves doing, that was our training."[28] Retrospectively, Stein refuses the possibility of the very slippages that underwrite "NMA" in the first place: the possibility even of simulating the hysterical symptom of automatism by appealing to the intractable conditions imposed by the place—the laboratory —and the experimenters' professionalism—their "training." Nor can Stein's retrospective representation of "NMA" be attributed to a late refusal of the "fractured" subject, for it is consistent with the direction she takes in the single-authored "CMA." Stein begins "Cultivated Motor Automatism" by characterizing it as an extension of "NMA," with a crucial difference: she uses many more subjects—forty-one men and fifty women.[29] This difference clearly rectifies a shortcoming in the earlier paper: "The only subjects we had [in 'NMA']," Stein notes apologetically, "were ourselves."[30]

Stein's single-authored paper, then, makes a move toward greater objectivity, which in turn enables a move toward more rigid typology. Central to "CMA" are the two character types that Stein identifies—"fire and phlegm," as Catharine Stimpson glosses them— which, as critics have noted, roughly correspond to the characters of Helen and Adele in *Q.E.D.* and, later, in its rewriting as *Three Lives*, Melanctha and Jeff.[31] Type I, Stein writes, is "nervous, high-strung, very imaginative, [and] has the capacity to be easily roused and intensely interested. . . . This type, although in some cases suggestible, is on the whole auto-suggestible rather than responsive to influences from without, unless the appeal is directed completely to the automatic personality"—that is, the automatic, purely physiological "personality" thought to have been identified in the earlier "NMA" experiments.[32] But while it is not surprising that the automatic personality is assumed to be physiological, it is notable that the tendency to be "very imaginative" and "intensely interested"—tendencies that anticipate the "complex, desiring" Melanctha—are routed through the quasi-physiological faculty of "attention" and are thus already part of, indeed distinguishing features of, a type.[33] Subjectivity is not imagined as exceeding typology. Type II, similarly, is defined by subjective states; the type is "distinctly phlegmatic. . . . If emotional, decidedly of a weakish sentimental order. . . . Their power of concentration is very small." Since the types, defined by capacities of attention, are rooted in the body, it is perhaps not surprising that Type II comes with explicit physical markers: "blonde and pale. . . . They may be either large, healthy, rather heavy and lacking in vigor, or they may be what we call anaemic and phlegmatic."[34] Finally, Type II is suggestible and similar to the type "described in books on hysteria"; the Type II subjects' "automatic personalities," owing to their weak powers of attention, easily overtake or merge with their "real" personalities.[35] Thus "CMA" is characterized by an overwhelming focus on typology, especially as compared to "NMA"; indeed, the thirteen cases described in the paper are first and foremost classified according to type, apart from one subject, who is oxymoronically designated as belonging to an "Intermediate Type."[36] This typing extends even to geographical region:

> A large number of my subjects were New Englanders, and the habit of self-repression, the intense self-consciousness, the morbid fear of "letting one's self go," that is so prominent an element in the New England character, was a constant stumbling-block. It usually took a New Englander a sitting longer to give a response than the other subjects. I could usually tell them as soon as I began the experiment by their resistance to my guidance. Afterwards I found that [psychologist G.] Stanley Hall, in his article on Fears, notes the fact that self-consciousness was dreaded by twenty-four boys in Cambridge, Mass., a thing unknown in Trenton or St. Paul.[37]

Of the typological theories suggested in Stein's article, the one that correlates character with geographical region has the least credibility today, yet it, like the other typological observations in "CMA," is made possible by the increased number of experimental subjects.[38] Objectivity creates a distance between the knower and the thing known; it does not, however, impose constraints on the kinds of data gathered, such as, for instance, the subject's geographical region of origin. The relatively greater objectivity of "CMA" discloses how little objectivity necessarily correlates with conclusions that appeal to contemporary theories of the subject (e.g., less rigid typological thinking); here, indeed, we see quite the reverse correlation. Far from producing enduring knowledge, greater objectivity has the effect of further embedding the study in historical contingency; the disciplinary conventions of the experiment's time, place, and institutional context; and contemporaneous neo-Lamarckian theories of environmental influence. Stein's solo article thus does not only mark a move away from the self-reflective radical empiricism of the earlier collaborative experiments and the reactions in which she is "supposed to be interested." It also moves her toward "the types of [the subjects'] characters" and a more objective methodology. Elsewhere in Stein's work we see the same logic emerge as racial typing, most notably in the formulaic epithets of "Melanctha," which are parodic, but no less racist for that.[39] Despite epistemic virtue's tendency to let epistemological soundness imply soundness in other registers, Stein's thinking shows why no such pattern obtains. Rather, Stein "exchang[es] a practice rooted in James's physiological psychology," as Steven Meyer puts it, not for a "subjective" science so much as for one whose very objectivity renders it problematic.[40]

Camera Work: Vision and Female Objectivity

At the beginning of this chapter, discussing Stein's *Q.E.D.,* I dismissed the idea that "the body of a coquette" was visualizable. Yet of course visualizing the body of the coquette, as a type, is exactly what the nineteenth-century traditions of physiognomy and anthropometrics tried to do. Moreover, concerns about the potential for dissonance between the visible body and its "true nature" were far from rare; indeed they were rampant—Zola's Nana (*Nana*, 1880), the "blonde Vénus" who is ultimately revealed as black earth, is only one example, and these concerns were not rarely but conventionally troped in the terms of racial passing.[41] A nineteenth-century tradition figures the body of the woman in particular as maddeningly unknowable, as in the case of the coyly titled "La femme sans nom" (Unnamed woman)—that is, the prostitute—described in the series of popular sociological sketches *Les français peints par eux-mêmes*:

> What name can we give to this type so rich and so miserable, so poetic and so abject, so moral and so repulsive; a living enigma that neither scientific research, nor the attentions of charity, nor the efforts of intelligence can illuminate? Already for a long time this woman, in which all devoutness and all baseness, all delicacies of passion and all corruptions of the soul are embodied, has been the study of [*se dérobera à*] the triple investigations of science, religion, and morality; she remains nonetheless one of the greatest mysteries of the human heart and of social necessity.[42]

As with Nana, the "femme sans nom" is thus imagined as the great focus of (male) scrutiny and the very thing that most baffles it, the unseeable spectacle that "se dérobera," will literally strip, before the triple gazes of science, religion, and society, who is fully visualized (figure 6) and yet remains fundamentally incoherent.[43] Nineteenth-century typology thus tries to make the visible body legible and does so precisely in response to the inevitably dissonant or unreadable body. This is not new; the tension between type and instance is a central productive force of the naturalist novel, and perhaps the novel in general. Indeed, we may understand the naturalist novel as an energetic narrative pressuring process, through which the human body is made to manifest its truth, as Nana finally does as she succumbs to disfiguring smallpox. "Elle est changée," Rose Mignon repeats over and over in Nana's last moments, but the joke is that Nana has not "changed" at all but simply revealed herself as diseased, the death-bound and infectious "golden fly" that she always was. "Melanctha" invites being read in the same tradition, suggesting that Melanctha's death at the end of the story is similarly the consummation of her constitutive malady. But unlike Nana's death scene, which is intricately staged and gruesomely visualized (Zola sent a friend to the hospital for details), Melanctha's death is quite abrupt and entirely *un*visualized.[44] The story ends, "They sent her where she would be taken care of, a home for poor consumptives, and there Melanctha stayed until she died."[45] The body is made to manifest no visible proofs.

But then, Melanctha's body was never precisely visualizable in the first place; instead, it is "half made with real white blood," as if mechanically composed out of genuine (invisible) ingredients, with colors signifying many things—but never actual, visible colors. Abstract typology rules in Bridgepoint; more precisely, it *rules visuality*. A visible body in "Melanctha" (and

Figure 6. *La Femme sans nom*. *Les Français peints par eux-mêmes*, vol. 1 (Paris: Curmer, 1840), plate between pp. 252 and 253. Gallica, Bibliothèque nationale de France.

elsewhere in *Three Lives*) is always first and foremost an abstracted body; to say that Melanctha is "pale yellow" does more to figure her race (with the associated stereotypes, in this case, of the tragic mulatta) than it does to describe her visually; "pale yellow" is not, after all, an actual skin color but rather a convention for naming a racialized category.[46] As Milton A. Cohen has shown, almost no one, down to the most minor characters (e.g., John the coachman), escapes color-coded racial stereotyping—descriptions that *invoke* the visual by using color words but that in fact *replace* the body's visible surface with its abstracted racial and characterological type.[47] Linguistically, this is achieved not only through visual cues that are always primarily racial cues but also through the repetition of those cues. Stein's use of repetition has been discussed at length, often brilliantly; Stein herself would later point to repetition as the stereotype by which she was conventionally parodied in the press.[48] In "Melanctha," repetition reveals character because it produces abstract racial types. Thus in "Melanctha" as in *Les français peints par eux-mêmes*, visualization directs us toward a type that encodes the truth of the body, rather than a literal and potentially duplicitous *view* of the body.

How does this resistance to the visible—a resistance that seems in sympathy with much earlier scientific protocols that quite literally objectify female bodies in particular—square with what I am arguing is Stein's increasing objectivity? To understand it, we must push further on the complex relationship between gender and objectivity—not only a philosophical relationship but also a very practical historical one bearing on what scientific activities counted as *work* (and should be published and paid for accordingly). As I noted at the opening of this chapter, because objectivity has often been taken to be the defining feature of science, feminist historians and philosophers of science, most notably Evelyn Fox Keller, Donna Haraway, and Sandra Harding, have argued that the invisibility of women in science has depended on the construction of femininity as by definition subjective and incapable of objectivity, whether because (as in the psychoanalytic model taken up in Keller's "Gender and Science") girls are actually developmentally disposed not to make sharp subject-object distinctions or because (as in Michèle Le Doeuff's reading) such an incapacity is merely attributed to women by a patriarchal society invested in defining the male as "the sex of knowing."[49] Exclude women from objectivity, the logic goes, and you exclude them from science. Yet as Naomi Oreskes has observed, the case of the women scientists in Stein's particular position troubles the question of objectivity, since their work was in many ways exemplary of the values of objectivity. "Broad historical generalizations are risky," she writes, "but, if anything, it appears that women in American science have been characteristically employed not in jobs that required a high degree of emotional involvement or contextual judgment [what feminist historians have called 'situated knowledge'], but precisely the opposite," especially "highly quantitative analytical and numerical work."[50] Moreover, contrasting with the objective scientific labor that was, as Oreskes points out, *typically* assigned to female scientists, there is an almost exclusively masculine tradition of "auto-experimentation"—experiments performed on oneself—that mobilizes heroic narratives in which "the auto-experimenter is portrayed as smarter than those surrounding him, possessed of an emboldening insight lacking in his colleagues," even though "the epistemological value of most auto-experiments . . . is certainly questionable"—as questionable as the objectivity of the auto-experimental "Normal Motor Automatism," in fact.[51] Examining the work of women scientists of the early twentieth century, Oreskes suggests that, contrary to dominant narratives of the role of gender in science, the exemplary agents of objectivity in the lab were not men but women.

These issues become especially salient in Stein's research at the Johns

Hopkins Medical School, where, as Maria Farland has outlined, Stein's supervisor, Franklin P. Mall, "single-handedly transformed medical training by inaugurating hands-on dissection and independent observation," effecting "a dramatic shift from a descriptive to an experimental" medical pedagogy.[52] It was there that Stein developed her self-described "reputation for original scientific work."[53] Stein's retrospective framing of those activities as "work" is notable, for as Farland also points out, the status of Stein's work there was fraught, in part because the *practice* of experimental science within the medical school was not only changing but also gendered:

> Paradoxically, in professional terms, the detailed manual labor and repetitive diagramming that Stein and [her colleague Florence] Sabin performed consigned them to the lower end of the manual-mental hierarchy. As Stein was reported to have pointed out, brain modeling was viewed as "purely mechanical work" performed primarily by female students and assistants; by contrast, "the men wouldn't waste their time on it." Stein herself dismissed the brain models and diagrams as an "excellent occupation for women and Chinamen"—an astonishing comment that further underscores the association of the production of models with the realm of manual labor.[54]

Although, as Lynn M. Morgan notes, "there were contradictory attitudes regarding the prestige attached to modeling" the brain, the "invisibility" of female scientific labor generally has long been a theme of feminist history and philosophy of science; women's scientific labor, precisely because it was done by women, frequently did not count as scientific labor.[55]

We can see these historical circumstances reflected in broader cultural discourses of female labor, especially repetitive, quasi-machinic labor. What Andreas Huyssen calls the "machine-woman" was a trope that arose "as soon as the machine came to be perceived as a demonic, inexplicable threat and as harbinger of chaos and destruction."[56] The modern machine-woman appears in the lab explicitly as an agent of objectivity; the "typewriter"—a female worker of the period named by the machine she operates—is the business-world analogue of another kind of (typically) female worker, the "computer." Before computers were machines they were people, typically women, whose work crucially enabled scientific research, especially in astronomy and physics, as early as the seventeenth century.[57] Leslie John Comrie, credited as "a pioneer in scientific computation," made his much-lauded strides in the 1920s by employing women's less expensive labor: "Almost all of Comrie's human computers were young, unmarried women."[58]

The work of these human computers contributed to Comrie's essentially managerial project of streamlining and automating scientific calculation, which involved not only repurposing a female labor force but also repurposing machines "such as the National machine and the Hollerith punched card equipment, for computational purposes far beyond the minds of the original designers of the machines."[59] Thus the female scientific "computer" was mobilized at the same time, in similar ways, and to similar ends as the early machine computers.[60]

Stein's work was not quantitative analysis but rather brain modeling, associated less with clerical work than with descriptive morphology and natural history illustration.[61] The underlying principle, however, is similar. Intellectual work that might be considered highly "objective," and therefore good science, could also be considered fundamentally mechanical, hence not really intellectual work at all. Indeed, mechanical work could potentially be framed as not even work. Stein herself described her brain sections as "purely mechanical work and rather restful," mechanization eliding the distinction between work and leisure.[62]

The problem comes into greater focus when we consider what is meant by "objectivity" here, especially with respect to "mechanical" labor. Daston and Galison describe a "mechanical objectivity" that rose to prominence in the second half of the nineteenth century, which relies on mechanical processes (such as photography) to filter out human intervention. Mechanical objectivity, just one version of "objectivity," usually depends on a distributed, alienated form of labor. "By *mechanical objectivity*," Daston and Galison write, "we mean the insistent drive to repress the willful intervention of the artist-author, and to put in its stead a set of procedures that would, as it were, move nature to the page through a strict protocol, if not automatically. This meant sometimes using an actual machine, sometimes a person's mechanized action, such as tracing."[63] Where humans were fallible, "patient, indefatigable, ever-alert" machines would take up the burden with their exemplary virtues of labor. "Of course," Daston and Galison note, "strictly speaking, no [moral] merit attached to these mechanical virtues, for their exercise involved neither free will nor self-command. But the fact that the machines had no choice but to be virtuous struck scientists distrustful of their own powers of self-discipline as a distinct advantage. Instead of freedom of will, machines offered freedom from will."[64] In such a context, Stein's shocking comment about brain modeling—that it was "excellent occupation for women and Chinamen"—comes into focus as the articulation of parallel stereotypes about women and about Chinese workers, both of whom were easily read as automata of one kind or another in discourses of the period, *requiring* no "powers of self-discipline" and therefore exemplary workers.[65] The female scientific laborer is represented less as a scientist than as a technician, less experimenter than experimental instrument, valuable less for her discernment than for her mechanical lack thereof.[66] By taking a picture of nature, she disappears from view: camera work.

As Huyssen and others have discussed, the machinic woman is a figure of modernity and a central preoccupation of what we have come to call modern*ism*. In "Melanctha," that modernity does not distance the work from literary naturalism and its types, but rather the reverse. Despite initial appearances, the unthinking (primitive) human animal of naturalism and the unthinking (modern) machine-woman are not so much opposites as translations of one another. It is in this context that we may understand Melanctha's position as both the abstracted "femme sans nom," subject to diagnosis, and an abstracted female knowledge worker. Phillipe Auguste Villiers de l'Isle-Adam's 1886 novel *L'Ève future* (*Tomorrow's Eve*) fictionalizes the American inventor par excellence, Thomas Edison, as a translator between the two archetypes, revealing their continuity. Villiers's Edison sets himself the task of understanding the Eve-like femmes fatales—chorus girls and prostitutes—who supposedly riddle major metropolises, posing a dire threat to masculine integrity and public order. Like Zola's Nana, such women are interpreted as animals, innocent insofar as they are not self-aware but poisonous all the same. Yet as Edison describes them to his friend Lord Ewald, the femme fatale is not only an animal, "less distant, in REALITY, from the animal species than from our own" and a monstrous "vampire" but also a technician, a sort of natural machine: "Look: the bee, the beaver, the ant do [*font*] marvelous things, but they do nothing else, and have never done anything else. The animal is exact; birth confers upon it, with life, this fatality. . . . The Animal does not err, does not oscillate! Man, on the contrary (and it is this which constitutes his mysterious nobility, his divine election) is subject to development and error. He is interested in all things and forgets himself in them."[67] What Marianne Moore would later celebrate as "unconscious/Fastidiousness" is here the mark of monstrosity, indeterminately either animal or machinelike, but in any case unconscious, hence incapable of human nobility or human error. The woman as object of scientific scrutiny is herself an engineer, Edison's own dark twin. Villiers's Edison thus logically reinvents the vampiric female animal as the "Eve of the future," the android Hadaly, literally automating unconscious fastidiousness and re-rendering a human chorus girl, Alicia, as the docile commodity-cum-worker she was always meant to be.

The abstraction of the mechanized worker and the abstraction that makes Melanctha an unvisualizable type—what we might call the story's modernist logic and its naturalist logic—thus map closely onto one another, for the repetition that reveals the bottom nature, as many critics have noted, also propels the narrative forward, constituting the labor of Melanctha's knowledge-gathering "wandering." Formally, to be a typed object of scientific scrutiny, "half made with real white blood," is also to be a repetitious wanderer, acquiring knowledge. Indeed, even the acquisition of knowledge for Melanctha is a doubled activity; knowledge is indivisible from sex, as Melanctha at first "trie[s] to learn the ways that lead to wisdom" from various men, and then begins "to see very clear" as a result of her affair with Jane Harden.[68] Thus to gather knowledge, for Melanctha, is simultaneously to become the pathologized figure of the sexually experienced woman, the "femme sans nom" who disrobes before, and yet baffles, the triple gaze of science, religion, and society. Gathering knowledge, she becomes knowledge's object.

The tension at the heart of mechanical objectivity, and the problem that it poses for Stein as for Melanctha, then, is that the very process of producing knowledge renders certain subjects pathological and object-like. As Friedrich Kittler argues in *Gramophone, Film, Typewriter*, the woman's supposed mechanicity is precisely what makes her valuable as a typewriter or stenographer. The woman-as-machine acts as an ideal amanuensis for nature, the interpreter who does not interpret but merely reveals. Figured as machine-like, the woman scientist has all the virtues of objectivity that the male scientist, "subject to development and error," notionally lacks; working in a laboratory, she is thus both the guarantee of scientific integrity and the herald of a technologized, fully automated modernity—the first step, as Stein might say, out of the nineteenth century and into the twentieth century in literature. Automatic writing, the natural product of quasi-hysteria, returns during Stein's time in medical school as the unique feminine contribution to the science of neuroanatomy, channeling results from sectioned brain samples, now, instead of one's own nervous system. Yet the issue of automatic writing points up the ambivalent status of the woman in the laboratory, for while Stein was a researcher of brain anatomy in medical school and of motor automatism as an undergraduate, she was also an experimental subject for the college experiments, and one laboratory role, as *L'Ève future* suggests, at times collapses into the other. Anticipating Villiers by two years, Stein strikingly represents the female experimental subject as a machine-woman in an 1894 lab report:

> This vehement individual is requested to make herself a perfect blank while someone practices on her as an automaton.
>
> Next she finds herself with a complicated apparatus strapped across her breast to register her breathing, her finger imprisoned in a steel machine and her arm thrust immovably into a big glass tube. She is surrounded by a group of earnest youths who carefully watch the silent record of the automatic pen on the slowly revolving drum.
>
> Strange fancies begin to crowd upon her, she feels that the silent pen is writing on and on forever. Her record is there she cannot escape it and the group about her begins to assume the shape of mocking fiends gloating over her imprisoned misery. Suddenly she starts, they have suddenly loosed a metronome directly behind her, to observe the effect, so now the morning's work is over.[69]

As Anne Raine points out, Stein stages this episode as "a gendered competition between internal and external perspectives" in which the female subject is "imprisoned . . . by the reduction of 'this vehement individual' to pure bodily phenomena."[70] What is most important in this gendering is the way in which it the woman in the laboratory is *simultaneously* "pure bodily phenomena" (as Raine puts it), "an automaton," and a (female) worker—just as the objects of the fictionalized Edison's scrutiny are workers. By being made into an object of science—here specifically the science of consciousness, experimental psychology—the woman is made into "an automaton," broken into her component parts and "surrounded," her sexually identificatory breast bound up in "a complicated apparatus." The woman in the lab, here as an experimental subject rather than as a researcher, is conscious of her unconsciousness as she engages in automatic writing that she cannot control, her "normal motor automatism," a mindless work of endless output from an "automatic pen" onto a "slowly revolving drum." Here the participation of the experimental *subject* is figured as labor, "the morning's work," but an unconscious labor—the automatic inscription of "her record" in an action parallel to that of the (supposedly) unthinking typist. Indeed, as Raine observes, Stein does not challenge the validity of the experimenters' knowledge so much as simply register its distance from the experimentee's subjective experience; although there is a gendered bifurcation of experience in the lab,

Stein does not exclusively endorse either one.[71] This serves as a reminder of the way that Stein herself moved between acting as the woman experimenter and the woman experimentee, each of which is, by this account—problematically—a kind of scientific worker. In other words, when conceived as a worker, the quasi-automatic female scientist is perilously close to the automated experimental subject. As we saw, Stein indeed occupied both positions in her research with Solomons, published in the same year as *L'Ève future*. What her 1894 lab report reveals is the way in which objectivity—conceived as separating the knower from the thing known—is rendered figuratively impossible for the woman integrated into a structure of "work" that depends on automating her body. Indeed, the narrative of mechanicity rendered Stein's work susceptible to being non-*read*, as in an incident that Meyer, Farland, Morgan, and Schoenberg have analyzed in some detail.[72] A minor controversy over whether some of Stein's work deserved to be published in the *Journal of Anatomy* centered on a question of whether it was "original" research or merely (unoriginal, copied from nature) data.[73] The work was not published; thus, outside the private exchange of letters between Lewellys Barker and Henry McElderry Knower, it never appeared as work at all. Stein's paper, the subject of Barker and Knower's epistolary exchange, is lost.

"To Make Confusion Clear": Wandering and Objectification

Stein left medical school in 1902, a year before she wrote *Q.E.D.*, on which "Melanctha" was later based. Meyer argues that Stein soon "exchang[ed] a practice rooted in James's physiological psychology and his subsequent research on 'extraordinary mental states' . . . for a practice more akin to the poetic science of Emerson and Whitman," one that resembles D. H. Lawrence's "subjective science."[74] The oneiric terror that suffuses Stein's 1894 description of research at the Harvard Psychological Laboratory certainly makes such a reading plausible. But a reading of *Q.E.D.* and especially "Melanctha" suggests a turn toward in what Jennifer Ashton has called "a mathematical independence from experience as such."[75] Like Ashton, I read in Stein's career a "logical turn," a turn to an abstract *lingua characterica*, but I will suggest that, when viewed as a performance of epistemic virtue, it is less a break with Stein's scientific training than a working out of that training to its logical consequences. Stein breaks with empiricism, radical or otherwise, but not with the objectivity that increasingly manifested in her scientific work—objectivity that led to her work, as late as 1902, being dismissed as insufficiently original.

The year 1902 was indeed a year of trading professional honors for objectivity.[76] Stein failed to graduate with her class but was offered the opportunity to recuperate her medical degree by undertaking an extra project in the sectioning and modeling of an embryo brain. Meanwhile, Florence Sabin, Stein's colleague and the soon-to-be first woman professor of medicine at Johns Hopkins, "set the standard against which [Stein's work] was judged."[77] When Mall found Stein's work unintelligible, he consulted Sabin, who had recently completed her important *Atlas of the Medulla and Midbrain*. As Sabin later recounted to a colleague, "I soon found out that she had bent the spinal cord of the soft brain forward, so that it protruded just under the frontal lobes before fixation, and that accounted for the strange and bizarre course of the tracts in her model."[78] Mall and Sabin discarded the whole project, ending Stein's last prospects for a medical degree. I do not suggest that Stein should have been awarded the degree or that hers was a good model. Rather, I wish to point out that it was mechanically objective—indeed, that Sabin and Mall discarded it because it was *too* objective. That Sabin was able to reconstruct the problem suggests that the model was not "fantastic," as Stein's classmate Dorothy Reed Mendenhall later reported, but rather an all-too-faithful representation of a damaged, hence atypical, specimen.[79] A guiding principle of mechanical objectivity is to "'let nature speak for itself,'" which "tend[s] . . . to shift attention to the reproduction of individual items—rather than types or ideals," even if those individual items are "inevitably flawed." The objective scientist would therefore use machines like the camera or, through heroic self-suppression, emulate such machines.[80] So far as we know, Stein's model of the brain fulfilled the values of mechanical objectivity to the point of uselessness. Sabin's *Atlas of the Medulla and Midbrain* offers a contrasting case, as one reviewer, describing one of Sabin's drawings, indicates: "A picture like this conveys a better idea of the convolutions of this body than can be obtained from a study of microscopial sections."[81] Sabin's clarifying and typifying representations of the brain mediated the messy contingency of actual microscopial sections, rendering them intelligible. Although Mall's pedagogy, which Stein praised in *The Autobiography of Alice B. Toklas*, emphasized the "hands-on," his most successful protégée, Florence Sabin, produced a pedagogical tool that registered and ameliorated the limitations of that very pedagogy—an atlas that could mediate and make sense of individual specimens.[82]

I do not, in this, mean to suggest that Stein was objective and that Sabin was subjective, or that Stein was somehow the "better" scientist. I wish to hold off the slippage that epistemic virtue enables, in which objectivity becomes equated with scientificity and various other values. Sabin, too, was an adherent of objectivity; several of her illustrations are carefully labeled tracings of sections prepared by John Hewetson; in tracing the sections, Sabin subordinated her judgment to the particularity of the specimen.[83] The tracings are mediations, of course, but they nonetheless seek to "let nature speak for itself." Moreover, Stein was evidently also a schematizer, or so she represented herself (whereas Sabin's illustrations are still widely available, Stein's are lost).[84] There is no evidence to suggest that Stein's drawings were stylistically different from Sabin's (though by most accounts they were less competent). What makes Stein's work more "objective" than Sabin's is Stein's willingness to copy the specimen before her, whatever its condition, declining (or, less charitably, unable) to correct or stylize by accounting for (discounting) a bent-back brain stem. Sabin's well-received atlas, in contrast, served as a visual aid that helped to impose legibility on a notoriously complicated organ. Her drawings refer not only to specimens but also to other drawings; a number of Sabin's illustrations are labeled "after Barker, L. F.: The Nervous System and its Constituent Neurones," just as many of Barker's illustrations in *The Nervous System and Its Constituent Neurones* are "after" the drawings of other anatomists.[85] This evidently widespread practice points to the ways in which visualizations of nature constantly had to be checked against *one another* as well as against specimens. Modeling the brain entailed building a communal consensus about what those models could look like. To censure this work as "subjective" would be to suppose that there necessarily existed in nature, and in every specimen, clearly defined objects that could be called the "inferior olive" or the "nucleus of Darkeschewitz" prior to their modeling and definition according to particular disciplinary norms. Stein's model of a brain with the brain stem bent back was objective yet also, because it was not intelligible in those terms, "fantastic." My point here is not that Sabin was (regrettably) a normalizer and Stein (virtuously) objective but rather that Stein was, by the end of medical school, beginning to push her objectivity beyond the norms of usable scientific practice—not retreating from objectivity but, if anything, rather aggressively, even destructively, exploring it further.

Stein's insistence that she *did* conform to the norms of her discipline both troubles and illuminates this account of objectivity in her work. In the controversy over whether her work might be published in the *American Journal of Anatomy*, Stein's final words on the subject—delivered immediately prior to leaving for France—curiously characterized her research as precisely the opposite of what her harshest reviewer, Henry Knower, deemed it to be. Knower wrote to Barker that Stein's paper contained excellent raw data that had not been adequately analyzed. It seemed to him "unfinished, and lacking in constructive thought," and he judged that the paper consisted primarily of "data" that needed to be "sifted more and worked up into a new or better mental picture."[86] In other words, Knower viewed Stein's paper as lacking in originality or critical thought, though rich in mimetic substance merely copied from nature. Stein's representation of her work strikingly inverts Knower's critique; *instead* of providing new data, she suggests, it provides new and clarifying analysis:

> The whole point of the adult [brain] series to me is not so much/that there is very/definite new|material although there is some of that but|that as far as xxxxxx xx/xx Ihavebeen able I have endeavored to expres[s]/a very clear image which exists in my own mind of a region which the existing literature of the subject leaves in a hopeless mess. My drawings are of course very much more diagram[m]aticxxxx than [Swiss anatomist Rudolph Albert] Von Kolliker's but it seems to me that they tell a clear story. [. . . M]y aim in writingthis article has been not so xxxxx much to give/new/matter but to make confusion clear.

Lacking reference to the original work, it is difficult to arbitrate between these two opposing accounts. What is striking about them is their complementarity, although as Meyer rightly observes, Stein's aggressively typo-ridden letter, ironically declaring the clarity of her work in flamboyantly unclear typography, performs something beyond what it says, suggesting, for instance, a message to Barker "that he and his kind can go to hell"—or, to put it in less oppositional terms, that she is not invested in whether her research is published.[87] Yet Stein's account seems to have something in common with Knower's—the idea that a "mental picture" is the form that knowledge takes. Given that a substantial portion of the work—"some manuscript and sixty-three drawings"—was *physical* pictures, literal images, it is curious that both Stein and Knower emphasize *mental* images.[88] Whereas Knower claims that the paper lacks "a new or better mental picture," Stein asserts that her work is the product of "a very clear image which exists in my own mind."

Evidently, Stein and Knower hold different notions of what a "mental picture" might be, what it ought to be doing for a scientific paper, and in whose mind it ought to reside. Each seems to conceive of the mental picture as something arising from empirical experience, drawn from the data at hand. But for Knower, the mental picture seems to be fundamentally a disciplinary picture, a locus of consensus, whereas for Stein it is evidently a private form of what James would call "knowledge of acquaintance." We have some sense of what Knower believed would impart the requisite mental picture from Sabin's *Atlas*, which Knower introduced as "offer[ing] a valuable and new remedy for" certain "difficulties," namely that "the descriptions [of the brain] in text-books or lectures are commonly so detailed, or so general or diagrammatic; that many students get but hazy ideas of what is shown in their preparations."[89] Sabin's work succeeds as an atlas because it is neither overly detailed nor overly schematic. Literally a happy medium, it offers enough detail to correlate the overwhelming particularity of the student's specimen with a mental picture that is not "hazy" but "clear."[90] The mental picture is something that the atlas can help the student to produce.[91] For Knower, the mental picture is both empirical and disciplinary; Sabin's *Atlas* offers a "new or better mental picture" because it builds a rapport between specimen particularity and anatomical generality. The mental picture, by this account, is enabled, indeed produced, by the physical pictures. This is why Knower could demand that Stein's submission be "worked up into a new or better mental picture"; the mental picture was conceived as something that could help make the specimen legible to the community and its neophytes.

Stein, in contrast, represents the mental picture as the *origin* of her manuscript: "I have endeavored to expres[s]/a very clear image which exists in my own mind of a region which the existing literature of the subject leaves in a hopeless mess." The site of Stein's mental picture, "my own mind," makes the image less a matter of correlating specimens with a professional visual idiom than of imparting to the community a "diagram[m]atic" schema of Stein's own knowledge of acquaintance. While Stein, perhaps even more than Knower, is concerned with clarity, her account of clarity is brusque, almost violent, not a matter of managing detail but of sweeping away the "hopeless mess" (as Mall and Sabin did with her hopeless mess of a brain model); her drawings thus "clear awaythe underbrush andleave a clear road."[92] This represents, I would argue, Stein's final shift in medical school toward an intensified objectivity, one that no longer attempts to represent specimens as such but rather turns to abstract mental structures, burning away contingency by way of "a clarifming process" and leaving pure structure. While Stein's knowledge of the brain is rooted in the hands-on work that she did, she conceives its final manifestation as a distilling. As the autobiographical

Adele puts it in her epiphanic moment in *Q.E.D.*, "Its like a bit of mathematics. Suddenly it does itself and you begin to see."[93] Here "see[ing]" is invoked as a metaphor for knowing; like the colors that are not colors in "Melanctha," the mental picture is no picture at all but an understanding produced by the extreme abstraction of a calculus that "does itself." Visuality itself cedes to —is subsumed by—ratiocination. Stein's emphasis on clarity, in her letter to Barker, is striking; "expres[sing]/a very clear image," Stein's "diagram[m]atic" images "tell a clear story" as they "clear awaythe underbrush andleave a clear road"; the aim of Stein's "clarif[y]ing process" is "to make confusion clear."[94] To make such insistent claims for clarity in such a typographically resistant letter is not only, as Meyer suggests, to make the social gesture of telling the medical school to "go to hell" but also to make a writerly gesture toward what critics have pointed to as a central conundrum of experimental writing, that clarity might be achieved only through obscurity.

Stein's abstraction in her early naturalist fiction has been examined in detail by a number of critics, perhaps most brilliantly by Jennifer Fleissner, who sees *Three Lives* and *The Making of Americans* as "representing the culmination and final transformation of the naturalist 'compulsion to describe.'"[95] The distinctive formal features of this period in Stein's career are well known: "rhythmic" repetition, the constant invocation of certainty, a thematics of taxonomy, the "continuous present," and a highly stylized syntax. What I hope my account of Stein's scientific work has by now suggested is that the features of this writing—I take "Melanctha" as my exemplar—can be theorized in the terms of an extreme objectivity that takes abstraction, or what Whitehead calls definition by "intension," as the guarantee of communicability.[96] The abstraction of language in "Melanctha" both figures and represents the abstraction of the body, an abstraction that, as a woman scientist, Stein had already learned to excessively and parodically enact.

This move toward an objectivity of abstraction is historically intelligible in the terms of what Daston and Galison call "structural objectivity," or what Martin Jay, in another context, has identified as a resistance to "the specter of psychologism."[97] Structural objectivity is suspicious of the objectivity of empirical data, indeed, of the possibility that experience can be communicated—a concern familiar to readers of "Melanctha." Because the senses are fallible, protocols for collecting data inevitably impure, mental heuristics misleading, and communication imprecise, adherents of structural objectivity —primarily, as Jay has pointed out, at the turn of the twentieth century—turned to the formal structures of mathematics and logic as the only possible guarantors of objectivity. Understanding the values being upheld in this model depends on distinguishing between objectivity and scientificity, suspending the assumptions that have so long attended the concept of objectivity. Indeed, many would argue that, by moving away from empiricism, these objective thinkers—notably Gottlob Frege, Henri Poincaré, and Bertrand Russell—were moving away from science itself. My purpose here is not to engage the ever-contested question of the boundaries of science but to track how an epistemic virtue, objectivity, took on a form that would eventually prove crucial in the development of logical positivist philosophy, computer science, and, as in Stein, one influential version of experimental writing.[98] I am arguing not influence but confluence; what I map in reading the structural objectivity of "Melanctha" is a formal correspondence between Stein's naturalist writing and the work of thinkers who hoped to use an objective language to mitigate "the specter of psychologism." The correspondences with Gottlob Frege's *Begriffsschrift* (Concept-writing) (1879) are particularly notable, but my aim is not solely to point out similarities. Rather, I take those similarities as evidence that Stein's naturalism is invested in a fairly counterintuitive set of values—Frege wished to banish psychology; Stein was trained in it, however unconventionally. To align Stein, and especially the Stein of "Melanctha," with an anti-psychologist like Frege may seem particularly perverse in light of many rich readings of "Melanctha" in the terms of Jamesian psychology (especially Lisa Ruddick's) as well as in light of the text's manifest interest in the "complex, desiring" Melanctha's interiority (not to mention Jeff's). Yet this interiority is as formalized as the body that determines it. As Jeff and Melanctha continue to attempt to communicate their interior states, they repetitively reveal and reinforce their own bottom natures. Psychology here does not counter the closed system but rather produces it. Or as Fleissner puts it, Stein is interested in "refiguring the meaning of the most apparently rigid taxonomization and repetition from within."[99] That rigid taxonomization is a concept-writing.

Frege's *Begriffsschrift* represents an attempt to construct a language to communicate ideas unambiguously. It is important to characterize this attempt fairly; Frege does not suggest that sense experience is irrelevant. His concern is not with gathering ideas (in which sense experience necessarily figures) but with proving their validity.[100] Nor does he entertain any fantasies that his *lingua characterica* is entirely unambiguous, and he explicitly denies that it can or should replace natural language. Rather, the uses of the

Begriffsschrift are specialized: is a regulator; it seeks "to provide us with the most reliable test of the validity of a chain of inferences and to point out every presupposition that tries to sneak in unnoticed, so that its origin can be investigated."[101] Frege's moral language around unlicensed intuitions and their tendency to "sneak in" puts the "virtue" in epistemic virtue. Importantly, however, for Frege, objectivity was determined not by images at all, machine aided or otherwise, but rather by communicability. The *Begriffsschrift* sought to guard against intuitions and psychologisms because they were *incommunicable*. Because they were not transferrable from one scientist to another, they were conceived as merely personal rather than objective.[102] To maintain structural objectivity, subjectivity of all kinds—including, ultimately, images—must be purged.

The *Begriffsschrift* has often been received as an early version of present-day quantificational logic, and it is often read through the lens of present-day usage (and the extent to which the 1879 *Begriffsschrift* lives up to it).[103] Frege's idiosyncratic two-dimensional notational system (figure 7), which is very different from present-day logical notation, has been a particular target of ridicule, although Frege himself recognized its alienating quality and defended it, later dryly remarking that "the comfort of the typesetter is certainly not the *summum bonum*."[104] As Danielle Macbeth has argued, it is worth taking Frege's logic "on its own terms," since a number of its features (the two-dimensional visual notation among them) cannot be explained in the terms of quantificational logic as we now know it.[105] Indeed, the alienating quality of Frege's notation, almost universally disparaged by philosophers and logicians alike, is, as Daston and Galison observe, part of its efficacy; the *Begriffsschrift* seeks to enforce *logical* connections in part by baffling psychological and heuristic connections, "break[ing] the domination of the word over the human spirit by laying bare the misconceptions that through the use of language often almost unavoidably arise concerning the relations between concepts and by freeing thought from that with which only the means of expression of ordinary language, constituted as they are, saddle it."[106] The *Begriffsschrift* is a positive construction in its own right, but its objectivity is guaranteed by its opposition to the powerful forces of psychology, "breaking" and "laying [them] bare" and "freeing thought from" them—clearing away the underbrush, as Stein might put it. Frege is thus perfectly aware that logicians may be "frightened off by an initial impression of strangeness."[107] The notation's alienating quality is part of what makes it objective, and I

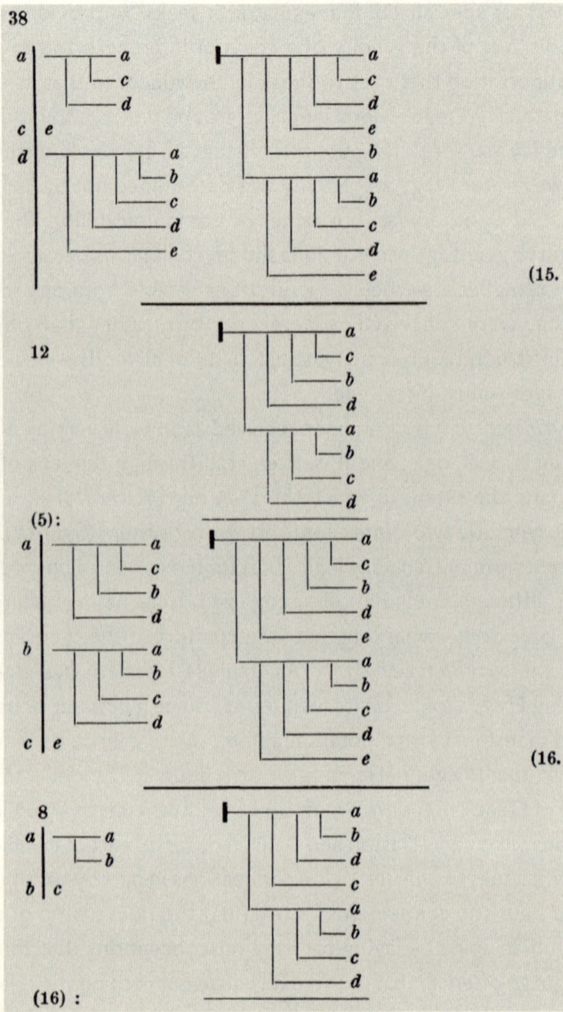

Figure 7. Gottlob Frege, notation from *Begriffsschrift* (formula 12), 1879. Image courtesy of Staats- und Universitätsbibliotek Göttingen.

would suggest that the stylized, alienating language in "Melanctha" operates in a similar way. Consider a paragraph like this one:

> Melanctha Herbert somehow had made him [Jeff] feel deeply just then, what very more it was that she wanted from him. Jeff Campbell now felt in him what

> everybody always had needed to make them really understanding, to him. Jeff felt a strong disgust inside him; not for Melanctha herself, to him, not for himself really, in him, not for what it was that everybody wanted, in them; he only had disgust because he never could know really what it was really right to him to be always doing, in the things he had before believed in, the things he before had believed in for himself and for all the colored people, the living regular, and the never wanting to be always having new things, just to keep on, always being in excitements. All the old thinking now came up very strong inside him. He sort of turned away then, and threw Melanctha from him.[108]

The Language poet Steve McCaffery might call this language "counter-communicative," even though it actually describes a scene of articulating (or attempting to articulate) knowledge.[109] The language is repetitive, lending it a disorientingly recursive quality. While critics like Michael North have productively analyzed the repetition of key lexical words (in the passage above, for instance, "feel"/"felt," "disgust," "strong," "really"), function words are equally if not more likely to be repeated in "Melanctha." Function words pervade everyday language, which is why they usually go unnoticed even when repeated. But here the repetition of function words, and the grammatical functions that they entail, assert themselves:

> Melanctha Herbert somehow had made him [Jeff] feel deeply just then, what very more it was that she wanted **from him**. Jeff Campbell now felt **in him** what everybody always had needed to make them really understanding, **to him**. Jeff felt a strong disgust **inside him**; not for Melanctha herself, **to him**, not for himself really, **in him**, not for what it was that everybody wanted, **in them**; he only had disgust because he never could know really what it was really right **to him** to be always doing, in the things he had before believed in, the things he before had believed in **for himself** and for all the colored people, the living regular, and the never wanting to be always having new things, just to keep on, always being in excitements. All the old thinking now came up very strong **inside him**. He sort of turned away then, and threw Melanctha **from him**.[110]

The repetition of the sequence **preposition + him[self]** works to communicate Jeff's psychological state as a set of unvisualizable spatial relationships. By constantly positioning ideas, feelings, and attitudes vis-à-vis "him," even when there can be no ambiguity about the indirect object, Stein anchors and solidifies Jeff, insisting upon his centrality and presence. Yet by exceeding grammatical necessity, these prepositional phrases become intrusive, interfering with the sense of the sentences. For instance, "Jeff Campbell now felt **in him** what everybody always had needed to make them really understanding, **to him**." Diegetic context illuminates the sense of the sentence: Jeff has learned that Melanctha's "understanding" (elsewhere "wisdom" and "learning") comes from her wide sexual experience and has extrapolated that such actions are *always* the condition of "understanding." Jeff apprehends this rather than knows it; he feels it "in him." The "to him" at the end of the sentence disrupts more than it clarifies; the most normative possible reading is that "to him" is redundant, and a more capacious reading would suggest that it raises semantic questions rather than putting them to rest: Does "to him" mean something different, in the context of the sentence, than "in him"? Does "to him" modify "understanding," so that the kind of understanding under consideration is specifically the kind approved by Jeff? The **preposition + him[self]** sequence in this passage thus impedes immediate grasp of the sentences' meaning, yet it does so not by "breaking" syntax but by reinforcing it, amping up its use of function words and *increasing* syntactic structure. We are, in other words, overloaded with syntactic cues, provided not with too few but with too many. This is especially true in the long, highly subordinated sentences that appear throughout the story, such as the one that forms the heart of the paragraph above:

> Jeff felt a strong disgust inside him; not for Melanctha herself, to him, not for himself really, in him, not for what it was that everybody wanted, in them; he only had disgust because he never could know really what it was really right to him to be always doing, in the things had had before believed in, the things he before had believed in for himself and for all the colored people, the living regular, and the never wanting to be always having new things, just to keep on, always being in excitements.

The sentence is complex; again we are prevented from forming a quick impression; again we must follow a complex logical tree to make sense of it. And again, the sentence is not difficult because it underspecifies but because it overspecifies; we already know, for example, Jeff's bourgeois opinion of how "the colored people" should "liv[e] regular," yet the sentence specifies these things at the *expense* of clarity. In this manner, the syntax of "Melanctha" performs the clarity-through-obscurity that also underwrites Frege's theory of objectivity.

While an emphasis on syntax—a well-documented feature of Stein's writing—already comports with Frege's project, even more salient are the particular syntactic features that Stein foregrounds. In addition to repetition, "Melanctha" also makes unusual uses of negation, nested syntax, quantification, and suspended judgment, all of which are features of formal logic generally and of Frege's logic in particular. Importantly, the features that make the linguistic environment of "Melanctha" similar to Frege's *Begriffsschrift* are also the features that make it difficult to parse and more or less unsummarizable. The use of negation, for instance, flamboyantly foregrounds the logical structures embedded in the writing: "I don't say it, no never to you, that that would not have been the right way for me to do, Melanctha."[111] Although the text occasionally uses the colloquial double negative ("I certainly never would have told you nothing"), the logical negative is by far the more pervasive structure.[112] Here negations seem to cancel one another out, yet the presence of the negations also necessitates longer and more complex sentences that impede reading. Moreover, while the negations seem to cancel one another out logically, the sequence of negations itself leaves an emotional trace; to not say that something is *not* true is a suspension of assertion, whereas to say it *is* true is to assert positively. And this emotional trace, like the alienation occasioned by overdetermined syntax, matters not only for a reader but also for the characters.

Indeed, the suspension of assertion, partly enabled by negation, is a key feature of the linguistic environment of "Melanctha." As in *Q.E.D.*, there is a constant desire to assign truth-values to the relationship between Melanctha and Jeff. "Tell me true," says Jeff repeatedly. "Tell me honest."[113] But somehow, it is never possible to "tell me true." As Jeff repeatedly complains, "I certainly don't know anything at all about you, and I certainly don't know which is a real Melanctha Herbert."[114] Jeff and Melanctha's declarations of love are couched in affirmations of certainty, negations, and truth-valuations, performing exquisite specificity; however, access to true feelings and desires can never be granted, because even the "true feelings" are uncertain. Though wrapped in tissue layers of counter-communicative specificity, the kernel is always an undefined variable rather than a truth value. Here is an example: "[Jeff] did not know very well what it was that he really wanted. He was very certain that he did not know very well what it was that Melanctha wanted."[115] Here, knowledge is attenuated by "very well," and desire is intensified by "really," but these specifying markers circle around a blank—"what it was." The second sentence reenacts this detailed statement of uncertainty, adding another layer of modification —"he was very certain."

Melanctha, for her part, handles questions about unknowns by keeping

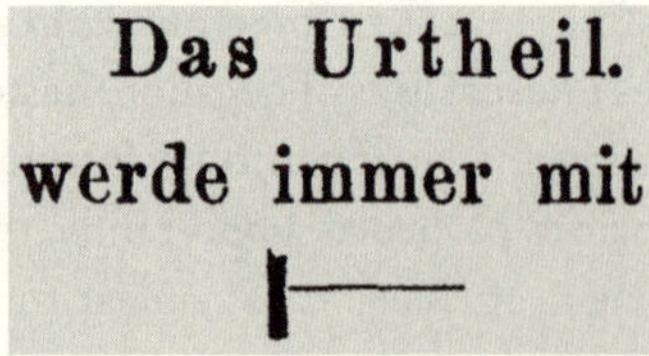
Das Urtheil.

werde immer mit

⊢

Figure 8. Gottlob Frege, "turnstile" (assertion with judgment stroke) from *Begriffsschrift*, 1879. Image courtesy of Staats- und Universitätsbibliotek Göttingen.

them as unknowns, by variable manipulation, as it were. Instead of specifying a value for *x*, Melanctha creates another expression involving *x*, referring the question back to the asker. "'You know very well Jeff Campbell,' said Melanctha, 'You certainly do know very well Jeff, you don't think really much, of my talking. . . . You know that's true what I am saying Jeff.'"[116] Jeff makes similar appeals to what Melanctha "already knows": "Sure Melanctha, you know that already."[117] But the "already" known is in fact never known but instead deferred. Consequently a truth-value cannot be determined; judgment is suspended. This feature of "Melanctha" corresponds to one of Frege's more idiosyncratic developments, what he called the "judgment stroke."[118] The turnstile symbol (figure 8), signifying assertion, was popularized in mathematical logic by Bertrand Russell, but Frege distinguished between the functions of the vertical and horizontal strokes, calling the horizontal stroke the "content" stroke and the vertical stroke the "judgment" stroke.

Frege therefore conceived the content of an assertion as distinct from actually asserting it. While this distinction has not been retained in quantificational logic—indeed, Ludwig Wittgenstein declared it "logically quite meaningless"—Frege's particular interest in the objectivity guaranteed by structure itself makes the distinction intelligible in the context of the *Begriffsschrift*.[119] This distinction is key in "Melanctha," in which entire waves of interaction between Jeff and Melanctha are sustained not on the basis of "what is true" but on the basis of the complex structures themselves. Indeed, in the world of "Melanctha," pure structure can and must signify. As the affair between Jeff and Melanctha dwindles, we find that "Jeff Campbell knew very well too now inside him, he did not really want Melanctha, now if he could no longer trust her."[120] Jeff's certainty is predicated on a judgment of desire that is predicated on a possibility—"*if* he could no longer trust her"—that is ultimately decided only by the structures around it. Structures alone are communicable, and they suffice as the basis for action.

So far I have discussed the "linguistic environment" of "Melanctha" as though it were homogeneous. Yet this is not quite true; for one thing, the sentence-level repetitions are augmented by larger-scale repetitions, most notably the recapitulation near the end of the story of the initial description of Melanctha's relationship with Rose Johnson. The environment of suspended judgment, what Lisa Ruddick and, to some extent, Michael North have read as a semiotically slippery "wandering" environment, is eventually shut down: one day someone does tell Melanctha something true—the dandy Jem Richards, with whom Melanctha has an affair after she breaks with Jeff at last. Jem begins a section of dialogue with Melanctha in the expected fashion: "Tell me Melanctha right and true, you don't care really nothing more about me now Melanctha."[121] Melanctha's evasion, like Jem's question, continues the pattern; she turns the question about herself into a question about Jem: "Why you ask me that, Jem Richards." But instead of wondering further or acting on partial knowledges built on unknowns, Jem expresses an unqualified feeling: "I just don't give a damn now for you any more Melanctha." The substitution of a value for a variable disables Melanctha's "wandering" strategy of interaction and the story's entire judgment-suspending modus operandi; "Melanctha never could have for this an answer."[122] The story quickly collapses after this episode, and Melanctha perishes within a page, a classic naturalist death. It is a fulfillment in a number of senses. In that it follows from the repetition of the novel's initial scenes with Rose Johnson, the final movement seems structurally mandated, just as it seems mandated on the sentence level when Jem finally assigns a truth-value to the omnipresent question of affection. And because Melanctha is constituted by these structures and by structured typologies (a Type I, in the terms of "CMA"), her death seems to arise out of her constitutive malady, her repetitious and "wandering" nature.

Yet this wandering also produces knowledge, the "understanding" that both comforts and horrifies Jeff by making him "see very clearly":

> Jane began to explain to Jeff Campbell how in every way, she Jane, had taught Melanctha. Jane then began to explain how eager Melanctha always had been for all that kind of learning. Jane Harden began to tell how they had wandered. . . . Jane began to tell all she knew of the way Melanctha had gone on, after she had left her. Jane began to tell all about the different men, white ones and blacks, Melanctha never was particular about things like that, Jane Harden said in passing, not that Melanctha was a bad one, and she had a good mind, Jane Harden

> never would say that she hadn't, but Melanctha always liked to use all the understanding ways that Jane had taught her, and so she wanted to know everything, always, that they knew how to teach her.[123]

Learning and understanding are of course euphemisms for sexual experience, but I wish to insist on the way that Stein frames sexual experience—specifically a promiscuous sexuality—as knowledge as well. Indeed, there is something remarkably industrious in Melanctha's learning, especially in the diversity of people with whom she sleeps. Melanctha, with her abstracted body, "half made with real white blood" and sustained by an abstracted language, is a gatherer of knowledge. That she is also in a sense a classic naturalist victim of her own constitution does not contradict her figuration as a (female) scientist. It is true that Melanctha, as a typologized and pathologized, impoverished, sexually promiscuous, bisexual woman of color, is a scientific *object* in much the same way as is Nana; indeed her name, a play on *melancthon* (Greek "black earth"), links her from the beginning to the dying Nana, a death-bound "mold of the earth."[124] Yet as I have argued above, the repetitious, compulsive modern woman, whether a typist or a scientist or merely—as Melanctha's promiscuity also suggests—a consumer, is undecidably both experimenter and experimentee. Indeed, it is never entirely clear whether Melanctha's behavior is really "wandering" or "learning"—whether it is leisure (and consumption) or industry (and knowledge production), dissipation or creativity. Melanctha ultimately dies of "consumption" (tuberculosis), and that consumption is her constitutive malady, not a self-consumption as Ruddick suggests but the consumption counterposed against productive labor, quite literally:

> Melanctha never killed herself, she only got a bad fever and went into the hospital where they took good care of her and cured her.
>
> When Melanctha was well again, she took a place and began to work and to live regular. Then Melanctha got very sick again, she began to cough and sweat and be so weak she could not stand to do her work.
>
> Melanctha went back to the hospital, and there the Doctor told her she had the consumption, and before long she would surely die. They sent her where she would be taken care of, a home for poor consumptives, and there Melanctha stayed until she died.[125]

Melanctha's death, then, is not simply tuberculosis but an oscillation between "work" and "consumption"—illness framed as work's inverse. The abstraction of "Melanctha," "the first definite step away from the nineteenth century and into the twentieth century in literature," thus models the abstraction of the modern knowing/known woman herself.[126]

Lest this abstraction appear neutral, however, it is important to remember what Melanctha's ability to inhabit a suspended, undecidable objectivity means. What permits it is, after all, a racialization and pathologization at the level of formal structures: Melanctha is a "complex, desiring" "Type I" whose pathologized mixed race, sexual promiscuity, and seemingly resultant (that is, always already latent) illness give her special access to a zone of meaning produced entirely out of communicable logical structures. Her diagnosis is her immiserated end. Charles Bernstein has suggested that although "[Stein's] attitude toward the poor and African Americans could be condescending, racist, and reactionary . . . her [literary] work radically contradicts such received ideas."[127] Although Bernstein's Stein scholarship is indispensable, this reading of her work does not, in my view, hold up. "Each sentence is a razor blade," the poet Dionne Brand writes of Stein's description of Rose Johnson. "What jaded poses dismiss all dreadfulness."[128] Rather, it is a case of epistemic virtue (objectivity) appearing to adequately proxy for political virtue even as, in this case, it actually produces the condescending, racist, and reactionary elements of her writing.

Seeing Clear: Portraits and Repetition

I have argued so far that Stein's experimentalism runs on a naturalist logic sustained by an anti-visual objectivity, the early traces of which can be seen in the scientific work that she completed prior to writing her major literary works. I have also argued for understanding this objectivity as a specifically female objectivity, not the situated knowledge of Harding and Haraway but one deeply embedded in social realities all the same. This "camera work" served to regulate and guarantee scientific objectivity and yet also tended to occlude the female scientist as such, to render her an instrument of science or even an object of science. If knowledge in "Melanctha" is, as I have outlined above, indivisible from sex, it is also indivisible from gender. For Melanctha, to actively work for "understanding"—an activity known in some contexts as "research"—is already to position herself as sexually promiscuous and pathologically repetitive, a hysterical typist with an automatic hand, a thing needing to *be* researched. To do camera work is to be abstracted and thereby dematerialized.[129]

Melanctha's abstracted and anti-visualized "pale yellow" body is therefore the concomitant of her wandering pursuit of understanding, her attempt to "see very clear."[130] To close, I wish to apply this reading of Stein's experimentalism as anti-visual structural objectivity to the numerous "portraits" that Stein wrote approximately around the same time as *Three Lives* was published. Two of these appeared in Alfred Stieglitz's journal *Camera Work: A Photographic Quarterly* in 1912; they were portraits of Matisse and Picasso, two painters with whom Stein has become permanently associated artistically as well as biographically. So our reading of Stein through the rubrics of objectivity should not preclude the notion that Stein's writing was invested in visuality, albeit an abstracted visuality; it clearly was.

Some important aspects of Stein's work, then, seem to run against the account I have given so far. If I have argued that camera work is a kind of exact repetition, for example, then we should look, in counterpoint, to Stein's self-representation in *The Autobiography of Alice B. Toklas* as someone constitutionally *incapable* of the machinic camera work of objectivity. "Gertrude Stein tried to copy Three Lives on the typewriter," we learn, "but it was no use, it made her nervous."[131] This inability to copy is later rooted in childhood with an anecdote in which Stein writes a description of a sunset that is "chosen to be copied out on beautiful parchment paper," but "after [Stein] had tried to copy it twice and the writing became worse and worse she was reduced to letting someone else copy it for her."[132] One way to read this retrospective self-presentation would be to see it as staking out a position of genius—a position staked out explicitly at the outset of *Alice B. Toklas* when Toklas's voice tells us, "The three geniuses of whom I wish to speak are Gertrude Stein, Pablo Picasso, and Alfred Whitehead."[133] The Stein of *Alice B. Toklas* is a genius, not an amanuensis. Moreover, the persona Stein constructs for *Alice B. Toklas* is not where it ends; in "Portraits and Repetition" (1935), Stein denies the possibility of copying altogether, explicitly in reference to her repetitive stylistics:

> Then also there is the important question of repetition and is there any such thing. Is there repetition or is there insistence. I am inclined to believe there is no such thing as repetition. And really how can there be. . . . [O]nce started expressing this thing, expressing any thing there can be no repetition because the essence of that expression is insistence, and if you insist you must each time use emphasis and if you use emphasis it is not possible while anybody is alive that they should use exactly the same emphasis.[134]

Repetition is not repetition even when it is exact, because the mere fact of its having been repeated changes its emphasis, turns it into "insistence." Stein's most noticeable and widely parodied formal trait, repetition, is thus embraced and, at the same time, rendered as something other than repetition. I would frame this not as a tension but as an explanation: repetition, the mechanical female scientific labor of abject mimesis, operates in Stein's essentially non-visual portraits to do something more than repeat: dispelling image, dispelling psychology, the camera work of repetition dwells in the subject-object collapse to which certain knowers are so prone. Repetition now not of the visual image (the traced brain section) but of verbal structures eliminates any trace of heuristics, instead inviting readers to register the shift in emphasis that inheres in each new repetition. Each repetition, as Stein's invocation of the cinema suggests, is like an anti-visual, abstracted photograph, capturing not only likeness but, as Roland Barthes puts it, the "this-has-been," a moment in time that can be neither erased nor recovered.[135] "I was doing what the cinema was doing," Stein writes. "I was making a continuous succession of the statement of what that person was until I had not many things but one thing."[136] Thus there are no shortcuts in reading the portraits, as in reading "Melanctha"; there is no possibility of summary or condensation, no picture worth these thousand-word portraits, no desire for flash. It is the mole's-eye view, precisely because it is *not* intuitable, that emerges as objective, portable because processual. "Melanctha Herbert never really killed herself," but her naturalist compulsion nonetheless produces an anti-psychological and anti-visual objectivity that makes Stein's portraits a way of "see[ing] very clear." It is precisely the absence of psychological shortcuts in Stein's structural objectivity that makes it "as exact as mathematics."[137] Thus Stein's abstract determinism—both typological and semiotic—is the surprising ground for an experimentalism that does not break with protocols—objectivity, repetition, camera work—but revels in them. Not against objectivity but through it, as Stein might say, "the difference is spreading."[138]

4 Precision

"These products of American distraction factories," Siegfried Kracauer wrote of the Tiller Girls, "are no longer individual girls, but indissoluble girl clusters whose movements are demonstrations of mathematics. As they condense into figures in the revues, performances of the same geometric precision are taking place in what is always the same packed stadium, be it in Australia or India, not to mention America."[1] Kracauer called the patterns formed by these "thousands of bodies, sexless bodies in bathing suits" the "mass ornament," an ornament made of a mass of people to be enjoyed by a mass of people: "The regularity of their patterns is cheered by the masses, themselves arranged by the stands in tier upon ordered tier."[2] But the value embodied by this sublime multiplicity is not that other epistemic virtue of the mass, flash. Instead of condensation, there's extension. Instead of instantaneity, duration. All the gory details.

But if mass echoes mass, it also is worth remarking that one of those masses, the dancers, is single sex, and the other, the audience, mixed. The precision dancers are "sexless," perhaps, and indeed "a linear system that no longer has any erotic meaning," but girls all the same, for Kracauer knows that the neutral body in a bathing suit is that of a woman—a pretty one.[3] Indeed, in the final, eponymous number of the 1934 Busby Berkeley film, Dick Powell's character, playing a movie producer, will shout loudly to an all-male board room that it is "DAMES" that make a show worth watching.[4] This spectacle of "dames" is what finally converts Powell's film character's wealthy, puritanical uncle Ezra (Hugh Herbert)—whose opposition to the young fellow's fast ways is the film's flimsy premise—to the pleasures of the theater. Sexless, then, but clearly not ungendered, and not without a certain sexual utility.

Sexless like machine parts, embodying the aesthetics of the machine, the female bodies of the mass ornament seem to be *culpably* unerotic to Kracauer, a bad use of attractive female bodies, a bad femininity. Kracauer's remarks on the Tiller Girls' purported "sexlessness" (Körpern . . . ohne Geschlecht) as they fall into "a linear system that no longer has any erotic meaning" disclose the expectation underpinning them: that a female body should be both sexed and erotic, that its failure to be so appears an uncanny gender transgression.[5] In conforming perfectly, the bodies deviate. Kracauer makes no such claims about military drills, a human mechanicity that he explicitly excludes from the category of the mass ornament on the thinnest of pretexts: its lines of male bodies are naturalized, rooted in a socially explicable "patriotic feeling."[6] No, the mass ornament is composed of feminine bodies unsexed by a rigidity, a hardness, an orderliness, morcellized into interchangeable "arms, thighs, and other segments"—feminine bodies queered by modernity.[7]

Is it an accident that the mass ornament and audience alike are arranged in tiers, in rows? That the dancers' vertical stacking comes to be flattened into two dimensions by an overhead lens that turns the bodies into diadems, rosettes, and wreaths, "resembl[ing] *aerial photographs* of landscapes and cities," a reductive schematization into two dimensions that nonetheless feels like omniscience?[8] I suggest not. The culpably unsexed feminine body, at once controlled and dismembered, with its alarming relation to and emblematization of the mass, with its evocation of the bomb's-eye view, with its disavowed resemblance to the military, has something to tell us about that so ambivalently valued poetic and scientific desideratum, precision.

Precision is widely accepted as an epistemic virtue with both moral and epistemological valences, but unlike objectivity, it is rarely considered the sine qua non of knowledge. It is a technical virtue, a way of improving on what is already good, often tautologically so: what is precise is better because it lets us know just how certain we are of what we know, which is to say because it is precise. As M. Norton Wise observes in his introduction to *The Values of Precision*, precision is widely distinguished from accuracy in that precision entails self-consistency (we get the same values every time), whereas accuracy implies adequation to an outside norm (the values match some expected target). In historical usage, however, this distinction is far from universal; thus "as a historical matter, precision has normally implied accuracy."[9] We may consider precision-and-accuracy as precision's fuller connotation, the one expected in discussions of precision weapons or precision tools; precision-and-accuracy, too, is the version of precision that, in introducing outside targets to which the precise act or object must be adequate, entails sociality and standardization: "Establishing precision," Wise continues, "is also a matter of establishing credibility and trust."[10]

If the "experimental tradition" has handed down an exemplary poet of precision, it is certainly Marianne Moore, and in descriptions of her poetics, precision has taken on just this valence of credibility and trust that Wise describes. The judgment of precision leaks out of critical readings of Moore's poems and into assessments of her selfhood, even Moore's very body. This is not the case for many other writers, including those conscripted into the experimental tradition. Poundian "sincerity" and Zukofskian "objectification," though likewise drawing on a nexus of epistemic virtues, are rarely described in the terms of precision. But with Moore it is everywhere. "We are now used to calling Marianne Moore an observer of unique precision," Evelyn Feldman and Michael Barsanti write, while Bonnie Costello writes that "precision is [Moore's] passion."[11] Kirstin Hotelling (Zona) asserts Moore's "lifelong devotion to scientific precision."[12] Linda Leavell notes in Moore a proclivity toward "observation, differentiation, and the precise diction of science."[13] Robin G. Schulze follows Lisa Steinman in arguing that Moore should be read in relation to the visual artists, including Charles Sheeler, Charles Demuth, and Joseph Stella, associated with early twentieth-century "precisionism," which undertook "a stripped-down rationalist aesthetic that valued the machine as an expression of pure intellectual order."[14] Schulze, furthermore, indicts Grace Schulman's edition of Moore's poems (2003) because, as she puts it, "the saddest argument that this entire edition makes is that Moore was not very precise."[15] Schulze's comment, suggesting that any half-awake reader of Moore should *know better* than to suggest that Moore was not precise, reveals how central the idea of precision has come to be in Moore's reception.

Moore encouraged this view herself. For example, her 1944 essay "Feeling and Precision" offers two poetic desiderata in ostensible harmony, yet relentlessly subsumes any valorization of feeling under the demands of precision.[16] Style, Roland Barthes has argued, always seems to "spring from the body and the past of the writer and gradually become the very reflexes of his [*sic*] art."[17] If this is the case—if precise style is "a radiograph of personality," as Moore suggests in "Feeling and Precision"—then precise style suggests a precise personality, an inner disposition that the author can but obey.[18] The problem of the elusiveness of feeling in Moore's poetry is as frequently commented upon as the prominence of precision, usually in conjunction with it, and, when strong feeling is attributed to Moore, it is often a feeling *about precision*, like the "passion" that Costello identifies or the "lifelong devotion" that Hotelling cites.[19] There is, then, a deferral in the way that Moore suggests, "Feeling at its deepest . . . tends to be inarticulate. If it does manage to be articulate, it is likely to seem overcondensed, so that the author"—obviously herself—"is resisted as being enigmatic or disobliging or arrogant."[20] The measures of precision, she seems to argue, index the deepest feeling, and yet, she admits, they do not *indicate* it. Thus "although Henry James was probably so susceptible to emotion as to be obliged to seem unemotional, it is a kind of painter's accuracy for Ezra Pound to say of him as a writer, 'Emotions to Henry James were more or less things that other people had, that one didn't go into.'"[21] The subterranean feelings that presumably underlie precision thus seem only to reverse the direction of causality and reveal precision to be the source of the feelings that are the source of precision.

When Moore's writing is called "precise," then, many other things are happening as well. A disturbing absence, displacement, or sublimation of feeling is also being identified; the disturbance, too, is being registered, and it is often also explicitly identified as being bound up in Moore's inhabitation of gender and sexuality, and indeed in her very body. Moore's precision is also the spectacle of a woman failing or, worse, refusing to emote in prescribed ways, even through the distancings of authorship or "modernist impersonality," and coming from a woman writer this is also framed as both an impossibility (there *must* be passion somewhere; perhaps it is a passion for precision) and a deviance.[22] And while Moore is often treated as an exceptional figure—the celibate always stands apart, is somehow *the only one* despite not, in fact, being anything like the only one—Moore's poetics helps to clarify the ways that precision has operated as a modern epistemic virtue not only (or even, perhaps, primarily) in literature but more broadly. Precision helps to name both an epistemological desideratum and a sexual unease in technological modernity, as perceptible in Kracauer's uncanny tower of identical dancing women as in the spinsterliness of Moore's infamous disclaimer at the beginning of her incomplete *Complete Poems* (1967): "Omissions are not accidents."[23] The production of Moore's persona, by herself and by her readers, reveals precision's complex gendering, the way that it is gendered feminine, but often deviantly so. It is important that precision, however associated with the feminine and the small and however desired as an epistemic virtue, is not, for all that, seen as harmless. Like "scissoring"—the lesbian sex act whose authenticity *as* a lesbian act (i.e., rather than a heterosexual male projection) is continually at issue, which proposes that when cis-bodied women copulate it is a form of cutting at the genitals—precision, to use Kenneth Burke's nervous verb, "snips."[24] As an epistemic virtue, precision confers a sense that Moore's poetry is authorizingly "scientific." Yet epistemic virtues also obfuscate their own specificity, occluding the ways that precision might work against other epistemic virtues. As an epistemic virtue, precision also suggests its own portability as a virtue, across aesthetic, ethical, and political domains. Yet precision will prove more congenial than not to the language of state atrocity that later experimental writers were concerned to oppose. Feminist theorists of both modernity and neoliberalism have taught us how little we can expect benignity from feminine forms; indeed, they can enable a genuinely menacing capitalist futurity or worse, as with the rise of drones and "precision" targeting, an all too mature and capably precise present.[25]

The First Grace of Style

"Complexity is not a crime," Moore writes in "In the Days of Prismatic Color" (1919), one of her many poems that deplore, while fully undertaking, a highly formal style. In the poem's postlapsarian aesthetic world we are all too prone to a "complexity . . . that has been committed to darkness instead of granting its-// self to be the pestilence that it is."[26] Not a crime, then, but not neutral, either; complexity is a pestilence that does not even do us the courtesy of admitting its own pestilential nature.[27] Carlo Ginzburg has pointed out how one fin-de-siècle evidentiary paradigm in aesthetics emerges from the modeling of judgment on the detection of crime; Moore's grudging exculpation, then, remains in the register of the aesthetic, a comment on style. In art as in crime, small or minor anatomical details give away the truth, making precision a valuable virtue.[28] Yet precision is not itself innocent; to detect the detail is to be *of* the detail, and precision therefore has much in common with complexity: "carry/it to the point of murki-/ness and"—tautologically—"nothing is plain."[29]

In this section I wish to specify what a precise literary style looks like—or rather, using the case of Moore, is *supposed* to look like, since, as I have discussed above, frequent appeals to form notwithstanding, precision is rarely separable from beliefs about precise persons. As with any epistemic virtue, precision binds epistemological values inhering in practices to ethical values inhering in persons, and in Moore's case this has signaled significant ambivalence, even danger. In mapping the production of the "precise"

Moore, then, I will also attend to the values entailed by precision—those moments when Moore's style is raised as evidence of "probity" or "scrupulousness," attributes that bespeak both soundness and, often, too, a threat: the myopic and unyielding knowledge practices of women, or the law, or more monstrously yet, both at once.[30]

Moore's twelve-line blazon "To a Snail" (1924) offers a sense of precise style in the way that it interleaves technics and ethics. Like many of Moore's poems, "To a Snail" focuses on an animal, imbuing the creature with epistemological and moral significance (both "knowledge" and "virtue") while thoroughly evacuating the poetic voice, so that an apostrophized invertebrate seems to take on all the poem's burdens of value:

> If "compression is the first grace of style,"
>   you have it. Contractility is a virtue
> as modesty is a virtue.
> It is not the acquisition of any one thing
> that is able to adorn,
> or the incidental quality that occurs
> as a concomitant of something well said,
> that we value in style,
> but the principle that is hid:
> in the absence of feet, "a method of conclusions";
> "a knowledge of principles,"
> in the curious phenomenon of your occipital horn.[31]

Praising piecemeal the body of a snail rather than that of a lover, Moore locates therein the principles of poetic craft. Cristanne Miller's description of "The Plumet Basilisk" could as well apply to the snail: "Like the poem itself, the basilisk that 'you' see . . . is a work of art, a moral guide, every bit as much as it is a creature scientifically observed and precisely rendered onto a page."[32] The values imputed to the animal are mirrored in the values performed by the "scientifically observed and precisely rendered" poem; precision is thus an ethical as well as a technical adequation to the specimen. Like the Tiller Girls, abstracted into series of morcellized legs and arms, the snail is divided into physical components: its "compression" and "contractility" in a shell, an "absence of feet," and an "occipital horn." These three physiological attributes quickly open out into aesthetic directives, each physical feature of the snail correlating with a poetic desideratum. Thus physical compression in a shell is simultaneously the verbal compression of poetry and the "modesty" that is "the first grace of style"; the absence of feet, in this unmetered poem, indicates "a method of conclusions"; and that most "curious" feature of the snail, the occipital horn, mysteriously suggests "a knowledge of principles."

We see in this poem all the hallmarks of Moore's precision, then: description that is not only detailed but disconnected, separated out, *sliced*, representing the snail not integrally but rather in parts; tidy parallelism across the whole poem, with each physical attribute paired with a philosophical one; and, in the final, elaborately hypotactic sentence, grammatical balance to match. Notwithstanding its brevity and its lauding of "compression," then, the poem flies in the face of the Poundian flash aphorism "Dichten = condensare." If Moore's style tends to be characterized by "despis[ing] connectives," it is not in the sense that Poundian parataxis (or, for that matter, the "New Sentence" of Language writing) eschews the forms of logical consequence and grammatical subordination; rather, grammatical parallelism and reversal produce a sense of separateness *within* hypotaxis.[33] There is a sense of completion, even, somehow, to excess; a *nicety* of detail that seems not only replete but inexorable.

Yet while the poem's punning references to poetic form suggest the snail as an allegory for poetry, as Schulze has put it, "Moore's animals remain animals."[34] Part of the force of the poem's poetic desiderata derives from their rootedness in the physical reality of the snail's body, and this, too, is part of precision (or rather, its concomitant, accuracy): its claim of adequation to a physical reality. Moreover, while the poem entertains the idea that the snail is merely a physical vehicle for more important intellectual abstractions, this reading is eventually punctured by the poem's delicately deferred final words, "your occipital horn." The attribute, named by a technical anatomical term, breaks the easy double meaning of the physical forms—compression, an absence of feet—named in the poem; its technical nature mitigates against the semantic doubleness on which punning depends. And because the chiasmus in the final lines defers the revelation of the "occipital horn" until the very end, the double reading of snail as poem is reduced suddenly; only at the end of the poem are we back to a physical fact, a snail, a specimen.[35]

But the occipital horn also introduces another problem: despite the anatomical terminology, despite the way that it so cleverly troubles the parallel between snail and poem, it is already a metaphor—for, strictly speaking, *snails do not have an occipital horn*. "Occipital" refers to the occiput, or back of the head—hence the "occipital bone" at the base of the skull and the "occipital lobe" of the brain, and even an "occipital horn syndrome" that manifests in calcium deposits on the occipital bone.[36] But snails do not have skulls, obviating the possibility of a horn; moreover, their tentacles are always in pairs and soft, unlike the "horn." In terms of physical resemblance, a better candidate for the "occipital horn" is perhaps the pointed apex of the snail's shell—though that would reduce "occipital" to a mere invocation of bone. In this final detail, then, concretion and abstraction meet in vertiginous confusion. The "occipital horn" is the aspect of the snail that is most apparently technical, and, owing to the narrowed semantic possibilities of the specialized anatomical terms, it is the detail that most strenuously resists assimilation into the analogy between snail and poem. Yet the occipital horn is also the least clearly referential detail of the snail that is named. The occipital horn, at once thoroughly specific and thoroughly vague, stages a crisis in naming, for the term's very specificity makes it unsuited to carry its semantic burdens; it *must* be a metaphor despite looking like anything but. Like a single snail specimen ("a Snail") representing the class Gastropoda, the occipital horn takes on an unwieldy task of signification, thus troubling the relationship between the particular and the abstract that the poem's earlier puns set up.

If "To a Snail" undermines its own tidy economies, it does so not by undoing precision but on precision's own terms: the overspecificity of the nonreferential occipital horn reenacts the problem presented by type specimens in natural history—individual, physical plants and animals that ground whole taxonomies. The "type specimen" (or "holotype") serves as a point of reference for any given species. The type concept in natural history is metonymic; as Lorraine Daston points out, the holotype need not be typical or particularly representative of the "essence" of the species; indeed, in species exhibiting sexual polymorphism, seasonal molting, or other variations, it would be an impossibility. It is not that the naturalist believes that the holotype is, or even could be, exemplary or typical of the species; rather, "the type specimen is only accidentally, not essentially, a representative sample of the species."[37] Indeed, the primary use of the holotype is to define species *nomenclature*, not the species per se. The fixity of the species *name* outweighs other considerations, so that the selection of the holotype is almost pointedly arbitrary. The use of the holotype constructs an unusually stable relationship between word and thing, because the name is fixed to a single specimen, just as the name "Duns Scotus"—to whom Moore misleadingly attributes quotations in "To a Snail"—may be affixed to a concrete pair of quotations.[38] In doing so, however, the holotype puts special pressure on the relationship between thing and concept—the concept, that is, of the species that the name is supposed to designate.

My point, here, is not to argue that natural history is precise and that Moore's poetics resembles natural history and is therefore (also) precise. Moore's (often "scientific") precision was agreed upon long ago and apart from any specific comparison to natural history, and in any case, I have no interest in *using* "precision" as a term of vague and semi-fearful praise. Rather, I am interested in *why* it functions as a term of vague and semi-fearful praise and what is its implication in a variety of scientific discourses (but a few in particular: natural history, embryology and cytology, measurement, military applications—the other side, in short, of the kinds of population thinking managed via flash) has to do with it. The function of holotypes in natural history makes evident the role of a law-giving arbitrariness in precision, for a type specimen is usually not the "best" or "most representative" specimen (by whatever criteria) but rather, simply, the *first*. The question of what constitutes a relevant detail, a *distinguishing feature*, in a specimen or a species can thus be a matter of mere chronological priority. Precision's probities—its high resolution, its detail, its consistency, its adequation to a norm—are thus always as self-undermining as an "occipital horn," in the sense that an element of arbitrariness grounds them.

This is perhaps why, as Naomi Schor argues, the detail belongs to "a larger semantic network . . . bounded . . . by the ornamental [and] the everyday."[39] Precision in Moore's poems depends substantially on *detail* as a concept and *details* as discrete components of the poem. This is certainly the case in "To a Snail," which renders the snail as a series of discrete details, however elusive some details may be. Yet detail stages its own well-known, and gendered, instabilities, for the poem uses details to set up an economy of value that can only put questions into motion. The tidy parallel between the physical detail (contractility, the absence of feet, the "occipital horn") and the abstract virtue (modesty, a method of conclusions, a knowledge of principles) is, in the poem, ostensibly hierarchical:

> It is not the acquisition of any one thing
> that is able to adorn,
> or the incidental quality that occurs

as a concomitant of something well said,
that we value in style,
but the principle that is hid[40]

The anatomical detail may take on the status of the mere "adorn[ment]," perhaps producing an "incidental quality" (not an essential one). The poem's precision, in using the detail, thus also raises the detail's problematic, the historical opposition between the detail as such and aesthetic order, what Moore might call "the first grace of style" and "the principle that is hid." The detail always verges on the merely ornamental, so that, as Svetlana Alpers puts it in her study of Flemish painting: "To say an art is for women is to reiterate that it displays not measure or order but rather . . . a flood of observed, unmediated details drawn from nature."[41]

Natural History; or, the Principle That Is Hid

"I never 'plan' a stanza," Moore is reported to say in a well-known 1961 *Paris Review* interview with Donald Hall. "Words cluster like chromosomes, determining the procedure."[42] In Moore's framing, art is supplanted by nature, the kind of "unconscious/ Fastidiousness" or "ambition without/ Understanding" that we might, as in Moore's poem "Critics and Connoisseurs," find in a swan or an ant. It is as if Moore the writer does not produce the words but rather looks down on them through the magnifying lens of a microscope as they gather by their own obscure mechanics.[43] The feature of Moore's poetic style most frequently associated with her "precision" is what has glibly come to be known as her "syllabics," the production of arbitrary stanzas measured in syllables, alluding to, without obeying, classical poetic meter. The importance of this form for Moore has been rather overemphasized in popular summaries of her work, the Hall interview included; in the "Marianne Moore" *Wikipedia* entry as of July 2016, for example, the entirety of the section labeled "Poetic Style" was given to generalities about Moore's alleged devotion to syllabic meter.[44] This is, moreover, a longstanding tendency; "those who have read some of the comments on Marianne Moore's poetry will recall a constant mention of her syllabic prosody," Robert Beloof noted in 1958.[45] This is curious, since many of Moore's most important poems, such as "An Octopus," are written in free verse, and many others (such as "When I Buy Pictures") were at first written in syllabic stanzas but were soon revised into free verse; indeed, it seems likely that Moore's chromosome simile functions to deflect the popular reduction of her poetics to "her meticulous counting."[46] Why are "syllabics" so popularly (and counterfactually) considered the first grace of Moore's style? And why might clustering chromosomes serve as the right explanation for them?

The way that "syllabics" and the fussy, obsessive counting that they seem to suggest have often been taken as exemplary of Moore's precision reveals more about precision generally than it does about Moore, for it is common to confuse precision with quantification. Introducing *The Values of Precision*, for example, Wise symptomatically slips into a discussion of quantification as if its relevance to precision were obvious.[47] Precision is not necessarily quantitative, but its association with quantification is powerful in part because of quantification's role in (as Theodore Porter has put it) "how science became technical"—where being "technical" enables the compact by which scientific research is accorded authority without public scrutiny, its inner machinations rendered both ratifying and dismissible: *don't worry about the technical details*.[48] Porter thus describes quantification as a means by which the sciences secured an advisory status vis-à-vis the state, adopting the role of "speaking precision to power."[49]

Precision's warrant for speaking to power comes at a cost: insofar as it a form of being technical, it asserts expertise by disavowing wider theoretical import or power relations of its own. Thus, as Jan Golinski points out, there have historically existed tensions, rather than the consonance we might assume, between claims to precision—sometimes derided as mere "nicety"—and claims to rigorous reasoning.[50] Randall Jarrell's discussion of Moore's precision likewise explicitly takes up the terms, and the trade-offs, of the technical:

> How much she cares for useless pains, difficulties undertaken for their own sake! Difficulty is the chief technical principle of her poetry, almost. (For sureness of execution, for originality of technical accomplishment, her poetry is unsurpassed in our time; Auden says almost that, and the author of "Under Sirius" ought to know. Some of her rhymes and rhythms and phrases look quite undiscoverable.) Such unnecessary pains, such fantastic difficulties![51]

Jarrell not only uses the language of technique but also registers deep reservations about Moore's vaunted *technical* excellence: it is, perhaps, *merely* technical, obeying arbitrary and superfluous ("needless," "unnecessary") laws, involving much "difficulty" and (twice) "pains." ("Technically it is a triumphant book," Bryher writes of Moore's *Poems*—a book that Bryher was herself instrumental in bringing out—as if judging a figure-skating competition and diplomatically withholding the artistic score.)[52] Jarrell's assessment of the "technical" quality of Moore's precision remarkably anticipates Porter's description of the same value in the history of the technocracy-leaning social and population sciences: "If we define the technical not just as what is difficult, but what is inaccessible and, by general consent, dispensable for those with no practical need of it," Porter writes, "then technicality may be less closely associated with an ideal of rigorous demonstration than with craft techniques and recipes. One great ambition of science since the eighteenth century has been to open up the private world of skill and guild secrecy by articulating, rationalizing, and systematizing technological processes."[53] In the domain of the sciences as well as of the arts, then, precision's (over)attention to the detail threatens to topple intellectualized masculine art into feminized craft, with its "recipes" and its "private world" of "secrecy."

Porter's description of the technical as what is, "by general consent, dispensable" adds another dimension to Schor's description of "the *detail as negativity* . . . bounded on the one side by the *ornamental*, with its traditional connotations of effeminacy and decadence, and on the other, by the *everyday*, whose 'prosiness' is rooted in the domestic sphere of social life presided over by women."[54] For while Porter is describing a zone of practice dominated by men (albeit men rhetorically demarcated on a class basis, so that early statisticians, for example, resisted "being reduced to 'hewers of wood and drawers of water' "), inferior ("dispensable") status, in this description, is clearly distributed on gendered terms.[55] This indicates how female intellectual work—Moore's precision in particular—might be legible primarily through an imputed obsession with counting, arbitrarily yet rigidly, syllable by syllable, a "technical" work of poetics that comports all too well with William Carlos Williams's description of the poet as lab tech: "With Miss Moore a word is a word most when it is separated out by science, treated with acid to remove the smudges, washed, dried and placed right side up on a clean surface."[56] Is she writing poetry, or is she *tidying up*? Precision—as "syllabics," as technics—thus emerges as a pathologically feminine pursuit, an attention to detail that models the technocratic dream of a wholly occluded, because merely technical, labor of the factual. Indeed, this is very nearly the account that Moore gives of herself, deflecting the image of herself as an obsessive counter by heightening it: "The words cluster like chromosomes," and the author disappears.

Moore's appeal to cell biology in the *Paris Review* interview, then, is not dissimilar to the appeal to a snail's verbally dissected parts in setting out an ars poetica. It is another instance of her characteristic gesture of dispelling style by attributing any formality to nature's perfect forms. It is not I who has style, Moore protests; it is nature. I am merely being precise. The very premise of precision as an epistemic virtue is that there is a fine-grainedness to nature that must be adequated. Precision itself thus functions to displace style—with its deep association with the author's body, "a radiograph of personality"—onto nature, away from the proclivities of the artist.[57] This phenomenon of displacement has perhaps been best explored in another author, who, like Moore, is known for projecting a "truly out-of-body voice": Jane Austen.[58] In D. A. Miller's powerful description, Austen Style pushes a feminine art—of the small, the detailed, the "lapidary"—to an extreme that takes on a quality of universal transcendence.[59] Miller's reading of Austen helps to explain why it might be desirable to displace style onto nature in the first place, for what Miller calls the "brute intimacy of style . . . with the body of its practitioner" draws attention to the body's forms, failures, and formalisms—to, in short, the overnice body of the spinster who sleeps alone—or worse, with her mother.[60] For Miller, the niceties of Austen Style mark "a failed, or refused, but in any case shameful relation to the conjugal imperative . . . like the Unheterosexual, the Spinster too resorts to Style, the utopia of those with almost no place to go."[61] Joseph Litvak, writing of stylistic "sophistication" and equally concerned with the ways in which style bespeaks the body, argues that "even the most celebratory invocations of sophistication as worldliness remain haunted by the guilty sense of sophistication as a deviation from, even a crime against, nature."[62] Style per se, insofar as it evidences *stylization*, threatens to disclose a body contra naturam in the sense that has so often attached to sexual deviance.[63] Consequently, Miller identifies "the first secret of Austen Style: its author hates style, or at any rate, must always say she does; she must always profess the values, and uphold the norms, of 'nature,' even as she practices the most extraordinarily formal art the novel had yet known."[64] An alignment with nature is often understood, as Alpers notes, as pathologically feminine, yet the pathologically feminine may be a needed alibi for a style that, in its disembodied mastery, betrays a body that is pathologically *unfeminine*—a body subject to (as Mina Loy would put it in her "Feminist Manifesto") "negation."[65]

We have already seen how Moore makes the same gesture over and over, from her grudging excusal of "complexity" (it is "not a crime") in "In the Days of Prismatic Color" to the refusal of adornment or the incidental in favor of "the principle that is hid" in "To a Snail." "My own fondness for the unaccented rhyme derives, I think, from an instinctive effort to ensure naturalness," Moore writes in "Feeling and Precision" (1944), deflecting another poetic practice onto nature, and even attributing that "effort" to "instinct." The persuasive power of precision, as I argued in the preceding section, lies in its claim to adequate a physical reality—a snail's body, a quotation about Duns Scotus. The force of the real lies behind precision's deflection of style.

To displace style onto nature raises two new problems, however. First, does nature really *have* the style, the "principle that is hid," that this gesture presupposes? Can nature plausibly take the credit, or the blame, for style's formalities? As Daston has framed the stakes of precision's historicity: "When did nature acquire sharp edges?"[66] And second, when is precision an epistemic virtue and when does it become a vice and a violence?[67] Or in other words, why does precision sometimes in fact fail to do the work of displacing style onto nature and redound back onto the pathological spinster observer-poet, becoming evidence of an "arid clarity" that is feared even in the midst of admiration?[68]

The answer is, simply, that precision's premise—that nature *does* have sharp edges, that it has a meaningful high resolution that should be adequated even to an infinitesimal degree—is not always granted, and it is, in particular, not always granted when women make the claim. James Elkins's rebuke to "overly precise" art historians (including himself—he unforgivingly cites his own PhD dissertation, which is "full of diagrams so intricate [that] I ran out of letters of the alphabet and started over with *aa*, *bb*, and so forth") offers a case in point.[69] Elkins thematizes geometry as "more a matter of duty than a pleasure," a matter of "technical details" literally presented as skippable: "If you are uninterested in technical details, and incurious about your uninterest, please leap ahead to section 3."[70] But despite his claim that "the annoying so-called trivia of lines and angles have been at stake all along," an intimation that perhaps it is those who are uninterested and incurious who are morally deficient, Elkins finishes by warning against the Pynchonesque mania for interpretation that such technical practices as perspectival diagrams bespeak.[71] The technical is at stake because it should not be, because a preoccupation with perspectival lines and vanishing points and "overly precise diagrams" dissolves into "the domain of forensic science," and "when all this starts to accumulate . . . it seems slightly fanatical," not to mention "annoying."[72] "Duchamp was clearly fascinated with popular science, in a way that Manet wasn't with perspective," Elkins argues, "but like Manet he knew when to stop—and, more important, when to stop caring. *The Large Glass* provokes thoughts of mechanisms, just as the *Bar* [*at the Folies-Bergère*] prompts us to think about optics, but we have to resist because, if we don't, we risk missing the real pleasure of the works, which is their precisely timed and beautifully balanced inattention to all things rigorous."[73] Taken as primary, and absolutely without question, in Elkins's analysis, is not nature but art. There is no question of Manet's shifting, subjectivity-unsettling perspective being culpably *off*. It is art. It is the critics, misrecognizing painting as a matter of science, who are pathological, "fanatical" "perspectival sleuths" whose "optical fervor is a matter of infection more than of truth," and if *A Bar at the Folies-Bergère* incites that fervor, it is the critics' weakness or indiscipline that allows them to succumb.[74]

This is not how the discourse of precision has operated with respect to Moore. Critics who misrecognize Manet's and Duchamp's precision, in Elkins's account, do not pathologize the artists as obsessive counters; the critics merely take it seriously, and in all sincerity become obsessive counters themselves—though the *critics'* dive into the technical is certainly pathologized by Elkins himself, in a way that echoes many recent calls for a "postcritical" reading.[75] If, for Elkins, artists like Manet and Duchamp intentionally allude to the technical to provoke our inner sleuths, they nonetheless know "when to stop" and "when to stop caring." Here is the contrast: Moore, readers seem to both hope and fear, doesn't, and it is she, the artist-deferring-to-nature, who is admirably or culpably, committedly, "technical"—"precise." D. A. Miller, reading the gendering of substanceless style in *Sense and Sensibility*, puts it this way: "Silly things cease to be silly simply by being done with all-sufficient, male authority."[76]

Perhaps it looks like a cop-out, in the end, to attribute interpretations of precision to a mere unsophisticated sexual hierarchy, to make of sex (as D. A. Miller does here) "the principle that is hid." And yet the systematic quality of misogyny—the ultimate denigration of the feminine, no matter how slippery "the feminine" as a category may be—deeply structures the ambivalences around precision that Moore's reception and Elkins's essay exemplify. Precision's technical nature bespeaks a modernity made feminine, predicated on the detail and on that which is inconsequential unless done with suitable "all-sufficient, male authority." Precision's premise, that nature has sharp edges that must be adequated, asserts a law and a lawfulness in nature that must in the end rest on itself. It is not, after all, necessarily the case that nature's details are infinitely, or infinitesimally, meaningful; to be precise is to assert a premise that is always perpetually in question. Thus Moore's jagged, "precise" poetic forms may be read as a perhaps too slavish representation of nature, detailed to be sure, but that may, as the artist Sir Joshua Reynolds argued, "by regarding minute particularities, . . . deviate from the universal rule, and *pollute [her] canvass with deformity*."[77] In an earlier version of this chapter, I called this potential for infinitesimal diversity an "empirical sublime."[78] But while I think something like this is invoked by precision, it does not fully explain the unease that precision occasions unless we understand this "sublimation," as Schor would put it, in relation to its ability to reorder hierarchy not only on gendered terms but also in terms of the hierarchies by which biological sex and sexuality are understood.[79] That is to say that, as Foucault so famously argued, sex is "*the* secret"; it *is* "the principle that is hid," and yet, too, it is what Benjamin Kahan calls an "empty secret," explaining next to nothing, or explaining it only tautologically.[80] That is to say, sex is often *the reason* for a power relation or hierarchy, but it is a reason that explains nothing, and to demand that it explain something would be, ultimately, to demand that misogyny make sense. In the end, it cannot.

Open Secrets of the Natural World

Does nature have a closet? Supposedly not, of course; why would it, when sexuality (as distinguished from sex) is so very *human*? Nature carries moral authority with it, as activist tactics have often shown by arguing that gay and lesbian people are "born this way" or by refusing the possibility of being queer by choice.[81] It seems more plausible, these tactics suggest, to root queer sexuality in nature than to unseat nature's moral authority over sexuality (since we cannot, ultimately, delimit sexuality from sex—"bodies and pleasures").[82] The challenge of the history of sexuality lies in the persistence of a desire for, and ultimate belief in, a prediscursive materiality that we could, if we were epistemically virtuous enough, simply *see*.[83] Consequently, despite the many arguments for understanding "nature" and "culture" as mutually constitutive concepts—especially Judith Butler's influential argument against the "misogynist dialectic" in which "materiality and meaning are mutually exclusive terms"—nature is often still tacitly framed as prediscursive and withholding, as *having secrets*—secrets, even, of sex, as in contemporary struggles to find a biological meaning of (usually binary) gender to apply to professional athletes, for example.[84] As Anne-Lise François points out, the early modern trope of the "book of nature" frames the natural world as simultaneously forthcoming and withholding, there in all its impassive "givenness."[85] Despite Foucault's profound influence on the history of science (the very concept of epistemic virtue is ultimately Foucault's), we have had difficulty coming to terms with the meaning of the open secret—that is, in Eve Sedgwick's useful framing, the epistemology of the closet—for the study of the natural world.

In other words, we have tended to read Foucault's history of sexuality in two different ways to support two different disciplinary lines of inquiry, resulting in the analysis of two different closet-like structures and two different (but formally resonant) systems of open secrets. The first, sexuality studies, has made particular strands of (usually white) gay male sexuality its canonical center, with the epistemology of a (canonically though not exclusively gay male) closet one of its chief sites of concern: the work of Sedgwick, Leo Bersani, Lauren Berlant, Michael Warner, Lee Edelman, and D. A. Miller come to mind here.[86] The second, feminist science studies, has given much more attention to gender than to sexuality, centering especially on the maternal body and the sciences of reproduction (e.g., anatomy, embryology, and genetics); here the work of Londa Schiebinger, Ludmilla Jordanova, Emily Martin, Evelyn Fox Keller, Sandra Harding, Donna Haraway, Anne Fausto-Sterling, and Katharine Park stands out.[87] Both strands crucially engage with the analytics of the public and the private and of knowing and unknowing, but by way of distinct exemplary objects. There are, to be sure, good reasons for the shapes of these trajectories. My intention is not to bemoan them but rather to point out their striking bifurcation.

In drawing out the implications of a "secret of sex" that is "inscribed not only in an economy of pleasure but in an ordered system of knowledge," then, sexuality studies has attended primarily to the dynamics of what were once called "crimes against nature" and the speaking of their unspeakability, while feminist science studies has attended primarily to the grounds on which femininity has historically been assimilated to *mere* nature. This latter is the urgent matter of decoding a sex/gender system whose laws seem ratified by nature, or the secret of sex*ism*, and it is a domain no less structured by open secrets than its ostensible opposite, the closet.[88] Thus, while Foucault's confessional *scientia sexualis* engages curiously little with it, gender is at the very center of the anthropologist Michael Taussig's account of the open secret, which I first took up in chapter 2. In the Tierra del Fuego societies that Taussig describes, the major open secret of the natural world—

that the "spirits" in the Big Hut are really the local men in costumes—is founded on gendered violence, an absolute categorization of gender in which the women's performance of "blind credulity" in the spirits is enforced by the threat of death. There is no use, as Taussig points out, in trying to determine whether the women "really know" the secret of the spirits; however unlikely the proposal that the women do not recognize their husbands in costume, the secret is unspeakable even among women—due in part to another knowledge: the threat of death—and so it functions to structure "woman" as the unknowing class no matter what is "known."[89]

Taussig's example shows how open secrets legislate who may and may not know, who may and may not speak, not so much along gender lines as in ways that reveal the boundaries of a sex/gender system. That open secrets structure gender as well as sexuality comes into further relief in other examples of the "secret of sex" as well. As Katharine Park has argued in *Secrets of Women*, for early (sixteenth-century) Italian anatomists, the gravid uterus was the paradigmatic human interior. The gravid uterus was a powerful figure for the secret of human life that was, in some instances, believed by the literate (male) physicians who wrote the early anatomies to be literally, and culpably, *kept secret* from men by women (mothers and midwives).[90] Human interiority, in Park's account of early anatomy, is a literal interior, a person's uterus containing a human embryo and, with it, the secret of life itself. The anatomies that Park describes are the very model of the kind of "depth" investigation that advocates of a postcritical reading attribute to "critique," and they echo a long-standing myth of the normatively female body as shell, closet, or dissembling surface. The fantasy of Denis Diderot's novel *Les bijoux indiscrets* (1748) is that vaginas (the *bijoux*, or "jewels," of the title) have secrets to tell and will only yield them when subjected to (male) magical powers.[91] Even when vaginal lips are forced to speak their secrets, moreover, they become not truthful but "indiscreet"; in the uncloseting of the feminine secret of sex, there is no outness that does not retain the trace of the interior, an uncanny hint that "that which should have remained secret and hidden . . . has come to light," as Freud puts it.[92] Indeed, Freud notes, "It often happens that neurotic men feel that there is something uncanny about the female genital organs. This *unheimlich* place, however, is the entrance to the former *Heim* [home] of all human beings, to the place where each one of us lived once upon a time and in the beginning. . . . In this case too, then, the *unheimlich* is what was once *heimisch*, familiar; the prefix '*un*' [un-] is the token of repression."[93] So powerful is the feminine open secret of sex—the open secret of generation—that its revelation only reinstates the mystery that has supposedly been unmasked.

Taussig explores another version of this belief in his discussion of the philosopher Arthur Schopenhauer's claim that men's beards exist to obscure the face, thereby making up for the disadvantage men have against women's "natural talent for dissimulation."[94] "Schopenhauer's beard," Taussig explains, "is not only nature's beneficent way of allowing men to compete with women's natural mastery of the arts of dissimulation, but is also the mask of castrated pussy that mimics deception itself."[95] Thus the secret of generation is *constitutively* secret, with "woman," with her propensity to dissemble, naming nature's native perversion, the natural thing that naturally behaves unnaturally. Peter Brooks examines the same trope in "narrative representations of unveiling the female body," particularly Émile Zola's *Nana*, arguing, "These narratives [of unveiling] must sooner or later reach the problem of unveiling the female sex, which they find to be itself a veil, perhaps from the anxiety that its final unveiling would reveal there is nothing to unveil. *Je sais bien, mais quand même*, runs the infantile response to the perception of anatomical difference."[96] Once again, the secret of sex is by no means demystified by its revelation. Rather, a system appealing to "nature" is reaffirmed. For example, among the human anatomies that Park examines, the most common reason for opening a woman's body was to remove and quickly baptize a fetus upon the mother's death during labor.[97]

One secret of sex—the unnatural, death-driven gay male or celibate closet—has typically been treated, then, as the other and opposite of another secret of sex, the "secret of life" allegedly hidden somewhere in a reproductive cis woman's uterus, which is, as it were, nature's perversity, nature's own law of abjection.[98] If one is supposedly a crime against nature, the other is supposedly legislated by it. In its tendency to undecidably teeter on the edge of epistemic virtue and vice, precision draws on both sides of this bifurcated history of the secret of sex, and it is for this reason that precision so consistently correlates with sexual unease. As we have already seen, a precision like Moore's—hyperformal, affectively abstemious, and by definition deflected onto nature (I am not being formal, merely precise; in fact, I am natural)—throws itself into question, at once offering nature as an alibi and entertaining the suspicion that what is at work here is something closer to what Elkins calls a "fanatical" and paranoid (or, to return to the recurrence of "syllabics," obsessive) sensibility or, alternatively and perhaps even more fully queerly, a maddening over-obedience to really existing detail that obliterates any sense of the whole.[99] Moore's precision thus entertains the possibility of being, on one hand, a scrupulously law-abiding appeal to nature's higher reality and, on the other hand, an unnatural, even criminal queer sophistication, in which scruples appear as a perverse end in themselves (that is, a fetish). "Such unnecessary pains, such fantastic difficulties!"—as if travailing endlessly to give birth to nothing.

As a poet, Moore, it is worth emphasizing, has always been read as closeted, no less pronouncedly so for the closet seeming to be empty. Leavell writes that "we have come to know Moore as a gendered poet but not yet as a sexual one. . . . We accept any sexual preference—except celibacy."[100] While Leavell's 2003 essay seems to have accelerated the trend toward discussing Moore as a "queer" poet, though, Moore has been discussed as a *closeted* poet since long before that—albeit often by way of armored animal proxies: her "Paper Nautilus," her "Pangolin," the spiny hedgehog or echidna of "His Shield."[101] It matters not that Moore's poems routinely empty those shelled spaces: "Pig-fur won't do; I'll wrap/myself in salamander-skin . . . a formula safer than//an armorer's: the power of relinquishing/what one would keep; that is freedom."[102] Randall Jarrell would unironically adapt the title of that poem for an essay, "Her Shield," essentially about Moore's self-protective style, which he describes as "the cool precise untouchedness, untouchableness, of fastidious rectitude."[103] The habit of describing Moore as shelled (and so closeted, covered by a moral alibi of "fastidious rectitude") correlates closely, moreover, with the habit of describing Moore as "precise"; as in Jarrell's description above, they are often imagined as concomitants.

We have already seen how precise style, in the sense of fastidiousness and superfluous formality, takes on "queer" resonances, an unnaturalness that Moore often repudiates and deflects back onto nature, without, however, fully succeeding in the way that Austen's deflections generally succeed.[104] If the closet rather famously has an epistemology, precision is one of its virtues. But this is far from straightforward: a queer virtue is sometimes no virtue at all. One reading of Moore's precision, a common one, is as a closeting, a means by which Moore poetically *constructs* the shells that she so often also (in pangolin-armor, in paper nautilus shells) describes. As Ellen Levy puts it, Moore's poetry of "armor, weapons, protection, places to hide" expresses "love . . . under the sign of negation."[105] Take, for example, Moore's one-sentence poem "An Egyptian Pulled Glass Bottle in the Shape of a Fish," which is dominated—in six out of a total of eight lines—by a long phrase modifying the "art" of the titular artifact, in Moore's characteristic elaborate hypotaxis. Within it, the bottle's art is compared first to a "wave," and then to another natural element,

> . . . that
> Spectacular and nimble animal the fish,
> Whose scales turn aside the sun's sword by their polish.[106]

It is as if the glass bottle receives not only its shape but its very glassiness from the fish's sheen. By describing descending sunlight as a "sword," Moore makes any surface it touches into armor. It is a battle waged in optics, but a battle nonetheless—an image of defense.

In Moore's proposed scenario, art (the bottle) imitates a nature conceived as agonistic, and yet the sword-on-scale defense that is being proposed as the bottle's original, despite its conceptual elevation, is also buried at the bottom of the poem, not just its linear *end* but also clinging to the fringes of its nearly empty grammatical core. Like the decorative glass bottle that it describes, the sentence is empty, all its lexical value pushed to the grammatical margins. The subject and verb—"Here we have"—that open "An Egyptian Pulled Glass Bottle in the Shape of a Fish" are but a placeholder subject (a "we" who will never reappear in the poem) and a dummy verb ("have"), more or less parallel to the French formula *il y a* ("there is," literally "it has there"). The poem is unpeopled except, perhaps, by a fictive aggressive sun and defensive fish; the "we" is not really a we, and the fake we does not really "have" anything. The long final sentence of "To a Snail" performs the same trick: while the sentence contains one lexical verb, "value," it is part of a subordinate clause; the main subject and verb of the exquisitely balanced nine-line sentence are "It is." Likewise at times in "The Plumet Basilisk": "In Costa Rica the true Chinese lizard **face/is found [*il y a*]**, of the amphibious falling dragon, the living fire-work."[107] The poems' richest, most striking images—images of battle and defense, descriptions of sun and flame, evocations of "a method of conclusions" and "a knowledge of principles"—take up residence in modifying phrases and clauses, pushed to a grammatical periphery and leaving a hollow grammatical core. Syntactically, in other words, Moore's sentences are often brightly jeweled, but empty, cases.

What imitation of nature could be more artificial? The syntactic depths of Moore's descriptions can be understood not only as a hyperspecificity but also as a way of pushing lexical richness to syntactic peripheries, creating syntactic open secrets in the process of specifying equally shelled and jeweled objects. This is a source of difficulty as well as of specificity; precision puts readers off, taking refuge in the "technical" and thereby transmuting style from the "radiograph of personality" that it might culpably be into a record of the intricacies (and insignificances) of nature. Insofar as precision repudiates its stylized formality by attributing it to nature, we can understand it as claiming a natural alibi for stylistic "unnecessary pains" that are crimes contra naturam.

Precision thus also illuminates the logic by which Moore's style (not just her biography) is so typically characterized as a kind of shelled self-protection bound up in Moore's very gender and sexuality. Precision collapses the distance in any allegorical parallel between shell and closet: hypotactic detail is the very material that wraps the empty secret; it *is* the full disclosure that, in being "technical," withholds. In an essay identifying Moore as one of "Three Hard Women," for example, Thom Gunn explicitly makes of Moore's style a self-protective celibacy:

> To resist marriage, to remain flexible, she had to be even harder than the statue of Daniel Webster [in her poem "Marriage"], hard as the armored animals that flocked into her poetry as she got older, protecting herself from the surrounding pressures: she would not marry; she would not give up her options. Neither would she, when she could help it, write as a woman any more than as a man, and so one of her forms of courage in *Observations* is to write virtually without gender. There is nothing wrong with that; after all, it is what many men do all the time. She is merely claiming as her own one of the privileges of the male.[108]

Gunn's assessment is riven with the usual contradictions. Moore is "hard" in order to be "flexible"; she writes "virtually without gender," which is "one of the privileges of the male," but of course this is marked as deviant ("hard") in a woman and is thus *entirely* gendered.[109] This is why Sandra Gilbert calls Moore a "female female impersonator": her persona of spinster celibacy repudiates gendered expectations in a distinctly gendered way, performing femininity in the breach.[110] Moore's precision can thus be seen as what makes her "hard," forming a protective shell of style—again, "the cool precise untouchedness, untouchableness, of fastidious rectitude."[111] But precision also supplies the form of deviance, *is* the deviance. The impenetrability, insignificance, or "unnecessary pains" (in Jarrell's words) of the closet are also the sign of what is queer about precision.[112] Precision cannot simply be an epistemic alibi (it is not I who is formal; it is nature; I am merely being precise), because it is also the symptom that requires closeting in the first place (being precise means being superfluously formal, means making a technical claim about nature that is "by general consent dispensable").[113]

Thus precision, so often achieved, in Moore's poems, through elaborate grammatical subordination at the expense of a grammatical core, takes on the qualities of "the spectacle of the closet"; the mark of insignificance or superfluity is also the sign of something queer. Such grammatical pyrotechnics mirror the role of the jeweled toothpick case that D. A. Miller finds in *Sense and Sensibility*, an empty box that is "blatantly outside donation, alliance, social function, and signification," unlike (say) a wedding ring and therefore, *because* of its meaningless elaboration, a "*bijou indiscret*" that reveals its owner as "impenetrable on the outside, but vacant within."[114] As Levy has argued, for Moore, the contradiction of having "no use value and a high exchange value"—being, in effect, an empty closet, a highly valued extravagance that always threatens to have no substance—is specially instantiated in jewels, for which she professed a fondness.[115] The epistemology of the closet, with what Sedgwick identifies as its "ineffaceable marking particularly of the categories secrecy/disclosure, knowledge/ignorance, private/public, masculine/feminine, majority/minority, innocence/initiation," etc., thus also marks the value through which Moore's poetics have most frequently been attributed a claim to knowledge—that is, precision.[116] At issue in the crisis of *nicety* around the representation of nature is just where the "secret of sex"—that is, as D. A. Miller argues, the secret of style: "the signs that, in anticipation of their social failure to signify, have already become signs of insignificance"—is located.[117] Hic et ubique: the snail's occipital horn is a nonreferential sign, an empty shell, an open secret.

There is no way out of precision's perversity, in short; its very performance of rigor, of obedience to law, of moral probity manifests as *bijoux indiscrets*, seeming to fetishize or even perversely create the laws that it obeys. It thereby implicates nature as an only intermittently convincing alibi, obedience to which points all the more persuasively to perversity. Moore's precision reveals her to be the Jamesian "bachelor" that she was styled in her intimate relationships, and when it does not, it discloses her, worse, as a woman.[118] Precision is an epistemic virtue of the closet insofar as it continually both speaks and reinstalls the open secret, seeming, in its disclosures of the natural world, to enact the power of demystification, "the power of the mystery," as Taussig puts it, "but without the mystery."[119] It is in this sense that precision also so often seems to give form to the sexual unease occasioned by technological modernity, a mastery of the natural world that threatens to unsex it, to submit female bodies to laws of precision—laws that pass themselves off as natural—and yet release them from any obligation to be erotic, as Kracauer complained, or even to be gendered at all.

Various Scalpels

What is precision's relationship to the law? I have circled around this question in the guise of considering precision's propensity to teeter on the edge of being an epistemic virtue or an epistemic vice—either adequately or excessively obedient to nature's details, depending on how sharp nature's edges—so often unseeable by the naked eye—are believed to be. Precision's technical nature, its status as not only unavailable but also *irrelevant* to the general public, is also its liability: not everyone can apply an eye to the microscope and agree that, yes, it really is just that detailed. Thus Moore's frequent alibi, her deferral of precision to nature itself when the words in her elaborate stanzas "gather like chromosomes," only intermittently succeeds in exculpating her style.

We may go further still, for we have seen that "precision snips," as Burke puts it. It is perfectly usual to see Moore's style described as "incisive," "acute," "keen," and otherwise bladed. Again, D. A. Miller's assessment of Austen is apposite: "The founding gesture of Austen Style," he writes, "is the cut (in testimony to which, every reader sooner or later resorts to calling it 'precise,' 'concise,' 'incisive')."[120] Moore, perhaps even more than Austen, is known for her poetic style's ability to cut, dissect, morcellize, or glint like a blade—to slice away, to relentlessly self-edit, and then to remorselessly affirm that "omissions are not accidents." As Emily Setina points out, in editing Moore's 1935 *Selected Poems*, T. S. Eliot complained that "Miss Moore exercised her own rights of proscription first, so drastically, that I have been concerned to preserve rather than abate."[121] Anthony Hecht likewise observes what Setina calls a "neat cruelty" in Moore's editing, which an important strand of Moore criticism has persuasively placed at the center of her poetics: "She has cut and trimmed in radical and merciless ways."[122] "*Détailler*: to cut in pieces," Schor notes.[123] When precision is an epistemic vice, then, it is not one of the vices of inattention, weakness, or passivity but rather a violent one—a perverse prosecution of the law to the letter, so intensively as, perhaps, to violate the spirit. If, as a virtue, precision obeys the law (of nature), as a vice it perverts the law by subordinating substance (that is, the spirit of the law) to *mere form*, performing an *arbitrary* fidelity of "unnecessary pains" (Jarrell again) and making the law itself criminally perverse.

This is why Elkins characterizes precision as "fanatical," making one into an "indefatigable investigato[r]," a "sleuth," or a cop—a Scarpio or a Javert who is interminably on the lookout for the Morellian detail or clue that incriminates.[124] The great open secret that the realist novel, as D. A. Miller would have it, must always both renew and give away is that of the difference between liberal and carceral subjects, which is "not substantive, but only effective."[125] How much more so, then, for the detail-ridden poem that declares (and then, through rigorous cutting, disavows) its allegiance to "the base-/ball fan, the statistician— . . . business documents and// school-books," for the poet who lives in a "thin glass shell"?[126] The liberal techniques of the self that make the epistemic virtue of precision are not so far off from the criminal tendencies that might land us in prison; the closet compasses both. In this sense my account of precision is distinct from Miller's argument in *The Novel and the Police*: precision does not so much unify discipline from without and from within as unify the positions of criminal and cop. Foucault's version of this phenomenon lies in the (as it were) sterile, masturbatory, and "formidable 'pleasure of analysis'" that the *scientia sexualis* affords in lieu of actual sex—the empty perversity of style and the queer insubstantiality of having (as Miller puts it) "nothing to say."[127] Thus the silence of that epistemic pervert and criminal master of material clues, Shakespeare's Iago, named for the saint whose symbol is a shell: "Demand me nothing. What you know, you know. / From this time forth I never will speak word."[128]

Precision's potential for criminality is thus a constant danger, as we see in Moore's "Four Quartz Crystal Clocks" (1940), a poem explicitly about precision. The poem's clocks, early instances of piezoelectric quartz movement, were advertised by Bell Labs (in a pamphlet that Moore cites) as "The World's Most Accurate Clocks." These real clocks were kept at a constant temperature at the labs, and, as Moore recounts, ordinary citizens could telephone to hear an automated voice read out the time, as determined by the clocks. Although the poem praises the new technology's precision, an undercurrent of anxiety about its superfluity—do we *need* to "punctualize the 'radio, cinéma,' and 'presse'" quite so precisely?—runs through the poem, culminating in the defensive declaration that "punctuality / is not a crime."[129] Who ever said that it was? It is the poem itself that raises the threat of criminality, in the course of lauding precision's power to distinguish small differences:

> The lemur-student can see
>   that an aye-aye is not
> an angwan-tíbo, potto or loris. The sea-
>   side burden should not embarrass
> the bell-boy with the buoy-ball
>   endeavoring to pass
> hotel patronesses[130]

Careful distinction folds into queerly gratuitous punning and alliteration here, as we are asked to "see" what is different about an "aye-aye" (eye) and, in an enjambed line, further clusters the homophonous "sea" with the lemurs, rather than with its semantic and syntactic relations, the bell-boy and the buoy-ball. The unusual level of sound-play in this poem—a poem that also punningly notes how "these worksless clocks work well" and names Jupiter the "jour pater, the day god" with a nearly Oulipian relish—rejoices formally in the sloppy slipperiness of sonic similarity even while thematically insisting on the value of crisp distinctions enabled by crystals kept cool.[131] Like celibacy, which undecidably both abides by the law (no sex here!) and perverts it (no sex here!), precision verges on criminality just when it is most obedient to nature.[132]

My point, then, is not that there is something queer about puns in general but rather that the elaborate superfluity of sonic wordplay in this poem—again, unusual for Moore—performs the stylistic function of what D. A. Miller identifies as a *bijou indiscret*; it is a semantically "empty" pleasure that reveals fine distinctions to be pleasurable above all in their violation. Can the clocks' precision, then, really be much use? "Punctualiz[ing]" the media (radio, cinema, press) that aspire to be "instruments of truth" and bringing disparate temporalities into alignment, these clocks can promise an assurance of noncriminality only by proposing criminality's possibility. Likewise, in the ostensible endorsement of epistemic innocence "In the Days of Prismatic Color," which I began discussing in the first section of this chapter, Moore offers a defense of complexity in the form of tautology—a form that is by definition both simple and needlessly complex (the alibi for, and charge against, precision): "complexity is not a crime, but carry/it to the point of murki-/ness and nothing is plain."[133] "In the Days of Prismatic Color," a Genesis story of the human fall from aesthetic simplicity ("prismatic color") into knowledge, stages, even more explicitly than the measurement of time in "Four Quartz Crystal Clocks," the dilemmas of postlapsarian epistemic virtue: when it comes to nature's unfathomable laws, crime's avoidance—or its fanatical prosecution—is also its commission.

When precision snips, then, it brings law into question, without, however, definitively landing on one side of the law or the other. Like an extrajudicial drone strike, precision violates the law that it so ardently obeys. Precision, in other words, becomes its own law, an epistemic virtue in service only to itself; to use a loaded term, it *perverts* the law. Under such circumstances, its machine aesthetics reign: to borrow a contemporary example from the film scholar Shohini Chaudhuri, the "precision" drone (no matter how many civilians it kills) is justified by its performance of technical modernity—its sheer efficiency at targeting and killing—whereas beheadings by sword, spectacularized by terrorist videos, are racialized and temporalized as "barbaric," an atavistic violation of modernity and modernity's régime of discipline—of epistemic virtues.[134] Paul Virilio has pointed out war's "origins in sympathetic magic." But if all war operates through what Virilio calls "pre-scientific . . . magical spectacle," those epistemic virtues that secure war's claims to technological modernity—precision above all—resignify its fundamental violence as technique.[135]

I would argue, then, that the sexual unease embedded in technological modernity, which precision names, also articulates the ways that precision conjoins the law with its violation. This is evident in precision's kitsch forms no less than in its avant-gardist ones. The machine aesthetics of early twentieth-century precision dancing, as in Kracauer's Tiller Girls or in the Ziegfeld Follies, not only offers a spectacle of sexual deviancy—a multiplication of exposed female bodies rendered curiously sexless—but also frequently produces these spectacles in support of fantasies of legal violence. Gilbert Seldes, Moore's colleague at the *Dial*, would write in his 1924 book *The Seven Lively Arts* that the Ziegfeld Follies, however orchestrally accompanied, really ran on "the steady, incorruptible purr of the dynamo"; for Seldes, the revue "shows a mania for perfection; it aspires to be precise and definite, it corresponds to those *de luxe* railway trains which are always exactly on time, to the millions of spare parts that always fit, to the ease of commerce when there is a fixed price. . . . [T]he revue is the most notable place in which this great American dislike of bungling, the real pleasure in a thing perfectly done, apply even vaguely to the arts." A machine dream, the Follies depart from the ideals of most art by making an aesthetics of a precision epitomized by capitalist modernity. Thus, Seldes writes, "the good revue pleases the eye, the ear, and the pulse; the very good revue does this *so well that it pleases the mind*."[136] "Apollonic, not Dionysian," the Follies' chief virtues are epistemic. These "*pleasure machines made of women*," as Joel Dinerstein calls the chorus lines, were themselves the products of Fordist discipline, as Florenz Ziegfeld "drew upon the raw, unrefined American women from the farm and the frontier, subjected them to a military regimen" and "transformed the ore into manufactured beauty."[137]

The question of the chorines' "sexlessness," declared by Kracauer and Edmund Wilson and contested by Seldes, as well as in the Busby Berkeley-choreographed *Dames*, about which Dinerstein seems ambivalent, is thus not a merely subjective matter of how titillated, or not, various men have been made by the shows (widely as they have discoursed on the subject).[138] Rather, "these products of American distraction factories," as Kracauer calls them, advance the erotism of withholding that underwrite celibacy's sexual ambiguity, a perversion that lies in its sheer normativity or in the way that, as one critic wrote, "the Rockettes seem . . . to exemplify the clean-limbed all-American girl at her brashest: each one, no doubt, able to step up front and recite her essay on Why America is Best."[139] The oddly frequently discussed question of whether early twentieth-century precision dancers were sexy is in fact nearly the same question as the one that has so long circulated around Moore's style: how her "precision" makes and unmakes her unsettlingly—unnaturally? naturally?—celibate female persona.

In addition to formally performing a Fordist version of precision, the Ziegfeld Follies also represented technological wonders like the telephone and the Panama Canal, as Dinerstein points out. The use of white female bodies to represent or embody technological modernity is nothing unusual in this period, as several scholars have shown.[140] But the representation of legal (military) violence in such spectacles is striking; for one 1909 Follies skit celebrating the US Navy, for example, chorines dressed as battleships; in another, in 1907, Dinerstein notes, "the girls dressed as dirigibles and each wore a 'sweeping searchlight moving over them against . . . a background of a burning city.'"[141] (As Paul Saint-Amour, writing of the British context, reminds us, bombers danced in formation too, in the spectacle of air shows.)[142] Withholdingly celibate, machinic in the precision of their movements, and all the same sexualized white female bodies thus perform precision's control and its excess, its normativity and its perversion.

While precision dancing has had a rich life on the stage—and, indeed, in the water, in the form of synchronized swimming—it is perhaps through the medium of cinema that precision's violent dimensions are made most fully evident. Aerial views make visible the dancers' technical proficiency, revealing a symmetry of motion that no individual chorine can see from her position on the ground. Precision is, indeed, located as much in the camera as in the dancers, as Busby Berkeley declared in a *Cahiers du Cinéma* interview: "A great part of my work has not been the work of a choreographer strictly speaking, because, for me, if I dare to say it, *it is the camera that must dance*."[143] For all the work of the chorines in motion, then, it is in a sense the camera that is the precision dancer; in the case of film, precision is a machinic embodiment that is shared across flesh and cinematic apparatuses, camera-eye and camera-object. In the Busby Berkeley film, precision is a coproduced happy adequation of precise viewer (the camera) to precise object (the mass of dancers), a representation as precise as the nature it represents, and a nature as precise as its representation. Like the overhead view of a microscope that discloses the ballet of dividing chromosomes at a level of detail that is really there but not visible to the ordinary eye, Berkeley's camera makes visible, as Jean-Louis Comolli put it in the same issue of *Cahiers du Cinéma*, "flowers of girls, forests of women in march with a single movement, dividing suddenly into equal masses, obeying in a mechanical ensemble the same abrupt starts and stops, breaking one another by the most abrupt angles or the contrary flowing along smooth curves."[144]

The ranks of female bodies, from the overhead view of the camera, thus take on organic and natural forms—radial symmetry especially, as in "flowers" (as Comolli puts it) or a Harold Edgerton strobe photograph of a droplet of milk breaking (figure 9).[145] The precision in the iconic star-shaped patterns of the Berkeley dance sequence (figure 10) echoes, too, the precision of bombardment, which, as Virilio argues, makes the action of bombing synonymous with the action of cinematography. Just as the camera makes the flower of girls, so the bomber makes a flower of its target, as Virilio points out in an example contemporaneous with Berkeley's Warner Brothers period:

> "I still remember *the effect I produced* on a small group of Galla tribesmen massed around a man in black clothes," reported Mussolini's son during the [Italo-]Abyssinian war of 1935–36. "I dropped an aerial torpedo right in the centre, and *the group opened up just like a flowering rose*." . . . [O]ne form suddenly dissolves before the war pilot's eyes, and in an extraordinary fade-out/fade-in another form

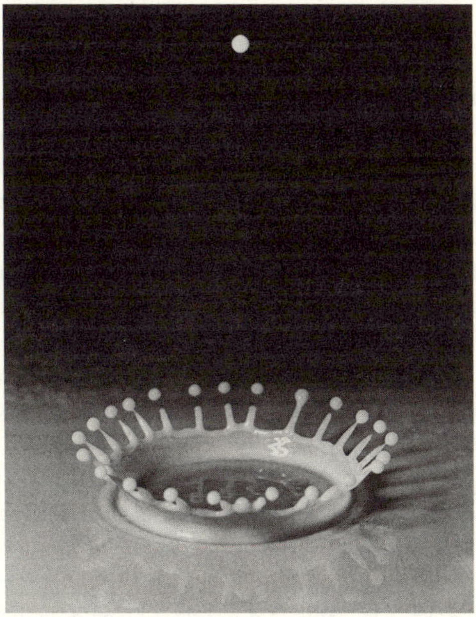

Figure 9. Harold Edgerton, *Milk Drop Coronet*, 1937. Davis Museum at Wellesley College, Wellesley, MA.

Figure 10. Rosette of precision dancers. Lloyd Bacon, director; Busby Berkeley, choreographer, *Footlight Parade*, Warner Bros., 1933.

> appears and reconstitutes itself. He has created it, just as a director working on a viewer can edit a scene in an aesthetically pleasing manner.[146]

Virilio's colonialist bomber is, here, a "director" producing a visual effect from above—but not just any visual effect. It may be more accurate to say that Mussolini's son, in this example, is a choreographer, making a flower of bodies by making his camera, the bomber, dance. A flowering rose—an object of beauty—appears as if the natural object of precision, the image of radial symmetry to be adequated by the overhead visual apparatus. But here precision's violence is at its clearest: the flowering rose is not adequated by precision but rather produced by it: "I dropped an aerial torpedo right in the centre." This is the endpoint of Elkins's caution about precision: its potential for fanatical epistemic overreach and its ability to hopelessly confound cause and effect, criminal and cop.

"An Octopus // of ice. Deceptively reserved and flat": the 1924 poem often described as Moore's masterpiece opens with an evocative description of the glacier atop Mount Rainier as an octopodal specimen of radial symmetry—a view of the glacier only available from the air (figure 11).[147] Precision is an epistemic virtue that operates by its potential for violence. The literature on the history of precision focuses primarily on two areas: precision measurement—as in the "Four Quartz Crystal Clocks" at Bell Labs—and precision weaponry. The categories are, in fact, varieties of one another: after all, the distinction between an instrument and a weapon lies in the intentions surrounding it, and they may be indistinguishable. As Elaine Scarry explains, "The weapon and the tool seem at moments indistinguishable, for they may each reside in a single physical object . . . and may be quickly transformed back and forth, now into the one, now into the other. . . . What we call a 'weapon' when it acts on a sentient surface we call a 'tool' when it acts on a nonsentient surface."[148] As Caren Kaplan has observed, many technologies that offer "precision" knowledge, such as geographic information systems and the Global Positioning System, are military in origin, and as Kaplan argues, "geographically based location technologies that draw on discourses of precision make possible the subjects of both consumption and war."[149] While these discourses of precision are often associated with recent technologies of surveillance and information retrieval, precision's status as an epistemic virtue with military connotations can be traced much earlier; as Conrad Crane establishes, in representations of World War I bombardment, the technical quality of precision (depending primarily on math-

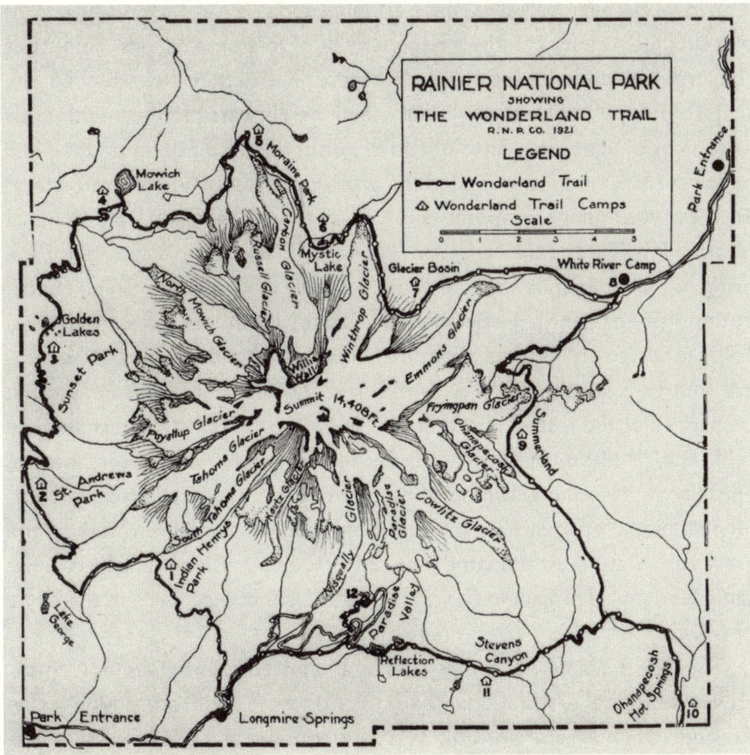

Figure 11. Map of the Wonderland Trail, Mount Rainier, circa 1921. National Park Service.

ematical calculation) came to be assimilated to American "frontier" values of heroic marksmanship—values that are clearly gendered and that recontextualize what it means to call a female poet "armored."[150] The work required to regender aerial bombardment as masculine—gender work that has been more recently renewed in relation to drone piloting—discloses how implicitly precision destabilizes gender norms.[151]

The work of the MIT photographer and engineer Harold Edgerton testifies to precision's link between aesthetics and violence, and offers some insight into its relationship to flash. A pioneer of precision measurement, Edgerton is perhaps best known for striking photographs of objects in motion, taken with extraordinarily precise timing. While he was particularly known for flash photography, his great innovations lay less in creating images of a sublime totality than in the refinement of instruments' precision; thus "Edgerton did not invent the stroboscope. . . . Rather, he extended the range of its application through the use of mercury-arc rectifiers-with-grids as sources of light in order to obtain impulses of shorter duration than had been possible. He thus facilitated the precision measurement of rotor-stator angles of machinery in operation."[152] In 1939 he began working on aerial photography for the US Army Air Force and, in 1947, on "a system for the firing of atomic bombs" for the Atomic Energy Commission.[153] The contribution that Edgerton's precision made was significant. As the *Science News-Letter* reported on his innovations in military aerial photography, "The camera shutter is synchronized with the flash assembly, so that each picture is snapped at the instant the xenon flash bulb reaches its greatest sun-like brilliance."[154] Although it is literally flash photography, we can see how the epistemic virtue of precision, not flash, predominates here: exact synchronicity, not the adequate partial representation of a sublime whole, is the great desideratum. At the same time, Edgerton's precision is engaged in the same biopolitical project as flash, creating tools that slice finely in the name of population health.

The values bound up in precision as an epistemic virtue are not simply arbitrary cultural associations, then; they do work. As Donald MacKenzie has argued in his history of Cold War intercontinental ballistic missiles, the development of precision targeting was intimately linked with a policy premise: that the missiles would in fact be fired. In contrast with a strategy of mutually assured destruction, wherein the purpose of stockpiling missiles was to deter their firing on either side, the development of increasingly precise missile targeting presupposed a *need* for such precision—that the missiles would be fired "strategically," destroying specific targets.[155] More recently, critics such as Rey Chow have elaborated how powerfully the concept of precision weaponry, via the "surgical strikes" made possible by increasingly "advanced" missiles and drones, has operated to ratify a vision of killing that appears bloodless and contained, wounding only to heal, and thus, in Scarry's terms, rhetorically transforming weapons into (scientific, "precision") tools and their targets from people into "nonsentient surfaces."[156] In such cases, then, precision, ever so precariously, determines the legality of killing: a "precise" ("surgical") strike makes the weapon into a tool, reframing killing as hygienic mending and bringing it under the sign of the biopolitical maximization of life. In this context, Williams's admiration for a relentlessly hygienic Moore begins to look more chilling: "With Miss Moore a word is a word most when it is separated out by science, treated with acid to remove the smudges, washed, dried and placed right side up on a clean surface."[157] She begins to look like the Moore who taught at Carlisle's United States Industrial Indian School for three years, privately critical of its abuses but silently complicit in its project of cultural genocide at work.[158]

Yet Moore's own poetry does not unambiguously embrace such a precision, primarily because precision does not for Moore entail unambiguous positioning—quite the reverse, in fact. Thus her poem "Those Various Scalpels" (1909) may be read as a different version of "To a Snail," another blazon that figures a body as all aesthetic shell. The ambiguously gendered "you" of "Those Various Scalpels" is, like the snail, a site of both aesthetic negotiation and an epistemology of the closet, for the poem renders hair, ears, eyes, and cheeks as formalized stone surfaces, "sculptured scimitars," "lances . . . submerged beneath emeralds from Persia," and, in an image recalling the radiating glacier of "An Octopus," "flowers of ice / And / Snow." The body "itself" is thus absorbed into the decorative—but also, clearly, substantive—shell materials at its periphery: clothing, jewelry, weaponry.[159] "Are they weapons or scalpels?" the poem finally asks of these "uniform / And at the same time diverse" accoutrements, centralizing precision's moral undecidability. "Those Various Scalpels" emerge as the objects of a fascinated gaze drawn to their "brilliance" but always epistemologically suspect in the sense that they may be "instruments . . . more highly specialized than the tissues of destiny itself."[160]

The 1923 notebook from which both "An Octopus" and "Marriage" emerged describes the top of Mount Rainier as "An octopus of ice / so cool in this the age of violence."[161] This draft notebook discloses the interarticulation of the different valences of precision that I have been considering so far. Moore's draft recognition of "this the age of violence" situates "An Octopus," with its rich description of the national project of enclosing wilderness spaces as national parks—like the new Paradise Park that supplies so much of the material for the poem—in relation to the recent war that had pioneered aerial bombardment. The "cool" quality attributed to the glacier in the notebook resonates with other descriptions of the glacier's "reserv[e]," its "sacrosanct remoteness— / like Henry James 'damned by the public for decorum,'" and its "relentless accuracy," features of what Levy calls Moore's sexual "ambivalence" and the personal qualities associated with Moore's precision.[162] In its coolness, then, the glacier, first viewed aerially as "an octopus/of ice," exhibits the precision that it also evinces as a (visual) target, the floriform flat image adequated and constituted by a bomb's-eye view. And if we may at first be tempted to see the glacier's coolness as a *contrast* with "this the age of violence," the poem soon sets us right: it is

> "a mountain with those graceful lines which prove it a volcano,"
> its top a complete cone like Fujiyama's
> till an explosion blew it off.[163]

The flowerlike pattern atop the mountain, "this fossil flower" that is the glacier, is created not by aerial bombardment or by bombardment's camera eye but from below; all the same, the withholding coolness of the glacier, "deceptively reserved and flat," is not violence's inverse but its concomitant; thus the poem closes with an avalanche of snow, a bombardment of coolness that falls violently "with a sound like the crack of a rifle,/in a curtain of powdered snow launched like a waterfall."[164]

"An Octopus" does not, of course, offer an exclusively aerial view, and despite its many horizontal planes (including the "smoothness" beloved of "the Greeks"), Moore's vision of Mount Rainier is as interested in verticality as in two-dimensional projections.[165] As Patricia Willis has argued, the poem's series of mountain fauna and flora are ranged by elevation, producing multiple vertical and horizontal views:

> Like the mountain itself, this poem is not truly symmetrical but marked by what might be called various elevations. It first presents the whole mountain as seen from a great distance; then it draws the reader close to the base and moves upward to the mountain goat near the peak. Next, it returns to the forest floor to examine its flora, only to ascend again to an orchid above the timberline. At the end, the poem steps back to the long view of the mountain and shows an avalanche that falls from the peak down to the claw of a glacier.[166]

The resemblance between Moore's technique, which Willis, as if insisting on Moore's precision, describes as an adequation of "the mountain itself," and that of Berkeley's precision-dancing camera ("*it is the camera that must dance*") is striking.[167] The resemblance is not, of course, due of any particular flow of influence but rather because a devotion to precision in the early twentieth century is likely to manifest in a specific range of formal qualities determined by the uses to which precision was put (precision weaponry, precision tools). Like Berkeley's camera, Moore's depiction of the mountain is not a single aerial image but rather an insistent toggling between an abstract, two-dimensional floriform surface and the three-dimensional bodies that compose it. Setina has identified this positional toggling in Moore's correspondence with Marsden Hartley as well, noting the many ways that, as Hartley's relentlessly "precise" editor, Moore was positioned at a "height."[168] As Martin Rubin points out, Berkeley's dance sequences are characterized by their tendency to "collaps[e] depth into surface" by turning white female bodies into images, and vice versa.[169] Precision guarantees the reality of the two-dimensional abstraction, a reduction of detail (in that one dimension, height, has been projected down onto a two-dimensional plane) that nonetheless offers *superior* detail, and that, it must constantly be proven and re-proven, can always be resolved back into its real, three-dimensional counterpart. Berkeley's swooping camera thus continually demonstrates that the abstract flowers and chains that cover the screen are made of precise, technically proficient women's bodies, tiered like a cake or visualized in serial smiling, near-identical close-ups (figures 12–14). Precision dancing is only dancing if it is really done by bodies and only precision if those bodies can be seen from afar in abstract patterns.[170]

The common origins of "An Octopus" and "Marriage" in a single notebook, where lines that would later find their ways into the separate poems commingled before diverging, first in an intense and long drafting of "Marriage" and later turning again toward "An Octopus," suggests reading across the two poems. If one poem conjoins a detailed accounting of a natural (but, as always for Moore, mediated) environment with aeriality, the queer epistemological chastity of Henry James and "the Greeks," and violent explosions, the other centralizes the problematics of marriage and criminality. It is from the latter that Levy takes the title of her study *Criminal Ingenuity*, a phrase that Levy adopts to describe Moore's ambivalence toward aesthetic and sexual institutions: marriage is the "institution . . . requiring all one's criminal ingenuity/to avoid!"[171] What the poem suggests, though, is that, much like "Henry James, 'damned by the public for decorum';/not decorum but restraint" (in "An Octopus"), the kind of avoidance of sexual commitment that "criminal ingenuity" achieves is a form of rectitude, just as Moore's protestation that "punctuality is not a crime" in "Four Quartz Crystal Clocks" suggests that it may just as easily be taken for one.

Figure 12. Dancers in vertical tiers. Lloyd Bacon, director; Busby Berkeley, choreographer, *Footlight Parade*, Warner Bros., 1933.

Figure 13. Aerial view of tiers of dancers, flattened into two dimensions. Lloyd Bacon, director; Busby Berkeley, choreographer, *Footlight Parade*, Warner Bros., 1933.

Figure 14. Views of the whole are followed by sequential close-ups of individual dancers. Lloyd Bacon, director; Busby Berkeley, choreographer, *Footlight Parade*, Warner Bros., 1933.

Distrust of Merits

"Wars," Susan Schweik has pointed out, "have a way of revealing with special clarity how men as well as women are both intensely and uneasily gendered."[172] Building on Foucault's insights into the structuring role that the discourse of sexuality has played in the making of knowledge practices, I have argued so far that precision is an epistemic virtue that easily slides into vice because the epistemological pleasures it affords have the effect of collapsing the positions of perverse criminal and law-enforcing cop. I have also argued that, while this particular scene of perversion has been most powerfully theorized in relation to a paradigmatically male epistemology of the closet, the language of precision is equally at home in the feminized, unruly detail-scape of the natural world, which in its own way veils "the" secret of sex. In her "criminal ingenuity," Moore never lost her celibacy and, if anything, only came to seem more celibate as she aged; she never lost her reputation for precision either.[173] But this is not to say that her poems, or their reception, did not change, and the increased "accessibility" and "popular" orientation of the "late" Moore are frequently remarked. As Elizabeth Gregory has argued, the period of Moore's postwar fame can be read as a period of disclosure (albeit crafted disclosure) aligned with the contemporary emergence of confessional poetics—disclosure, in Moore's case, not so much of sexuality, reproduction, or the body (as in the writing of Anne Sexton and Sylvia Plath) as of a radical celibacy of aging femininity, or what Gregory calls "the scandal of age."[174] While Gregory is particularly interested in Moore's postwar period, she rightly points out that this transition begins with her World War II poetry. "What is our innocence, / what is our guilt? All are / naked, none is safe," Moore writes in "What Are Years?" (1940).[175] Although the poem continues earlier engagements with questions of rectitude (and is contemporary with some poems that I've discussed above, like "Four Quartz Crystal Clocks"), this is a startling moment of shell-lessness that explicitly raises a term—"innocence"—that often circulates only covertly in Moore's poetry (especially in restaging the garden of Eden).[176] If the sunbeams of the early "Egyptian Pulled Glass Bottle in the Shape of a Fish" offer agonistic play, by the time of "'Keeping Their World Large'" (1944), they are asked to "Shine, o shine, / unfalsifying sun, on this sick scene." The best disinfectant, in the wartime poems that presage Moore's late style, seems to be applied to every closet.

Moore's later style of disclosure—often realized in an "accessibility" that also means the stripping of her sentences' customary grammatical insulation —coexists with an ongoing exploration of her earlier, more involuted style. Moore herself described "In Distrust of Merits" as "sincere" but not "a poem," a framing of the poem as pure expression echoed by critical assessments of the poem as "the direct communication of honest feeling."[177] But to simply contrast these early and later styles would wrongly suppose that all that is needed to reveal a secret is disclosure, as if disclosure and surfacing were not themselves part of the logic of the closet, incitements to speech that constitute what is confessed as interior in the first place. Rather, we might ask what is at stake in a precise and "armored" poet's claim to transparency in the context of war.

Randall Jarrell's infamous critique of "In Distrust of Merits" crucially turns on denying any straightforward shift from precision to limpidity in the poem, despite acknowledging that Moore appears "honest and lovable" therein.[178] Rather, he characterizes the poem as a turn to "abstractions that she is unfamiliar with" that neither achieves transparency on its own terms nor adequately repudiates Moore's earlier style, which (he suggests) the context of war reveals as a culpably mannered and fussily feminine precision: "For this poem Miss Moore has given up her usual method, because of the emotion and generality that have overwhelmed her. I wish that she had—as the world has—taken her little animals, her bric-a-brac with all their moral and aesthetic qualities, her individuals with their scrupulous virtues, and shown them smashed willy-nilly, tortured, prostituted, driven crazy—and not for a while but forever; that is, till the day they died."[179] Critics including Schweik and Rachel Galvin have elaborated the gendered contours of war poetry and the problematic role that the poet's (sexed and gendered) body plays in the representation of a scene of destroyed bodies.[180] And certainly, Jarrell's reading of "In Distrust of Merits" can fruitfully be read as resisting a female poet's fussy, trivial incursion into the male domain of war morality. In support of this reading, Schweik quotes Cynthia Enloe's observation that the gendering of war precedes its content, such that, as Schweik puts it, "Jarrell's actual distance from the 'front lines' matters very little, while Moore's matters very much."[181] "The military," Enloe explains, "has to constantly redefine 'the front' and 'combat' as wherever 'women' are not."[182]

Jarrell's extraordinarily gendered attack on Moore's precision, though—signaled in particular by the wish to see its chastities "prostituted"—suggests another dimension as well. Jarrell is himself the author of a celebrated war poem, "The Death of the Ball Turret Gunner," which appeared in the same 1945 issue of the *Partisan Review* as his critique of "In Distrust of Merits."[183] Jarrell's adult-yet-fetal posthumous narrator can reproach the "State" for having aborted his life: "When I died they washed me out of the turret with a hose."[184] The chaotic "black flak and the nightmare fighters" of the ball turret gunner's experience is miles away from the aestheticized precision that has been invested in aerial bombardment, as in Virilio's example: "I dropped an aerial torpedo right in the centre, and the group opened up just like a flowering rose."[185] Yet the image of Jarrell's pregnant ball turret seems to recognize that precision's *claim* to efficacy—aerial warfare's claim to be "surgical," to make perfect rosettes of bodies; the claim that legitimates putting the smallest, perhaps youngest, soldier in a fetal position in order to man an aerial machine gun—is a feminized one. If one version of the "secret of sex" is enclosed not by the closet but in the uterus (with its dissembling external beard, as Taussig notes), the pregnant ball turret places aborted life at its center. Jarrell thus angrily gives the lie to precision's claims by peopling the ball turret womb with an adult speaker who should not be able to speak because he is not only *dead* but also, not quite figuratively, a fetus—rendered by his youth as the kind of proto-life that is, in the words of anti-abortion rhetoric, an "innocent life," despite also being a designated combatant tasked with firing a machine gun. In such a scenario, feminine precision, as enacted in Moore's poetics, is not only not innocent but at fault as the deviantly unprotecting, unreproducing, responsibilized mother who, in "sleep," crèches an equally unawake fetus in the fatal surrogating belly of the state.[186] It is difficult to miss the echoes of Moore's own metal-shelled moral center, one decidedly less innocent than Jarrell's fetal soldier:

> Hate-hardened heart, O heart of iron,
> iron is iron till it is rust.
> There never was a war that was
> not inward; I must
> fight till I have conquered in myself what
> causes war, but I would not believe it.
> I inwardly did nothing.
> O Iscariot-like crime!
> Beauty is everlasting
> and dust is for a time.[187]

Another wartime shell, another "crime"—but there is no innocent within, only a culpability ("what/causes war") that more culpably still lies unprosecuted and unaccused: "I inwardly did nothing," undecidably suggesting both innocence ("I did . . . nothing") and failure to hold oneself accountable. Nor is there durability for the metallic shell either, which promises to become "rust," oxidizing from solid metal into "dust": this is a scenario of disclosure that can disclose only by destroying its own terms of inner and outer, confession and law, leaving no accusable aborting mother (it is the wrong empty organ), no salvable fetal center, only the conclusion—exceptionally dissatisfying in wartime—that *ars longa, vita brevis*.[188] If Moore's "little animals, her bric-a-brac with all their moral and aesthetic qualities, her individuals with their scrupulous virtues" deserve to be shown tortured and destroyed by the scenario of war, in Jarrell's logic, it is because they are, as "inward" elements that cannot be distinguished from their coy shells, finally war's agents. Moore is thus not unqualified to speak of war because, as a female noncombatant, she is innocent or ignorant of its depredations (Enloe again: "The military has to constantly redefine 'the front' and 'combat' as wherever 'women' are not"); rather, she is unqualified because she is guilty. In the scenario that Jarrell constructs, war has become deviantly feminine, rendered indistiguishable from peace by the bad undecidability embodied in niceties like Moore's. Thus, Jarrell writes, "It is the peace of which we were guilty."[189]

Jarrell—long one of Moore's most sympathetic readers—thus proposes a troubling reversal by which the male combatant in war is a fetal innocent, while celibate women poets' literary precision makes them culpable abortive mothers, whose surgical niceties (and failed mothering) deserve violent reprisal. (Earlier in the essay, Jarrell describes Moore's form as "fix[ing] her specimens on her slides," attributing to her yet another gesture of cold vertical visualization.)[190] Ideological as Jarrell's reversal is, however, it also perceptively registers the *reversibility* that precision carries with it and the deep sexual perturbation that it thereby occasions. Jarrell is not wrong to suggest that precision's very nicety stages an epistemological and moral undecidability that, far from being unacceptable in wartime, rather constitutes modern war logics: "A noiseless piano, an / innocent war."[191]

What is at stake in a claim to transparency in wartime poems like "In Distrust of Merits" and "'Keeping Their World Large,'" then, is something akin to the way that the notion of being "technical," in Porter's sense, constitutes precision's alibi, provides an out for precision's transgressions. For if, as Moore acknowledges in poems like "Those Various Scalpels" and "Four Quartz Crystal Clocks," precision can exceed nature and impose its own perverse law, the *technical* supplies a line of demarcation that brackets away, encloses, or enclosets any perversely excessive precision, without, however, seeming to keep a secret. You could look at the details—technically—but why would you? To be technical is to be available to all yet irrelevant to most. Precise style is not only the aesthetic version of the technical but the rendering of the aesthetic per se *as* technical, for good and ill. In this scenario, the poet becomes a kind of specialist, the technician whose work may be incomprehensible, but more to the point, in a certain basic sense, none of your business: as Moore so notoriously put it, "Omissions are not accidents."

5 Contact

In 1920, William Carlos Williams announced the first run of his little magazine *Contact*, coedited with Robert McAlmon, as "a place . . . [f]or native work," "insisting on that which we have not found insisted upon before, the essential contact between words and the locality that breeds them, in this case America."[1] In the *Dial* a year later, W. C. Blum would lovingly mock the "modest quality of realness" about Williams's poetry, "which he attributes to 'contact' with the good Jersey dirt."[2] Williams's engagement with contact as a poetic principle spanned multiple stages of his career, from the time of *Kora in Hell* (1920) into his later involvement with the Objectivists, including but not limited to two separate little magazines called *Contact* coedited by Williams, the first an irregular five-issue run from 1920 to 1923, and the second a run of three issues begun at the invitation of publishers promising to back the venture, in 1932.[3] Williams's "Americanness" in the face of the kind of modernist cosmopolitanism represented by Eliot and Pound has been much remarked, and recent turns toward regional, local, and "peripheral" modernisms have reframed critical perceptions of a poetics of "contact" located within a blossoming empire. After all, "contact" is a term whose neutrality occludes the possibility of unequal relations of power, not to mention the question of who is contacting whom.

I wish to make three initial points about "contact." First, contact is imagined as a relation of simplicity and immediacy, in which place engenders word. It is, in essence, an appeal to nature, if an oblique one, calling upon an appropriative fantasy of indigeneity.[4] Second, in contrast with "local color" writing, which was often feminized and read as provincial and nostalgic, the kind of localism associated with "contact" was a modern one, engendering the fresh and the new, often on violently masculinist terms. (Indeed, *Contact* repudiated any hint of melancholic effeminacy: "lady lyricists . . . boys with gusto . . . cynical adolescents and Oxfordian . . . satyrists [*sic*].")[5] And finally, this modernity was a function of contact's status as an epistemic virtue, promising privileged access to reality precisely through eschewing idealism and abstraction. Blum's parody, attributing a "modest quality of realness" to "'contact' with the good Jersey dirt," captures the ethical quality of humility ("modest," "good Jersey dirt") embedded in contact's claim to epistemological value ("realness"). Williams would put it another way: "no ideas but in things."

Contact is thus an epistemic virtue wherein touching or physical contiguity with the material world guarantees the knowledge status of the language that emerges from that touching. Its epistemological guarantees, though already clearly affirmed by Williams and McAlmon, become even more evident in the newly fieldwork-oriented discipline of anthropology, which had, under the influence of Bronislaw Malinowski in Britain and Franz Boas in the United States (among others), moved away from the comparatism of Émile Durkheim, James Frazer, and E. B. Tylor. In contrast with the earlier, comparatist division of labor between the missionaries, merchants, and locals supplying ethnographic material and the "armchair" anthropologist who wrote from England or France, the fieldwork ethnographer embodied both poles, the near and the far.[6] As Joshua Schuster has argued, "Anthropology [according to Franz Boas] means attention to 'contact,' exactly what Williams expounded in aesthetic terms."[7] Indeed, it is almost a cliché to read Williams through the anthropology of the same era, which Marc Manganaro and Susan Hegeman have so persuasively identified as modernism's interlocutor and twin.[8] In another moment of close twinning of literary and ethnographic pursuits, the *Writing Culture* moment of the 1980s, James Clifford famously opened *The Predicament of Culture* with a reading of a poem from *Spring and All* (the one eventually titled "To Elsie"), calling Williams a "doctor-poet-fieldworker" and using the poem to launch a discussion of the quandaries presented by the very idea that America has "pure products."[9] Whereas some argument is required to establish the relevance of other scientific traditions and their associated epistemic virtues for experimental writing, for anthropology, that argument has already been made in several ways.[10]

Yet reading poetic contact alongside contact as a contemporaneous ethnographic virtue does not simply map out a happy transdisciplinary consilience of the 1920s and 1930s. Nothing makes this more evident than the ways that Zora Neale Hurston—an ethnographer who studied under Franz Boas himself *and* a formally interesting and well known writer of the 1920s and 1930s who, moreover, blended ethnography with creative writing—does *not* fit in well with an analysis of "contact" as an epistemic virtue or within a narrative of "experimentalism" as it is currently constituted. Although Hurston has become increasingly canonical as a "modernist" in recent decades, she has not been a major figure of "experimentalist" recovery either by Language writers or by ethnographers in the 1970s and 1980s.[11] (Neither, for that matter, has Ruth Benedict, Boas's student and a prominent anthropologist, who wrote poetry under the pseudonym "Anne Singleton"; despite an embrace of scientific associations, experimental writing has not historically been understood to benefit from "really" doing science.) Hurston, like Williams, was an object of recovery in the later twentieth century—in fact, she is perhaps *the* canonical figure of recovery—but on very different terms than the kind of recovery we see at work with experimentalism's white canon. In one such act of experimentalist recovery, Charles Bernstein averred at the 1983 MLA convention that Williams's "intervention . . . against static forms of knowledge" "is heard but not listened to," emphasizing Williams as an epistemological innovator.[12] In contrast, Alice Walker wrote of her search for Hurston's grave, "As far as I'm concerned, she *is* my aunt—and that of all black people as well," asserting a literal kinship relation on the basis of racial identity, terms that Language writers considered more or less antagonistic to what they saw as a project of more fundamental critique at the level of language and thought.[13] Meanwhile, in another register of recovery—their 1986 account of "experimental" ethnography—the anthropologists George Marcus and Michael Fischer note that their project occasions numerous returns to the classic ethnography of the 1920s and 1930s, but the only "experimental" ethnographic forerunner they cite is the British-American anthropologist and information theorist Gregory Bateson's monograph *Naven* (1936).[14] Hurston does not appear in the book's index.

This is not to castigate either anthropologists or Language writers for missing Hurston out, though the role of white historical obliviousness in Hurston's reception overall certainly should not be discounted.[15] (Indeed, this is why she was a figure of African American womanist recovery in the first place.) Rather, my point is that while, biographically, Hurston would seem to be an ideal figure for both literary and ethnographic moments of "experimental" recovery, she was not—and not only because of her complex politics (including seeming justification of the US occupation of Haiti in *Tell My Horse*), with which her critics and admirers continue to grapple.[16]

Hurston's noninclusion in either anthropological or literary "experimentalist" canons in the later part of the twentieth century tells us something about the delimitations of experimentalism. A further exploration of contact will show why contact's ostensible simplicity might not suit an African American woman who often wrote about the folklore of the communities from which she hailed. Hurston, I suggest, did not centralize "contact" as a virtue; in fact, it would be fair to say that Hurston—a collector of "lies"—was not terribly interested in performing epistemic virtue at all in her writing. There are good reasons why she would not be interested in contact and Williams would be, which an examination of William's notion of contact in relation to ethnography helps to unfold.

Contact and First Contact

In the second issue of *Contact*, McAlmon deprecated how T. S. Eliot "continually relates literature to literature, and largely overlooks the relation of literature to reality," just as, in the opening issue, Williams announced the magazine's commitment to the aesthetic standards that emerge from "reality" and (jarringly) "indigenous . . . experience," in preference to the "mere mental exercise" of any other aesthetic standard.[17] In articulating the principles of contact, Williams and McAlmon thus echoed the early modern experimental rhetoric of the "book of nature" and the Royal Society's repudiation of discourse in favor of demonstration, as advertised in their motto, *Nullius in verba* (on no one's word).[18] Even to be "scientific," moreover, warranted further qualification through binding to the real, "exist[e]nce," and the "local": Williams averred that the works that would appear in *Contact* would "be scientific insofar as medium is concerned, but their substance [would be] no more scientific than is that of existance [*sic*]."[19] The writing of *Contact*, in its formal diversity, would thus be contained by obedience to the real; in contrast with precision, contact would never be technical or risk having sharper edges than nature itself.[20] The appeal to reality through contact was thus staged as a simplicity as well as an epistemic virtue.

Contact in anthropology made similar claims. The historian of anthropology George Stocking has identified "three looming archetypes" that dominate anthropology's own account of itself: the preprofessional or amateur ethnographer (missionaries, travel writers, and the like), the armchair comparatist, and the professional fieldworker, of which the last—the academically trained fieldworker—is both the most "modern" and the most "scientific." Though there are many candidates for the "first" academic fieldworker and the development of professional norms around fieldwork was gradual, Stocking suggests that "the emerging 'moment' of the archetypal fieldworker is the decade or so following World War I."[21] The epistemic virtue of contact made it possible for fieldwork to be experimental without doing experiments. "Those who went out from the university into the field in the 1920s," Stocking argues,

> were confident that they were doing ethnography in a different, more efficient, more reliable, more "scientific" way than the travellers, missionaries, and government officials whom they were pushing to the margins of the discipline. Expressed in the metaphor of the ethnographic field as a "laboratory," in which a distinctive method was employed to test previously assumed comparative (or merely culturally traditional) generalizations about human behavior, this disciplinary self-image was projected with considerable success outward to the surrounding social sciences, and even beyond to the general intellectual and literate public.[22]

The metaphor of the laboratory (and the "test") produced contact with a locality as an epistemological guarantee: to know a culture was to go there. Moreover, that guarantee was based on constraint: just as the *Dial* characterized Williams's "realness" by the "modest quality" produced by contact, ethnographic contact with singular localities ensured an epistemological sobriety that comparatists like Frazer, ranging over the globe's cultures from their armchairs, lacked.[23] Fieldwork became "the basic constituting experience both of anthropologists and of anthropological knowledge" to the exclusion, or at least the bracketing, of other sources of knowledge, like older, amateur ethnographic accounts whose undisciplined contact, colored by missionary and imperial aims, was suspect.[24]

Yet like early modern appeals to the book of nature, contact's simplicity is complex. It is a simplicity produced by self-conscious disciplining and the containment of spatial and temporal difference. Such difference runs across Williams's characterizations of an "American" aesthetic that he repeatedly calls "native" or "indigenous."[25] In a typescript from around the time that he was considering the second run of *Contact*, for example, Williams advanced a notion of a particularly modern "American language," arguing that "the impetus to the new poetry[—] . . . which[,] if it did not originate in America[,] found, at least, its natural habitat here[—]was linguistic."[26] Williams holds in uneasy suspension the contradiction of a "natural habitat" that is not a place of origin, registering but not acknowledging that, like the eucalyptus that thrives in California, the "American language" is an invasive species. Signifying while disavowing intercultural power relations, contact is both a principle of modernity and a way of accessing a distant past; it is both "local" and defined by travel to a distant location. Williams's *In the American Grain* (1925), a hyperbolically settler-oriented history, thus stages and restages the "discovery" of America, beginning with Viking settlements and moving through Columbus, Cortéz, Ponce de Léon, de Soto, and so on, stretching into the mid-nineteenth century and producing a long and palimpsestic sequence of scenes of contact.[27] Even American slavery is perversely and offensively staged as an episode of arrival and discovery: "These were just men of a certain mettle who came to America in ships, like the rest."[28]

The epistemological sobriety that contact offers is thus deceptively simple, using specific scenes and localities to tether down any potential for unrestricted comparison, universalism, or ideological projection—the epistemological excesses attributed to "armchair anthropology" and the Eliotic poetics that so self-consciously referenced it—but only by investing scenes of contact with temporal and spatial self-difference. The *scene* of contact implies, but also occludes, travel; the *moment* of contact implies and occludes previous moments of contact that must be discounted. As Mary Louise Pratt has argued, ethnographic fieldwork in the early twentieth century conventionally defined itself against the "unscientific" contact of explorers, travel writers, and missionaries; "This picture is false," Bronislaw Malinowski wrote in his 1922 *Argonauts of the Western Pacific*, "and like many other falsehoods, it has been killed by Science."[29] At the same time, however, the narration of ethnographic contact has often recapitulated the literary tropes of narratives of first contact; thus, Pratt argues, Raymond Firth's *We, the Tikopia* (1936) closely echoes what she calls "the classic Polynesian arrival scene . . . commonplace in the literature of the South Sea explorations of Cook, Bougainville and others in the 1760s and 70s."[30] As Pratt continues, "Firth reproduces in a remarkably straightforward way a utopian scene of first contact that acquired mythic status in the eighteenth century, and continues with us today in the popular mythology of the South Sea paradise. . . . Far from being taken for a suspicious alien, the European visitor is welcomed as a messiah by a trusting populace ready to do his or her bidding."[31] For Pratt, the persistence of literary tropes of first contact in classic ethnographies —or even their self-conscious inversion in later ethnographies like Marilyn

Shostak's *Nisa: The Life and Words of a !Kung Woman* (1981)—is a sign of the unscientific subjectivity that the professional fieldworker must live with (as part of the participant-observer method) but deflect in the writing of the monograph.[32] The legacies of colonialism, exoticist travel writing, and proselytization are to be disavowed as "killed by Science," yet insofar as those legacies are disavowed, the fieldworker is constrained to represent ethnographic contact as *first* contact—first, in that preceding episodes of contact do not "count." Pratt's account helps to illuminate the dimension of constraint and disavowal in ethnographic contact of the 1920s and 1930s. Breaking with a prescientific legacy, professional fieldwork was forced to "make it new"—that is, make contact anew, make ethnographic contact into first contact, as if in ignorance or repudiation of preceding scenes of cultural interface or migration.

This double move—the "making new" of ethnographic contact by a disavowal that cites the previous contact being disavowed—discloses the temporal complexity of ethnographic contact in the early twentieth century. This complexity does not disqualify or "debunk" contact as an epistemic virtue, for in-person participant observation, with its commitment to seeing for oneself, remains central to ethnographic method. Contact was *and has remained* a source of epistemic guarantee. Rather, contact's doubleness as always both original and repetition helps us to see why modern ethnography comports so well with what Rosalind Krauss has called the "modernist myth" of originality.[33] Moreover, its structure of disavowal and citation reveals the constraint that underlies contact, which might otherwise be construed as a purely positive principle of encounter. Williams stages this principle through his familiar slogan "no ideas but in things," whose negative structure is brought into relief by its presentation in the opening of *Paterson* I (1946): "—Say it, no ideas but in things—."[34] Set off, at first, by dashes, the line appears as a subversive suggestion, the words "say it" nearly a dare. The words recur even more emphatically in repetition: "Say it! No ideas but in things." While Bill Brown rightly cautions that "'no ideas but in things' doesn't mean no ideas," the repeated injunction to "say it" registers the self-discipline, even self-coercion, involved in such an insistence.[35] To repeat "no ideas but in things" is to renounce all those ideas that might not be tethered to things, to place materiality at the center of one's epistemology through an act of negation. Pace Brown, the possibility of "no ideas" is indeed temporarily entertained: ideas are first banished ("no ideas"), *then* allowed to reenter through an exception ("but in things"). Contact thus contains now and then, here and away, touching and that which is off limits or unavailable to touching, in an oscillatory structure whose very internal tension is made into the condition of knowledge production.

Nakedness and the Form of Contact

Contact's ability to render spatial and temporal difference as simplicity and immediacy has a name: primitivism. Primitivism in both early twentieth-century writing and ethnography has been well studied.[36] What their pairing brings into relief, however, is the ways in which primitivism functions as a form of *rigor* that lies at the center of an epistemic virtue that remains operative today, rather than its embarrassing exception. The "spare" quality of Williams's form and language; his often openly exoticizing images, especially of Black and Native American women; and his claims to linguistic indigeneity are all features of a valorization of contact as an epistemic virtue. "Where but in [A]merica," Williams writes, "would you expect the naked word itself to work such miracles[?]"[37] This is the nakedness of a word like "sky" stripped of "association" and returned to "the residual contact between life and the imagination which is essential to freedom" in *Spring and All*, as well as the nakedness of Adolf Loos's architectural cladding that Anne Cheng has read as a "second skin," the bareness that is a covering and the primitive form that is the form of modernity.[38]

"Nakedness" can, of course, take many different forms; its translatability into a variety of registers is what enables its ubiquity and makes it so difficult to pin down. Across early ethnography and Williams's writing, though, the minimal form of concatenation—the mere linking of one thing to the next and thus a nakedness at the level of relation—is contact's most powerful manifestation. In early twentieth-century anthropology, the (literary) form of contact is certainly the "one ethnographer / one tribe" monograph—or, as Pratt revises it, the pairing of the ethnographic monograph with the personal memoir of time spent in fieldwork, the gap between them marking the split ethnographic self produced by contact.[39] Yet these are preceded by a more minimal form, concatenation, which exists in ethnography and which Williams develops as a site of experimental poetic "discovery." "Discovery," here, should be understood not as pure epistemological realization but in the palimpsestic, deeply compromised sense implied by the historical senses of contact that I discussed in the previous section. Given that it is barely a form at all, I wish to explain what I mean by proposing concatenation as the "form" of contact. First, concatenation *enacts* contact through juxtaposition, effecting syntagmatic encounters between the arbitrary and unlooked-for; to form a line is by definition to create encounters between unlike things. Second, it has a privileged form in the concatenation of arbitrary events through the passage of calendar time, in the chronicle or logbook—the ethnographer's logbook, to be sure, but also—as in the long passages in the voice of Christopher Columbus's logbook in *In the American Grain*—that of the disavowed yet ever-present prescientific explorer.[40]

These elements are visible in the practices of early twentieth-century anthropology as well as in Williams's contactual poetics, but it would also be fair to say that concatenation can be detected in *almost anything*: the placing of one thing after another is an obligatory form present in any linear sequence, offering little in the way of structure and thereby accommodating of a great deal of contingency. There is a basic insufficiency in describing any sequence as "concatenated"; unlike the way that "sonnet" might serve as an account of the structure of fourteen lines or even the way that "Language poetry" is sometimes taken as a sufficient description of *any given instance of Language poetry*, we learn nothing from the description "concatenated" until we learn what has been linked to what. Concatenation thus recedes as a form, foregrounding instead the contingent elements that constitute it. Merely paratactic, concatenation makes a principle of proximity, a formal rather than a logical relation, and thus courts insignificance; as a structure it is everywhere and intrinsically means nothing. This recessiveness is important: it is a nonstyle, a form of formlessness, and thus telegraphs the commitment to "the naked word" that Williams claims for contact.[41] It is therefore also a form of abjuration and constraint, marking the way that contact operates as an epistemic virtue to manage the tense relation between contingency and meaning at the heart of the science of culture.

Williams's "By the road to the contagious hospital," the first poem in *Spring and All* (1923), offers a view of contact as a principle of poetic form:

> They enter the new world naked,
> cold, uncertain of all
> save that they enter. All about them
> the cold, familiar wind —
>
> Now the grass, tomorrow
> the stiff curl of wildcarrot leaf

One by one objects are defined —
It quickens : clarity, outline of leaf

But now the stark dignity of
entrance—Still, the profound change

has come upon the[m] : rooted they
grip down and begin to awaken[42]

Williams's description of spring's unfurling takes the form of a logbook, concatenating events by the sequence in which they transpire and deliberately staging their stepwise emergence. "Now," "tomorrow," "one by one," "but now," the disparate, contingent events of springtime are cataloged in order, culminating in the "profound change" that makes the newly revived plants "grip down and begin to awaken." These events are linked by juxtaposition in time, a contingent touching without a necessary internal logic or even sameness of kind. Grass is followed by wildcarrot leaf, but these are followed by the abstraction of "clarity" and "outline," and then the affective register of "dignity": heterogeneity is brought in line, but only just. In this, concatenation accommodates the realism of contingency, what Fredric Jameson, glossing Barthes's "reality effect," calls "the irreconcilable divorce between intelligibility and experience," giving form to contingency without canceling its essential resistance to meaning.[43]

Here, as in his "Note," Williams confounds contact and first contact, locality with foreign shore; the things of spring "enter the new world naked," citing, with "the new world," a European colonizer's perspective on the "good Jersey dirt" and, by making them "enter" that "new world," aligning the new growths with an exploring or colonizing force. Yet they enter the new world by being born into it, "naked," the wind's chilly touch familially "familiar": colonization is made continuous with indigeneity, first contact with contact. They therefore occupy what Hegeman has identified as "the peculiar historical position of the Native American in the Anglo-American settler-colonial imagination, as both the despised, displaced native other and the noble model of a landed national American identity."[44] Both "rooted" and "grip[ping] down," native to the soil and seizing it, the denizens of this soil make an ambiguous contact that structures the poem's unfolding.

Spring and All stages its essential newness repeatedly, announcing that "THE WORLD IS NEW."[45] But like the classic ethnographies that Pratt examines, "By the road to the contagious hospital" also declares its own disavowed precedents, not only Eliotic "roots that clutch" but an even earlier and less "scientific"—more fully mythic—precedent.[46] The poem's opening "under the surge of the blue/mottled clouds driven from the/northeast—a cold wind. Beyond, the/waste of broad, muddy fields" echoes the opening of the book of Genesis, "the earth being unformed and void, with darkness over the surface of the deep and a wind from God sweeping over the water," with corresponding blobby, indistinct earth, water, and wind.[47] In this originary logbook, the events of each day are recorded sequentially: "And there was evening and there was morning, a first day," and later "and there was evening and there was morning, a second day" (and so forth), with the biblical separations of light from darkness, water from sky, and so on, anticipating the "clarity, outline of leaf" with which "objects" in the poem come into distinctness.[48] The poem thus restages, and thus cancels and supersedes, an originary minimal sequence of separations and distinctions as a newness that is itself destined to be superseded—spring.

The first contact lurking within contact helps to explain why concatenation is contact's privileged form (insofar as it *is* a form). Contact is not only a relation of affinity between language and land, a principle of harmony or unity, as Williams sometimes suggests, but also a generator of temporal and spatial difference. The "local" is thus always also the locality to which some participant observer has traveled, making contact in a "now" that supersedes earlier, prescientific contact, and thus reenacts the first contact that it disavows.[49] To explain this further, I wish to turn to Michael Taussig's argument that "mimesis, as either an unadorned human faculty or one revived in modernity by mimetic machines . . . alerts one to the contactual element of the visual contract with reality."[50] Mimesis is an aesthetic principle—one that, in the specialized, primitivist sense in which Taussig uses it, draws its power to work in the world not solely from a representational realism but also from the "contact" that it effects between different bodies, in a "seemingly limitless" "chain" of "sympathetic associations."[51] This sympathetic chain, like the concatenations we have just examined, is drawn together not by resemblance or similarity but by contact, literal or metaphorical touching.[52] Drawing on the pre-Boasian, primitivist account of "sympathetic magic" in Frazer's *Golden Bough*, Taussig identifies mimesis—first, as attributed to "primitives" in Frazer and, later, in the mimetic machines that Walter Benjamin, in his media theory, identifies as harbingers of modernity—as rooting resemblance in a "contactual element." Countering the conventional belief that mimesis is the special province of the "native," Taussig sees mimesis as "curiously baseless, so dependent on alterity that it lies neither with the primitive nor with the civilized, but in the . . . space of First Contact. . . . [I]t was above all that auratic moment of 'first contact' with the primitive that gave Europeans their first image of the mimetic treasure which lay, if not within, then between the collective bodies in contact with one another."[53] The "sympathetic chain" of contact through which mimesis is effective always refers back not to an original but to "first contact," an encounter of alterity.

There seems to be a difference between the magical sympathetic chain that Taussig identifies (that is, borrows from Frazer and the earlier, disavowed, prescientific anthropology that he represents) and the concatenation that Williams effects, for Williams's "modern," epistemically virtuous sequences are characterized by a sense of arbitrariness and *resistance* to meaning that is nearly the opposite of the way that sympathetic magic works. Sympathetic magic is what contact seems to define itself *against*. As Michel Foucault describes sympathy in another context, "It alters [things], but in the direction of identity, so that if its power were not counterbalanced it would reduce the world to a point, to a homogeneous mass, to the featureless form of the Same."[54] Williams's objects, in contrast, retain their disunity and their distinction: "clarity, outline of leaf." Indeed, in *Spring and All* this resistance is marked and deliberate, as sections of the book bear section headings that not only lack ordinal sequence but also belong to different sequencing systems (roman and arabic numerals, occasional headings printed upside-down, etc.), as if to repudiate the order that is manifestly imposed by any linear arrangement. Not all concatenation is the same.

Yet to take Taussig's account seriously is to resist the distinction between a "primitive mind" that believes in sympathetic magic and the powers of mimesis, and a "civilized mind" that is modern, fallen from an originary state of unity between signs and things, and therefore disenchanted with resemblance, seeing reality instead in nonmeaning and contingency.[55] If we agree that mimesis is not uniquely "primitive" but rather a product of alterity in encounter, then we ought to recognize the double character of the sympathetic chain as both "primitive" and "modern," oscillating between the registers of visual resemblance (representation, realist to greater or lesser degrees) and physical contact, *and always liable to translate one into the other*. As Seb Franklin has suggested, the limen between form and formlessness is a historical phenomenon, marking the simultaneity of racialized alterity and capitalist primitive accumulation: the "raw" and "formless" is that which is, *in a particular historical moment*, rendered conceptually available to capture at the site of, yes, contact. "Comprehensibility," Franklin argues, "is . . . determined not by universal criteria but by historically specific coordinates that can in themselves reveal much about the conditions under which certain systems of thought, and representation become established and normalized."[56] And in this sense, the "modern" concatenation of arbitrary or seemingly unpatterned units *is* the same as the sympathetic chain that always risks reduction to "the featureless form of the Same," for a minimal form looks remarkably similar to an overdetermined one.[57] The modernity signaled by the deliberate arbitrariness of Williams's concatenations thus reenacts, replaces, and disavows the primitive unmodernity of the sympathetic chain.

The minimal "nakedness" of concatenation as a form also offers some insight into the primitivism that so widely characterizes Williams's writing, especially the exoticization of nonwhite women across his oeuvre. As Marjorie Perloff has blandly put it, "Expressions of sexual desire for a 'dark woman' are ubiquitous" in Williams.[58] From the "Arab / Indian / dark woman" "rich in savagery" to whom the "Black eyed susan" of *Spring and All* is compared, to the "Colored Girls of Passenack," to *Paterson*'s Beautiful Thing, "black plush, a dark flame" who is both a raped woman and the animating force of a fire that rips through Paterson, Williams's poetics of contact are persistently routed through the sexual exoticization of nonwhite feminine figures.[59] Like Loos with his minimal architectural cladding, Williams produces a form of modernity that relies absolutely on a nakedness not only performed but narrated and located in the bodies of women represented as "primitive" and (therefore) natural sites of violence and abjection:

> the guys from Paterson
> . . . socked you one
> across the nose
> Beautiful Thing
> for good luck and emphasis
> cracking it
> till I must believe that all
> desired women have had each
> in the end
> a busted nose.[60]

Contact's function as an epistemic virtue tends to occlude—or excuse—its potential to violently relegate a "contacted" party to abjection. As Franklin's analysis of the limen between form and formlessness suggests, primitivism's realization as form does not render it benign. Thus while a distinction between "modern" and "primitive" will continue to prove useful for discussing an early twentieth century pattern of thinking that depended on it, it is a distinction that we should hold very much in suspension. As W. J. T. Mitchell suggests, "When students scoff at the idea of a magical relation between a picture and what it represents, ask them to take a photograph of their mother and cut out the eyes."[61]

Recovery, Salvage, and the Untimeliness of Contact

In 1989, four Language poets—Michael Davidson, Lyn Hejinian, Ron Silliman, and Barrett Watten—traveled to Leningrad for an international conference on culture and poetics. The conference brought the writers, so influenced by both Russian and American avant-gardes of an earlier moment, into direct personal contact with the Russian avant-garde's Cold War–era successors. In *Leningrad*, the book that they wrote collaboratively about the experience, Ron Silliman explicitly frames the conference in world-historical and, specifically, Cold War terms: it occurs "during that brief window in world history between the Tiananmen Square massacre in Beijing and the fall of the Berlin Wall and the Eastern bloc," and although the conference is conceived as "international," Lyn Hejinian observes that "the French were right in saying that the conference was more a dialogue between Russians and Americans."[62] Ever aware of their own situatedness in history, the Language writers sought to effect a cultural encounter outside the terms of a state ideology that they saw as fully complicit with mass atrocity, most notably in Vietnam.

As Silliman's self-historicization—placing the Leningrad conference between the events at Tiananmen Square and the Berlin Wall—attests, Language writing's sense of its own historicity is explicitly a sense of what Benedict Anderson identified as the simultaneity of homogeneous, empty time—the time of nation and the time of empire.[63] Things are happening "at the same time," so that Language's sense of the simultaneity of homogeneous, empty time emerges in what Sianne Ngai has intriguingly called its "paranoid" sensitivity to "bad timing": "why is it that at the same time . . . ?"[64] Thus, for instance, the poet Tom Mandel observes of the programmer Bob Frankston that "while we were creating 'Language poetry' he was writing Visicalc," the popular spreadsheet software released in 1983.[65] This sense of simultaneity, that while this happens, that happens too, and that these events may be causally connected *but they also may not*, pervades Language writing.[66] Ted Pearson would retrospectively note that

> the period in question [the early days of Language poetry] began at the end of the postwar "economic miracle" and at the onset of a long and devastating recession, deepened by the astronomic debt and social misery that resulted from the pursuit of imperial ambition, if not yet, as is now clear, overtly global hegemony—a pursuit that barely paused to reload when Saigon "fell."...
>
> *Not coincidentally, it was also the moment when* the nation's "unlimited drift/to the right" emerged from conservative think tanks and fundamentalist pulpits.[67]

Not coincidentally, but not altogether causally either. Thus Language's self-historicization projects a deep formal inhabitation of the structures of national time and a regretful awareness that "bad timing" is, so to speak, the way time works now.[68] Language writers understood themselves to be in and of US empire even as they opposed it.

"It was also the moment" when many prominent US anthropologists—James Clifford, Mary Louise Pratt, George Marcus, Michael Fischer, Paul Rabinow, Dell Hymes, and others—first articulated the terms on which I have read Williams in this chapter, in the course of delineating an "experimental" practice that reconsidered early twentieth-century ethnography. The important anthology *Writing Culture: The Poetics and Politics of Ethnography* (1986—"also the moment of" *Star Trek IV: The Voyage Home*) challenged the very grounds of epistemological security in ethnography by retracing a disciplinary counterdiscourse that included Michel Leiris's *L'Afrique fantôme* (1934, reissued with a new preface in 1981), Claude Lévi-Strauss's *Tristes Tropiques* (1955), Laura Bohannon's fictionalized *Return to Laughter* (1954), and Bronislaw Malinowski's fieldwork diaries (published in 1967).[69] It was at the level of "writing culture"—of poetics, discourse, and textual production—that the authorizing epistemological force of contact, so central to early twentieth-century anthropology's claim to epistemic virtue, was revealed as questionable and in need of rehabilitation through critique. Anthropological critiques included Johannes Fabian's analysis of the "denial of coevalness" built into ethnographic conventions and Clifford's own challenge to a poetics of "salvage" that made the ethnographer into the heroic and authoritative preserver of an otherwise disappearing culture.[70] These were predominantly, in other words, reassessments of the role of temporality in theorizing contact and attempts to "historiciz[e] the ethnographic present."[71] With the increasing prominence of reflexive ethnographic texts, Clifford writes, "an implicit question mark was placed beside any overly confident and consistent ethnographic voice. What desires and confusions was it smoothing over?"[72] The anthropologists involved in the *Writing Culture* conversation thus attempted to acknowledge and reckon with contact's acts of containment—containment, above all, of anthropology's debts to earlier, often colonial or missionary, scenes of contact.

Importantly, this did not mean jettisoning contact as an epistemic virtue in the 1980s, either for Language writers or for anthropologists. Rather, for both, it meant, first, acknowledging the messiness that earlier instantiations of contact had labored to contain; and, second, attempting to imagine better, more potentially liberatory ways to effect contact that, through a reflexivity that destabilizes the coherent authorial (whether ethnographic or poetic) voice. Although this trope of the destabilized authorial voice is by now a cliché in poetics and while, as Kim Fortun observes in her introduction to the Twenty-Fifth Anniversary Edition of *Writing Culture*, ethnographic reflexivity "can be just another device for establishing authority," it is important to understand what it seemed to offer in these moments of recovery. Reflexivity in the 1980s was a way of acknowledging, if not unkinking, the doubled-over temporality that had always been built into contact. It was thus a technique for rehabilitating contact as an epistemic virtue—for holding open the possibility of a contact that did not efface violent histories and that thus might yield the knowledge that intercultural exchange and material immediacy promised, without the power relations that it had so far manifestly entailed.[73] Reflexivity promised to put the virtue back in epistemic virtue.

Like their anthropologist contemporaries whose "literary turn" manifested in the intensive self-scrutiny and self-historicization of *Writing Culture* and related work, Language writers sought to construe their own encounters with the ethnographic "others" reflexively. Ron Silliman's long poem *Ketjak* (1978), for example, is often considered an exemplary instance of what Silliman called the "new sentence," a technique for disrupting hegemonic logics by limiting what he calls "syllogistic movement" (the resolution of sentences into narrative and consequential continuities) in order to "[keep] the reader's attention at or very close to the level of language, that is, most often at the sentence level or below."[74] The new sentence is, in other words, a way of preventing the consolidation of an authoritative authorial "voice" through what I have described above as concatenation. Laid end to end, the structures of the new sentence are concatenated, but only just, resisting higher-level integration or allowing it only in ways that will soon be dispelled. "The sole precedent I can find for the new sentence is [William Carlos Williams's 1920 book] *Kora In Hell: Improvisations* and that one far-fetched," Silliman writes.[75] Williams's concatenated discontinuities in *Kora in Hell* thus offer a precedent but not quite a model for the version of contact that Silliman seeks. *Ketjak* produces its "new sentences" procedurally by iterating its paragraphs, each paragraph interspersing the sentence of the previous paragraph (or variations on those sentences) with new ones, thus couching repetition in constant recontextualization and unsettling narrative and voice alike. Thus the sentence "We ate them" reappears as gruesome comedy in the next paragraph, when a new preceding sentence is introduced: "Look at that room filled with fleshy babies. We ate them."[76] It is a new context that does not last long, as the poem's observations, often recognizably and directly of the San Francisco Bay Area, accrue in increasingly granular ways. The new sentence concatenates, insisting on sequences that are just barely sequences, thus reenacting the logic of contact by way of repudiating the primitive magics of ideology.

The forms through which *Ketjak* works to dispel ethnographic authority, then, also reproduce early twentieth-century forms of contact. Moreover, these ambivalences pervade the poem, which takes its title from a Balinese dance and chant—spelled using Dutch orthography—that Silliman first encountered through the Nonesuch Explorer Series, what Silliman describes as "the first great project of widely available field recordings of world music." Balinese *ketjak* (or *kecak*) is a chant that, like Steve Reich's *Drumming* (itself an "ethnographic" work developed by Reich after observing drumming in Ghana), modeled for Silliman a dynamic mode of repetition from which he developed *Ketjak*'s iterative new sentence structure.[77] Although the Nonesuch Explorer Series positioned its listeners as "explorers" and the recordings themselves as "field recordings," Silliman notes in 2003:

> Not long after I composed the poem *Ketjak,* I came across some articles on the dance & learned that (as [David] Lewiston insinuates without fully acknowledging in his marketing-driven liner notes) *Ketjak* was by no means an instance of "native" or "tribal" culture, but had in fact been constructed precisely to perform for tourists in search of the exotic. While its origins began with Sang Hyang exorcism ritual dances, a Javanese choreographer, Sardono Kusumo, made modifications sometime in the early 20th century. In the 1930s, Limbak and at least two westerners, Walter Spies and Katherine Mershon, transformed the ceremony by

> inserting a danced narrative from an entirely different tradition, the Ramayana. The two layers, each of which entails both singing & dance, occur *simultaneously*. The very opposite of "indigenous authenticity," *Ketjak* is a modern—even post-modern—pastiche targeted directly for the tourist dollar.[78]

What is at first taken to be the product of an ethnographic "first contact" (field recordings) reveals itself to be a palimpsestic composite of engagements between Balinese art, colonialism, and what Clifford has called the "art-culture system"—"a machine for making authenticity" through recontextualizations and remediations on the global art market.[79] It is no wonder that Marcus and Fischer responded with some annoyance to "quibbles that authors of pioneering descriptive accounts of other cultures such as E. E. Evans-Pritchard, Bronislaw Malinowski, Franz Boas, or Gregory Bateson already 'said something like that,' or that experimentation in ethnographic writing is as old as anthropology," above all because such "quibbles" were not wrong.[80] Formal strategies for reflexivity did not so much undo contact's layers as add more of them. Thus Alice Notley's *Dr. Williams' Heiresses* opens its concatenated fragments of dialogue on the ways that a female poet might "use" Williams with an act of recovery—the writing of an American poetic genealogy beginning with Poe (whom Williams, in *Spring and All* and *In the American Grain*, anointed as the first genuinely American poet)—that is staged as an origin myth.[81] Notley's Williamsian cosmogony begins with Poe mating "with a goddess" and then reproduces a mostly familiar "experimental" trajectory as literal kin, descending from mostly male poetic parents who mate with goddesses who are "mostly evaporative non-parental types." "You could use [Williams] to sound entirely new if you were a woman," says one of the voices in *Dr. Williams' Heiresses*, proposing newness through a contact that pastiches "primitive" myth.[82]

The perfect coexistence of reflexivity and the dimensions of contact that reflexivity aimed to ameliorate—its tendency to appeal to simplicity and immediacy—emerges in the Language writers' collaborative account of their visit to Russia in 1989. *Leningrad* is framed as a provisional, reflexive mini-ethnography; as Hejinian introduces the volume: "This collaboration is about that week [of the conference], about juxtaposition, happenstance, double vision, vistas, and a flow of observations and expectations kept in suspense."[83] Hejinian presents the encounter as one with knowledge at stake, writing, "I've been back since, but I don't know any more [than I did before]." Or, as Watten names the epistemological hope invested in contact:

"There is a history of cultural figures that have developed from the Cold War for the dilemma of Us/Them, and these figures have left residual traces that must be renegotiated when faced with the real Soviet Union. To do so is to confront the fantasy and dread occasioned by such denial with *real knowledge.*"[84] Seeing for oneself—contact—is an epistemic virtue that dispels fantasy and state propaganda. Yet this is also an encounter in which knowledge is gathered by "juxtaposition, happenstance, double vision," and, in "this collaboration," through writing itself. Thus, in the book's introductory section, all the authors reflect on what the Russian avant-garde has meant to their poetics—famously, a great deal—and all of them introduce this engagement by historically situating it against Vietnam, the Cold War, or both.[85]

These gestures both "historiciz[e] the ethnographic present," in Marcus and Fischer's terms, and, at the same time, repeatedly stage the authors' awareness of at least some of the limitations entailed by their visit to the Soviet Union, deliberately effacing their authority in the process.[86] Watten, for one, reflects on *Leningrad* as "a first moment in this as-yet-undetermined genre" of "accounts of the 'opening' of the Soviet Union," a genre that he places in parallel with the "substantial literature—often written along romantic, nineteenth-century travel narrative lines—of the reencounter of China by the west in the 1970s." Aiming to deflect any hint of a conquering Robinson Crusoe–like subject in this qualified first contact, Watten argues that the Soviet case "will necessitate other and more difficult figures for interpretation than those of a Third World-oriented neocolonialist fantasy." Hejinian, likewise, qualifies her own relation to Russian literature and avows her own situatedness in an American literature "contextualized by the social and political life of the time." "I myself," she writes, "had a fantastic rather than a comprehensive relationship with the works of someone like Velimir Khlebnikov . . . because I had no Russian context for understanding the scale and intentions (and hence the meaning) of his work."[87]

Such gestures suggest that Language's investment in contact as an epistemic virtue is a critical one that imagines writers "inside as well as outside the histories of contact on which they follow," as Pratt puts it.[88] Effacing authorial identity emerges here as a feature of a renewed and rehabilitated understanding of contact for the Language writers. Pratt describes how, in *Nisa: The Life and Words of a !Kung Woman* (1981), Marjorie Shostak produces an arrival scene that almost brutally renounces the production of ethnographic contact as first contact, her informants gushing about the last ethnographers who came through and the gifts of "Western commodities" that the ethnographers gave them. "It is an awful scene, a real return of the repressed," Pratt writes, and for the authors of *Leningrad*, something like this renunciation is important enough to be staged repeatedly, both in the introduction and across the text.[89] As Davidson frames the doubleness of encounter, "The city is given to us as part of the collective unconscious of a generation growing up during the Cold War. By the time we step off the plane, we have, to some extent, already arrived."[90]

The necessity of reflexivity is evident, in *Leningrad*, in the ways that the poetic language-game of experimentalism is severely tested by contact with Leningrad itself. Like Hejinian, Silliman writes of his fascination and identification with avant-gardist Russian poetry and scholarship, only to affirm the strain that the visit to Leningrad places on that identification. "When, in 1982, the first issue of *Poetics Journal* published Richard Sheldon's translation of Shklovsky's 'Plotless Literature,' I read it . . . as though the text were speaking of my own poetry directly," Silliman writes, situating his visit in a history that includes both attachment and a dependence on translation. "This, however," he adds, "is not the Marxism of which Leningrad poets speak, nor with which Russians have had to contend for more than seventy years."[91] Many of the writers that the Language poets meet have distanced themselves from the Russian historical avant-garde, "largely because it is perceived by them, in the end, to have served the state," as Watten puts it.[92] The Language poets' Russian-derived aesthetic tools for resisting the totalizing logic of the Cold War have less utility in Russia itself. This necessitates what Watten calls an "ethics of partial knowledge" made available, not quite by the Russian avant-garde, but by a contemporary rereading of it, "available if one cares to read it in that tradition of Russian literature inaugurated by Shklovsky."[93] Responding to political necessity means reinterpreting the historical avant-garde's legacy—an act of "white recovery," as I have suggested—to make its historically situated knowledge production available to a new political situation. As Davidson puts it, "The [Russian] formalist generation's aesthetic motivation becomes our generation's critical goal."[94] In *Leningrad*, this tension between the Language writers' faith in the political purchase of their experimental poetics and their apprehension of their Soviet counterparts' skepticism—*both* of which arise from a commitment to contact—is never resolved, only held in reflexive suspension.

The Final Frontier

Above all other epistemic virtues explored in this book, contact supplies the form and rationale for the kinds of time travel (or recovery) undertaken by late twentieth-century writers who sought to renegotiate their place within the homogeneous, empty time of empire. But although I have been at some pains to demarcate the centrality of "experimental" discourses in discussing contact, contact was widely embraced as an epistemic virtue, especially in that other Cold War cultural phenomenon that appealed to the sciences—science fiction. Science fiction's purchase on twentieth-century American anxieties about technology, alterity, and futurity are well documented, but its relationship to literary experimentalism has usually been thorny at best; unlike experimental writing, twentieth-century American science fiction has often been tacitly or explicitly congenial both to capitalism and to US empire, thematically, stylistically, and in relation to the book market. It is true that science fiction was rarely concerned to enact epistemic virtues at the level of language in the ways that experimental writing was. Yet if experimental writing laid a claim to the forms of scientific modernity, science fiction laid a claim to its contents. Furthermore, mainstream liberal fictions that tried to imagine benevolent, or nonimperialist, forms of contact often shared experimentalism's "paranoid" sensibility in relation to homogeneous, empty time; its essential faith in epistemic virtue (if not as actually practiced in the present, as they might be realized in an enlightened, "modern" future in which science and politics could be kept apart); and even in certain forms.[95]

Concatenation—minimal though it is—proves a resilient form of contact across "experimental" and mainstream works alike. The concatenations of the explorer's notebook are thus reenacted in the typical voice-over introduction in the television series *Star Trek* (1966–1969), "Captain's log, star date . . ." The dates that begin most episodes situate the crew of the *Enterprise*, *Star Trek*'s benevolent quasi-anthropological explorer protagonists and representatives of the interplanetary Federation, in a homogeneous, empty time that is not only world-historical but, in the show, literally universal. The episodes' discontinuous, nonprogressive structure, meanwhile, resists higher-level integration, as contact with various worlds—and the difficulties of abiding by the Federation's noninterventionist Prime Directive—is restaged over and over.[96] As Kevin McGeough puts it, "The *Enterprise*'s explorations are encounters with anachronism," wherein the "future" in which the series is set is marked by uneven developments that supply alterity.[97] Quite often, the *Enterprise*'s alien encounters are with the Earth of the past.

Even more ambitiously, Ursula K. Le Guin's Hugo and Nebula Award-winning 1969 novel *The Left Hand of Darkness* tries to imagine benevolent contact through its participant-observer narrator, Genly Ai. Ai is the first emissary of an interplanetary organization, the Ekumen, to a cold world called Gethen. He is, then, Gethen's "first contact." Le Guin is at pains to efface the possibility of nefarious political (especially imperialist) motives, which the inhabitants of Gethen reasonably fear, in the Ekumen, by minimizing the Ekumen's status as a political entity and rendering it as a neutral technocratic facilitator of "open trade."[98] Thus, Ai explains that the oddly Hayekian Ekumen is "not essentially a government at all. . . . The motives of communication and cooperation are of its essence, and therefore in another aspect it's a league or union of worlds. . . . It does not enforce laws; decisions are reached by council and consent."[99] Through such disclaimers, Le Guin minimizes the power relations that a single planet's entry into a larger union might entail and floats the possibility of pure mutuality.[100] "My job here, really," Ai says, "is to find out if you're willing to communicate with the rest of mankind."[101] More fundamentally, the novel's narrative of Ai's self-transformation, published two years after Malinowski's incendiary fieldwork diaries, resembles the kinds of reflexive narratives of ethnographic contact that the *Writing Culture* group cites as placing "a question mark . . . beside any overly confident and consistent ethnographic voice."[102] Ai's Ekumen not only espouses its own version of *Star Trek*'s Prime Directive, the Law of Cultural Embargo, but further guards against imperialist potential by sending a solitary emissary to make first contact.[103] "Alone, I cannot change your world, but I can be changed by it," Ai tells Estraven. "Alone, I must listen, as well as speak. Alone, the relationship I finally make, if I make one . . . is individual, it is personal, it is both more and less than political."[104] For Le Guin, contact guarantees knowledge when it is "more and less" than, not equal to, the political.

Le Guin's formal strategies for centralizing contact as an epistemic virtue, while at the same time fending off compromising political motives, strikingly anticipate those of anthropology and experimental writing in the 1980s. (Indeed, Fredric Jameson insistently likens the sex/gender system on Gethen to a thought experiment that is "experimental" in Émile Zola's sense.)[105] Reflexivity pervades Ai's musings, as he (usually unsuccessfully) tries to unseat his attachment to a familiar Terran sex/gender system in the face of Gethen's much different norms. The novel also adopts strategies of narrative discontinuity, interrupting a mostly first-person account with field reports and ethnographic material in the form of Gethenian hearth stories, supplied with metadata about the time and place of collection. Although these punctuating interruptions do not by any means prevent the kind of narrative integration that Language writing's new sentence is meant to prevent, they betray the novel's ongoing preoccupation with homogeneous, empty time and the difficulty of rendering time commensurable across cultures. The novel opens with the metadata of Ai's report, which "starts on the 44th diurnal of the Year 1491," performing the role of a logbook and, with the year "1491," setting up and just barely sidestepping a comparison to 1492, famously the year of Christopher Columbus's landing at Hispaniola and one of the many settler origin myths of the Americas that Williams takes up in *In the American Grain*.[106] Interplanetary travel allows the difficulty of coevalness to become literal, as different planets necessarily reckon time differently. An appendix to the novel describes the "Gethenian calendar and clock" whose terminology are used throughout, and especially in the logbook that Therem Estraven, the Gethenian with whom Ai ultimately becomes closest, keeps during the novel's most intense meditations on intercultural contact, their long and difficult trek across a glacier.

Once inside the diegesis, the first thing that Ai narrates about Gethen is the concatenated sequence of a parade in the Gethenian state of Karhide: "Next come the lords and mayors and representatives. . . . Next, a troop of jugglers. . . . Next, forty men in yellow, playing gossiwors. . . . Next, the royal party . . ."[107] For a solid four paragraphs, Ai's narration is paratactic, its polysyndeton and repetition of "next" merely listing and describing the marchers in the alien parade in the seemingly arbitrary order that they appear, and thus undertaking the "naked" style that we have come to expect from the performance of contact as an epistemic virtue. In *The Left Hand of Darkness*, Ai, though flawed, is authorized and made sympathetic through the constraints of contact: his attempts at "no ideas but in things," his self-historicization, and his reflexivity about many of the ways that those attempts fail.

Le Guin likely borrowed the name Ekumen from the concept of "ecumene" (or *oikumene*), which her father, Alfred L. Kroeber, a student of Franz Boas and the first appointee to the University of California, Berkeley, Department of Anthropology, brought into use in American anthropology to describe "the total area of traceable diffusion influences from the main higher centers of Eurasia."[108] Le Guin's anthropological imagination is often remarked in criticism, and as a participant observer, Ai clearly wrestles with what, in a talk delivered at the hundredth anniversary celebration of the Berkeley Department of Anthropology, Le Guin identified as the risk of "the exploitation of real people."[109] But more important than Le Guin's personal connection to disciplinary anthropology (in the same Bay Area that would become an epicenter for Language writing and the fictional home of the United Federation of Planets in *Star Trek*) is the popularity of *The Left Hand of Darkness* (it has never been out of print) and the legibility of the encounters with alterity that it proposed. In *Star Trek IV: The Voyage Home*, the crew of the *Enterprise* returns to 1986 San Francisco to find the resources to survive a new kind of first contact (with a space probe that speaks only the language of the extinct humpback whale). Rewriting contact as comedy, *Star Trek IV: The Voyage Home* uses time travel as a device both for historicizing the 1980s late Cold War milieu as contingent and temporary, and for proposing a liberal future whose science, and whose contact, are benevolently post-political.

Distinct as *Star Trek*'s liberal vision is from that of the Language writers, both hoped for a knowledge that was "modern" in Bruno Latour's sense: epistemically virtuous and thereby free from state violence and its motives.[110] In the (terrible) 1996 film *Star Trek: First Contact*, Captain Picard and the android officer Data travel back to the year 2063 and reenact a scene that Carol Cohn describes in her ethnography of Cold War defense intellectuals: "patting the missile."[111] Their mission in the past is to ensure that an Earth human, Zefram Cochran, succeeds in launching his invention, a space flight technology "advanced" enough to attract the attention of passing alien ethnographers, initiating the titular first contact and Earth's entry into a new age. First contact, *Enterprise* officer Deanna Troi tells Cochran, "unites humanity in a way that no one ever thought possible when they realize they're not alone in the universe. Poverty, disease, war—they'll all be gone in fifty years." The Federation, like Le Guin's Ekumen, represents a post-political future in which scientific knowledge and technology can be wholly and unproblematically directed toward the common good. And while Language writers did not share the liberal politics of a "post-political" contact, they shared its hope that contact might rearrange or disestablish oppressive power relations. Attending to popular science fiction such as *The Left Hand of Darkness* and the Star Trek franchise discloses how investments that are often treated as arcane and minor—experimental aesthetics—were in reality pervasive. The scene of "patting the missile" in *Star Trek: First Contact* both emblematizes this hope and performs contact's characteristic containment of previous, disavowed scenes of contact. Cohn, embedded for a year (1984-1985) among nuclear defense strategists, recounts the repeated language and practice of "patting the missile"—laying hands on bombs—both for one's own satisfaction and to provide assurance to allied powers. For Cohn, "patting the missile" is both a scene of all-male bonding and a way of minimizing the destructive power of the bombs.[112] In *Star Trek: First Contact*, Picard reverently touches Cochran's space vessel, telling Data that he's always wanted to touch it. The vessel is, of course, a repurposed nuclear warhead, and "it is a historical irony," as Data says, "that Dr. Cochran would choose an instrument of mass destruction to inaugurate an era of peace." Touching the vessel/warhead that they have traveled back in time to protect, Picard and Data enact contact through recovery, explicitly in the interests of a "first contact" that promises to replace Earth's primitive politicization of technology, signified by the repurposed warhead, with benevolently pure knowledge, a future contact free from oppressive power relations. Much as this scene of contact aims to replace the fruits of the military-industrial complex (and implicitly, though not historically, the logic of Cold War defense strategists) with an epistemically uncompromised version of contact, however, it also reenacts the very 1980s defense strategy scene of "patting the missile" that it aims to replace, down to its white, masculine homosociality.[113]

Contact, for Williams and McAlmon, could unite the positions of indigenous and discoverer through a linguistic principle of the "naked word," the site of what Taussig would later call "mimesis and alterity" and what Cheng would call the primitivism of the "modern surface." Already for Williams it was a principle of recovery as much as of discovery, animating excavations of the American archive for *In the American Grain* and of Paterson, New Jersey, for *Paterson*. Such gestures of recovery were widespread in the late twentieth century, including the Language writers' production of an "experimental tradition" of which Williams was a part. The Star Trek franchise and *The Left Hand of Darkness* show what liberal science fiction of the second half of the twentieth century had in common with experimental writing despite otherwise very different politics and aesthetics: a conception of futurity whose hopes rested in the Latourian modernity of rehabilitated epistemic virtue. It was a hope that sought to overcome, but also frequently reenacted, the logics of difference—primitive and modern, self and other, salvage and progress—that had so often authorized contact as an epistemic virtue in the first place.

Coda
Future Texts

> What are the dimensions of the field? They've put me here in the tallest grasses and strangest fruit and have demanded at gunpoint that I bend into it over and over, but I'm so tired, and my limbs are sore, and I feel disconnected, or I disintegrate, a shadow figure towers over me as I exhaust, body buckle, ballast removed.
>
> Dawn Lundy Martin, "WITHOUT KNOWING THE SLIGHTEST THING ABOUT WAR, I FIND MYSELF AN INSTRUMENT OF LABOR, INVESTIGATION, AND EXPERIMENT"

In Ralph Ellison's *Invisible Man* (1954), the protagonist shares an embarrassed moment with a fellow communist activist, Brother Tod Clifton, after an encounter with the Afrocentric West Indian radical Ras the Exhorter, who compares the well-proportioned Clifton to an African king.[1] "It's a wonder he didn't say something about 'Ethiopia stretching forth her wings,'" Clifton murmurs to the protagonist.[2] The Invisible Man and Clifton—both young Black men well trained in the Marxist "science" of the Brotherhood—see Ras as too promiscuously mingling history and science with mysticism and religious prophecy, as evidenced in the phrase, "Ethiopia stretching forth her wings," a quotation from Psalm 68 that many turn-of-the-century Black activists were known to quote, and a key scriptural foundation for late nineteenth-century Ethiopianist and AME Christian theology.[3] Ras the Exhorter's evocation has clear roots in nineteenth-century Afrocentric discourses that are also associated with more credited Pan-Africanists like W. E. B. Du Bois, a sociologist to whom are now attributed important innovations in statistical methods in social science.[4] But the modern distinction between "the scientific power charged with representing things and the political power charged with representing subjects" quickly runs aground when it comes to people whose status as representable subjects (as opposed to representable objects) is already in question.[5] Ras's identitarian appeal to Clifton's black body, situated in a mythic Africa and invoked as grounds for a political realignment, avows an unscientific politics, one that lets knowledge and politics get not so much hybridized as confused, rendering his knowledge and politics alike unmodern. In their exchange, Clifton and the protagonist register their embarrassment at this epistemically unvirtuous unmodernity, which they feel they must quickly repudiate. Tellingly, the protagonist calls Ras "crazy," casting his call to pan-African solidarity out of epistemological bounds entirely.

Yet as misguided as Ras seems to be in *Invisible Man*, the protagonist and Clifton's belief in the "science" of the Brotherhood also proves misguided. As Michel Foucault puts it, specifically in relation to the question of whether Marxism is a "science":

> Even before we know to what extent something like Marxism or psychoanalysis is analogous to a scientific practice in its day-to-day operations, in its rules of construction, in the concepts it uses, we should be . . . asking ourselves about the aspiration to power that is inherent in the claim to being a science. The question or questions that have to be asked are: "What types of knowledge are you trying to disqualify when you say that you are a science? What speaking subject, what discursive subject, what subject of experience and knowledge are you trying to minoritize when you begin to say: 'I speak this discourse, I am speaking a scientific discourse, and I am a scientist.'"[6]

And indeed, Ras speaks directly to technoscience's violence-enforced hierarchy, waving his fist at a transport plane flying overhead ("Hell with him, some day we have them too!") and challenging the Brotherhood's ideology as "some blahsted lies in some bloody books written by the white mahn in the first place"—a challenge that Clifton can answer only with a fist.[7] As the novel unfolds, Ras's warning is perversely borne out, as the Brotherhood's universalizing "science" ultimately emerges as its own end, with the specific concerns of Harlem ending up as collateral damage on the way to furthering it. Although that turn in the novel is widely read as a critique of Marxism, as Scott Selisker has persuasively argued, moments like Ras's appeal show why the novel stages less a critique of Marxism per se than of the impulse within it to allow a techno-scientific vanguardism to stand in for, and indeed run roughshod over, more local and specific political commitments.[8] The language of the future is not enough. As I have aimed to show in this book, experimental writing is prone to the same fallacy, as well as to similar modes of hope, possibility, and strength. To put it another way, experimental writing is far from the first writing to make a claim to material efficacy via form; what sets it apart is the intensity of its claim to do so secularly, as technology rather than as magic. And that claim depends on a "modern" distinction between technology and magic that has never not been subtended by hierarchies of race, gender, and coloniality.[9] As Nathaniel Mackey has observed, notwithstanding the consistent if marginalized presence of Black American writers in and around the domain of US experimental writing, wherever experimentalism is understood as a "complex accommodation between technique and epistemological concerns, between ways of telling and ways of knowing, especially where knowing is less the claim than a nervousness about it"—that is, an aspiration toward epistemic virtue—"the investment in [racially] segregated categories dies hard."[10] I have aimed to map out the ways that that investment lies less in any specific attitude toward race per se (indeed, most experimental writers are avowed anti-racists) than in a belief—consolidated long before, in the period from which key experimental texts emerged—in epistemic virtue's power to proxy for political virtue. In their postmodern mode, experimental languages of the future are a hierarchy masquerading as continuity, avowing the "hybridization" of epistemology and politics only insofar as epistemology is tacitly allowed to take the lead.[11]

To counter the language of state violence on its own experimental terms, then, is perhaps already to concede too much. Experimental poetry criticism bingo has become too familiar (not to reduce all experimental poetry criticism to it, of course): the text foregrounds the materiality of language, it disrupts traditional syntax or traditional associations, it's self-canceling, it draws attention to language as a process/as material/as indeterminate, it refuses closure/opens up to contingency, and, most hackneyed of all, it challenges the lyric subject.[12] Each iteration proffers the text as an instantiation of an ethically endorseable right knowledge practice, producing the hermetic hermeneutic that Sianne Ngai points out in her essay "Paranoia": we don't even necessarily need the poem in hand to do a reading; each experimental text risks being no more than an instantiation of the—and it is all too nearly *the*—reading, even as experimental poetry criticism bingo never really seems to capture the genuine pleasure and possibility in so much "experimental" writing (which I hope some of my readings of retroactively claimed experimentalists have brought to the fore).[13] The bad good timing of a certain version of language philosophy's historical coincidence with Language writing produces, in Ngai's words, "a fit that seems too close. I could say: 'In its privileging of the letter and constant deferral of stabilized meanings, Lyn Hejinian's *Writing Is an Aid to Memory* produces a heterogeneous flow of matter and signs in order to break down normative frameworks of reference and sense-making.' And you might well respond: 'Tell me something I don't already know!'"[14] Indeed, these tendencies have also long been endemic to criticism of experimentalism's most celebrated foremother, Gertrude Stein, whose recovery was deeply implicated in this same confluence of academic and creative writing. Stein's writing has often been subject to the strategy of "sampling" her ostensibly homogeneous (because always legible under the sign of a certain experimental theory of language, and *only* legible under that sign) corpus, anticipating criticism of the later experimental writing toward whose history Stein's work was marshaled.[15] Although it seems paradoxical that "experimental" works would come to be conventionally read as instantiations of a default organizing theoretical rubric, their very secularism makes it almost inevitable: in their epistemically virtuous resistance to impositions of authoritative meaning, that resistance itself takes the place of meaning, becomes the meaning. Resisting "the language of Auschwitz" through epistemic virtue, like the science of the Brotherhood, emerges as its own end.

The exception to this, and Ngai's focus in "Paranoia," is the relative success with which white feminist experimentalisms have met. Juliana Spahr and Stephanie Young's celebrated essay-performance "Foulipo" pointedly enacts the ideological underpinnings of what counts as "avant-garde": highly masculinized Oulipian writing is literally older than 1970s feminist body art, yet its styles and methods remain signifiers of the "new" even as feminist body art is deprecated as hopelessly "dated."[16] Yet in the end, Spahr and Young stop short of attempting to dismantle the temporal framework implied by Oulipo's mysterious perpetual youth (that is, the implicit white maleness of futurity), "scaed of" what that dismantling might foreclose:

> And then we stopped shot of asking the question, is Oulipo pehaps toubled by an uninvestigated sexism and thus not capable of being a pat of ou witing life in any way, a question we didn't eally want to ask because we wee scaed of the answe and what it would deny us and we wee all about the "& and." We instead wondeed if thee could be a new goup fomation, a sot of feminist Oulipo, some-

> thing we jokingly began calling "foulipo" because we didn't want it to be women only; we didn't want oulipuss. We just wanted something that engaged the elation between fomalism and body at and saw both as pat of a tadition that was complicated and inteconnected. We did not think it made any sense to cay only oulipo fowad and not cay the body at fowad.[17]

Even Spahr and Young's astute gender analysis of the "new" in experimental poetics—an analysis whose analogues in the domain of science studies were at that point well established—was not conceded by those who argued that "gender has little to do with it."[18] Yet in the end, theirs is a mild critique that hopefully imagines a resolution in "ca[rr]y[ing] the body a[r]t fo[r]wa[r]d" along with the male neo-avant-garde (whatever else may be left behind). The centrality of epistemic virtue—so often manifested, as in "Foulipo," as a concern to dispel "narcissism"—in formulations of the "experimental" also disclose their limit, then. Recuperating the "primitive" (whether as *écriture féminine*, as Ngai discusses; via an embodied "foulipo"; or in the ways that experimental writers from about 1990 began to retcon in writers of color with whom they had previously engaged little) and restoring it to the status of the genuinely modern only reinscribes the ideology of modernism to which experimentalism is indebted—a primitivist ideology, as so many important scholars of modernism have shown.[19] For this reason, contemporary experimental writing cannot be understood without the (modernist) genealogy that it created for itself. Rather, its attempts to grapple with a bad capitalist modernity on the terrain of its structures of power/knowledge—that is, on the terrain of language—have tended to repeat the modernist double bind of primitivism—the double bind in which modernity cannot be imagined without projecting an originary simplicity to be recovered and "made new." Its attempts to recuperate or recover abjected terms have thus succeeded only incompletely, leaving intact the temporal framework that abjected them in the first place. To be clear, experimental writing did *not* aim merely to rescue itself from abjection; it aimed to use language and newly revealed continuities between epistemology and politics to comprehensively jam the system that produces such hierarchies. Their aspirations were nothing so liberal or so commonplace as, for example, Gene Roddenberry's space multiculturalism. The question, then, is why, with a surprising preponderance of reason to suppose that such experimental writing would be politically efficacious, it, by and large, was not. As "Foulipo" apophastically acknowledges, the answer is that experimentalism's mechanism for jamming the system—epistemic virtue—leaves much more of the original apparatus in place than late twentieth-century experimentalists supposed.

Not this. What then?[20]

I have argued that the power of the "experimental" and the epistemic virtue that it implies is that it brings disparate practices under an apparent unity of purpose, as if to align varying epistemological practices and dispositions not only with one another but also with ethical and political virtue. Disarticulating the often competing values of epistemic virtue—flash against precision, objectivity against contact—may, then, help us reach some clarity about the circumstances under which those values may give rise to opportunities to make political choices—or may force them. Yet, as I hope the arguments in this book make clear, a more granular understanding of epistemic virtues only partly decenters experimentalism's seeming monopoly on the language of the future. Experimental writing was, after all, far from the only recovery project of the late twentieth century, and concurrent work discloses other ways that scientific modernity and the arts' place within it was negotiated. The Afrofuturist jazz musician Sun Ra's 1974 film *Space Is the Place*, set mostly in Oakland, California, offers a third interpretation of the kind of disruptive counter-communication explored, in their different ways, by Language writers and by *Star Trek IV: The Voyage Home*. As the film opens on a distant planet, Ra, playing himself, explains his plan to bring Black people to the planet, where the "vibrations" are better. The mode of transport? "Teleportation, transmolecularization, or better yet . . . music."[21] Music, Ra's chosen art, is represented as the parallel and opposite to the US government's civilian space program, and fully as capable of transporting people through space. Like language for the Language writers and in *Star Trek IV*, music in *Space Is the Place* does not *represent* the world but rather *intervenes* in it. In an early scene in a Chicago night club, Ra's dissonant piano playing brings material destruction to the environment, as wine glasses burst and the building begins to crumble. Conversely, later in the film, two US government agents capture and paranoically interrogate Ra about the possibility that "Africa" has a space program, using music as their instrument of torture.[22] The music's square style—a peppy oompah—asserts its rectilinearity against Ra's free-form jazz, nearly, though not quite, to the point of overwhelming the offending tune itself, the blackface minstrel song and Confederate anthem "Dixie."[23] The film thus aligns the US space program, widely represented as big science's friendly civilian face and a site of national virtues of courage, aspiration, and (of course) epistemic virtue, not only with Cold

War cultural diplomacy and "soft power" but also the more explicitly violent state apparatuses of CIA covert operations, which developed a program of "no-touch torture" including music since the 1950s.[24]

Other moments in the film likewise refuse a distinction between an ostensibly civilian space program, on one hand, and state violence against African Americans at home and purported enemies abroad, on the other. For example, an interviewer asks Ra, "Why are you talking to ghetto Blacks? Why shouldn't you be talking to, say, white nuclear physicists?"—tellingly eliding two notionally very different kinds of "rocket science"—nuclear physics and astrophysics—and bringing the civilian, "peaceful" astrophysics enterprise under the umbrella of the more overtly military domain of nuclear war. Notwithstanding the actual historical presence of African Americans in US government jobs, including as scientists (in 1972, the year *Space Is the Place* was filmed, NASA took out a full-page ad filled with photographs of Black NASA workers in the sixteenth annual Career Edition of the *Afro American*), the film represents state-sponsored science as inimical to the kind of music-driven space flight and Black "freedom and peace and liberty" at the center of Ra's project.[25] Ra's music, in this context, appears as the equal and opposite force to the idiom of state violence, much as the experimental new sentence aims to oppose and undo the state language of "fraud."

What distinguishes Ra's counter-communicative, dissonant artistic project of refusing the language of state violence from the strand of American writing, primarily poetry, that has come to be called "experimental"? For *Space Is the Place*, there is no cherishing of a future knowledge practice whose political virtue rests on its truth-telling capacity and thus also no repudiation of unmodernity (the repudiation that, in a poetic register, Gillian White has explained as "lyric shame").[26] On the contrary, *Space Is the Place*, and much of Ra's persona throughout his career, is self-consciously goofy, mingling its futurism with the hokey—identitarian, perhaps—Afrocentrism of ancient Egyptian symbolism, eschewing claims to epistemic virtue in favor of purely political aims.[27] "You're not in a place where truth can do you any good," Ra tells a questioner in a 1971 lecture at Berkeley, "so you're going to have to come to me privately, and we'll talk about things that can *help* the Black race."[28] Later, we might see an echo of this sentiment in the figure of the what-sayer, the anti-soothsayer ("sooth," of course, meaning "truth" or "revelation") in Nathaniel Mackey's long poetic sequence *The Song of the Andoumboulou*, based on a Dogon cosmology whose sources are themselves questionable.[29] "I was the what-sayer./ Whatever he said I would/ say so what."[30]

Epistemic virtue, for Ra, is a losing proposition in the face of long-standing historical marginalization. "I'm dealing with equations. I can't go around and tell you I'm right, or good, when the dictionary's telling everybody in the world everything black is evil and wicked, so then I'm gonna say yes. So what. Yes, I'm wicked. Yes, I'm evil. . . . I don't want to go to heaven."[31] Positioning himself against an authoritative edifice of Eurocentric knowledge that is hierarchical in advance, Ra disavows any hope that a pursuit of a more genuine epistemic security might equate to political liberation. Sylvia Wynter has argued that "all human orders . . . have mapped their 'descriptive statements' or governing master codes on the heavens . . . enabling them to be experienced by each order's subjects as if they had been supernaturally (and, as such, extrahumanly determined) criteria."[32] It is within this context that Ra renounces heaven even as he reinscribes in mythic terms (as his Berkeley lectures were titled) "the Black man in the cosmos": for Ra, the secularized heavens of state-sponsored big science are no more recuperable—even via a cleansed language of the future, as in *Star Trek: First Contact*'s repurposing of a nuclear missile for space travel and a putatively post-political intergalactic liberalism—than a religious heaven. Thus no effort is made (as it is in *Star Trek*) to rescue a truer, more epistemically virtuous version of techno-science from the ruins of the politically interested present. Ra suggests, rather, that *only* partial and interested knowledges are possible: NASA is already war by other means.[33]

Similarly, Ishmael Reed's novel *Mumbo Jumbo*—itself dated to Berkeley, 1971—cheerfully performs epistemic unvirtue, for example, breezily dismissing the great European theorist of the irrational, Sigmund Freud, as an "Atonist" surrounded by "professors of New York University or people from Columbia University."[34] Openly unfair and reductive as the novel's dismissal of psychoanalysis is, it is at the same time staged in a way that makes it impossible to ignore that dismissal's symmetry with scientific dismissals of animism and African-influenced knowledge systems, especially Vodou. The novel's protagonist, the "obeah-man" PaPa LaBas, approaches Freud "to teach him The Work; but he couldn't gain entrance to the hotel suite, which was blocked by ass-kissers. . . . They had told LaBas to take the back elevator even though some of them prided themselves on their liberalism."[35] Set mostly in the 1920s and drawing heavily on Zora Neale Hurston's ethnography, *Mumbo Jumbo* recovers an Afrocentric America, but unfaithfully and in many ways flippantly, simultaneously satirizing and obliquely enshrining James Weldon Johnson's account of African American culture as something that, like the minstrel figure Topsy, "jes grew."[36] Thus whereas Hurston dedicates her ethnography *Tell My Horse* (1938) to Carl Van Vechten, the white author, photographer, and patron of the arts who was also one of Gertrude Stein's greatest champions, Reed ruthlessly satirizes Van Vechten (as the Atonist operative Hinkle Von Vampton) as a cynical negrophile whose main relationship to the Harlem Renaissance was one of opportunism, theft, and political containment. Epistemic virtue, the novel suggests, is not a reasonable demand in a situation in which one's words—science, magic, The Work—are already read in advance as "mumbo jumbo."

What the novel proposes instead is not a sober restoration of truth; rather, it offers nothing less than a sprawling conspiracy theory about the global suppression of Black art since the time of ancient Egypt, with the Wallflower Order (a thinly veiled Ivy League) enforcing an epistemic marginalization that is both presented in esoteric, ridiculous terms (Knights Templars, Von Vampton's diet of creepy crawlies, and the like) and in many ways undeniable as historical fact (the looting and violence that make Western art museums into prisonlike "Center[s] of Art Detention").[37] Reed's paranoid counterhistory of Western civilization is openly biased yet discloses its alternatives as no less so. If experimentalism replaces grand narratives with multiple and heterogeneous epistemic virtues (flash, precision, objectivity, contact) that only notionally align, yet which are bound by modalities of self-denial and epistemic ascesis, Ra and Reed stage knowledge practices that are self-consciously and suspiciously *invested*. The point is not that knowledge is worthless but that attempts to protect its virtue, to cordon science off from magic or history from conspiracy theory, are themselves tacitly invested in the presupposition that we can reliably identify some knowledge as unknowledge and some history as myth—distinctions that often fall along lines of racial domination. As John Corbett writes of the outer space mythologies of Ra, Lee Perry, and George Clinton, such challenges to epistemic virtue as such acknowledge "the fundamental *unreality* of existence for people imported into New World servitude and then disenfranchised into poverty. . . . *Is life on this planet not an unreasonable, otherworldly existence in itself?*"[38]

These are in some ways easy examples, assimilable to the much broader arc of postmodern refusals of grand narratives, and thus of a more general defeat of epistemological stability in the face of indeterminacy. A screaming comes across the sky: a weapon, a dissonant language. Jean-François Lyotard described the postmodern "interlinkage between the kind of language called science and the kind called ethics and politics," which experimental writing took up as its ground and its site of intervention, and it is by no means my purpose to reduce that moment.[39] Here is the difference: it's true that fringe and conspiracy theory *in general* may bespeak a loss of faith in epistemological stability. But stability is neither the beginning nor the end of epistemic *virtue*; indeed, as I have suggested, epistemic virtue is powerful in just those places in which stability is unavailable or undesirable, serving as a provisional unifying rubric for wildly divergent practices and forms. As I suggested of Language writing in the previous chapter, epistemological crises can, moreover, be reflexively reincorporated *as* occasions for epistemic virtue, as a further disenchantment that can be met by all the more comprehensive techniques of the self. Consequently, a general postmodern loss of grand narratives is fully compatible with the rise of a technocratic neoliberalism, in which agnosticism about method or theory becomes itself a performance of epistemic virtue, as in the rise of "big data" and attendant ecstatic claims to have slipped the bonds of human ideation at last, allowing "the data itself" to speak.[40]

Afrocentric, anticolonial, queer, and feminist conspiracy theory, in contrast, roots epistemological instability not in a general condition of unknowability but rather in a specific critique of epistemological marginalizations so systematic and long lived as to throw basic categories of validity into question (indeed, this is also deconstruction's foundational gesture, although the specificity of its critique is not always preserved).[41] Epistemically unvirtuous moves like Ra's and Reed's register how, as Lisa Marie Cacho has put it, "race, gender, and sexuality are *ways of knowing* that make sense of social reality in the United States."[42] Eve Sedgwick opens her influential essay on "paranoid reading" with an anecdote aimed at deflating the import of "strong theory": in the words of the activist Cindy Patton, supposing that a conspiracy theory about the origins of HIV turned out to be true, "what would we know then that we don't already know?"[43] But the question can as easily be turned on its head: What reason is there to place faith in official accounts of HIV's origins when we already know (in Patton's words again) that "the lives of Africans and African Americans are worthless in the eyes of the United States; that gay men and drug users are held cheap where they aren't actively hated; that the military deliberately researches ways to kill noncombatants whom it sees as enemies; that people in power look calmly on the likelihood of catastrophic environmental and population changes"?[44] These facts—which are already in evidence—are not the upshot or the surprising revelation of conspiracy theory but rather their condition. It is not necessarily the case that we might want to know the origins of HIV mainly in order to find out whether the state is violent toward certain categories of human beings. Rather, starting with the knowledge that it absolutely is, we might then wish to know how—or why—to (virtuously) know anything about the origins of HIV at all. As Suzanne Canally has described epistemic marginalization's overdetermination: it is the state of knowledge produced when O. J. Simpson did it *and* was framed.[45] Responsible epistemological practices won't save anyone from irresponsible epidemiological practices; perhaps, in that case, pressure on what constitutes responsibility is in order. Sedgwick's question, then—"What does knowledge *do*?"—not only reinstates the experimental hierarchy of action over contemplation (see chapter 1) but in doing so effaces the complexity and compromise embedded in a "knowledge" already admitted to be "conspiracy theory" within a situation of avowed epistemic marginalization. One thing that such "knowledge" (which relinquishes its claim to being knowledge) does for Ishmael Reed in *Mumbo Jumbo*, for example, is make space for the unmodern not by way of tokenistic "inclusion" or elevation to the status of modern but by reorganizing the epistemological ground rules.

In this relation it is useful to consider Stefano Harney and Fred Moten's concept of "experiment[s] of hold," which draws on the work of Frank Wilderson to intervene in modernity's distinction between the domain of science (representing objects) and the domain of politics (representing subjects) at the site of its founding move: the capture and sale of "commodities, the ones that could speak," explored so well in recent years by Ian Baucom, Lisa Lowe, and Christina Sharpe, among others.[46] For Harney and Moten, the triumph of capitalist modernity in its latest phase—global just-in-time logistics managed by supply chain software like SAP—only continues the covert ways that racialized labor has long been shuttled into the category of object: the shipping container, no less than the hold, contains hyperexploited and socially dead laborers.[47] "Logistics," they argue, "wants to dispense with the subject altogether. This is the dream of the newly dominant capitalist science."[48] In that context, Harney and Moten suggest, striving for inclusion in (neo)liberal subjectivity—the attempt, that is, to climb out of being an object of a logistical science in order to become a subject of political representation—offers little in the way of liberation, whatever else it might bring. Nor, indeed, does the experiment of the hold itself, in Harney and Moten's sense, liberate; rather, it offers a compensation—"hapticality, the touch of the undercommons"—and thus an extension of the unmodern magic of "a shaman, a witch, a seer, a poet."[49] We might see this as one realization of Hejinian's call to foreignness, importantly, however, addressed in the first instance to a condition of having no choice about one's foreignness.[50]

Harney and Moten's "experiments of hold" are one way to use language to dislodge modernity's violences without holding out for epistemic virtue. Other thinkers have proposed related and diverging modes of disarticulating epistemic virtue's premises. What Christina Sharpe calls "wake work," which she reads in works by Dionne Brand, M. NourbeSe Philip, June Jordan, and Kamau Brathwaite (among others), for instance, depathologizes what Anne Cheng has termed "the melancholy of race," the need not only for grievance but for grieving (in Cheng's memorable formulation) in the face of racial injury.[51] Sharpe takes "the wake of slavery" not as a scene to be superseded but as an analytic for encountering the "spatial, legal, psychic, material, and other dimensions of Black non/being as well as . . . Black modes of resistance."[52] In wake work, it is not humorous hokeyness or conspiracy theory but a persistent recurrence to the logic of resemblance that makes space for the unmodern in Sharpe's reading, confronting as figure that which it would be no use to render as fact.[53] In a different but related vein, Anthony Reed unfolds in Kamau Brathwaite's poetry of the 1990s a "plural instant": "Rather than a logic of time or modernity the plural instant is a graph of temporality" that produces synchronicities.[54] My point is not that this is work that can be read as "experimental" and should be included in its rubrics (although it increasingly is). Rather, if we are attached to the term "experimental," this is work whose experimentalism is generally uninvested in—or critical of—the core investment of literary experimentalism as it has largely been constituted since the 1970s, namely epistemic virtue. This uninvestedness is not (necessarily) due to a lack of investment questions of knowledge, but rather to an awareness that epistemological guarantees do not contain or entail a politics—that, indeed, the structures that give epistemic virtues their value are often the problem.

This awareness is evident when Dawn Lundy Martin asks, "What are the dimensions of the field?," in her poem "WITHOUT KNOWING THE SLIGHTEST THING ABOUT WAR, I FIND MYSELF AN INSTRUMENT OF LABOR,

INVESTIGATION, AND EXPERIMENT," the penultimate work in her 2015 book *Life in a Box Is a Pretty Life*.[55] One way to read *Life in a Box Is a Pretty Life* is as an extended exploration of the experimental "trajectory" and the violent pleasures that are embedded in its aspirations to epistemic virtue, especially precision, an epistemic virtue of biopolitics, as I explored in chapter 4. "Life in a box" evokes both the Joseph Cornell box and the modernist grid, which "functions to declare the modernity of modern art."[56] "Pretty," it is a site of aesthetic experience. But, too, life in a box is life incarcerated, life shipped, life subject to logistics, as in the book's opening poem, "MO[DERN] [FRAME] OR A PHILOSOPHICAL TREATISE ON WHAT REMAINS BETWEEN HISTORY AND THE LIVING BREATHING BLACK HUMAN FEMALE," which makes explicit that the book responds to Carrie Mae Weems's 1996 photograph series *Framed by Modernism*.[57] And as Sharpe argues, the "box" that is the hold is also the maternal body, insofar as the racialization of criminality is made hereditary in the "wake" of chattel slavery: the doctrine of *partus sequitur ventrem* (the child follows the condition of the mother) works to "turn the womb into a factory producing blackness as abjection much like the slave ship's hold and the prison . . . still ushering their children into their condition."[58] Dotted across Martin's book are excerpts, sometimes altered and manipulated, from Frederick Starr's "The Degeneracy of the American Negro" (1897), J. L. M. Curry's "The Negro Question" (1899), and Frederick L. Hoffman's *Race Traits and Tendencies of the American Negro* (1896), what we might call modernist works of race theory.[59]

Remediating epistemic virtue with an eye toward systematically increased susceptibility to social and bodily death, Martin scrutinizes the affordances of the glass box, the grid, and "the field." The "field," so often invoked by experimental writers looking to Black Mountain "open field poetics," emerges in "WITHOUT KNOWING" as anything but neutral ground: the site of backbreaking agricultural labor and "strange fruit," the field is another version of "life in a box," the modernist frame or the hold.[60] It is a reminder that Charles Olson's open field is also a grid of typewriter monospacing and carriage returns: "It is the advantage of the typewriter that, due to its rigidity and its space precisions, it can, for a poet, indicate exactly the breath, the pauses, the suspensions even of syllables."[61] The field thus, like the grid, contains the contradiction that Rosalind Krauss notes of all grids, that they are at once "centripetal" and "centrifugal," enclosing as well as suggesting infinite outward extension.[62] Martin's field shows that this is not necessarily a scenario of equal, undecidable impulses inhering in a neutral form; as Weems's series suggests, some people are more likely than others to be "framed by modernism," made "at gunpoint" to "bend into it over and over."[63] To be framed is to be criminalized and thus subject to the kind of carceral logic that we already see at play in Marianne Moore's punctiliousness, but without the undecidability that precision so privileges.[64] For whereas precision offers the "technical details" that are disclosed but that may as well be in a black box, Martin insists on the ways that the black box has been literalized in the supply chain—enslavement, the hold, the container ship—as the open secret of capitalist modernity. Contra Robert Duncan's "return to a meadow," in which a field suggests expanse and pastoral enchantment, then, the connotations of a field are, for Martin, anything but "open."[65] Rather, it suggests "complete enclosure"—capitalism's mechanism for securing land and labor alike, the violence of primitive accumulation.[66]

Martin thus takes up the pleasures of precision—its queerness, its femininity, its sharp edges, its real capacity for violence—and opens out another dimension, showing that there are relations to epistemic virtues besides having them, or wanting to. Made an "INSTRUMENT OF LABOR, INVESTIGATION, AND EXPERIMENT," the poem's "I" is an intermediary apparatus—a weapon or tool—caught between subject and object, and in no position to lay a claim to virtue one way or another. For if "labor, investigation, and experiment" suggest an epistemological undertaking, the poem's title hints that there is some contradiction in undertaking it in a state of not "knowing the slightest thing about war." Agnosis about war is not innocence; neither is it any barrier to being made modernity's agent or to being made a party to its violence: "A dead fawn under machinery. I am the machinery. Am also the end of the sentence."[67] The flip side of precision's legal tautology, its tendency to seem to unnaturally *make* the natural law that it too avidly obeys, is the racialized logic of criminalization, which renders certain groups, in Cacho's words, "criminal by being, unlawful by presence, and illegal by status[;] *they do not have the option to be law-abiding.*"[68]

Life in a Box thus engages precision consistently, without, however, either agreeing to enter its population logic or seeming free to evade it. In "MO[DERN] [FRAME]," Martin introduces a voice that seems to ask to be framed by modernism by offering itself as nature, object, and muse: "My body aflame with it, can't you see? Make an outline around my form. Use your chisel. I will indulge your every little fit, I, your perfect muse, your ____ ____, your everything, also your nothing."[69] This voice appears to speak for a sharp-edged nature who requires precision, a tight fit made by a cutting tool, a chisel. "Adequate me," this voice seems to say. Yet "your every little fit," precision's offices of adequation to the real, must be "indulge[d]," and thus seem indistinguishable from fits of rage, which impose a form rather than accurately meet a preexisting one (as, indeed, chisels usually do). The enclosure of an "outline around my form" is reprised as literal black boxes on the page. The "black box" in engineering is a modular unit whose workings are unknown and need not be known; in other words, it contains the technical details that can only ever matter to a specialized few. Yet here, the technical details have a voice—what, just earlier in the poem, is called by another voice "the object" that "lures us into a belief that she is indeed human."[70]

The poem does not stage moral indignation at a person being treated like a thing, then, so much as an inhabitation of the space of the commodity that speaks, in the knowledge that such enclosures of human life are indeed capitalist modernity's "everything, also [its] nothing," precision ironized by who, or what, has been constituted in advance as a "nature" that talks back, but only just.[71] In this way, Martin's poems offer a critique of epistemic virtue in the philosophical sense, an unfolding of its seduction scene in all its gory detail. The poems thus enact what Mackey might call a "discrepant engagement," open to "noise," in Mackey's sonic register, perhaps, yet equally in the informatic register of potentially *bad data*, not to jam the signal (noise is already part of the signal) but because epistemic virtue is not necessarily a matter of choice.[72]

A screaming comes across the sky: not a weapon and yet a weapon. Where does it land? Precision targeting claims: "just where we want it to land, strategically, smartly, cleanly."[73] Experimentalism says: with the right counter-communication, by repurposing epistemic virtue, we can reroute the bomb, take it away, perhaps usher in intergalactic peace, and prove ourselves speakers of the language of the future. But with slow violence now everywhere more visible, we might say: the bomb has already landed; it never stops exploding, and we are in its wreckage.[74]

Now what?

Notes

Preface

1. With apologies to Steven Shapin, from whom this line is stolen. Shapin, *The Scientific Revolution*, 1.

2. Latour, *We Have Never Been Modern*.

3. The phrase is originally attributed Plato, in the *Phaedrus*. See also Campbell, O'Rourke, and Slater, *Carving Nature at Its Joints*. On technologies that work, see canonical anthropological studies of technologies of divination and ritual that work, e.g., Rappaport, *Pigs for the Ancestors*; Lansing, *Priests and Programmers*; Dove, "Uncertainty, Humility, and Adaptation in the Tropical Forest"; Helmreich, "Power/Networks."

4. I am mindful of Kyla Schuller's caution that gender is already a racialized category. Schuller, *The Biopolitics of Feeling*, 17.

5. Dimock, "Education Populism."

6. Michelle Murphy insightfully discusses the GDP as a "phantasmagram," a social science metric invested with affective charge. Murphy, *The Economization of Life*, 24–25.

7. Gallagher, "Formalism and Time," 231.

8. Taussig, *Defacement*, 1.

9. E. Wilson, "The Theatre," 421–22.

10. I refer here to Achille Mbembe's concept of "necropolitics" as the biopolitics' concomitant, the management of premature death and prevented life. Mbembe, "Necropolitics."

11. Dimock's recent writing on "experimental humanities" merges the older "experimental" discourse with funding-scarce post–Cold War formations that emphasize foundation funding and one-off grants. The language of virtue pervades this work. See Dimock, "Experimental Humanities"; Dimock, "Education Populism."

12. See, for example, Hejinian, "En Face."

13. Harney and Moten, *The Undercommons*, 97–98; Sharpe, *In the Wake*.

14. I. Reed, *Mumbo Jumbo*, 204. *Mumbo Jumbo* has become a touchstone for discussions of Afrofuturism; see especially A. Nelson, "Introduction: Future Texts."

Chapter 1. Experimental

1. Speaking with cetaceans was the dream of the neurophysiologist and renegade marine biologist John C. Lilly, founder of the Communications Research Institute, which was funded by, among others, the Office of Naval Research, the National Science Foundation, and NASA. D. Graham Burnett argues that Lilly's research programs should be "understood not as madcap '1960s-style' *antitheses* to the buttoned-down world of military bioscience, but rather as their very apotheosis." Lilly, *Man and Dolphin*, 159; Burnett, *The Sounding of the Whale*, 582.

2. R. Mitchell, *Experimental Life*, 5. See also Díaz, *The Experimenters*, 3.

3. By this I mean not only poetic form but also the formalism of attaching literary experimentalism to "the scientific method," a form that requires historicization and serious reconsideration. For examples of formalist accounts of experimentalism, see, for example, Golding, "Experimental Modernisms"; Drucker, "Experimental Writing (or Poetry Lab)"; Viegener, "Experimental Writing"; Bray, Gibbons, and McHale, *The Routledge Companion to Experimental Literature*.

4. The subtitle to Ron Silliman's Language anthology *In the American Tree* points to the centrality of "realism" in conceptions of the experimental. Silliman, *In the American Tree*. See also Hejinian, "Two Stein Talks."

5. Silver, "September 24, 1960."

6. In reality, the *Enterprise* was deployed during the time of shooting, and scenes were instead filmed on the USS *Ranger* (CV-61). See Rayner, *The Naval War Film*, 165. Rayner incorrectly names the setting of *Star Trek IV* as "San Diego."

7. Capshew and Rader, "Big Science," 4.

8. Audra J. Wolfe provides an invaluable bibliography on big science and the military-industrial complex in *Competing with the Soviets*, 145–48.

9. Ghamari-Tabrizi, *The Worlds of Herman Kahn*; Wolfe, *Competing with the Soviets*; Wolfe, *Freedom's Laboratory*; Erickson et al., *How Reason Almost Lost Its Mind*; Collignon, *Rocket States*. On the "cultural cold war," see, for example, Winks, *Cloak & Gown*; Saunders, *The Cultural Cold War*; Barnhisel, *Cold War Modernists*; Price, *Cold War Anthropology*.

10. Even extremely scrupulous studies, like Peter Middleton's *Physics Envy*, often default to the language of "experiment" as a generic description for "testing out" literary and conceptual forms. Middleton, *Physics Envy*, 47.

11. On ideologies of invention and their contradictions, see, primarily, de Man, "Literary History and Literary Modernity." For examinations in modernism in particular, see Levenson, "Novelty, Modernity, Adjacency"; North, *Novelty*; Rasula, "Make It New."

12. This is, of course, again overlaid by what *I* am ready to see.

13. Baucom, *Specters of the Atlantic*, 29.

14. Clover, "The Genealogical Avant-Garde."

15. Baucom, *Specters of the Atlantic*, 43–44; Chandler, *England in 1819*.

16. Baucom, 43. My emphasis.

17. As I discuss below, the rejection of typicality is one reason experimentalism has had such difficulty imagining "identity categories" as amenable to experimental modes.

18. Grimstad, *Experience and Experimental Writing*, 42–64; Hejinian, "Two Stein Talks"; Zola, *Le roman expérimental*. A second version of this genealogy, forwarded by Marjorie Perloff, Paul Stephens, Craig Dworkin, and some others, dwells more extensively on the European avant-garde and especially the French 'pataphysical tradition. Engaging fully with this tradition is beyond this book's scope. For the moment, I will say that this investment in experimentalism's purported internationalism effaces, willingly or otherwise, the intertwining of the "experimental tradition" with US hegemony in the twentieth century, which this book is concerned to draw out. James Laughlin in particular was actively involved in Cold War cultural diplomacy. See Perloff, *The Poetics of Indeterminacy*; Stephens, "What Do We Mean by 'Literary Experimentalism'?"; Dworkin, *Reading the Illegible*.

19. Pound, "How to Read," 17.

20. "The Egoist"; "Are You a Connoisseur of Art?"; Winters, "Primitivism and Decadence." Although *Primitivism and Decadence* was first published as a standalone by Arrow Editions (1937), other works in the collection in which it soon after appeared, *In Defense of Reason*, were first published by New Directions (*Maule's Curse*, *The Anatomy of Nonsense*).

21. Barnhisel, *Cold War Modernists*, 179.

22. Stephens, "What Do We Mean by 'Literary Experimentalism'?," 146. There are a few salient counterexamples, probably the most famous of which is Wallace Stevens's (postwar) aphorism in the posthumously published *Adagia*, "All poetry is experimental poetry." On the trope of experiment in midcentury performance-oriented arts, see especially Eva Díaz's *The Experimenters*. Stevens, *Opus Posthumous*; Díaz, *The Experimenters*.

23. If, as Anthony Reed has observed to me in conversation, accounts of experimental writing too often lead to Language writing as its logical end point, this is by design: what we now call "experimental writing" is a retrospective history largely instituted by Language writers (in their capacities both as creative writers and as critics) and sympathetic critics including Jed Rasula, Marjorie Perloff, Jerome McGann, and Alan Golding. There is no reason to suppose that this self-justifying critical project was undertaken in bad faith or for self-serving ends; indeed, there are strong historical motivations that warrant it, although Language has also been justly subject to criticism as well.

24. Kane, *"Do You Have a Band?,"* 197.

25. C. Bernstein, "Poetry Scene Investigation," 240. Bernstein is referring to his MLA address "The Academy in Peril."

26. Perelman, *The Marginalization of Poetry*, 12.

27. Perloff, "Pound/Stevens," 486.

28. Perloff, *The Poetics of Indeterminacy*, 44.

29. McGann, "Contemporary Poetry, Alternate Routes," 626.

30. I use "post-Vietnam" here and throughout to provisionally indicate the late Cold War period, in part for convenience and in part because the Vietnam War serves as such a powerful political touchstone for late twentieth-century experimental writers. I wish to acknowledge, however, that the "post-" greatly oversimplifies that war and its aftermath.

31. Sorensen, *Ethnic Modernism and the Making of US Literary Multiculturalism*, 140.

32. Lyotard, *The Postmodern Condition*, 5.

33. Lyotard, 8.

34. Lyotard, 3.

35. Cohn, "Sex and Death in the Rational World of Defense Intellectuals," 687.

36. Cohn, 704.

37. Cohn, 709.

38. McGann, "Contemporary Poetry, Alternate Routes," 643. McGann's position here was opposed soon thereafter, notably by Charles Altieri, but viewing it in a historical light, McGann's assessment of the logic of experimentalism is basically sound. See also Altieri, "An Idea and Ideal of a Literary Canon."

39. Saunders, *The Cultural Cold War*; Barnhisel, *Cold War Modernists.*

40. Shapin and Schaffer, *Leviathan and the Air-Pump*, 332.

41. Wittgenstein, *Philosophical Investigations*, 6.

42. Wittgenstein, 7; Jameson, *The Political Unconscious.*

43. Cohn, "Sex and Death in the Rational World of Defense Intellectuals," 687. More recently, Mark Seltzer has theorized such language games as hypertrophied autonomous art works. See Seltzer, *The Official World.*

44. Hejinian, "Barbarism," 325.

45. Ngai, *Ugly Feelings*, 303–4.

46. Melley, *Empire of Conspiracy*, 2.

47. Erickson et al., *How Reason Almost Lost Its Mind.*

48. Hejinian, "Barbarism," 323–24.

49. On Language writers' centering of knowledge, see also Middleton, *Physics Envy*, 21.

50. McGann, *Towards a Literature of Knowledge*, 7. My emphasis.

51. Hacking, *Representing and Intervening*, 23. Emphasis in the original.

52. Hacking, 24.

53. We could map this opposition to the structuralist opposition between writing and speech that Jacques Derrida deconstructs in *Of Grammatology*.

54. Silliman, "Poetry and the Politics of the Subject," 62.

55. Lyotard, *The Postmodern Condition*, 3.

56. Cantor, "The Rhetoric of Experiment"; Gooding, Pinch, and Schaffer, *The Uses of Experiment*; Shapin and Schaffer, *Leviathan and the Air-Pump*; Daston and Galison, *Objectivity*.

57. Nimoy, *Star Trek IV*.

58. Marshall, *American Experimental Poetry and Democratic Thought*, 1–2. Marshall thus also subtly implies that, e.g., Whitman and Dickinson are not "innovative," revealing how these terms can strategically shift roles from historical (here "innovative" is used to mean "early-twentieth-century modernist") to transhistorical and back.

59. Perelman, "My Avant-Garde Card," 881.

60. There is substantial criticism on early twentieth-century literature and science, much of which I discuss in the chapters that follow. See, for example, Albright, *Quantum Poetics*; Bell, *Critic as Scientist*; Ebury, *Modernism and Cosmology*; Fleissner, *Women, Compulsion, Modernity*; Hegeman, *Patterns for America*; Manganaro, *Culture, 1922*; Paul, *Poetry in the Museums of Modernism*; Seitler, *Atavistic Tendencies*; Seltzer, *Bodies and Machines*; Whitworth, *Einstein's Wake*.

61. Shapin, *The Scientific Life*, 32. Shapin is alluding to the seventeenth century, but the statement applies perhaps even more aptly to the turn of the twentieth.

62. Rudolph, "Epistemology for the Masses," 345; Porter, "How Science Became Technical," 296; Cowles, "Hypothesis Bound," 636; Bacon, *Francis Bacon*.

63. Such characterizations looked back to Baconian induction as an intellectual resource, including the suggestion that a single inductive method could be equally applied to political and moral problems. Yeo, "Scientific Method and the Rhetoric of Science in Britain, 1830–1917," 260, 262.

64. Yeo, 262.

65. Montessori, *The Montessori Method*, 16, 9.

66. Rudolph, "Epistemology for the Masses," 365–66.

67. Rudolph, 366.

68. Rudolph, 368.

69. Rudolph, 372.

70. Pearson, *The Grammar of Science*, 12.

71. Pearson, 35.

72. Freud, *Introductory Lectures on Psycho-analysis*, 19.

73. Freud, 21, 23.

74. Freud, 23.

75. Freud, 24.

76. Montessori, *The Montessori Method*, 5.

77. Montessori, 12.

78. Montessori, 7, 9, Montessori's emphasis.

79. Michel Foucault has outlined how the emergence of the "human sciences" in the early part of the nineteenth century may be understood as resulting from discoveries that "knowledge has anatomo-physiological conditions"—that, in other words, knowledge cannot be altogether independent of the knower's body. As Jonathan Crary glosses the situation in his account of "subjective vision," "the viewing body and its objects begin to constitute a single field on which inside and outside are confounded. Perhaps most importantly, both observer and observed are subject to the same modes of empirical study." Foucault specifies that the "human sciences" do not extend scientific positivity to a preexisting domain ("man" [*sic*]), "for man did not exist"; rather, for Foucault, the emerging human sciences call their domain of study ("man" [*sic*]) into being, insofar as they construct human beings as the site of knowledge and "the foundation of all positivities." Foucault's caution—fundamentally a historicist one—is important. Yet I also wish to account for the ways that Pearson, Freud, and Montessori (and many more) explicitly describe the expansion of the sciences in exactly the terms that Foucault defends against. See Foucault, *The Order of Things*, 344–45; Crary, *Techniques of the Observer*, 73.

80. Zola's essays should not necessarily be taken as reliable indicators of his thought. The Goncourt brothers, in particular, reported in their journal that Zola himself disclaimed his theoretical writings as "just so much charlatanism to puff my books." Puff his books they did, however, in the process becoming one of the most famous early statements on literary experimentalism. Goncourt and Goncourt, *Pages from the Goncourt Journal*, 229.

81. Bernard, *Introduction à l'étude de la médecine expérimentale*.

82. Zola, *Le roman expérimental*, 59. Translations from French are my own unless otherwise noted.

83. Bridgman, *Gertrude Stein in Pieces*, 357. Psychology would not become an autonomous department at Harvard until 1934, when Stein was already famous as the author of *The Autobiography of Alice B. Toklas*. See Pattullo, "About the Department."

84. Pearson, *The Grammar of Science*, 24.

85. This is not to minimize the dynamism of the physical sciences in this period. Additionally, not all physical sciences were stably experimental—the "physical science" of astronomy is, in 1865, Claude Bernard's canonical example of an "observational" science. Schuster and Watchirs, "Natural Philosophy, Experiment and Discourse," 1; Bernard, *Introduction à l'étude de la médecine expérimentale*, 30.

86. Bernard, 20.

87. On the fallacies and limitations of this narrative, see, e.g., Bensaude-Vincent, "A Historical Perspective on Science and Its 'Others.'"

88. On popularization in the United States, see Pandora, "Popular Science in National and Transnational Perspective"; Lucier, "The Professional and the Scientist in Nineteenth-Century America"; Pandora and Rader, "Science in the Everyday World."

Pandora thoughtfully parallels the Gilded Age turn to professionalization/popularization in the sciences to the divergence of the cultural "brows" mapped by Lawrence Levine. I would add a third parallel: Leonard Diepeveen's focus, specifically, on the "professionalizing" effects of modernist difficulty. See Pandora, "Popular Science in National and Transnational Perspective," 357; Levine, *Highbrow/Lowbrow*; Diepeveen, *The Difficulties of Modernism*, 96–104.

89. Cecire, "Marianne Moore's Precision," 98–101.

90. On the role of technicians in scientific practice, see, among others, Shapin, "The House of Experiment in Seventeenth-Century England"; Daston and Galison, *Objectivity*.

91. Daston and Galison, 39.

92. Daston and Galison, 40.

93. Against epistemic virtues, historians of science have also detected a countervirtue, or what Matthew Hunter, in a study of Restoration experimental science, has called a "wicked intelligence" with which certain practitioners "effectively courted a shady reputation," in a manner that perhaps anticipates experimental writing's embrace of the "oppositional." Hunter, *Wicked Intelligence*, 22.

94. Daston and Galison, *Objectivity*, 41.

95. Daston and Galison, 41.

96. Wordsworth and Coleridge, *Wordsworth and Coleridge*, 287.

97. Poovey, *A History of the Modern Fact*, 327.

98. Altieri, "What Theory Can Learn from New Directions in Contemporary American Poetry," 65; Hinton and Hogue, *We Who Love to Be Astonished*.

99. Retallack, *The Poethical Wager*, 3.

100. Watten, *The Constructivist Moment*, 16–25.

101. Perloff, "Language Poetry and the Lyric Subject," 433.

102. G. C. White, *Lyric Shame*, 4–5. See especially White's valuable account of Perloff and others' reinterpretation of M. H. Abrams on the lyric (214–23). Even Keston Sutherland, a contemporary experimental writer who is a tireless defender of Wordsworth and of Romantic lyric in general against what he has argued are lazy and under-nuanced characterizations, does so against a general anti-Romantic grain. See, e.g., Sutherland, "A Response to Jasper Bernes, Joshua Clover and Juliana Spahr."

103. This relentless disidentification may have something to do with the Romantic lyric's status as a privileged object of deconstructive criticism, an intellectual current with which Language writing has long been associated. I am grateful to an anonymous peer reviewer for this observation. Ironically, however, deconstructive criticism has tended to read the Romantic lyric subject as anything but unitary.

104. Retallack is a salient example. See *The Poethical Wager*.

105. One affordance of the "epistemic virtue" as an analytic tool is that it, too, can accommodate a wide variety of forms.

106. See, for example, Abrams, *The Mirror and the Lamp*; N. Jackson, *Science and*

Sensation in Romantic Poetry; R. Mitchell, *Experimental Life*. For the application of the "scienciness" criterion of experimentalism in a nineteenth-century US context, see Grimstad, *Experience and Experimental Writing*.

107. Oreskes and Conway, *Merchants of Doubt*.

108. See, for instance, Alder, "The History of Science as Oxymoron"; Daum, "Varieties of Popular Science and the Transformations of Public Knowledge"; Gordin, *The Pseudoscience Wars*; Latour, *We Have Never Been Modern*; Wallis, *On the Margins of Science*; Wallis, "Science and Pseudo-science." Gordin gives a particularly useful brief overview of the debate, including the place of the oft-cited Popperian "falsifiability" within it.

109. A classic example of such codetermination is elaborated in Shapin and Schaffer, *Leviathan and the Air-Pump*. See especially Shapin and Schaffer's account of Robert Boyle's "literary technology."

110. I. Armstrong, *Victorian Glassworlds*; Beer, *Darwin's Plots*; Beer, *Open Fields*; DeWitt, *Moral Authority, Men of Science, and the Victorian Novel*; G. L. Levine, *One Culture*; G. L. Levine, *Dying to Know*; G. L. Levine, *Realism and Representation*; G. L. Levine, *Darwin Loves You*; Otis, *Membranes*; Shuttleworth, *The Mind of the Child*.

111. Hejinian notes Zola's "experimental novel" as a forebear to the experimentalism in which she is interested (and which she will trace in Stein), largely on the basis of what I would call Zola's commitment to epistemic virtues. But she balks at the level of form, arguing that, pace the French naturalists, "it is precisely a special way of writing that realism requires." "Two Stein Talks," 89.

112. Pound, "How to Read," 17–18.

113. Laughlin, *Spearhead*, 10.

114. I am indebted to Daniel Kane for this observation.

115. Stephens, "What Do We Mean by 'Literary Experimentalism'?," 149–50; Perloff, *The Poetics of Indeterminacy*; Perloff, *Unoriginal Genius*; Wertheim and Viegener, *The Noulipian Analects*. I would argue that the 'pataphysical tradition running from Jarry through the Oulipo to conceptualism is invested in an altogether different epistemological frame than is experimentalism—what I call "puerility"—but an exploration of this mode is beyond the scope of this book.

116. Ross, *Fast Cars, Clean Bodies*, 176–96. See also Liu, *The Freudian Robot*, 167.

117. Barnhisel, *Cold War Modernists*, 182; Laughlin, *Spearhead*.

118. This whiteness is complicated by the shifting status of American Jewishness over the twentieth century.

119. Perelman, *The Marginalization of Poetry*, 11.

120. I take this version of the formulation from Nicholls. Nicholls, "Difference Spreading." See also Nicholls, "Beyond the Cantos," 152.

121. See Ferguson, *The Reorder of Things*.

122. Epstein, "Verse vs. Verse," 46.

123. Epstein, "Verse vs. Verse," 48. For a thoughtful treatment of creative writing

pedagogy's relationship to poets' institutionalization in the academy, see Andrews, "Trade Secrets."

124. Many experimental writers have been critical of the poetry workshop model, while also being implicated in it. See, for example, Juliana Spahr's economic and political critique of the MFA structure. Spahr, "How to Teach Writing."

125. C. Bernstein, "The Academy in Peril," 244.

126. Perelman, *The Marginalization of Poetry*, 15.

127. For some analyses of the ways that recovery projects produce the conditions of legibility for recovered texts, see Carby, "The Politics of Fiction, Anthropology, and the Folk"; Limón, "The Return of the Mexican Ballad"; Sorensen, *Ethnic Modernism and the Making of US Literary Multiculturalism*. For a critique of producing legibility in the terms of "theory," see Christian, "The Race for Theory."

128. There are some productive sites of overlap and dissent in these structures that are beyond the scope of this book. Theresa Hak Kyung Cha's *Dictée* has had a double life across ethnic studies and experimental writing, as Timothy Yu has explored, for example. Another avenue of inquiry might be the lesbian communist poet Karen Brodine, a co-founder of Berkeley's Kelsey Street Press. Brodine writes in her poem "Response to L-A-N-G-U-A-G-E" of the contrast between its "experimental" stance toward language and the violent physical silencing of gay women workers. Yu, *Race and the Avant-Garde*, 100–37; Brodine, *Illegal Assembly*, 51–52; Solomon, "Offsetting Queer Literary Labor," 260.

129. See Rakosi, *Collected Prose*; Heller, *Carl Rakosi*, and Silliman, *In the American Tree*.

130. National Poetry Foundation, "NFP Alumni." Although the 2000 conference claims a whole decade, the title "The Opening of the Field"—the title of a book by Robert Duncan—clearly announces some affinities.

131. *Sagetrieb* was retired in 2014, its scope folded into *Paideuma*. Bernstein notes *Sagetrieb*, along with *Credences* and *boundary 2*, as a home for "other traditions" that "flourish outside official verse culture." C. Bernstein, "The Academy in Peril," 248.

132. Here, as elsewhere, there is, if not gender parity, a nontrivial attention to white female writers, including H.D., Marianne Moore, Gertrude Stein, and Denise Levertov. Attention to writers belonging to racial minorities, in contrast, is minimal.

133. Harris, "Editing after Pound," 108.

134. Such journals include *Open Letter*, *This*, *How2*, *Poetics Journal*, and of course *L=A=N=G=U=A=G=E*.

135. Hejinian, "En Face."

136. Mullen, "Untitled," 11. "Official verse culture" is a term popularized by Charles Bernstein.

137. D. Wang, *Thinking Its Presence*, xxii. On the integration of white feminism, we can draw attention to the prominence of Lyn Hejinian, Joan Retallack, Susan Howe, Fanny Howe, Johanna Drucker, Carla Harryman, Rae Armantrout, Kathleen

Fraser, and Juliana Spahr, among others, in experimentalist anthologies and criticism, as well as the pride of place that Gertrude Stein has taken in Language's critical construction of an early twentieth-century experimental tradition. See also Hinton and Hogue, *We Who Love to Be Astonished*; Bergvall et al., *I'll Drown My Book*. This is not to say that this integration was not hard won or is uncontested even now, but there is a long-standing, identifiable, and prominent white feminist strain in experimental discourses. See, e.g., Armantrout, "Why Don't Women Do Language-Oriented Writing?"

138. See especially D. Wang's response to Steve Evans, in *Thinking Its Presence*, 15.

139. D. Wang, 31–32.

140. See, e.g., Silliman, "Poetry and the Politics of the Subject."

141. Mackey, *Discrepant Engagement*; Moten, *In the Break*; A. Reed, *Freedom Time*; Shockley, *Renegade Poetics*; D. Wang, *Thinking Its Presence*; Yu, *Race and the Avant-Garde*. See also Gladman and singleton, "Expanding the Repertoire." For a succinct, widely read account, see Hong, "Delusions of Whiteness in the Avant-Garde."

142. A. Reed, *Freedom Time*, 216–17n15.

143. Bradway, "Introduction," 2.

144. Wang has similarly pointed out instances of "myopic cluelessness" among white contemporary writers; she is right to identify them, of course, but I hope to explain here why it is not the whole story. See D. Wang, *Thinking Its Presence*, 15.

145. See, for example, C. Bernstein, "Gertrude Stein's War Years." For a nuanced look at Stein's wartime politics, see "Gertrude Stein and the War She Saw," in Galvin, *News of War: Civilian Poetry, 1936–1945*, 278–305.

146. Mullen, "Poetry and Identity," 31; Heim, "Race and the Poetic Avant-Garde." Another signal intervention is the *Tripwire* special issue "Expanding the Repertoire," based on a 2000 conference hosted by Small Press Traffic and New College in San Francisco.

147. For an analysis of a generalized oppositionality in relation to anticapitalist activism, see Kreiner, "The Politics of Language Writing and the Subject of History."

148. Here I use "white" catachrestically to denote racial unmarkedness in a US context; it is not, obviously, a stable category.

149. Pound, "Commission," 10.

150. Interpreting modernist form as embodying liberation and freedom would come to be a standard move of the cultural Cold War, though Pound himself, recently convicted of treason, was persona non grata among CIA- and Congress for Cultural Freedom–sponsored activities. See Barnhisel, *Cold War Modernists*, 28, 114.

151. Pound, "How to Read," 21; Pound, *ABC of Reading*, 32, 20.

152. Spahr, *Everybody's Autonomy*.

153. Yu, *Race and the Avant-Garde*, 58. These racist, misogynistic, and homophobic slurs are spelled out in the original. I have chosen to elide them here.

154. This is not to discount their real political marginalization as anti-war protestors and, in many cases, communists.

155. Yu, *Race and the Avant-Garde*, 3.

156. Hale, *A Nation of Outsiders*.

157. Yu, *Race and the Avant-Garde*, 60.

158. 8C. Bernstein, "The Academy in Peril," 246.

159. Yu, *Race and the Avant-Garde*, 14. 16.

160. Watten, "The Turn to Language and the 1960s," 189.

161. Retallack, *The Poethical Wager*, 3.

162. Retallack, 3.

163. Retallack, 3.

164. McGann, "Contemporary Poetry, Alternate Routes," 625. I am deliberately aligning this narrative of an opposition between "oppositional" ("experimental") and "accommodationist" ("expressive," "Official Verse Culture") poetics with C. P. Snow's "two cultures" thesis: "scientific" and "humanistic" cultures and temporalizations are in fact exactly what are being claimed for these two poetic strands.

165. McGann, 643.

166. Wittgenstein, *Philosophical Investigations*, 7; Shapin and Schaffer, *Leviathan and the Air-Pump*, 332.

167. C. Bernstein, "The Academy in Peril," 245; Barnhisel, *Cold War Modernists*, 247-48, Barnhisel's emphasis. For a view of midcentury *attacks* on "experimental" modernism that saw modernist form as a proxy for communism, see Filreis, *Counter-revolution of the Word*.

168. C. Bernstein, "The Academy in Peril," 244, my emphasis.

169. My point is not that Williams lacked political virtue—he had his moments—but rather that we need not assume that it derives from his poetics.

170. C. Bernstein, "The Academy in Peril," 245, Bernstein's emphasis.

171. Sorensen, *Ethnic Modernism and the Making of US Literary Multiculturalism*, 125-126, 131.

172. Nguyen, *The Gift of Freedom*, x.

173. Charette, "The STEM Crisis Is a Myth."

174. Holsinger, *Neomedievalism, Neoconservatism, and the War on Terror*.

175. For example, the authors of the "Ecomodernist Manifesto" name their embrace of technology and (concomitantly) of capitalist growth as a "modernism." See Asafu-Adjaye et al., "The Ecomodernist Manifesto."

176. I am grateful to Lindsey Andrews for pointing this out.

177. Bray, Gibbons, and McHale, *The Routledge Companion to Experimental Literature*; Emerson, *Reading Writing Interfaces*, 76-77.

178. There is, of course, something tendentious in seeing electronic literature as any more "technology bound" than other "born-digital" contemporary literature—

say, the novels of Salman Rushdie, composed in Microsoft Word. See Emory University Library, "Finding Aid, Salman Rushdie Papers."

179. Sidney, *The Defense of Poesy*, 2.

180. Sidney, 4.

181. Peacock, "The Four Ages of Poetry," 15.

182. Foucault, *The Order of Things*, 31.

183. Foucault, 42–43. My emphasis.

184. Consequently, the contemporary practice among politicians and education officials of warning students that taking arts and humanities subjects will ruin their futures is not just a symptom of recent neoliberal cynicism (although it is that too); it rests on a literally centuries-old belief about the temporal structure of the disciplines. Hutchison, "Education Secretary Nicky Morgan"; Kennicott, "President Obama Disses Culture with 'Art History Degree' Punch Line"; Murai, "Subsidies Used as Carrot to Prod National Universities to Streamline, Ditch Humanities."

185. Perelman, "My Avant-Garde Card," 893; Hejinian, "Some Notes toward a Poetics," 241.

186. Hejinian, "Barbarism," 325–26, emphasis in the original.

187. Luxemburg attributes the formulation to Friedrich Engels, although the source has not been located. The phrase was later taken up in condensed form by the French radical group Socialisme ou Barbarie. Adorno, "Cultural Criticism and Society," 35; Luxemburg, *The Crisis in the German Social-Democracy*, 18.

188. De Man, "Literary History and Literary Modernity," 148. Note that only a few years later (2000), Hejinian drops the trope of "barbarism" in favor of *xenos*. See Hejinian, "Some Notes toward a Poetics," 235.

189. Harding, *Sciences from Below*, 1. See also Latour, *We Have Never Been Modern*, 73.

190. So far the humpback whale is not yet extinct.

191. Nimoy, *Star Trek IV*; Nichols, *The Day of the Dolphin*. According to Burnett, "at least two" Marine Mammal Program dolphin training programs "were operationalized as navy 'systems'; and . . . by 1970–1971, a number of navy dolphins accompanied a specialized team of navy divers to Cam Ranh Bay, in Vietnam, where they were deployed in a program to stop Vietcong sappers," although "the actual deployment in Vietnam . . . remains clouded in rumor." *The Day of the Dolphin* is loosely based on the life of John C. Lilly, the aforementioned director of the government-funded Cetacean Research Institute who sought to communicate with dolphins. See Burnett, *The Sounding of the Whale*, 598, 621.

192. Latour, *We Have Never Been Modern*, 93.

193. As noted above, the *Enterprise* was deployed during the time of shooting, and scenes were instead filmed on the *U.S.S. Ranger* (CV-61). The resonance between the two *Enterprise*s is very deliberate, however; the aircraft carrier's name and hull classification symbol, CVN-65, are clearly visible in some shots. "CVN" indicates "Air-

craft Carrier, Nuclear-powered"; the *Ranger* was not nuclear powered and could not have fulfilled the nuclear power subplot. See Rayner, *The Naval War Film*, 165.

194. Nimoy, *Star Trek IV*.

195. Sun Ra's *Space Is the Place* (1974), which is set primarily in Oakland, is an instance of the related but different strategies attempted by Afrofuturism: Sun Ra's dissonant jazz has the same destructive power as whale song. The complexities of Afrofuturism in general and Sun Ra's persona in particular are well beyond the scope of this chapter, but it seems telling that even *Space Is the Place* requires a vision of a colony elsewhere, ready for the taking. Coney, *Space Is the Place*.

196. Laughlin, *Spearhead*, 10.

197. Perelman, "My Avant-Garde Card," 881.

198. Perelman, "My Avant-Garde Card," 882.

199. Ahmed, *The Promise of Happiness*, 143.

200. For Ahmed, this melancholia appears to be only alleged, a misreading of present grievance as an inappropriate pastness. Cheng's slightly stickier and perhaps more ambitious project is to take seriously the pathological morphology of racial injury without pathologizing those who experience it or "naturalizing that pain." Thus, for Cheng, racial melancholia is real, experienced by both injurers and injured, and requires a thoroughgoing rethinking of temporality altogether. See Cheng, *The Melancholy of Race*, 14, 7.

201. The concept of the "denial of coevalness" is elaborated in reference to the history of anthropology in Fabian, *Time and the Other*, 30. Dipesh Chakrabarty develops this further as "historicism" in *Provincializing Europe*, 8–9.

202. Nguyen, *The Gift of Freedom*, 17.

203. Paz, *Alternating Current*, 19.

Chapter 2. Flash

1. Poe, "The Man of the Crowd," 392.

2. Benjamin, "On Some Motifs in Baudelaire," 326.

3. Benjamin, *The Arcades Project*, 531 (Q2,6); Poe, "The Man of the Crowd," 392.

4. Poe, "The Man of the Crowd," 396.

5. Sekula, "The Body and the Archive," 55.

6. Crane, *Correspondence*, 310.

7. Because Lorraine Daston and Peter Galison's work has been so crucial to this project, it seems worth observing that their 2007 study *Objectivity* begins with a flash of light—"[the British physicist Arthur Worthington] lit his laboratory with a powerful millisecond flash" (11). For Daston and Galison, this flash is incidental, a means by which Worthington first observes the motion of droplets of liquid and then, in 1894, photographs it. The latter use of flash introduces into Worthington's investigations a version of objectivity, the scientific value that Daston and Galison are con-

cerned to historicize in their study. This chapter considers flash as not a stepping stone to objectivity but rather as an epistemic virtue in its own right, a set of protocols for seeing what might otherwise be missed. One of Harold Edgerton's updates to the Worthington liquid droplet images is the cover image for this book, and it is discussed briefly in chapter 4.

8. In this sense, Stephen Crane stands as a privileged example, although he is rarely called an "experimental" writer: his writing has been called "realist," "naturalist," "impressionist," and "modernist," such that critics like Michael Warner have concluded by eschewing literary-historical labels altogether. See Warner, "Value, Agency, and Stephen Crane's 'The Monster,'" 76–77.

9. As Seitler has succinctly observed, the idea of a sharp rupture between naturalism and modernism/avant-gardism is itself a historical artifact. Following Seitler and others, I believe that this sense of rupture should be acknowledged and examined, but not simply accepted. Seitler, *Atavistic Tendencies*, 16; Steinlight, "Populating the Novel," 3.

10. Pound, "I Gather the Limbs of Osiris (I–II)," 130.

11. Hacking, *Representing and Intervening*.

12. Hales, *Silver Cities*. Riis occasionally accidentally set the buildings he was photographing on fire.

13. Riis, "Flashes from the Slums," 10.

14. Kate Flint has usefully put pressure on just how instantaneous photographic flash has historically been. Flint, *Flash!*, 87–88.

15. Monteiro, *Stephen Crane*, 82. The majority of notices of *Maggie* appeared upon its reprinting in 1896, after the success of *The Red Badge of Courage*. Apart from the important notice of William Dean Howells, there was little critical reception of the novel on its first printing in 1893.

16. Riis, *How the Other Half Lives*.

17. Alan Trachtenberg echoes this assessment in 1974: "The story is, in effect, a retelling of a familiar plot: Maggie (the name itself was virtually generic), pure blossom of the slums, is driven—by indifference, selfishness, and sexual exploitation—first to streetwalking then to suicide in the East River. For Crane, the plot was an occasion to tell a familiar tale with vividness, with exactness of observation, and most of all, with sufficient irony to make it apparent that the characters themselves viewed their world melodramatically, through lenses blurred with the same false emotions they inspired—as 'low life'—in the many popular tellers of their tale." Trachtenberg, "Experiments in Another Country, 145."

18. On the realism of brief moments in fiction, see Underwood, "Why Literary Time Is Measured in Minutes," 357–59.

19. Monteiro, *Stephen Crane*, 4.

20. Weinstein, "How Many Others Are There in the Other Half?"

21. Riis, *How the Other Half Lives*, 5.

22. Weinstein, "How Many Others Are There in the Other Half?," 197.

23. Riis, *How the Other Half Lives*, 102.

24. Weinstein, "How Many Others Are in the Other Half?," 197, 201.

25. Riis, "Flashes from the Slums," 10.

26. Baer, "Photography and Hysteria," 42, 45.

27. Baer, 49.

28. Bourneville and Regnard, *Iconographie photographique de la Salpêtrière*.

29. Cady, introduction, xxiii.

30. Goldsby goes on to critique the mode of the sketch for its indirection, arguing that its light touches are complicit in white silence around antiblack terrorism (lynching). The sketch's affinity with other image-texts of the period, many of which explicitly work to encode whole arguments for social and racial normalization into single images, should offer another insight in to the ways in which the social knowledge it helped to produce was a racist one. The literary sketch's status as a form of flash is at once the grounds of its experimentalism (what Goldsby identifies as Crane's "modern" quality and his "literariness") and its indebtedness to a biopolitical knowledge that was fundamentally racist in its assumptions. This is not an argument about Crane's personal and explicit feelings about race, which would be beyond the scope of this book; rather, it is an argument about the formal structures of social thought in which he participated. Goldsby, *A Spectacular Secret*, 132.

31. Goldsby, 131.

32. Monteiro, *Stephen Crane*, 39.

33. I use "reality effect" not in Roland Barthes's sense of signifying a divorce between reality and meaning but rather to indicate that these are effects that suggest special purchase on reality. Barthes, "The Reality Effect."

34. "To create poetry = to condense." Pound, *ABC of Reading*, 36.

35. Porter, *The Rise of Statistical Thinking, 1820–1900*, 134; Mayr, *The Growth of Biological Thought*, 45–47.

36. Bigg, "The Panorama, or *La Nature à Coup d'Oeil*," 84.

37. Daston, "On Scientific Observation," 108.

38. Alexander Galloway, in the context of the numerous network visualizations that "all seem to resemble a large cauliflower floating free somewhere beyond the solar system," has called flash's attachment to the sublime an aesthetics of "unrepresentability." Galloway, *The Interface Effect*, 82, 86.

39. Murphy, *The Economization of Life*, 25.

40. Griffiths, *Wondrous Difference*, 4.

41. Lucas, *The Story of Museum Groups*, 32.

42. Battle scenes were a conventional subject of panoramas in the nineteenth century; two of the few presently surviving American panoramas are the Gettysburg Panorama, depicting the Civil War Battle of Gettysburg, and the Atlanta Cyclorama, depicting the Battle of Atlanta. War was also a favorite subject of cinema, and, as

Walter Benjamin argued, "mass movements, and above all war, are a form of human behavior especially suited to the camera." See Schwartz, *Spectacular Realities*, 153–54; B. Brown, *The Material Unconscious*, 134–35; Benjamin, "The Work of Art in the Age of Its Technological Reproducibility," 133n37.

43. Crane, "Death and the Child," 962.

44. Bigg, "The Panorama, or *La Nature à Coup d'Oeil*," 94. The contemporary was John D. Barry, in a letter to Crane (Monteiro, *Stephen* Crane, 3).

45. Crane, "Death and the Child," 950.

46. Crane, 946.

47. Crane, 963.

48. Seltzer, *Bodies and Machines*, 100.

49. Fried, *Realism, Writing, Disfiguration*, 141.

50. For example, Susan Mizruchi has emphasized the powerful strain in late nineteenth-century social science, endorsed by the influential British theorist Herbert Spencer, that imagined the diversity of US immigrants converging toward a homogeneously "American" subject position, conducing to what Mizruchi identifies as a "wholesale containment of subjective understanding." Mary Poovey has likewise described the authority of a nineteenth-century statistical discourse in which "the individual human being . . . is obliterated by the numerical average or aggregate that replaces him." See Mizruchi, "Cataloging the Creatures of the Deep," 278–79; Poovey, "Figures of Arithmetic, Figures of Speech," 414.

51. Calhoun, *Sociology in America*, 1–2, 13. As Calhoun points out, "sociology" at the turn of the twentieth century was deeply interarticulated with a variety of popular and professional practices and discourses; in particular, "sociology," the discipline to which Mizruchi alludes, and "statistics," which is Poovey's area of consideration, were understood as closely overlapping domains.

52. Hewes and Gannett, *Scribner's Statistical Atlas of the United States*, 18–20.

53. Hewes and Gannett, 20.

54. Gannett, *Statistical Atlas of the United States*.

55. Gannett, *Statistical Abstract of the World*, iii.

56. Gannett, *Statistical Abstract of the World*, iii.

57. Gannett, *Statistical Abstract of the World*, iii.

58. Daston, "On Scientific Observation," 108.

59. The title "Visible Darkness" seems to intentionally evoke John Milton's description of hell in *Paradise Lost*. On "Flashes from the Slums," see, e.g., Stange, "Jacob Riis and Urban Visual Culture," 280.

60. Hales, *Silver Cities*, 173.

61. Jones, *Cassell's Cyclopaedia of Photography*, 258.

62. Flint, "Surround, Background, and the Overlooked," 457.

63. Bazin, *What Is Cinema?*

64. Maren Stange has argued that Riis's live presentations also adopted the conventions *of* literary realism. Stange, "Jacob Riis and Urban Visual Culture," 291.

65. Kasson, *Rudeness & Civility*, 75–76. See also Flint's discussion of Helen Campbell's *Darkness and Daylight; or, Lights and Shadows of New York Life* (1891). Flint, *Flash!*, 102–6.

66. Kasson, *Rudeness & Civility*, 77.

67. Trotter, "Becoming Media."

68. "The Birth of a Nation."

69. Cohen et al., *The Flash Press*.

70. Crane, *Maggie*, 15. Subsequent references are made parenthetically in text.

71. Flint, *Flash!*, 103.

72. Monteiro, *Stephen Crane*, 50.

73. B. Brown, *The Material Unconscious*, 142.

74. Steinlight, "Populating the Novel," 8–9.

75. Poe, "The Man of the Crowd."

76. Murphy, *The Economization of Life*, 79.

77. Murphy, 135.

78. Silliman, *The New Sentence*, 11. It bears pointing out that the infographic is now a staple of "daily journalism."

79. On information, see Benjamin, "The Storyteller," 147–48.

80. Auerbach, *Scenes from the Drama of European Literature*, 34.

81. Bersani, *The Culture of Redemption*, 53.

82. Cooter and Pumphrey, "Separate Spheres and Public Places"; Gordin, *The Pseudoscience Wars*; Kohlstedt, "Parlors, Primers, and Public Schooling"; Wallis, "Science and Pseudo-science."

83. Daum, "Varieties of Popular Science and the Transformations of Public Knowledge," 320.

84. Pandora, "Popular Science in National and Transnational Perspective," 350.

85. Small, "The Era of Sociology," 6.

86. Murphy, *The Economization of Life*, 79.

87. Strictly speaking, Foucault is referring to discipline in this quotation, but, as he makes clear, the power he describes operates through "the body as one pole and the population as the other." Foucault, *"Society Must Be Defended,"* 37, 253.

88. Beasley, *Ezra Pound and the Visual Culture of Modernism*, 1, 51–54.

89. Harris, "Editing after Pound," 107. Over time, as Harris documents (114), *Sagetrieb*'s scope broadened to the "Pound—H.D.—Williams tradition" (1984), the "imagist/Objectivist tradition" (1987), and finally "poetry and poetics after modernism" (1999), before eventually being retired in a 2013 double issue with *Paideuma*, the Pound studies journal, which was to take on *Sagetrieb*'s former scope.

90. My treatment of Pound here is abbreviated, but it is worth pointing out a

further consonance between Pound's "luminous detail" and Benjamin's flash: their separate temporary uses of the "vortex" as a cognate figure. See Weigel, "The Flash of Knowledge and the Temporality of Images," 356-58.

91. Coyle, *Ezra Pound, Popular Genres, and the Discourse of Culture*, 121-47.

92. Pound, "I Gather the Limbs of Osiris (I-II)," 130.

93. Pound, "A Few Don'ts by an Imagiste."

94. Bateson, *Steps to an Ecology of Mind*, 459.

95. Pound, "I Gather the Limbs of Osiris (I-II)," 130. Beasley attributes some of this language to Hudson Maxim's *The Science of Poetry and the Philosophy of Language*, which Pound reviewed in 1910. Beasley, *Ezra Pound and the Visual Culture of Modernism*, 52-53.

96. Pound, *ABC of Reading*, 52.

97. Pound, *ABC of Reading*, 21.

98. Pound, *ABC of Reading*, 36; Pound, "A Few Don'ts by an Imagiste," 200.

99. Sherry, *Ezra Pound, Wyndham Lewis, and Radical Modernism*, 83.

100. Taussig, *Defacement*, 1.

101. Taussig, *Defacement*, 3, Taussig's emphasis.

102. Taussig, *Defacement*, 3.

103. Coyle, *Ezra Pound, Popular Genres, and the Discourse of Culture*, 141.

104. Tiffany, *Radio Corpse*.

105. Pound, *ABC of Reading*, 43.

106. Pound, *ABC of Reading*, 34.

107. Pound, *ABC of Reading*, 45, Pound's emphasis.

108. Daston, "Rev. of M. Norton Wise, Ed., *The Values of Precision*," 108.

109. Benjamin, "The Work of Art in the Age of Its Technological Reproducibility," 119.

110. Benjamin, "On the Concept of History," 390.

111. Weigel, "The Flash of Knowledge and the Temporality of Images," 344-45, Weigel's emphasis. In contrast with the genealogy of flash I have outlined in this chapter, Weigel sharply defends against an association between Benjamin's flash and the eighteenth-century *coup d'oeil*, with its suggestions of a divine "sovereign gaze," reading the Benjaminian flash (rightly, I think) not as a godlike view, but rather as aligned with the *reception* of divine revelation. Yet, following Taussig, I would put pressure on Weigel's distinction, given the remarkable reversibility of sacred and profane in the specific context of the kind of distinguishing knowledge that flash secures. Flash's optimistic, informational appeal to a clarity couched in darkness is not the Enlightenment *coup d'oeil*'s opposite but rather a later and fuller account of it, one that effects frequent reversals of seer and seen. See 348; Taussig, *Defacement*, 52.

112. Benjamin, "On the Concept of History," 396.

113. Benjamin, "On the Concept of History," 391.

114. Benjamin, "On the Concept of History," 390.

115. Gunning, "In Your Face," 25.

116. Taussig, *Defacement*, 3, 224.

117. Benjamin, "The Work of Art in the Age of Its Technological Reproducibility," 108.

118. Fried, *Realism, Writing, Disfiguration*, 99-101.

119. Tiffany, *Radio Corpse*, 2.

120. Genette, "Figures," 47, Genette's emphasis.

121. Genette, 49. Thus Lyn Hejinian castigates Zolian naturalism for failing to go far enough in his naturalist "experimental novel": "It is in Paul Alexis's statement that we see the limitations of the project already defined: 'a need to analyze in order to know, but not a special way of writing.' In fact, it is precisely a special way of writing that realism requires." Hejinian, "Two Stein Talks," 89.

122. On the figure's dubious supersessions, see also Snediker, "*Pierre* and the Non-transparencies of Figuration."

123. Taussig, *Defacement*, 53.

124. Warner, *Publics and Counterpublics*, 24.

125. Taussig, *Defacement*, 37.

126. Taussig, 51, Taussig's emphasis; Foucault, "Preface to Transgression," 35.

127. Foucault, *The History of Sexuality*, 1:25.

Chapter 3. Objectivity

1. Stein, *Writings, 1903-1932*, 4.

2. Nicholls, "Beyond *The Cantos*," 152.

3. Davidson et al., "Reading Stein."

4. C. Bernstein, "Gertrude Stein's War Years." On this controversy, the best account is Rachel Galvin's. Bernstein has also more recently traced the false allegation that Stein nominated Adolph Hitler for the Nobel Peace Prize to a single source, a "Gustav Hendrikssen," who, according to a dean at the Swedish university where he is supposed to have worked, appears to be "made up." Galvin, "Gertrude Stein, Pétain, and the Politics of Translation"; C. Bernstein, "Gertrude and Alice in Vichyland."

5. C. Bernstein, "Gertrude and Alice in Vichyland."

6. Hejinian, "Two Stein Talks," 89.

7. Keller, "Gender and Science."

8. Keller, "Gender and Science," 187.

9. Daston and Galison, *Objectivity*.

10. Daston and Galison, *Objectivity*, 198.

11. Eliot, "Tradition and the Individual Talent," 10-11. C. Miller takes this question up at length in *Marianne Moore*.

12. See Maria Farland's well researched account of Stein's attempt to publish during medical school in "Gertrude Stein's Brain Work," 124-25.

13. Stein, *Everybody's Autobiography*, 267.

14. It is worth pointing out that Barker, in addition to being an eminent physician, was an active eugenicist who translated the German physician and eugenicist Hermann W. Siemens's proto-Nazi treatise *Grundzüge der Rassenhygiene, zugleich Einführung in der Vererbungslehre* in 1924. Siemens, *Race Hygiene and Heredity*.

15. Stein, *Writings, 1932–1946*, 271.

16. On the importance of the idea of a split self in the nineteenth century, see Harrington, *Medicine, Mind, and the Double Brain*.

17. Unfortunately, it is beyond the scope of this chapter to explore in detail the way in which distraction was secured, namely through the reading of fiction, evidently popular fiction. "For distracting attention," Solomons observes, "literature that is easily followed and emotional in character is by far the best" (508). This literature played a crucial role in the experiment, and indeed in maintaining the scientific character of the experiment, since it was only through its distraction that the elements of "second personality" might be simulated at all. But the main criteria for identifying such scientifically useful literature were not the criteria of literary evaluation but rather its demands on cognition (ideally low) and affect (ideally high). The kinds of literature described by Solomons and Stein as useful for the experiment indeed seem distinctly pot-boilerish, and one throw-away comment—"dialect stories do not go well at all" (504)—attests to the eclecticism and openness to popular literature that may have attended the experiments. The literature of distraction used by Solomons and Stein may well be the same literature of distraction critiqued by social theorists like Walter Benjamin, who lamented "the replacement of the older narration by information, of information by sensation." Jonathan Crary has argued persuasively that the distraction that Benjamin diagnosed was only a part of a broader, pervasive dialectic of attention and distraction that rose to prominence at the end of the nineteenth century. See Crary, *Suspensions of Perception*, especially 49–51. Tim Armstrong, in a chapter titled "Distracted Writing," takes up Crary's critique with specific reference to "Normal Motor Automatism," arguing that Solomons and Stein's experiments in attention and distraction help map out the shift from the nineteenth-century notion of double personality into what Kittler calls the "discourse network circa 1900," in which writing is reconceived as "pure behavior." Armstrong, *Modernism, Technology, and the Body*, 205; Benjamin, "On Some Motifs in Baudelaire," 315.

18. Solomons and Stein, "Normal Motor Automatism," 493.

19. Solomons and Stein, 502, emphasis in the original.

20. Solomons and Stein, 511, emphasis in the original.

21. As Kittler wryly points out, "While German universities still trembled at the thought of the chaos women students would provoke, the Harvard Psychological Laboratory had long been desexualized. In their test report, Solomons and Stein are referred to throughout as 'he.' The scientific discourse gives only hints that during

this strange cooperation the man dictated and the woman wrote." Kittler, *Discourse Networks 1800/1900*, 227. The hints to which Kittler alludes appear on pp. 500 and 506 of "Normal Motor Automatism." Kittler's observation about the gendering of the paper's language—always a pseudo-neutral "he"—is well taken, but his suggestion that Stein was *always* the subject, and Solomons always the experimenter, is by no means clear from the article. According to Wilma Koutstaal, Solomons and Stein "served, in turn, as investigators and subjects." Stein's characterization of the study in "CMA," where she notes that the subjects were "ourselves," supports this view (295). Koutstaal, "Skirting the Abyss," 13.

22. Solomons and Stein, "Normal Motor Automatism," 496.

23. Solomons and Stein, 493.

24. Kittler, *Discourse Networks 1800/1900*, 219.

25. T. Armstrong, *Modernism, Technology, and the Body*, 198.

26. Will, *Gertrude Stein, Modernism, and the Problem of "Genius,"* 32–33.

27. Will, 34.

28. Stein, *Everybody's Autobiography*, 231.

29. Stein, "Cultivated Motor Automatism," 295–96.

30. Stein, "Cultivated Motor Automatism," 295.

31. Stimpson, "The Mind, the Body, and Gertrude Stein," 498.

32. Stein, "Cultivated Motor Automatism," 297.

33. Crary's study of modern fascination with the attention/distraction dialectic takes up many of the ramifications of this conception of attention that are beyond the scope of this chapter. See Chapter 1 of *Suspensions of Perception*.

34. Stein, "Cultivated Motor Automatism," 297.

35. Stein, "Cultivated Motor Automatism," 298.

36. Stein, "Cultivated Motor Automatism," 304.

37. Stein, "Cultivated Motor Automatism," 299.

38. Will, *Gertrude Stein, Modernism, and the Problem of "Genius,"* 33.

39. In this I follow L. Doyle, "The Flat, the Round, and Gertrude Stein," 263.

40. Meyer, *Irresistible Dictation*, 55–56.

41. Zola, *Nana*, 438. Sander Gilman discusses this moment in *Difference and Pathology*, 105. For a helpful reading of "Melanctha" through Nella Larsen's *Passing*, in the context of passing narratives of the period, see Blackmer, "African Masks and the Arts of Passing."

42. Delord, "La femme sans nom," 245. My translation.

43. Peter Brooks reads Nana in precisely this way in Brooks, "Storied Bodies, or Nana at Last Unveil'd."

44. The friend was Henri Céard. See F. Brown, *Zola*, 433–34.

45. Stein, *Writings, 1903–1932*, 239.

46. See also the numerous Harlem Renaissance narratives, for instance in Nella

Larsen's *Quicksand* or Jessie Fauset's *Plum Bun*, that describe light-skinned African Americans as being "yellow as a banana"—an image that, outside the slang conventions of the period, presents a jarring image.

47. M. A. Cohen, "Black Brutes and Mulatto Saints."

48. Stein, *Writings, 1932–1946*, 288.

49. Keller, *Reflections on Gender and Science*; Haraway, *Modest_Witness@Second_Millennium*; Harding, *The Science Question in Feminism*; Le Dœuff, *The Sex of Knowing*.

50. Oreskes, "Objectivity or Heroism?," 89.

51. Oreskes, "Objectivity or Heroism?," 106–7.

52. Farland, "Gertrude Stein's Brain Work," 134, 120. On the emphasis on research in the study of medicine at Johns Hopkins, see also Harvey, "A New School of Anatomy"; Harvey, "Creators of Clinical Medicine's Scientific Base."

53. Stein, *The Autobiography of Alice B. Toklas*, 82.

54. Farland, "Gertrude Stein's Brain Work," 123. Florence Rena Sabin (1871–1953) was, in Morgan's words, "a classmate of Stein's at Johns Hopkins. Sabin was three years older than Stein and a year ahead of her in medical school. They were acquaintances, thrown together with the other female students, yet their medical careers took different paths. Sabin was a talented embryological anatomist 'who is credited with discovering that the lymphatic vessels arise from endothelial budding from embryonic veins—a discovery that was confirmed only as late as 1999.'" She became "the first woman appointed to the Johns Hopkins medical faculty." Morgan, "The Embryography of Alice B. Toklas," 311–12.

55. Morgan, "The Embryography of Alice B. Toklas," 311n5. See also Morgan, *Icons of Life*, 101–4. On women's work in the sciences, see Rossiter, *Women Scientists in America*; Schiebinger, *The Mind Has No Sex?*; Kass-Simon, Farnes, and Nash, *Women of Science*; Oreskes, "Objectivity or Heroism?"; Galison, *Image and Logic*.

56. Huyssen, *After the Great Divide*, 70. As Georges Canguilhem has suggested, it is not so much that people and other organic beings are figured as machines as that machines are modeled on living beings in the first place. Canguilhem, "Machine and Organism." On women as figures of capitalist modernity, see F. Brown, *Zola*, 198; Felski, *The Gender of Modernity*; Fleissner, *Women, Compulsion, Modernity*; Huyssen, *After the Great Divide*.

57. See, for example, Grier, *When Computers Were Human*; and Hayles, *My Mother Was a Computer*.

58. Massey, "Leslie John Comrie, 1893–1950," 101; Campbell-Kelly and Aspray, *Computer*, 58. On women's computing in the British context, see Hicks, *Programmed Inequality*.

59. Massey, "Leslie John Comrie, 1893–1950," 99.

60. As Oreskes demonstrates in her case study of Eleanor Lamson—who was included in the 1927 edition of the unfortunately titled *American Men of Science*—women who were hired as "computers" were not necessarily engaged in machinic or

automatic tasks but in scientific research per se. Oreskes, "Objectivity or Heroism?," 91. The reality of the computer, like that of the typewriter, did not necessarily map accurately onto the narratives by which she was described (or paid). This reality does not, however, negate the power with which an allegedly machinic and unthinking female worker might come to signify a specifically scientific modernity. On women's work with typewriters, see Keep, "The Cultural Work of the Type-Writer Girl"; Thurschwell, "Supple Minds and Automatic Hands"; Price and Thurschwell, *Literary Secretaries/Secretarial Culture*.

61. Farland, "Gertrude Stein's Brain Work," 123.

62. Quoted in Schoenberg, "Gertrude Stein's Neuroanatomic Investigations," 251.

63. Daston and Galison, *Objectivity*, 121.

64. Daston and Galison, 123.

65. The stereotype of Asian labor as mechanical (and correspondingly rigid and uncreative) has a long history. See, for example, Lye, *America's Asia*, 5; Nakamura, *Cybertypes*, 22–26; Galloway, *The Interface Effect*, 133–37.

66. On the problematic of the technician more generally, see Latour and Woolgar, *Laboratory Life*; Latour, *Science in Action*; Pickering, *Constructing Quarks*; Pickering, *Science as Practice and Culture*; Shapin, "The House of Experiment in Seventeenth-Century England"; Shapin, "The Invisible Technician." On female scientific illustrators, see Daston and Galison, *Objectivity*, 89; see also B. Gates, *Kindred Nature*; Shteir and Lightman, *Figuring It Out*.

67. Villiers de L'Isle-Adam, *L'Ève future*, 255–59. My translation.

68. Stein, *Writings, 1903–1932*, 137, 139.

69. Raine, "Science, Nature Work, and the Kinaesthetic Body in Cather and Stein," 808. Raine's source is Brinnin, *The Third Rose*, 30–31.

70. Raine, "Science, Nature Work, and the Kinaesthetic Body in Cather and Stein," 809.

71. Raine, 809.

72. Stein's later reputation as "unreadable" has been central to her reception as an "experimental" writer. See Cecire, "Ways of Not Reading Gertrude Stein."

73. See especially Meyer, *Irresistible Dictation*, 90–91.

74. Meyer, 55.

75. Ashton, *From Modernism to Postmodernism*, 28.

76. For other accounts of this episode, see Bridgman, *Gertrude Stein in Pieces*; Farland, "Gertrude Stein's Brain Work"; Meyer, *Irresistible Dictation*; Schoenberg, "Gertrude Stein's Neuroanatomic Investigations."

77. Meyer, *Irresistible Dictation*, 85.

78. Morgan, "The Embryography of Alice B. Toklas," 315.

79. Meyer, *Irresistible Dictation*, 85. That the specimen was damaged was likely Stein's own fault, but many specimens came to the laboratory already damaged. See Morgan, "The Embryography of Alice B. Toklas," 309, 316.

80. Daston and Galison, *Objectivity*, 121, 151.

81. Meyer, *Irresistible Dictation*, 86.

82. Stein, *The Autobiography of Alice B. Toklas*, 81.

83. Sabin, *An Atlas of the Medulla and Midbrain*, 121.

84. Although Barker cites Stein's studies twice in his *Nervous System and Its Constituent Neurones*, he does not include any of her drawings.

85. Sabin, *An Atlas of the Medulla and Midbrain*, 121.

86. "To Lewellys Barker," April 7, 1902, The Alan Mason Chesney Archives, The Johns Hopkins Medical Institutions, Baltimore. Rpt. in Schoenberg, "Gertrude Stein's Neuroanatomic Investigations," 254, 256.

87. Meyer, *Irresistible Dictation*, 101. Stein also seems to implicitly compare her work to Sabin's, saying that "[her] object has been to save the next man from a longp Xperlimanarywork"; Sabin's *Atlas* was similarly meant to "save the student much time for real study, now often spent in getting started." Knower, editor's preface, 5.

88. Stein, "To Lewellys Barker," repr. in facsimile in Schoenberg, "Gertrude Stein's Neuroanatomic Investigations," 254, 256.

89. Knower, editor's preface, 5.

90. Knower, 5.

91. As Daston and Galison put it, "For initiates and neophytes alike, the atlas trains the eye to pick out certain kinds of objects as exemplary (for example, this 'typical' healthy liver rather than that one with cirrhosis) and to regard them in a certain way. . . . The atlases drill the eye of the beginner and refresh the eye of the old hand." The figure of "the eye of the old hand" is unfortunate. Daston and Galison, *Objectivity*, 22.

92. Stein, "To Lewellys Barker," repr. in facsimile in Schoenberg, "Gertrude Stein's Neuroanatomic Investigations," 255–56; Meyer, *Irresistible Dictation*, 94–95.

93. Stein, *Writings, 1903–1932*, 13.

94. Stein, "To Lewellys Barker," repr. in facsimile in Schoenberg, "Gertrude Stein's Neuroanatomic Investigations," 255–56.

95. Fleissner, *Women, Compulsion, Modernity*, 254.

96. Intension, as opposed to extension, defines a class of objects by its characteristic properties rather than by attempting to enumerate (as Stein claims to attempt in *The Making of Americans*) its constituent elements. See Jennifer Ashton's in-depth discussion of intension in Stein in chapter 1 of *From Modernism to Postmodernism*. On the influence of Whitehead see also chapter 4 of Meyer, *Irresistible Dictation*.

97. Jay, "Modernism and the Specter of Psychologism."

98. As Daston and Galison hasten to point out, structural objectivity was not a "movement" but a value (or a set of values), and to say that two different thinkers—say, Frege and Poincaré—both interested themselves in structural objectivity is not at all to suggest that they had a tendency to agree on other things.

99. Fleissner, *Women, Compulsion, Modernity*, 302n27.

100. Frege, *Begriffsschrift*, 5.

101. Frege, 6.

102. Daston and Galison, *Objectivity*, 270.

103. Jean van Heijenoort's influential collection *From Frege to Gödel* suggests a clear trajectory of influences, but it is not entirely uncontroversial. On the *Begriffsschrift*'s contemporary reception, see Vilkko, "The Reception of Frege's *Begriffsschrift*." On Russell and Whitehead and Stein, see Ashton, *From Modernism to Postmodernism*.

104. Frege, *Begriffsschrift*, 364.

105. Macbeth, *Frege's Logic*, vii, 1. The literature on Frege is too vast to summarize here, but see especially Sluga, *Gottlob Frege*; Dummett, *Frege*; Dummett, *Frege and Other Philosophers*. In their account of structural objectivity, Daston and Galison follow Sluga in attributing Frege's understanding of objectivity to that expounded in Hermann Lotze's 1843 *Logik* (Daston and Galison, *Objectivity*, 266). In his essay "Objectivity and Reality in Lotze and Frege," Michael Dummett dissents, pointing to a key distinction between Lotze's and Frege's uses of the term *wirklich* (usually translated "real"). Dummett argues that, unlike for Lotze, "for Frege, physical objects are objective as well as *wirklich*" (114). The material point for the present study, however, is that, for Frege, that which is objective *need* not be real. Dummett's and Sluga's positions represent an ongoing debate about Frege's realism. See Sluga, "Frege as a Rationalist"; Dummett, *Frege*; Sluga, *Gottlob Frege*; Dummett, "Frege as a Realist," in Dummett, *Frege and Other Philosophers*.

106. Frege, *Begriffsschrift*, 7.

107. Frege, 7.

108. Stein, *Writings, 1903–1932*, 178.

109. McCaffery, "The Death of the Subject," 62.

110. Stein, *Writings, 1903–1932*, 178.

111. Stein, *Writings, 1903–1932*, 175.

112. Stein, *Writings, 1903–1932*, 175.

113. Stein, *Writings, 1903–1932*, 165.

114. Stein, *Writings, 1903–1932*, 165.

115. Stein, *Writings, 1903–1932*, 163.

116. Stein, *Writings, 1903–1932*, 161–62.

117. Stein, *Writings, 1903–1932*, 95.

118. On the judgment stroke, see chapter 3, W. M. Martin, *Theories of Judgment*.

119. Macbeth, *Frege's Logic*, 184n7.

120. Stein, *Writings, 1903–1932*, 134.

121. Stein, *Writings, 1903–1932*, 237.

122. Stein, *Writings, 1903–1932*, 238.

123. Stein, *Writings, 1903–1932*, 168–69.

124. Zola, *Nana*, 438.

125. Stein, *Writings, 1903–1932*, 238–39.

126. Stein, *The Autobiography of Alice B. Toklas*, 54.

127. C. Bernstein, "Gertrude and Alice in Vichyland."

128. Brand, *The Blue Clerk*, 117, 116.

129. In this dimension my reading parallels Bill Brown's reading of *The Monster*, in which the now-faceless black servant, abstracted into a generic "monster," acts as a site where black minstrelsy and the freak show converge, producing an absolute (abject) spectacle that, Brown argues, comes "to allegorize the process of photographic development as facial disfigurement" as well as "to develop a figure for the new theatricalizing apparatus, the camera: an eye without a face." I have left the element of minstrelsy out of my discussion, since it has been very competently taken up elsewhere (e.g., North, *The Dialect of Modernism*; and L. Doyle, "The Flat, the Round, and Gertrude Stein"), but it seems to me that the confluence of race and gender in "Melanctha" helps define the possibility of doing the camera work of objective science. Brown, *The Material Unconscious*, 236.

130. Stein, *Writings, 1903–1932*, 139.

131. Stein, *The Autobiography of Alice B. Toklas*, 52. See also Steven Meyer's provocative discussion of these passages in *Irresistible Dictation*, 102–3.

132. Stein, *The Autobiography of Alice B. Toklas*, 75–76.

133. Stein, *The Autobiography of Alice B. Toklas*, 5.

134. Stein, *Writings, 1932–1946*, 288.

135. Barthes, *Camera Lucida*, 79.

136. Stein, *Writings, 1932–1946*, 294.

137. Stein, *How Writing Is Written*, 157.

138. Stein, *Writings, 1903–1932*, 313.

Chapter 4. Precision

1. Kracauer, "The Mass Ornament," 75–76. John Tiller was actually British, but there were several American precision dance troupes active in the early twentieth century, including what would eventually become the Radio City Music Hall Rockettes. "All these ensembles stressed the virtues of precision, synchronization, and regimentation." See M. Rubin, *Showstoppers*, 76.

2. Kracauer, "The Mass Ornament," 76.

3. Kracauer, "The Mass Ornament," 77.

4. Enright and Berkeley, *Dames*.

5. Kracauer, "Das Ornament Der Masse," 51; Kracauer, "The Mass Ornament," 76–77.

6. Kracauer, "The Mass Ornament," 77.

7. Kracauer, "The Mass Ornament," 78.

8. Kracauer, "The Mass Ornament," 77. Kracauer's emphasis.

9. Wise, *The Values of Precision*, 8.

10. Wise, 9.

11. Feldman and Barsanti, "Paying Attention," 7; Costello, *Marianne Moore*, 38.

12. Hotelling, "'The I of Each Is to the I of Each,'" 77.

13. Leavell, *Holding On Upside Down*, 165.

14. Moore, *Becoming Marianne Moore*, 490.

15. Schulze, "How Not to Edit," 132.

16. Moore, *Complete Prose*, 396, 398.

17. Barthes, *Writing Degree Zero*, 10.

18. Moore, *Complete Prose*, 396.

19. "What William James calls the 'passion for distinguishing,'" Leavell writes of Moore, "is almost by definition celibate." Leavell, "Marianne Moore, the James Family, and the Politics of Celibacy," 238.

20. Moore, *Complete Prose*, 396. Mark Seltzer has recently pointed out a male version of this phenomenon in Patricia Highsmith's *The Talented Mr. Ripley*, in which an all-male "human pyramid" "eroticizes a failure of self-difference, in the aggregate, as a failure of sexual difference." Seltzer, *The Official World*, 12.

21. Moore, *Complete Prose*, 401.

22. Moore's sexuality—her celibacy—has always been implicated in assessments of her style, from Ezra Pound's praise of her "arid clarity" and Marion Strobel's denunciation of the poet as a "well-muscled lady in tights" to Sandra Gilbert's reading of Moore as a "female female impersonator" and more recent queer-theoretic approaches to Moore's celibacy. See Pound, "Marianne Moore and Mina Loy," 2003, 23; Monroe, "A Symposium on Marianne Moore," 210; Gilbert, "Marianne Moore as Female Female Impersonator"; Leavell, "Marianne Moore, the James Family, and the Politics of Celibacy"; C. Miller, *Cultures of Modernism*; Leavell, "Frightening Disinterestedness"; McCabe, "Survival of the Queerly Fit"; Levy, *Criminal Ingenuity*; Kahan, *Celibacies*; Arckens, "In This Told-Backward Biography"; Mak, "On Falling Fastidiously."

23. Moore, *Complete Poems*.

24. Osworth, "You Need Help"; Burke, "Likings of an Observationist," 126.

25. N. Armstrong, *Desire and Domestic Fiction*; Fleissner, *Women, Compulsion, Modernity*; Felski, *The Gender of Modernity*; James, *Resilience & Melancholy*; Chow, *The Age of the World Target*.

26. Moore, "In the Days of Prismatic Color."

27. On criminality and sexuality in Moore, which I will take up further later in the chapter, see Ellen Levy's fascinating study *Criminal Ingenuity*. Levy reads this line slightly differently than I do (121–22).

28. Ginzburg, *Clues, Myths, and the Historical Method*, 97–98.

29. Moore, *Complete Poems*, 41.

30. Stevens, "A Poet That Matters," 113, 117.

31. Moore, *Becoming Marianne Moore*, 65.

32. C. Miller, *Marianne Moore*, 45. It is worth noting how Miller, like so many other

critics, characterizes Moore's description as "precise" without specifying what that precision entails. As I hope I am making clear, Miller's distinction between a "precise" and "moral" approach to the animal does not hold up. Throughout the chapter, to avoid confusion, I will refer to various Millers (Cristanne and D. A.) by their full names.

33. W. C. Williams, "Marianne Moore," 313.

34. Schulze, "Marianne Moore's 'Imperious Ox, Imperial Dish' and the Poetry of the Natural World," 5.

35. An earlier draft, titled "Snail.," does not insist upon or even much support the parallel between snail and poem; though Moore mentions compression, absence of feet, and the occipital horn in the draft, all three appear in the draft's first three lines, obviating the possibility of sustaining any puns until the end. Moreover, in the draft, the puns would not function in the first place. As Costello notes, the draft is longer (less "compressed") than the later version (*Marianne Moore*, 52); moreover, the draft poem is arranged in syllabic stanzas that less distinctly manifest an "absence of feet" than the later free verse version of the poem. A facsimile of the draft, housed at the Rosenbach Museum and Library's Marianne Moore archive, is reprinted in Costello, "'To a Snail,'" 12.

36. Horn and Tümer, "Menkes Disease and the Occipital Horn Syndrome," 651.

37. Daston, "Type Specimens and Scientific Memory," 162.

38. I discuss Moore's use of citation at greater length in an earlier version of this chapter. See Cecire, "Marianne Moore's Precision."

39. Schor, *Reading in Detail*, xlii.

40. Moore, *Becoming Marianne Moore*, 65.

41. Alpers, *The Art of Describing*, 195, qtd. in Schor, *Reading in Detail*, 20.

42. Hall, "Marianne Moore, the Art of Poetry No. 4," reprinted as Moore and Hall, "The Art of Poetry," 34.

43. Moore, "Critics and Connoisseurs," 77.

44. "Marianne Moore."

45. Beloof, "Prosody and Tone," 144.

46. Gilbert, "Marianne Moore as Female Female Impersonator," 43.

47. Wise, *The Values of Precision*, 5.

48. Porter, "How Science Became Technical," 293–94.

49. Porter, "Speaking Precision to Power."

50. Golinski, "'The Nicety of Experiment,'" 75. On the "*nicety* in experiments," Golinski is quoting Robert Harrington, *The Death-Warrant of the French Theory of Chemistry*, 1804. See Golinski, 72.

51. Jarrell, "Her Shield," 121.

52. Quoted in Monroe, "A Symposium on Marianne Moore," 209.

53. Porter, "How Science Became Technical," 298.

54. Schor, *Reading in Detail*, xlii.

55. Porter, "Speaking Precision to Power," 1276–77.

56. W. C. Williams, "Marianne Moore," 318.

57. On Moore's frequent figuration as, herself, an animal and the use of this figuration as a deflection of or replacement for sexuality, see Mak, "On Falling Fastidiously"; C. Miller, *Cultures of Modernism*, 73–80.

58. D. A. Miller, *Jane Austen, or The Secret of Style*, 1.

59. D. A. Miller, *Jane Austen, or The Secret of Style*, 23. The association between Austen and the detail, and especially her infamous self-description as a miniaturist in her letter to her nephew James Edward Austen, has been much discussed. See also Schor, *Reading in Detail*, 16.

60. D. A. Miller, *Jane Austen, or The Secret of Style*, 20. Linda Leavell details how radically Moore's body was subject to the control and surveillance of her mother, Mary Warner Moore, through most of her life up until Mary's death in 1947. Leavell, *Holding On Upside Down*, 162–67.

61. D. A. Miller, *Jane Austen, or The Secret of Style*, 28–29. I have written, with slightly different emphasis, on this point elsewhere as well; see Cecire, "Habemus PM; or, Irritation after the EU Referendum."

62. Litvak, *Strange Gourmets*, 4.

63. See Puff, "Nature on Trial," 234; Foucault, *The History of Sexuality*, 1:38. Pound also famously invokes the phrase to refer to "usura" in his Canto XLV. See Pound, *The Cantos of Ezra Pound*, 229–30.

64. D. A. Miller, *Jane Austen, or The Secret of Style*, 26–27.

65. Ramazani, Ellmann, and O'Clair, *The Norton Anthology of Modern and Contemporary Poetry*, 923.

66. Daston, "Rev. of M. Norton Wise, Ed., *The Values of Precision*," 517.

67. An interesting project, beyond the scope of the present one, might be to take up the study of epistemic vices. The history of literary criticism is filled with accusations of epistemic vices: being "ahistorical," being "positivist," etc. The postcritical turn is especially marked by a moralizing tone, as it accuses critics of being "suspicious" and "paranoid." It is clear from the literary critical examples how specific and local a vice may be. Clear, too, that we are often more attached to our vices than to our virtues.

68. Pound, "Marianne Moore and Mina Loy," 23.

69. Elkins, "Precision, Misprecision, Misprision," 175n9.

70. Elkins, 169–70.

71. Elkins, 170.

72. Elkins, 171–72, 174.

73. Elkins, 175.

74. Elkins, 174, 176.

75. See, e.g., Felski, *The Limits of Critique*.

76. D. A. Miller, *Jane Austen, or The Secret of Style*, 19. Incidentally, Elkins's essay on precision literally does not cite or even mention a single woman, except for the

barmaid at the center of Manet's canvas and, in passing, the abstract bride of Duchamp's *Large Glass*. It is an all-male world of (authoritative) artists and (misled, secondary) critics. On gendered questions of authority run through Moore's poems, see C. Miller, *Marianne Moore*.

77. Reynolds, *Literary Works*, 2:135, quoted in Schor, *Reading in Detail*, 9. Schor's emphasis.

78. Cecire, "Marianne Moore's Precision," 90.

79. Schor, *Reading in Detail*, 36.

80. Foucault, *The History of Sexuality*, 1:35; Kahan, *Celibacies*, 3.

81. Walters, "You Say Nature, I Say Nurture . . . Let's Call the Whole Thing Off."

82. Foucault, *The History of Sexuality*, 1:159.

83. Sara Ahmed has pointed out a characteristic gesture of "new materialist" criticism that accuses, variously, feminism, "theory," or "cultural criticism" of failing to account for a prediscursive material remainder. "By turning matter into an object or theoretical category, in this way," Ahmed writes, "the new materialism reintroduces the binarism between materiality and culture that much work in science studies has helped to challenge. Matter becomes a fetish object: as if it can be an 'it' that we can be for or against." Notably, as Ahmed points out, the new materialist gesture all too frequently occurs by way of imputations of epistemic unvirtue: "The idea that such feminist responses are knee-jerk and automatic implies they are unthinking, perhaps even bodily responses." As Heather Love has acknowledged, exhortations to "reparative" reading practices also tend to be heavily moralized. Ahmed, "Some Preliminary Remarks on the Founding Gestures of the 'New Materialism,'" 35, 27; Love, "Truth and Consequences," 237.

84. Butler, *Gender Trouble*, 48; Keller, *The Mirage of a Space between Nature and Nurture*; Fausto-Sterling, *Sex/Gender*; J. Doyle, "Dirt off Her Shoulders"; Pieper, *Sex Testing*.

85. François, *Open Secrets*, 7.

86. This is not to discount the crucial work of lesbian and transgender studies, but rather to acknowledge the predominant focus of some of the most prominent scholars in the field. Foucault himself tended to focus on gay men, especially in *The History of Sexuality*, vols. 2 and 3. I am thinking in particular of the canonicity of works like Bersani, "Is the Rectum a Grave?"; Bersani, *The Culture of Redemption*; Sedgwick, *Between Men*; Sedgwick, *Epistemology of the Closet*; Berlant and Warner, "Sex in Public"; Edelman, *No Future*; Edelman, "Against Survival"; D. A. Miller, *The Novel and the Police*.

87. These are not mutually exclusive categories, but the two fields, engaged with different questions, do tend to operate in relative (pretended) ignorance of one another. For examples of prominent works, see Schiebinger, *Feminism and the Body*; Schiebinger, *Nature's Body*; Jordanova, *Sexual Visions*; Jordanova, *Nature Displayed*; Keller, *Reflections on Gender and Science*; Keller, *Secrets of Life, Secrets of Death*; Keller

and Longino, *Feminism and Science*; Haraway, *Primate Visions*; Haraway, *Modest_Witness @Second_Millennium*; E. Martin, "The Egg and the Sperm"; Harding, *The Science Question in Feminism*; Harding, *Sciences from Below*; Fausto-Sterling, "Science Matters, Culture Matters"; Park, *Secrets of Women*.

88. Foucault, *The History of Sexuality*, 1:69. I am using Gayle Rubin's concept of the sex/gender system provisionally, with awareness of the ways that sex as well as gender are constructed. I think it is useful, in this context, to entertain provisionally the concept of a presocial biological sex because of that concept's influence in the history of women and for its historical utility in beginning to trace the construction of gender, acknowledging, however, the ways that it ultimately does not hold up. Butler's *Gender Trouble* and *Bodies That Matter*—now so canonical as to be curiously unseeable—are precisely an attempt to reckon with the (biological) secret of sexism and the place of the so-called female body in it. Ahmed notes the urgency with which feminist activists have engaged with biological science as a matter of self-preservation. See Rubin, "The Traffic in Women," 159; Butler, *Gender Trouble*; Butler, *Bodies That Matter*; Ahmed, "Some Preliminary Remarks on the Founding Gestures of the 'New Materialism,'" 29–30.

89. This regime, moreover, rests on a founding myth in which the original keepers of the secret were the women, against whom the men rose up, seizing the secret and slaughtering all but the youngest girls. Taussig, *Defacement*, 104–6, 109–10.

90. Park, *Secrets of Women*, 77ff.

91. I am indebted to Nihad Farooq for prompting me to think further about Diderot's novel.

92. Freud, "The 'Uncanny,'" 225.

93. Freud, "The 'Uncanny,'" 245.

94. Taussig, *Defacement*, 95.

95. Taussig, *Defacement*, 97.

96. Brooks, "Storied Bodies, or Nana at Last Unveil'd," 29.

97. Park, *Secrets of Women*, 64.

98. Susan Fraiman, among others, has critiqued queer studies on the grounds that it reinstates the marginalization of women that its antecedent, women's studies, aimed to unseat. These questions are bound up in the contestations around disciplinary shifts from "women's studies" to "gender studies" and "gay and lesbian studies" to "queer studies," which are beyond the scope of this chapter. See Fraiman, *Cool Men and the Second Sex*, 122–55; Walters, "From Here to Queer"; M. Nelson, *The Argonauts*. Against this tendency, see Mavor, *Reading Boyishly*; Parker, *The Theorist's Mother*. Freud's essay on the uncanny compasses both versions of the secret of sex—both the *heimisch/unheimlich* vagina discussed above and the compulsion to repeat that is the sign of the death drive that is so central to classic accounts of male homosexuality. See Freud, "The 'Uncanny,'" 238. For another view of nature's perversions, see Porzak, "Inverts and Invertebrates."

99. Elkins, "Precision, Misprecision, Misprision," 174.

100. Leavell, "Marianne Moore, the James Family, and the Politics of Celibacy," 220.

101. In 1998, for example, Robin G. Schulze identified a critical "camp" "exemplified by T. S. Eliot, R. P. Blackmur, Charles Molesworth, and . . . feminist critics Adrienne Rich and Suzanne Juhasz . . . [who] claim that Moore's creatures serve principally as vehicles for covert or repressed self-expression." Schulze, "Marianne Moore's 'Imperious Ox, Imperial Dish' and the Poetry of the Natural World," 4. On queer uses of animal proxies, see Stockton, "Why the (Lesbian) Child Requires an Interval of Animal."

102. Moore, *Complete Poems*, 144.

103. Jarrell, of course, quotes "His Shield" and acknowledges that Moore "put[s] no trust in armour." The Moore-like pileup of attributes here, conjoining temperature, morality, a haptic quality, and epistemic strength, is worth noting. Jarrell, "Her Shield," 122–23.

104. The difference: Austen deflects onto *human* nature; Moore rather insistently deflects onto what is inhuman in nature, and thus invokes the *technical* in a way that Austen never does.

105. Levy, *Criminal Ingenuity*, 64.

106. Moore, *Becoming Marianne Moore*, 62.

107. Moore, *Complete Poems*, 20.

108. Gunn, "Three Hard Women," 44.

109. Gunn's disclaimer rhymes with the refrain in *Seinfeld* regarding gayness, in the 1993 episode "The Outing": "Not that there's anything wrong with that!" See "The Outing (*Seinfeld*)."

110. Gilbert, "Marianne Moore as Female Female Impersonator," 34–35.

111. Jarrell, "Her Shield," 122–23.

112. In fact, it may be the *only* thing that signifies what is queer about precision; as D. A. Miller points out of *Sense and Sensibility*: "The labor of constructing a closet leaves Robert no leisure for committing the indecencies to be shut in there." Miller, *Jane Austen, or The Secret of Style*, 16.

113. Porter, "How Science Became Technical," 298.

114. Sedgwick, *Epistemology of the Closet*, 213–59; D. A. Miller, *Jane Austen, or The Secret of Style*, 12–14. Linda Leavell has speculated, based on Moore's unpublished, semiautobiographical novel *The Way We Live Now*, that Scofield Thayer once proposed to Moore by offering her (as recounted in the scene) a small round box "of ivory lined with velvet, the fine-fitting edges beveled to sharpness; . . . it held a pendant of square emeralds set in greenish gold filigree." Though this (sharp-edged!) box is not empty, its contents and the offer it represents, coming as they do from a married man, are, as Leavell argues, evacuated by their impropriety. Leavell, "Frightening Disinterestedness," 69.

115. Levy, *Criminal Ingenuity*, 120–24. Moore professes this fondness to Elizabeth Bishop.

116. Sedgwick, *Epistemology of the Closet*, 11.

117. D. A. Miller, *Jane Austen, or The Secret of Style*, 17.

118. On Moore's self-styling as a "bachelor," and her affinity with Henry James in particular, see Leavell, "Marianne Moore, the James Family, and the Politics of Celibacy."

119. Taussig, *Defacement*, 159.

120. D. A. Miller, *Jane Austen, or The Secret of Style*, 34.

121. Eliot, introduction, xiv, quoted in Setina, "'Mountains Being a Language with Me,'" 173–74.

122. Quoted in Moore, *Becoming Marianne Moore*, 1; Setina, "'Mountains Being a Language with Me,'" 181n76. On Moore's revisions and editing, see Setina, "'Mountains Being a Language with Me,'"; Schulze, "How Not to Edit"; Schulze, "Marianne Moore's 'Imperious Ox, Imperial Dish' and the Poetry of the Natural World."

123. Schor, *Reading in Detail*, 53.

124. Elkins, "Precision, Misprecision, Misprision," 174–75.

125. D. A. Miller, *The Novel and the Police*, 220.

126. Moore, *Becoming Marianne Moore*, 72; Moore, *Complete Poems*, 121.

127. Foucault, *The History of Sexuality*, 1:71; D. A. Miller, "Foutre! Bougre! Ecriture!," 503. It should be obvious that the pleasures of analysis can exceed those of "actual sex," and it is not particularly in the interests of the scholarship on sexuality to privilege bodily pleasures above intellectual ones, however "empty."

128. Shakespeare, *Othello*, 1443 (5.2.303–4.) The saint is Santiago de Compostela.

129. Moore, *Collected Poems*, 116.

130. Moore, *Collected Poems*, 115–16.

131. François Le Lionnais endorses homophonic translation (of which Moore's Jupiter/jour pater is an example) in the second Oulipian manifesto. Motte, *Oulipo*, 31. In the poem, the crystals' constant temperature is described as a "coolness," with the quartz described as a "water/clear 'crystal' as the Greeks used to say,/this 'clear ice' must be kept at the/same coolness." In these lines, we can see the quartz regulators being associated with the cool reserve of the glacier of "An Octopus" (complete with a characterization by "the Greeks"). It is worth noting, though, that the "coolness" at which these clocks were held was 41°C—and as a Bell Labs representative wrote to Moore in 1946, apparently in response to an inquiry on her part, "I would hardly call 41 degrees centigrade 'cool.'" Paul B. Findley to Marianne Moore, April 30, 1946, Rosenbach Library Moore XIVb: 01: 11. This may simply be a mistake on Moore's part (thinking in Fahrenheit rather than Celsius), but it may also be a deliberate return to the thematics of crystalline coolness that emerge across her poems.

132. My account of celibacy is indebted to Kahan's. See Kahan, *Celibacies*.

133. Moore, "In the Days of Prismatic Color."

134. Chaudhuri, "Nine Cinematic Devices for Staging (In)Visible War and the (Vanishing) Colonial Present," 173.

135. Virilio, *War and Cinema*, 5.

136. Seldes, *The Seven Lively Arts*, 133, my emphasis. While Moore and Seldes were friends and colleagues, I have encountered no evidence in their correspondence (either in the Marianne Moore papers at the Rosenbach Library or the Scofield Thayer/*Dial* papers at the Beinecke Library) that they discussed *The Seven Lively Arts* or the Follies. My argument is not that Moore held any particular views on precision dancing—in fact, archival evidence seems to suggest that she was not interested in it at all—but rather that the significance of precision in the twentieth century is something bigger than Moore and crosses several milieux. The only reference to precision dancing that I could find in the Marianne Moore papers is an October 1924 entry from her conversation notebook; her interlocutors, Paul Rosenfeld and Seldes's friend and frequent interlocutor (and *Dial* contributor) Edmund Wilson, declare the Follies interesting "fr the point of view of production" and compare the "girls" to "animals in the circus" (Wilson: "I feel sorryer for the girls than for the animals"). See Rosenbach Library Moore VII: 11: 01 1250/25 Conversation Notebook 82r–82v.

137. Dinerstein, *Swinging the Machine*, 200–201, Dinerstein's emphasis. Dinerstein also argues that the unerotic quality of this precise "pleasure machine" depended on a fetishization of whiteness, performing an "energized" quality very different from that exhibited by the African American vogue in shows like *Shuffle Along*. Precision's construction as white is an important point that I will not have space here to explore in depth, but the racialized dynamic of the "precise" drone versus the messily "medieval" killing technologies of those who are bombed (the sword, the suicide bomb) clearly carries this logic forward. Precision is attached to whiteness in the way that dominant concepts of technological modernity always attach to racial whiteness. See Dinerstein, 192.

138. Kracauer, "The Mass Ornament," 76; Seldes, *The Seven Lively Arts*, 131; Dinerstein, *Swinging the Machine*, 196.

139. Dinerstein, 197.

140. See, for example, Fleissner, "Dictation Anxiety"; Thurschwell, "Supple Minds and Automatic Hands"; Thurschwell, *Literature, Technology, and Magical Thinking, 1880–1920*; Fleissner, *Women, Compulsion, Modernity*; Goble, *Beautiful Circuits*; Cecire, "Ways of Not Reading Gertrude Stein."

141. Dinerstein, *Swinging the Machine*, 191.

142. Saint-Amour, *Tense Future*, 76.

143. Brion and Gilson, "A Style of Spectacle," 28. My emphasis.

144. Comolli, "Dancing Images," 24.

145. Edgerton's milk droplet photographs followed from photographs produced by Arthur Worthington in the 1890s. See Worthington, *The Splash of a Drop*.

146. Virilio, *War and Cinema*, 19. The first emphasis is Virilio's; the second is mine.

147. Moore, *Becoming Marianne Moore*, 125.

148. Scarry, *The Body in Pain*, 173.

149. Kaplan, "Precision Targets," 696.

150. Crane, *Bombs, Cities, and Civilians*, 20. Kaplan, "Precision Targets," 700.

151. Bayard de Volo, "Unmanned?," 57; Daggett, "Drone Disorientations," 374.

152. Stratton, "Harold Eugene Edgerton," 446.

153. Stratton, 447–48.

154. "Aerial Photos at Night."

155. MacKenzie, *Inventing Accuracy*, 1–4.

156. Chow, *The Age of the World Target*, 12, 27–32.

157. W. C. Williams, "Marianne Moore," 318. Williams's semi-ironic genocidal fantasies in *Spring and All* also take on a new light when we see precision in this way. W. C. Williams, "Spring and All," 90–91.

158. Leavell, *Holding On Upside Down*, 116–19; Phillips, "The Students of Marianne Moore."

159. Moore, "Those Various Scalpels."

160. Moore, *Becoming Marianne Moore*, 262. Moore retains "tissues" through the poem's publication in *Observations* (1924), but in the 1967 *Collected Poems*, "the tissues" become less fleshy "components." Moore, *Complete Poems*, 51.

161. Rosenbach Library Moore VII: 04: 04 Poetry Notebook 1251/7 p. 2v. See also P. C. Willis, "The Road to Paradise," 247.

162. Moore, *Becoming Marianne Moore*, 131.

163. Moore, *Becoming Marianne Moore*, 127.

164. Moore, *Becoming Marianne Moore*, 131, 125, 132.

165. Moore, *Becoming Marianne Moore*, 130.

166. P. C. Willis, "The Road to Paradise," 249.

167. Patricia Willis, like many other Moore critics, has a tendency to insist on Moore's precision even in less-than-likely scenarios. For example, commenting on Moore's early poem "A Jellyfish," Willis writes that Moore "for her junior year course in comparative anatomy drew a precise jellyfish in her laboratory notebook." Although Moore certainly drew the jellyfish, Willis's characterization of the drawing as "precise," especially in comparison with the much more detailed and carefully labeled drawings to be found in (for example) the biologist Edmund Beecher Wilson's notebooks across town at the American Philosophical Society, is puzzling. Willis and Moore, *Marianne Moore*, 34.

168. Setina, "'Mountains Being a Language with Me,'" 161.

169. M. Rubin, *Showstoppers*, 112.

170. In "By a Waterfall," the middle number of the three stacked spectacles at the end of *Footlight Parade* (Warner Bros., 1933), Dick Powell summons his lover, played

by Ruby Keeler, with the lines "By a waterfall/I'm calling you." If at first Keeler responds, sitting by Powell's side and singing him to sleep, she soon hears other, female voices calling and ditches the napping Powell for an all-female world of singing nymphs, their bathing caps and swimsuits stylized so as to appear to be nothing but long, flowing hair. Keeler joins them in the long water spectacle to follow. The sequence includes one section in which two long rows of dancers face each other, their legs stretched out in the water and interlocked like DNA base pairs. A diver swims down the middle, breaking apart the tightly knit row of legs, only to swim back up as the helix reknits. In another section, shot from underwater, a diver swims through the corridor created by a long row of women's spread legs. Is this an all-female utopia of pleasure or just—as Powell waking up at the end of the scene suggests—a man's fantasy?

171. Levy, *Criminal Ingenuity*, xxii, 36; Moore, *Becoming Marianne Moore*, 115. Moore's drafts for "Marriage" more explicitly stake a position against marriage than the published versions; three times, the lines that would become "I wonder what Adam and Eve/think of it by this time" are followed by "I don't think much of it." See Rosenbach Library Moore VII: 04: 04 Poetry Notebook 1251/7 1v, 2v, 12r. Leavell has convincingly read "Marriage" as at least partly motivated by anger at a proposal of marriage that Moore received from Scofield Thayer; some readings of this episode in Moore's life have concluded that the poem is less a celebration of restraint than a rejection of insufficiently passionate marriage. I am not willing to take Leavell's documentation to quite that conclusion, especially given the various references to male power that dot the notebook, which survive intact in the lines "men have power/and sometimes one is made to feel it." Leavell, "Frightening Disinterestedness"; Leavell, *Holding On Upside Down*; Gregory, "'Still Leafing,'" 73n5; Moore, *Becoming Marianne Moore*, 120. See also Rosenbach Library Moore VII: 04: 04 Poetry Notebook 1251/7 2r, 8v, 11v, 14v, 15r, 16r, 17r, 18v.

172. Schweik, *A Gulf So Deeply Cut*, 3.

173. On Moore's aging, see Kahan, *Celibacies*; Gregory, "'Still Leafing.'"

174. Gregory, "'Still Leafing.'"

175. Moore, *Complete Poems*, 95.

176. "In the Days of Prismatic Color" and "Marriage" are the most prominent examples of this. On Moore's lapsarian poetics, see also Benjamin Johnson, "The Poetics of the Fall in Marianne Moore's 'The Jerboa.'"

177. O. Williams, *The War Poets*, 6, quoted in Schweik, *A Gulf So Deeply Cut*, 33. Schweik points out the poem's ambivalence toward the very concept of "inwardness" (38).

178. Jarrell, "Poetry in Peace and War," 122.

179. Jarrell, "Poetry in Peace and War," 122. On Jarrell's critique, see also Gregory, "'Still Leafing,'" 59; Setina, "Marianne Moore's Postwar Fables and the Politics of Indirection," 1261–63.

180. Schweik, *A Gulf So Deeply Cut*; Galvin, *News of War*, 251–77.

181. Schweik, *A Gulf So Deeply Cut*, 38.

182. Enloe, *Does Khaki Become You?*, 15, quoted in Schweik, *A Gulf So Deeply Cut*, 38.

183. Jarrell, "The Death of the Ball Turret Gunner."

184. See also Fuss, *Dying Modern*, 62–63.

185. Virilio, *War and Cinema*, 19.

186. In contrast, as Schweik points out, Jarrell's authorized (male) speakers, the ones who are *really* in a war, "bear for years and die forever," taking up the good pregnancy at which precision fails. Jarrell, "Poetry in Peace and War," 121; Schweik, *A Gulf So Deeply Cut*, 50. On the biopolitical responsibilization of women, see Deutscher, *Foucault's Futures*, 116, 186–88.

187. Moore, *Complete Poems*, 138.

188. In this sense, though pointedly nonreproductive, the poem echoes the ambivalent dynamic that Barbara Johnson describes in women's abortion poems in "Apostrophe, Animation, and Abortion."

189. Jarrell, "Poetry in Peace and War," 122.

190. Jarrell, "Poetry in Peace and War," 120.

191. Moore, *Complete Poems*, 145. The quotation is from "'Keeping Their World Large.'"

Chapter 5. Contact

1. W. C. Williams, "Further Announcement." By "native," Williams essentially means "settler." Williams coedited *Contact* with Robert McAlmon until 1923; in 1930 Richard Johns started *Pagany: A Native Quarterly*, titled in homage to Williams's 1928 novel *A Voyage to Pagany*, with Williams's editorial involvement. It ran until 1932. Williams was approached to edit a new run of *Contact*, now titled *Contact: An American Quarterly* and coedited with Nathanael West and (nominally) McAlmon; this ran for three issues in 1932. On these magazines, see Mariani, *William Carlos Williams*, 312–35; Perloff, "'Barbed-Wire Entanglements'"; E. White, "In the American Grain"; E. White, *Transatlantic Avant-Gardes*; Metzler Sawin, "Making *Contact!*"

2. Blum, "American Letter," 566, quoted in Green, "The Comedian as the Letter C, Carlos, and Contact," 263. Blum goes on to praise Williams as a poet.

3. The publishers were David Moss and Martin Kamin. Metzler Sawin, "Making *Contact!*," 337. Schulze locates Williams's obsession with contact in a passage from Henry David Thoreau's *The Maine Woods*. Schulze, *The Degenerate Muse*, 208.

4. Despite an emphasis on Americanness in both series of *Contact*, the final issue of the first series was published in Europe, and McAlmon's Contact Editions (1923–29) was located in Paris.

5. McAlmon, "Contact and Genius," 16.

6. Pratt, "Fieldwork in Common Places," 32; Manganaro, *Culture, 1922*, 79.

7. Schuster, "William Carlos Williams, *Spring and All*, and the Anthropological Imaginary," 121.

8. Manganaro, *Culture, 1922*; Hegeman, *Patterns for America*.

9. Clifford, *The Predicament of Culture*, 6. On the cross-fertilizations of literary studies and anthropology in the 1980s, see Evans, "Introduction"; Hymes, "Anthropology and Poetry."

10. In addition to Manganaro, *Culture, 1922*; Schuster, "William Carlos Williams, *Spring and All*; and the Anthropological Imaginary." See Hegeman, *Patterns for America*; Manganaro, *Modernist Anthropology*; Stocking, "The Ethnographic Sensibility of the 1920s and the Dualism of the Anthropological Tradition"; Shelton, "Primitive Self." It is notable that Manganaro and Hegeman also read a number of other modernists, especially T. S. Eliot, in relation to ethnography. While they make persuasive arguments about Eliot's indebtedness to an anthropological discourse, Williams's poetics of contact was often explicitly positioned *against* Eliot's modernism. While both poets are, I think, engaged with anthropological questions, only Williams is particularly concerned with contact as an epistemic virtue.

11. A full accounting of the politics of "globalizing" modernism is beyond the scope of this chapter, but I consider it an adequate shorthand to concur with Leif Sorensen's preference for "provincializing rather than expanding modernism," "accept[ing] that modernism is one response to modernity among many while recognizing that what makes many modernist experiments powerful and compelling is their hubristic refusal to acknowledge their limitations." Sorensen, *Ethnic Modernism and the Making of US Literary Multiculturalism*, 18.

12. C. Bernstein, "The Academy in Peril," 244, 251.

13. Walker, "Looking for Zora," 102.

14. Marcus and Fischer, *Anthropology as Cultural Critique*, 40. As Marcus and Fischer note in the preface to the second edition, their notion of an "experimental ethnography" was deeply indebted to the literary notion of experimentalism (xxxi).

15. Hegeman observes that Hurston's relationship with Columbia's anthropology department was significantly less well supported than those of white women like Ruth Benedict, Margaret Mead, and Elsie Clews Parsons. "Not only was Hurston's academic career so plagued by financial troubles that she left Columbia without ever taking an advanced degree," Hegeman notes, "but she occupied a strange status in anthropology . . . as both anthropologist and a species of native informant." Hegeman, *Patterns for America*, 217n17; Gordon, "The Politics of Ethnographic Authority," 148–50.

16. Hazel V. Carby, for example, compellingly critiques Hurston as an ethnographer and suggests that it is precisely her ability to render Blackness through an anthropological gaze—a "romantic and, it must be said, colonial imagination"—that has

made her so widely available to recovery by institutions. Carby, "The Politics of Fiction, Anthropology, and the Folk: Zora Neale Hurston," 80.

17. McAlmon, "Modern Artiques"; W. C. Williams, "Issued."

18. The early modern "book of nature" formulation is, of course, not as straightforward as was often claimed; rather, as Peter Dear has argued, the "book of nature" required "new techniques of exegesis." Dear, "Totius in Verba," 146.

19. W. C. Williams, "Issued."

20. It is worth noting that Williams repeatedly recurs to Marianne Moore's poetry as exemplary of the aesthetic he has in mind for *Contact*, and "Those Various Scalpels" and "In the Days of Prismatic Color"—two poems that I have considered under the rubric of precision—both appear in the second issue of *Contact* (first series). Precision, I have argued, is a virtue that always runs the risk of exceeding nature's bounds, in contrast with contact's claim to be bound by locality; clearly, I disagree with some of Williams's perceptions of Moore's poetics.

21. Stocking, "The Ethnographic Sensibility of the 1920s and the Dualism of the Anthropological Tradition," 281.

22. Stocking, 281.

23. The frequent invocation of the "armchair" stereotypes the comparatist as essentially engaging in leisure, not work, suggesting another aspect of contact's virtue and professionalism.

24. Stocking, 282.

25. W. C. Williams, "Issued."

26. W. C. Williams, "Note."

27. The often white supremacist ideological investments in Viking settlements in histories of the "discovery" of the Americas are a complex issue beyond the scope of this chapter. See Kolodny, *In Search of First Contact*.

28. W. C. Williams, *In the American Grain*, 208. The contentious question of whether enslaved people should be understood as settlers is beyond the scope of this chapter, but for a sensitive consideration of the relationship between antiblackness and settler colonialism, see Day, "Being or Nothingness."

29. Malinowski, *Argonauts of the Western Pacific*, 11, quoted in Pratt, "Fieldwork in Common Places," 27.

30. Pratt, 35.

31. Pratt, 36.

32. Pratt, 44.

33. Krauss, *The Originality of the Avant-Garde and Other Modernist Myths*.

34. W. C. Williams, *Paterson*, 6.

35. B. Brown, *A Sense of Things*, 1.

36. See, for example, Torgovnick, *Gone Primitive*; Flam and Deutch, *Primitivism and Twentieth-Century Art*; Shelton, "Primitive Self"; Hegeman, *Patterns for America*;

Fabian, *Time and the Other*; Clifford, *The Predicament of Culture*; Clifford and Marcus, *Writing Culture*.

37. W. C. Williams, "The American Language—Again," n.d., YCAL MSS 116 Box 30 Folder 890, Beinecke Library. The word "naked" is inserted by hand in the typescript.

38. W. C. Williams, "Spring and All," 100; Cheng, *Second Skin*.

39. Stocking, "The Ethnographic Sensibility of the 1920s and the Dualism of the Anthropological Tradition," 282; Pratt, "Fieldwork in Common Places," 31.

40. W. C. Williams, *In the American Grain*, 7–26.

41. W. C. Williams, "The American Language—Again."

42. W. C. Williams, *Spring and All*, 12–13.

43. Jameson, *The Antinomies of Realism*, 37. He is paraphrasing Barthes, "The Reality Effect."

44. Hegeman, *Patterns for America*, 26.

45. W. C. Williams, *Spring and All*, 11.

46. Eliot, *The Waste Land and Other Poems*, 55.

47. Genesis 1:1. Tanakh, 3.

48. Genesis 1:5, 8. Tanakh, 3. On separations in Genesis, see also Douglas, *Purity and Danger*.

49. Paul de Man describes this temporal structure as "modernity" and examines it in some detail in *Blindness and Insight*. See de Man, "Literary History and Literary Modernity."

50. Taussig, *Mimesis and Alterity*, 70.

51. Taussig, *Mimesis and Alterity*, 72. I have had to chop this quotation up for concision's sake. Taussig writes: "'We find,' [Mauss and Hubert] write with respect to the magicians' Law of Contact, 'that both individuals and objects are theoretically linked to a seemingly limitless number of sympathetic associations. The chain is so perfectly linked and the continuity such that, in order to produce a desired effect, it is really unimportant whether magical rites are performed on any one rather than another of the connections.'"

52. To concatenate is literally to "chain together."

53. Taussig, *Mimesis and Alterity*, 72–73.

54. Tellingly, Foucault is describing premodern Europe. Foucault, *The Order of Things*, 24.

55. Foucault, *The Order of Things*, 43.

56. Franklin, "The Contexts of Forms," 2.

57. Foucault, *The Order of Things*, 43.

58. Perloff, *The Poetics of Indeterminacy*, 136.

59. W. C. Williams, *Paterson*, 128. For a reading of one of Williams's more explicit attempts to engage race, see Mackey, *Discrepant Engagement*, 246–52.

60. W. C. Williams, *Paterson*, 128.

61. W. J. T. Mitchell, *What Do Pictures Want?*, 9.

62. Davidson et al., *Leningrad*, 8, 54.

63. B. Anderson, *Imagined Communities*, 24–26. Contra Language's stated aesthetic affiliations, Anderson identifies this temporality as essentially novelistic, perhaps explaining why Language's version of national simultaneity is experienced in "paranoid" rather than naturalized terms. On temporality and periodization in Language writing, see also Watten, "Presentism and Periodization in Language Writing, Conceptual Art, and Conceptual Writing."

64. Ngai, *Ugly Feelings*, 303–4.

65. Watten et al., *The Grand Piano*, 2:45.

66. Indeed, acausality, in the refusal of the syllogism, is a central principle of what Silliman theorized as "the new sentence," on which more below. See Silliman, *The New Sentence*, 79.

67. Watten et al., *The Grand Piano*, 2:21–22. My emphasis.

68. On paranoia as a Cold War phenomenon, see Melley, *Empire of Conspiracy*.

69. Clifford and Marcus, *Writing Culture*, 13–14. On the recovery structure of the first and 1981 editions of Leiris's *L'Afrique fantôme*, and for a critique of its reception, see Shelton, "Primitive Self."

70. Fabian, *Time and the Other*; Clifford, "On Ethnographic Allegory," 112–13.

71. Marcus and Fischer, *Anthropology as Cultural Critique*, 95.

72. Clifford and Marcus, *Writing Culture*, 14.

73. Clifford and Marcus, xiii.

74. Silliman, *The New Sentence*, 91. On the effects of the new sentence in *Ketjak*, see, for instance, Epstein, *Attention Equals Life*, 208.

75. Silliman, *The New Sentence*, 63. Silliman in fact adduces several other precedents throughout the essay, in poems by Fenton Johnson, Hannah Wiener, Stéphane Mallarmé, Gertrude Stein, and others.

76. Silliman, "*Ketjak*," 4–5.

77. Epstein, *Attention Equals Life*, 207.

78. Silliman, "Untitled."

79. Clifford, *The Predicament of Culture*, 222–26. Clifford uses the phrase "a machine for making authenticity" in the Greimas diagram on p. 224.

80. Marcus and Fischer, *Anthropology as Cultural Critique*, ix.

81. "It is the New World, or to leave that for the better term, it is a *new locality* that is in Poe assertive; it is America, the first great burst through to expression of a re-awakened genius of *place*." W. C. Williams, *In the American Grain*, 216.

82. Notley, *Dr. Williams' Heiresses*. Nathaniel Mackey, in his *Song of the Andoumboulou*, draws critically on the French ethnographer Marcel Griaule, even as he acknowledges the field's reflexive turn "since Griaule's day." Like Notley and Silliman, Mackey engages reflexively with ideas of contact. Unlike Silliman and Notley, how-

ever, Mackey also directly addresses the politics of ethnography. Mackey, *Discrepant Engagement*, 181. On Mackey's uses of ethnography, see Ellis, *Territories of the Soul*, 171–76.

83. Davidson et al., *Leningrad*, 7–8.

84. Davidson et al., 24. My emphasis.

85. Davidson et al., 2, 10, 17, 21. On the Dragomoshchenko-Hejinian collaborations, see especially chapters 2 and 3 of Edmond, *A Common Strangeness*.

86. Marcus and Fischer, *Anthropology as Cultural Critique*, 95.

87. Davidson et al., *Leningrad*, 22–23, 2–3.

88. Pratt, "Fieldwork in Common Places," 49.

89. Pratt, 44.

90. Davidson et al., *Leningrad*, 17. Hejinian had previously visited in 1983.

91. Davidson et al., 12.

92. Davidson et al., 29.

93. Davidson et al., 28.

94. Davidson et al., 21.

95. On the desire for clear demarcations between science and politics, see Latour, *We Have Never Been Modern*.

96. The Prime Directive, introduced in the *Star Trek* episode "Return of the Archons" (season 1, episode 22; February 1967), is defined in "Bread and Circuses" (season 2, episode 25; March 1968) as "No identification of self or mission. No interference with the social development of said planet. No references to space or the fact that there are other worlds or civilizations."

97. McGeough, "Victorian Archaeologies, Anthropologies and Adventures in the Final Frontier," 232.

98. Le Guin, *The Left Hand of Darkness*, 133.

99. Le Guin, *The Left Hand of Darkness*, 132. On Hayek's vision of the market as information-machine, see Hayek, "The Use of Knowledge in Society."

100. It is telling, however, that this vision of pure mutuality looks so much like the neoliberal ideal of a market, which in practice and by design exacerbates economic inequality.

101. Le Guin, *The Left Hand of Darkness*, 134.

102. Clifford and Marcus, *Writing Culture*, 14.

103. Le Guin, *The Left Hand of Darkness*, 132.

104. Le Guin, *The Left Hand of Darkness*, 245.

105. Jameson, *Archaeologies of the Future*, 270. I use the term "sex/gender system," which is somewhat outdated, in part because the conceptions of sexuality and gender in *The Left Hand of Darkness* reflect the American feminist thinking of its period. Gethenians essentially only have gender when they have sex and reproduce. Gayle Rubin's term, derived in part from her reading of Claude Lévi-Strauss, thus fits Le Guin's project well. Rubin, "The Traffic in Women."

106. Le Guin, *The Left Hand of Darkness*, 7.

107. Le Guin, *The Left Hand of Darkness*, 8–9.

108. Hannerz, *Writing Future Worlds*, 167; Kroeber, *Anthropology*, 423.

109. Le Guin, "Indian Uncles," 14. On Le Guin's engagement with anthropology, see Clifford, *Returns*, 91–191; Fayad, "Aliens, Androgynes, and Anthropology"; Senior, "Cultural Anthropology and Rituals of Exchange in Ursula K. Le Guin's *Earthsea*." Kroeber's legacy has been a site of ongoing controversy, especially in relation to his dealings with "Ishi," a California Native American of disputed ancestry who was represented and studied as the "last wild Indian" of California, and whose remains were later autopsied and treated as research materials. Le Guin defends her father's friendship with Ishi and his attempts to prevent Ishi's autopsy in "Indian Uncles." Le Guin's mother, Theodora Krakow Kroeber Quinn, wrote two popular books about Ishi, *Ishi in Two Worlds* (1961) and *Ishi, Last of His Tribe* (1964). On the Ishi controversy, see Rockafellar and Starn, "Ishi's Brain"; Scheper-Hughes, "Ishi's Brain, Ishi's Ashes"; Kenny, Killion, and Scheper-Hughes, "'Ishi's Brain, Ishi's Ashes'"; Clifford, *Returns*.

110. Latour, *We Have Never Been Modern*, 37.

111. Frakes, *Star Trek*.

112. Cohn, "Sex and Death in the Rational World of Defense Intellectuals," 695–96.

113. A full account of the many layers of contact embedded in *Star Trek: First Contact* is beyond the scope of this chapter. In the film, the "good" first contact (with the logical Vulcans, who are essentially ethnographers in this instance) must be preserved to prevent a "bad" contact with the Borg, who have traveled back in time to disrupt first contact and thus immeasurably weaken Earth before "assimilating" its inhabitants into its quasi-communist collective. The film thus represses what anthropology of the same period had already come to critique reflexively—the intertwining of ethnography with colonialism—and insists on a sharp distinction between benevolent, "scientific" ethnographic contact and rapacious colonialism.

Coda

Epigraph. D. L. Martin, *Life in a Box Is a Pretty Life*, 70.

1. Ellison, *Invisible Man*, 372. Ras's self-chosen name is an Ethiopian honorific (as in Ras Tafari).

2. Ellison, *Invisible Man*, 376.

3. Shilliam, "Ethiopianism, Englishness, Britishness," 250–51; Shilliam, "'Ethiopia Shall Stretch Forth Her Hands unto God,'" 109; Sundquist, *To Wake the Nations*, 551–63.

4. Morris, *The Scholar Denied*; S. Wilson, "Black Folk by the Numbers." It is worth noting that Du Bois turned away from academic social science to pursue political

advocacy more fully, and Eric Sundquist notes Du Bois's "increasing reliance on visionary language." Sundquist, *To Wake the Nations*, 540.

5. Latour, *We Have Never Been Modern*, 29.

6. Foucault, *Society Must Be Defended*, 10.

7. Ellison, *Invisible Man*, 374–76. By writing Ras's speech as "dialect," Ellison minoritizes him and makes him a bearer of unmodernity formally as well as thematically. Clifton himself is later killed in the most stereotypical possible way, by a white policeman, for peddling without a license.

8. Selisker, *Human Programming*, 81.

9. See, for a few indicative examples, Oldenziel, *Making Technology Masculine*; Palmié, *Wizards and Scientists*; Jasanoff, *States of Knowledge*; Harding, *Sciences from Below*.

10. Mackey, "Expanding the Repertoire," 7, 8.

11. Cf. Latour, *We Have Never Been Modern*, 34.

12. On contingency and the "open" text, see G. C. White, "Poetics of Contingency," 531. White describes the contingency argument as follows: "If one does the right things to 'keep' the contingency of things in a poem, the logic goes, then one has opened poems and whatever reality inspired them to myriad readings, assuring through form a poem's ability to sustain multiple readings across time and space, and guarding those originary things from ill-use." This account discloses how the appeal to "contingency" registers a sense of ethical responsibility to the real that amounts to epistemic virtue.

13. Ngai, *Ugly Feelings*, 308.

14. Ngai, 309.

15. Cecire, "Ways of Not Reading Gertrude Stein," 292.

16. Spahr and Young, "Foulipo." For a plea to not concede Oulipian writing to hegemonic masculinity, see Leong, "Oulipo, Foulipo, Noulipo."

17. Spahr and Young, "Foulipo." This excerpt comes from one of the essay's "slenderizing" passages, which borrows the Oulipian technique of eliminating a letter (in this case, the letter *R*).

18. Goldsmith, "A Response to Foulipo."

19. For example, Torgovnick, *Gone Primitive*; Hegeman, *Patterns for America*; Cheng, *Second Skin*.

20. Silliman, *Tjanting*, 16. This line opens the poem and recurs throughout.

21. Coney, *Space Is the Place*.

22. Zambia had a space program begun by Edward Mukuka Nkoloso in 1964. See Serpell, "The Zambian 'Afronaut' Who Wanted to Join the Space Race."

23. The song would later notoriously be weaponized against African American Senator Carol Moseley Braun by her white colleague Senator Jesse Helms. Associated Press, "Helms Sings a Song of 'Dixie': Moseley-Braun Looks Away."

24. McCoy, *A Question of Torture*, 7; Cusick, "Music as Torture / Music as Weapon"; Grant, "Pathways to Music Torture." For a celebration of the US space program as a site of "experimental" virtue, see Dimock, "Experimental Humanities."

25. "NASA: Yes! We Are Involved!"

26. G. C. White, *Lyric Shame*.

27. This is not to suggest that the film's politics are necessarily ideal (its misogyny is notable, for instance), only that politics are prioritized over epistemology; epistemology is not allowed to stand in for a politics in the film.

28. Ra, *Untitled*.

29. Ellis, *Territories of the Soul*, 174–76.

30. Mackey, *Whatsaid Serif*, 22.

31. Ra, *Untitled*.

32. Wynter, "Unsettling the Coloniality of Being/Power/Truth/Freedom," 271.

33. Here I am drawing on Michel Foucault's account of subtexts of biopolitical thinking, for example, the biopolitics of Jim Crow and its aftereffects, to which Ra is responding. Foucault, *Society Must Be Defended*, 108–11. I am bound to be met by objections, at this point, about one of the great watchwords of the present moment, "fake news," by which is meant a general social failure to agree on facts. Even in some scholarly circles, a (seemingly) new rise in epistemological instability has been blamed on "postmodern theory" and science studies' analysis of the political nature of knowledge. This is, however, precisely to confuse the dog for its tail. Returning to liberal neutrality is not an option because liberal neutrality was never very neutral in the first place; the difference, now, is that the political nature of knowledge is being avowed openly (if only partially). We ought not repeat the mistake of experimental writing in supposing that purifying our epistemological practices will engender political rectitude; on the contrary, the allegedly epistemological problem of lies in the public sphere should be understood as the much more specific *political* problem of *the ability to force people to treat statements as if they were true regardless of whether they are believed or believable* through disproportionate influence on the law, ownership of media properties and infrastructures (including digital), and intimidation and bullying through political, physical, and economic power. For example, in 2015 the UK government affirmed a requirement to vet and monitor university activities, including research events, under the "anti-terrorist" so-called Prevent duty. While the government guidance briefly mentions "far-right extremism," definitions of extremism as a departure from "British values" clearly indicate how, in practice, it legally intensifies the surveillance of Muslim students, staff, and faculty. At the same time, former Universities Minister Sam Gyimah has condemned and sought to (somehow) disallow the practice of "no-platforming," i.e., the refusal to invite speakers thought to be demeaning to an institution's members. This practice is most often used by student groups to refuse a platform to anti-trans, anti-Semitic, and racist speakers.

Thus certain university events (many Muslim cultural events, panels on Palestinian occupation, events critical of settler colonialism) are disallowed by law, whereas other kinds of events ("controversial" speakers questioning the humanity or rights of queer, trans, immigrant, racialized, and other populations), it is proposed, should not only be allowed but required to be supported. Indeed, as the BBC reports, "The new higher education watchdog, the Office for Students, has a responsibility for protecting free speech," as evidenced in the government's rushed appointment of professional provocateur and avowed racist, eugenicist, and misogynist Toby Young to the Office for Students in 2018. Treating such a scenario as a matter of competing, perhaps insufficiently virtuous epistemologies when certain positions are backed by the force (and budget) of the state seems to me to get the situation backwards. Coughlan, "Free Speech Pledge for Universities"; HM Government, "Revised Prevent Duty Guidance," 5. On irregularities in the appointment of Toby Young to the Office for Students, see especially paragraphs 21–28 in the "Findings" section of Riddell, "The Commissioner for Public Appointments Report on the Recruitment Campaign for the Office for Students."

34. I. Reed, *Mumbo Jumbo*, 45.

35. I. Reed, 45. The classic reading of *Mumbo Jumbo* as a "signifyin(g) text" is in chapter 6 of H. L. Gates, *The Signifying Monkey*.

36. I. Reed, *Mumbo Jumbo*, 11. The line "jes grew" is from *Uncle Tom's Cabin*, but Topsy's long afterlife as a figure of racist minstrel entertainment and material commodification is detailed in R. Bernstein, *Racial Innocence*.

37. I. Reed, *Mumbo Jumbo*, 42; H. L. Gates, *The Signifying Monkey*, 225. On American universities' direct involvement with chattel slavery, see Wilder, *Ebony & Ivy*.

38. Corbett, *Extended Play*, 8–9. See also Mackey, *Discrepant Engagement*, 234.

39. Lyotard, *The Postmodern Condition*, 8.

40. This argument was most influentially advanced, in a short essay touchingly innocent of philosophy of science, by the then editor in chief of *Wired* magazine, Chris Anderson, in 2008. "The End of Theory."

41. On postmodern conspiracy theory in general, see Melley, *Empire of Conspiracy*. On the decolonial potential of deconstruction, see Spivak, "Can the Subaltern Speak?"

42. Cacho, *Social Death*, 2. My emphasis.

43. Sedgwick, "Paranoid Reading and Reparative Reading," 123. On the deflationary power of anecdote, see Katherine Parker-Hay, PhD diss., forthcoming.

44. Sedgwick, "Paranoid Reading and Reparative Reading," 123.

45. Canally to Cecire, "OJ Theory."

46. Harney and Moten, *The Undercommons*, 97; Baucom, *Specters of the Atlantic*; Lowe, *The Intimacies of Four Continents*; Sharpe, *In the Wake*.

47. The classic account of social death is Patterson, *Slavery and Social Death*. See also Agamben, *Homo Sacer*; Butler, *Frames of War*; Cacho, *Social Death*. On supply

chains, see Cowen, *The Deadly Life of Logistics*; and Posner, "The Software that Shapes Workers' Lives."

48. Harney and Moten, *The Undercommons*, 87.

49. Harney and Moten, 98.

50. Hejinian, "Barbarism."

51. Cheng, *The Melancholy of Race*, x.

52. Sharpe, *In the Wake*, 14.

53. For example, Sharpe reads an image of a Haitian girl who, in the aftermath of the 2010 earthquake, has had the label "ship" applied to her forehead as a figural repetition of Phillis Wheatley's renaming by her owners after the *Phillis*, the slave ship that brought her to the Americas. Sharpe, 43–48.

54. A. Reed, *Freedom Time*, 63.

55. D. L. Martin, *Life in a Box Is a Pretty Life*, 70.

56. Krauss, *The Originality of the Avant-Garde and Other Modernist Myths*, 9. On Joseph Cornell and the artist most associated with precision, Marianne Moore, see Levy, *Criminal Ingenuity*.

57. D. L. Martin, *Life in a Box Is a Pretty Life*, 1. Martin also notes this in her acknowledgments.

58. Sharpe, *In the Wake*, 74.

59. D. L. Martin, *Life in a Box Is a Pretty Life*, 92; Starr, "The Degeneracy of the American Negro"; Curry, "The Negro Question"; Hoffman, *Race Traits and Tendencies of the American Negro*. Modernist studies has been eager to welcome W. E. B. Du Bois—who reviewed Hoffman—into the fold of "modernists"; less so his openly racist interlocutors. Du Bois, "*Race Traits and Tendencies of the American Negro*. By Frederick L. Hoffman, F.S.S. [Review]."

60. "Strange fruit" refers to the 1939 Billie Holiday song of that title, which is about Jim Crow–era lynching.

61. Olson, "Projective Verse," 393.

62. Krauss, *The Originality of the Avant-Garde and Other Modernist Myths*, 17.

63. D. L. Martin, *Life in a Box Is a Pretty Life*, 70.

64. Here I draw on Angela Y. Davis's insight that the criminalization of racialized populations has its roots in chattel slavery and the right of the free to control and monitor the movements of the unfree. Davis, *Are Prisons Obsolete?* See also Browne, *Dark Matters*, Cacho, *Social Death*; J. Wang, *Carceral Capitalism*. For a nuanced explanation of why contemporary criminalization cannot simply be shorthanded as a "new Jim Crow," see Gilmore, *Golden Gulag*, 20–29.

65. Duncan, *The Opening of the Field*.

66. D. L. Martin, *Life in a Box Is a Pretty Life*, 72.

67. D. L. Martin, 75.

68. Cacho, *Social Death*, 8. Emphasis in the original.

69. D. L. Martin, *Life in a Box Is a Pretty Life*, 3.

70. D. L. Martin, 2.

71. Martin uses the word "precision" and its variants only a few times in the book. See D. L. Martin, 25, 33, 55.

72. Mackey, *Discrepant Engagement*, 20. On noise and damage *as* neoliberal signal, see James, *Resilience & Melancholy*.

73. I follow Caren Kaplan in understanding "precision targeting" as referring not only to bombs but also to other military location technologies, including consumer GPS and data targeting (as in election analytics, consumer profiling and ad targeting, and "predictive" algorithms such as credit scores and recidivism risk algorithms. Kaplan, "Precision Targets." On the power of "predictive" algorithms to act as self-fulfilling prophecies, see J. Wang, *Carceral Capitalism*, 47–51.

74. Nixon, *Slow Violence and the Environmentalism of the Poor*.

Bibliography

Abrams, M. H. *The Mirror and the Lamp: Romantic Theory and the Critical Tradition*. New York: Oxford University Press, 1953.

Adorno, Theodor W. "Cultural Criticism and Society." In *Prisms*, translated by Samuel Weber and Shierry Weber, 19–34. Cambridge, MA: MIT Press, 1983.

"Aerial Photos at Night." *Science News-Letter* 47, no. 8 (1945): 116.

Agamben, Giorgio. *Homo Sacer: Sovereign Power and Bare Life*. Stanford, CA: Stanford University Press, 1998.

Ahmed, Sara. *The Promise of Happiness*. Durham, NC: Duke University Press, 2010.

———. "Some Preliminary Remarks on the Founding Gestures of the 'New Materialism.'" *European Journal of Women's Studies* 15, no. 1 (February 1, 2008): 23–39. https://doi.org/10.1177/1350506807084854.

Albright, Daniel. *Quantum Poetics: Yeats, Pound, Eliot, and the Science of Modernism*. New York: Cambridge University Press, 1997.

Alder, Ken. "The History of Science as Oxymoron: From Scientific Exceptionalism to Episcience." *Isis* 104, no. 1 (March 1, 2013): 88–101. https://doi.org/10.1086/669889.

Alpers, Svetlana. *The Art of Describing: Dutch Art in the Seventeenth Century*. Chicago: University of Chicago Press, 1983.

Altieri, Charles. "An Idea and Ideal of a Literary Canon." *Critical Inquiry* 10, no. 1 (September 1, 1983): 37–60.

———. "What Theory Can Learn from New Directions in Contemporary American Poetry." *New Literary History* 43, no. 1 (January 1, 2012): 65–87.

Anderson, Benedict. *Imagined Communities: Reflections on the Origin and Spread of Nationalism*. Rev. and extended ed. New York: Verso, 1991.

Anderson, Chris. "The End of Theory: The Data Deluge Makes the Scientific Method Obsolete." *Wired*, June 23, 2008. https://www.wired.com/2008/06/pb-theory/.

Andrews, Kimberly Quiogue. "Trade Secrets: Poetry in the Teaching Machine." *New Literary History* 49, no. 1 (Spring 2018): 71–91.

Arckens, Elien. "'In This Told-Backward Biography': Marianne Moore against Survival in Her Queer Archival Poetry." *WSQ: Women's Studies Quarterly* 44, no. 1 (2016): 111–27. https://doi.org/10.1353/wsq.2016.0020.

"Are You a Connoisseur of Art?" *Poetry: A Magazine of Verse*, March 1921. Modernist Journals Project.

Armantrout, Rae. "Why Don't Women Do Language-Oriented Writing?" In *In the American Tree: Language, Realism, Poetry*, edited by Ronald Silliman, 518–20. 2nd ed. Orono, ME: National Poetry Foundation, 2002.

Armstrong, Isobel. *Victorian Glassworlds: Glass Culture and the Imagination 1830–1880*. Oxford: Oxford University Press, 2008.

Armstrong, Nancy. *Desire and Domestic Fiction: A Political History of the Novel*. New ed. New York: Oxford University Press, 1989.

Armstrong, Tim. *Modernism, Technology, and the Body: A Cultural Study*. Cambridge: Cambridge University Press, 1998.

Asafu-Adjaye, John, Linus Blomqvist, Stewart Brand, Barry Brook, Ruth DeFries, Erle Ellis, Christopher Foreman, et al. "The Ecomodernist Manifesto." ecomodernism.org, 2015. http://www.ecomodernism.org/manifesto/.

Ashton, Jennifer. *From Modernism to Postmodernism: American Poetry and Theory in the Twentieth Century*. Cambridge: Cambridge University Press, 2005

Associated Press. "Helms Sings a Song of 'Dixie': Moseley-Braun Looks Away." *Los Angeles Times*, August 6, 1993. http://articles.latimes.com/1993-08-06/news/mn-20952_1_carol-moseley-braun.

Auerbach, Erich. *Scenes from the Drama of European Literature*. Minneapolis: University of Minnesota Press, 1984.

Bacon, Francis. *Francis Bacon: The New Organon*. Edited by Lisa Jardine and Michael Silverthorne. Cambridge University Press, 2000.

Baer, Ulrich. "Photography and Hysteria: Toward a Poetics of the Flash." *Yale Journal of Criticism* 7, no. 1 (1994): 41–77.

Barnhisel, Greg. *Cold War Modernists: Art, Literature, and American Cultural Diplomacy*. New York: Columbia University Press, 2015.

Barthes, Roland. *Camera Lucida: Reflections on Photography*. New York: Hill and Wang, 1981.

———. "The Reality Effect." In *The Rustle of Language*, translated by Richard Howard, 141–48. Berkeley: University of California Press, 1989.

———. *Writing Degree Zero*. Translated by Annette Lavers and Colin Smith. New York: Hill and Wang, 1968.

Bateson, Gregory. *Steps to an Ecology of Mind: Collected Essays in Anthropology, Psychiatry, Evolution, and Epistemology*. New ed. Chicago: University of Chicago Press, 2000.

Baucom, Ian. *Specters of the Atlantic: Finance Capital, Slavery, and the Philosophy of History*. Durham, NC: Duke University Press, 2005.

Bayard de Volo, Lorraine. "Unmanned? Gender Recalibrations and the Rise of Drone

Warfare." *Politics & Gender* 12, no. 1 (March 2016): 50–77. https://doi.org/10.1017/S1743923X15000252.

Bazin, André. *What Is Cinema?* Translated by Hugh Gray. Vol. 1. 2 vols. Berkeley: University of California Press, 2005.

Beasley, Rebecca. *Ezra Pound and the Visual Culture of Modernism*. Cambridge: Cambridge University Press, 2007.

Becker, Daniel Levin. *Many Subtle Channels: In Praise of Potential Literature*. Cambridge, MA: Harvard University Press, 2012.

Beer, Gillian. *Darwin's Plots: Evolutionary Narrative in Darwin, George Eliot, and Nineteenth-Century Fiction*. 2nd ed. Cambridge: Cambridge University Press, 2000.

———. *Open Fields: Science in Cultural Encounter*. Oxford: Oxford University Press, 1996.

Bell, Ian F. A. *Critic as Scientist: The Modernist Poetics of Ezra Pound*. London: Methuen, 1981.

Beloof, Robert. "Prosody and Tone: The 'Mathematics' of Marianne Moore." In *Marianne Moore: A Collection of Critical Essays*, edited by Charles Tomlinson, 144–49. Englewood Cliffs, NJ: Prentice-Hall, 1969.

Benjamin, Walter. *The Arcades Project*. Edited by Rolf Tiedemann. Translated by Howard Eiland and Kevin McLaughlin. Cambridge, MA: Belknap Press of Harvard University Press, 1999.

———. "On Some Motifs in Baudelaire." In *Walter Benjamin: Selected Writings*. Vol. 4, *1938–1940*. Edited by Edmund Jephcott, Howard Eiland, and Michael W. Jennings, 313–55. Cambridge, MA: Harvard University Press, 2003.

———. "On the Concept of History." In *Walter Benjamin: Selected Writings*. Vol. 4, *1938–1940*, edited by Edmund Jephcott, Howard Eiland, and Michael W. Jennings, 389–400. Cambridge, MA: Harvard University Press, 2006.

———. "The Storyteller: Observations on the Works of Nikolai Leskov." In *Walter Benjamin: Selected Writings*. Vol. 3, *1935–1938*, edited by Howard Eiland and Michael W. Jennings, 143–66. Cambridge, MA: Belknap Press, 2006.

———. "The Work of Art in the Age of Its Technological Reproducibility." In *Walter Benjamin: Selected Writings*. Vol. 3, *1935–1938*, edited by Howard Eiland and Michael W. Jennings, 101–33. Cambridge, MA: Belknap Press, 2006.

Bensaude-Vincent, Bernadette. "A Historical Perspective on Science and Its 'Others.'" *Isis* 100, no. 2 (June 1, 2009): 359–68. https://doi.org/10.1086/599547.

Bergvall, Caroline, Laynie Browne, Teresa Carmody, and Vanessa Place, eds. *I'll Drown My Book: Conceptual Writing by Women*. Los Angeles: Les Figues Press, 2012.

Berlant, Lauren, and Michael Warner. "Sex in Public." *Critical Inquiry* 24, no. 2 (1998): 547–66.

Bernard, Claude. *Introduction à l'étude de la médecine expérimentale*. Paris: Baillière, 1865.

Bernstein, Charles. "The Academy in Peril: William Carlos Williams Meets the MLA." In *Content's Dream: Essays, 1975–1984*, 244–51. Los Angeles: Sun & Moon Press, 1986.

———. "Gertrude and Alice in Vichyland." Plenary lecture presented at the European Gertrude Stein Network, Paris, November 26, 2016. https://jacket2.org/commentary/gertrude-and-alice-vichyland.

———, ed. "Gertrude Stein's War Years: Setting the Record Straight." In *Jacket2*, 2012. https://jacket2.org/feature/gertrude-steins-war-years-setting-record-straight.

———. "Poetry Scene Investigation." In *Attack of the Difficult Poems: Essays and Inventions*, 239–55. Chicago: University of Chicago Press, 2011.

Bernstein, Robin. *Racial Innocence: Performing American Childhood and Race from Slavery to Civil Rights*. New York: New York University Press, 2011.

Bersani, Leo. *The Culture of Redemption*. Cambridge, MA: Harvard University Press, 1990.

———. "Is the Rectum a Grave?" *October* 43 (December 1, 1987): 197–222. https://doi.org/10.2307/3397574.

Bigg, Charlotte. "The Panorama, or *La Nature à Coup d'Oeil*." In *Observing Nature—Representing Experience: The Osmotic Dynamics of Romanticism, 1800–1850*, edited by Erna Fiorentini, translated by Julia Bernard and Eddie Crockett, 73–95. Berlin: Reimer, 2007.

"The Birth of a Nation." In *Kansas Board of Review Movie Index*. Topeka: Kansas Historical Society, 1923. https://www.kshs.org/statearchives/archives_board_of_reviews/search/film:birth%20of%20a%20nation/company:/star:/elimination:/begyr:/endyr:/submit:SEARCH.

Blackmer, Corinne E. "African Masks and the Arts of Passing in Gertrude Stein's 'Melanctha' and Nella Larsen's 'Passing.'" *Journal of the History of Sexuality* 4, no. 2 (October 1993): 230–63.

Blum, W. C. "American Letter." *The Dial; a Semi-Monthly Journal of Literary Criticism, Discussion, and Information* 70 (May 1921): 562–68.

Bourneville, Désiré Magloire, and Paul Regnard. *Iconographie photographique de la Salpêtrière*. Paris: Progrès médical, 1876.

Bradway, Tyler. "Introduction: The Promise of Experimental Writing." *College Literature* 46, no. 1 (January 9, 2019): 1–31.

Brand, Dionne. *The Blue Clerk: Ars Poetica in 59 Versos*. Durham, NC: Duke University Press, 2018.

Bray, Joe, Alison Gibbons, and Brian McHale, eds. *The Routledge Companion to Experimental Literature*. London: Routledge, 2012.

Bridgman, Richard. *Gertrude Stein in Pieces*. New York: Oxford University Press, 1970.

Brinnin, John Malcolm. *The Third Rose: Gertrude Stein and Her World*. Boston: Little, Brown and Company, 1959.

Brion, Patrick, and Rene Gilson. "A Style of Spectacle: Interview with Busby Berkeley." *Cahiers du Cinéma in English* 2 (1966): 26–37.

Brodine, Karen. *Illegal Assembly*. New York: Hanging Loose Press, 1980.

Brooks, Peter. "Storied Bodies, or Nana at Last Unveil'd." *Critical Inquiry* 16, no. 1 (1989): 1–32.

Brown, Bill. *The Material Unconscious: American Amusement, Stephen Crane and the Economies of Play*. Cambridge, MA: Harvard University Press, 1996.

———. *A Sense of Things: The Object Matter of American Literature*. Chicago: University of Chicago Press, 2003.

Brown, Frederick. *Zola: A Life*. New York: Farrar, Straus and Giroux, 1995.

Browne, Simone. *Dark Matters: On the Surveillance of Blackness*. Durham, NC: Duke University Press, 2015.

Burke, Kenneth. "Likings of an Observationist." In *Marianne Moore: A Collection of Critical Essays*, edited by Charles Tomlinson, 125–33. Englewood Cliffs, NJ: Prentice-Hall, 1969.

Burnett, D. Graham. *The Sounding of the Whale*. Chicago: University of Chicago Press, 2012.

Butler, Judith. *Bodies That Matter: On the Discursive Limits of "Sex."* New York: Routledge, 1993.

———. *Frames of War: When Is Life Grievable?* London: Verso, 2009.

———. *Gender Trouble: Feminism and the Subversion of Identity*. 10th anniversary ed. New York: Routledge, 1999.

Cacho, Lisa Marie. *Social Death: Racialized Rightlessness and the Criminalization of the Unprotected*. New York: New York University Press, 2012.

Cady, Edwin. Introduction to *Tales, Sketches, and Reports*, vol. 8. *The Works of Stephen Crane*. Charlottesville: University Press of Virginia, 1973.

Calhoun, Craig J., ed. *Sociology in America: A History*. Chicago: University of Chicago Press, 2007.

Campbell, Joseph Keim, Michael O'Rourke, and Matthew H. Slater, eds. *Carving Nature at Its Joints: Natural Kinds in Metaphysics and Science*. Cambridge, MA: MIT Press, 2011.

Campbell-Kelly, Martin, and William Aspray. *Computer: A History of the Information Machine*. The Sloan Technology Series. Boulder, CO: Westview, 2004.

Canguilhem, Georges. "Machine and Organism." Translated by Mark Cohen and Randall Cherry. In *Incorporations*, edited by Jonathan Crary and Sanford Kwinter, 45–69. Zone 6. New York: Zone, 1992.

Cantor, Geoffrey. "The Rhetoric of Experiment." In *The Uses of Experiment: Studies in the Natural Sciences*, edited by David Gooding, T. J. Pinch, and Simon Schaffer, 159–80. Cambridge: Cambridge University Press, 1989.

Carby, Hazel V. "The Politics of Fiction, Anthropology, and the Folk: Zora Neale

Hurston." In *New Essays on "Their Eyes Were Watching God,"* edited by Michael Awkward, 71–90. Cambridge: Cambridge University Press, 1991.

Capshew, James H., and Karen A. Rader. "Big Science: Price to the Present." *Osiris*, 2nd series, 7 (January 1, 1992): 2–25.

Cecire, Natalia. "Habemus PM; or, Irritation after the EU Referendum." *Jacket2* (blog), July 11, 2016. http://jacket2.org/commentary/habemus-pm-or-irritation-after-eu-referendum.

———. "Marianne Moore's Precision." *Arizona Quarterly: A Journal of American Literature, Culture, and Theory* 67, no. 4 (2011): 83–110.

———. "Ways of Not Reading Gertrude Stein." *ELH* 82, no. 1 (2015): 281–312.

Chakrabarty, Dipesh. *Provincializing Europe: Postcolonial Thought and Historical Difference*. Princeton, NJ: Princeton University Press, 2000.

Chandler, James K. *England in 1819: The Politics of Literary Culture and the Case of Romantic Historicism*. Chicago: University of Chicago Press, 1998.

Charette, Robert N. "The STEM Crisis Is a Myth." *IEEE Spectrum*, August 30, 2013.

Chaudhuri, Shohini. "Nine Cinematic Devices for Staging (In)Visible War and the (Vanishing) Colonial Present." In *Disappearing War: Interdisciplinary Perspectives on Cinema and Erasure in the Post-9/11 World*, edited by Christina Hellmich and Lisa Purse, 170–90. Edinburgh: Edinburgh University Press, 2017.

Cheng, Anne Anlin. *The Melancholy of Race*. Race and American Culture. Oxford: Oxford University Press, 2000.

———. *Second Skin: Josephine Baker and the Modern Surface*. New York: Oxford University Press, 2011.

Chow, Rey. *The Age of the World Target: Self-Referentiality in War, Theory, and Comparative Work*. Durham, NC: Duke University Press, 2006.

Christian, Barbara. "The Race for Theory." In "The Nature and Context of Minority Discourse," edited by Abdul JanMohamed and David Lloyd. Special issue, *Cultural Critique* 6 (Spring 1987): 51–63.

Clifford, James. "On Ethnographic Allegory." In Clifford and Marcus, *Writing Culture*, 27–50.

———. *The Predicament of Culture: Twentieth-Century Ethnography, Literature, and Art*. Cambridge, MA: Harvard University Press, 1988.

———. *Returns: Becoming Indigenous in the Twenty-First Century*. Cambridge, MA: Harvard University Press, 2013.

Clifford, James, and George E. Marcus, eds. *Writing Culture: The Poetics and Politics of Ethnography*. Berkeley: University of California Press, 1986.

Clover, Joshua. "The Genealogical Avant-Garde." *Lana Turner*, no. 7 (2014): 224–26.

Cohen, Milton A. "Black Brutes and Mulatto Saints: The Racial Hierarchy of Stein's 'Melanctha.'" *Black American Literature Forum* 18, no. 3 (Autumn 1984): 119–21.

Cohen, Patricia Cline, Timothy J. Gilfoyle, and Helen Lefkowitz Horowitz. *The Flash*

Press: Sporting Male Weeklies in 1840s New York. Chicago: University of Chicago Press, 2008.

Cohn, Carol. "Sex and Death in the Rational World of Defense Intellectuals." *Signs* 12, no. 4 (Summer 1987): 687–718.

Collignon, Fabienne. *Rocket States: Atomic Weaponry and the Cultural Imagination*. New York: Bloomsbury, 2014.

Comolli, Jean-Louis. "Dancing Images: Busby Berkeley's Kaleidescope." *Cahiers du Cinéma in English* 2 (1966): 22–25.

Coney, John. *Space Is the Place*. Video recording. Plexifilm, 2003.

Cooter, Roger, and Stephen Pumphrey. "Separate Spheres and Public Places: Reflections on the History of Science Popularization and Science in Popular Culture." *History of Science* 32 (1994): 237–67.

Corbett, John. *Extended Play: Sounding Off from John Cage to Dr. Funkenstein*. Durham, NC: Duke University Press, 1994.

Costello, Bonnie. *Marianne Moore: Imaginary Possessions*. Cambridge, MA: Harvard University Press, 1981.

———. "'To a Snail': A Lesson in Compression." *Marianne Moore Newsletter* 3, no. 2 (Fall 1979): 11–15.

Coughlan, Sean. "Free Speech Pledge for Universities." *BBC News*, May 3, 2018, sec. Family & Education. http://www.bbc.co.uk/news/education-43989236.

Cowen, Deborah. *The Deadly Life of Logistics: Mapping Violence in Global Trade*. Minneapolis: University of Minnesota Press, 2014.

Cowles, Henry M. "Hypothesis Bound: Trial and Error in the Nineteenth Century." *Isis* 106, no. 3 (2015): 635–45.

Coyle, Michael. *Ezra Pound, Popular Genres, and the Discourse of Culture*. University Park: Pennsylvania State University Press, 1995.

Crane, Conrad. *Bombs, Cities, and Civilians: American Airpower Strategy in World War II*. Lawrence: University Press of Kansas, 1993.

Crane, Stephen. *The Correspondence of Stephen Crane*. Edited by Stanley Wertheim and Paul Sorrentino. New York: Columbia University Press, 1988.

———. "Death and the Child." In *Prose and Poetry: Maggie: A Girl of the Street; The Red Badge of Courage; Stories, Sketches and Journalism; Poetry*, 943–63. Edited by J. C. Levenson. New York: Library of America, 1984.

———. *Maggie: A Girl of the Streets*. In *Prose and Poetry: Maggie: A Girl of the Streets; The Red Badge of Courage; Stories, Sketches and Journalism; Poetry*, 5–78. Edited by J. C. Levenson. New York: Library of America, 1984.

Crary, Jonathan. *Suspensions of Perception: Attention, Spectacle, and Modern Culture*. Cambridge, MA: MIT Press, 1999.

———. *Techniques of the Observer: On Vision and Modernity in the Nineteenth Century*. Cambridge, MA: MIT Press, 1990.

Curry, J[abez] L[amar] M[onroe]. "The Negro Question." *Popular Science Monthly*, June 1899, 177–85.

Cusick, Suzanne G. "Music as Torture / Music as Weapon." *Trans: Revista Transcultural de Música*, no. 10 (2006). https://www.sibetrans.com/trans/articulo/152/music-as-torture-music-as-weapon.

Daggett, Cara. "Drone Disorientations." *International Feminist Journal of Politics* 17, no. 3 (July 3, 2015): 361–79. https://doi.org/10.1080/14616742.2015.1075317.

Daston, Lorraine. "On Scientific Observation." *Isis* 99, no. 1 (March 1, 2008): 97–110.

———. "Rev. of M. Norton Wise, Ed., *The Values of Precision*." *Isis* 87, no. 3 (September 1, 1996): 517–19.

———. "Type Specimens and Scientific Memory." *Critical Inquiry* 31, no. 1 (2004): 153–82. https://doi.org/10.1086/427306.

Daston, Lorraine, and Peter Galison. *Objectivity*. New York: Zone Books, 2007.

Daum, Andreas W. "Varieties of Popular Science and the Transformations of Public Knowledge: Some Historical Reflections." *Isis* 100, no. 2 (June 1, 2009): 319–32. https://doi.org/10.1086/599550.

Davidson, Michael, Larry Eigner, Bob Perelman, Steve McCaffery, Peter Seaton, Rae Armantrout, Dick Higgins, Jackson Mac Low, Carl Andre, and Robert Grenier. "Reading Stein." *L=A=N=G=U=A=G=E* 6 (1978). http://eclipsearchive.org/projects/LANGUAGEn6/pictures/001.html.

Davidson, Michael, Lyn Hejinian, Ron Silliman, and Barrett Watten. *Leningrad: American Writers in the Soviet Union*. San Francisco: Mercury House, 1991.

Davis, Angela Y. *Are Prisons Obsolete?* New York: Seven Stories Press, 2003.

Day, Iyko. "Being or Nothingness: Indigeneity, Antiblackness, and Settler Colonial Critique." *Critical Ethnic Studies* 1, no. 2 (2015): 102–21. https://www.jstor.org/stable/10.5749/jcritethnstud.1.2.0102.

Dear, Peter. "Totius in Verba: Rhetoric and Authority in the Early Royal Society." *Isis* 76, no. 2 (June 1985): 145–61.

Delord, Taxile. "La femme sans nom." In *Les français peints par eux-mêmes: Encyclopédie morale du dix-neuvième siècle*, 1:244–56. Paris: L. Curmer, 1840. http://gallica.bnf.fr/ark:/12148/bpt6k1025067f.

de Man, Paul. "Literary History and Literary Modernity." In *Blindness and Insight: Essays in the Rhetoric of Contemporary Criticism*, 142–65. 2nd ed., rev. Minneapolis: University of Minnesota Press, 1983.

Deutscher, Penelope. *Foucault's Futures: A Critique of Reproductive Reason*. New York: Columbia University Press, 2017.

DeWitt, Anne. *Moral Authority, Men of Science, and the Victorian Novel*. Cambridge: Cambridge University Press, 2013.

Díaz, Eva. *The Experimenters: Chance and Design at Black Mountain College*. Chicago: University of Chicago Press, 2015.

Diepeveen, Leonard. *The Difficulties of Modernism*. New York: Routledge, 2003.

Dimock, Wai Chee. "Education Populism." *PMLA* 132 (October 2017): 1089–96.

———. "Experimental Humanities." *PMLA* 132, no. 2 (March 1, 2017): 241–49. https://doi.org/10.1632/pmla.2017.132.2.241.

Dinerstein, Joel. *Swinging the Machine: Modernity, Technology, and African American Culture between the World Wars*. Amherst: University of Massachusetts Press, 2003.

Douglas, Mary. *Purity and Danger: An Analysis of Concepts of Pollution and Taboo*. Routledge Classics. London: Routledge, 2002.

Dove, Michael R. "Uncertainty, Humility, and Adaptation in the Tropical Forest: The Agricultural Augury of the Kantu.'" *Ethnology* 32, no. 2 (1993): 145–67. https://doi.org/10.2307/3773770.

Doyle, Jennifer. "Dirt Off Her Shoulders." *GLQ: A Journal of Lesbian and Gay Studies* 19, no. 4 (January 1, 2013): 419–33. https://doi.org/10.1215/10642684-2279897.

Doyle, Laura. "The Flat, the Round, and Gertrude Stein: Race and the Shape of Modern(ist) History." *Modernism/Modernity* 7, no. 2 (April 1, 2000): 249–71. https://doi.org/10.1353/mod.2000.0032.

Drucker, Johanna. "Experimental Writing (or Poetry Lab)." In *The Noulipian Analects*, edited by Christine Wertheim and Matias Viegener, 75. Los Angeles: Les Figues, 2007.

Du Bois, W. E. B. "*Race Traits and Tendencies of the American Negro*. By Frederick L. Hoffman, F.S.S. [Review]." *Annals of the American Academy of Political and Social Science* 9 (January 1897): 127–33.

Dummett, Michael A. E. *Frege and Other Philosophers*. Oxford: Oxford University Press, 1991.

———. *Frege: Philosophy of Language*. 2nd ed. Cambridge, MA: Harvard University Press, 1981.

———. "Objectivity and Reality in Lotze and Frege." *Inquiry* 25, no. 1 (1982): 95–114.

Duncan, Robert. *The Opening of the Field*. New York: Grove Press, 1960.

Dworkin, Craig Douglas. *Reading the Illegible*. Avant-Garde & Modernism Studies. Evanston, IL: Northwestern University Press, 2003.

Ebury, Katherine. *Modernism and Cosmology: Absurd Lights*. New York: Palgrave Macmillan, 2014.

Edelman, Lee. "Against Survival: Queerness in a Time That's out of Joint." *Shakespeare Quarterly* 62, no. 2 (2011): 148–69. https://doi.org/10.1353/shq.2011.0015.

———. *No Future: Queer Theory and the Death Drive*. Durham, NC: Duke University Press, 2004.

Edgerton, David. "C. P. Snow as Anti-historian of British Science: Revisiting the Technocratic Moment, 1959–1964." *History of Science* 43, no. 2 (2005): 187–208. https://doi.org/10.1177/007327530504300205.

Edmond, Jacob. *A Common Strangeness: Contemporary Poetry, Cross-Cultural Encounter, Comparative Literature*. New York: Fordham University Press, 2012.

"The Egoist: An Individualist Review." *Little Review: A Magazine of the Arts*, August 1915. Modernist Journals Project.

Eliot, T. S. Introduction to *Selected Poems*, by Marianne Moore. New York: Macmillan, 1935.

———. "Tradition and the Individual Talent." In *Selected Prose of T.S. Eliot*, edited by Frank Kermode, 37–44. New York: Harcourt, Brace, Jovanovich, 1975.

———. *The Waste Land and Other Poems*. Edited by Frank Kermode. New York: Penguin, 1998.

Elkins, James. "Precision, Misprecision, Misprision." *Critical Inquiry* 25, no. 1 (October 1, 1998): 169–80.

Ellis, Nadia. *Territories of the Soul: Queered Belonging in the Black Diaspora*. Durham, NC: Duke University Press, 2015.

Ellison, Ralph. *Invisible Man*. Penguin Essentials. New York: Penguin, 2014.

Emerson, Lori. *Reading Writing Interfaces: From the Digital to the Bookbound*. Minneapolis: University of Minnesota Press, 2014.

Emory University Library. "Finding Aid, Salman Rushdie Papers: Born Digital Materials," n.d. http://findingaids.library.emory.edu/documents/rushdie1000/series11/.

Enloe, Cynthia H. *Does Khaki Become You? The Militarisation of Women's Lives*. London: Pluto Press, 1983.

Enright, Ray, and Busby Berkeley, dirs. *Dames*. Warner Bros., 1934.

Epstein, Andrew. *Attention Equals Life: The Pursuit of the Everyday in Contemporary Poetry and Culture*. Oxford: Oxford University Press, 2016.

———. "Verse vs. Verse: The Language Poets Are Taking Over the Academy, but Will Success Destroy Their Integrity?" *Lingua Franca* (September 2000): 45–54.

Erickson, Paul, Judy L. Klein, Lorraine Daston, Rebecca Lemov, Thomas Sturm, and Michael D. Gordin. *How Reason Almost Lost Its Mind: The Strange Career of Cold War Rationality*. Chicago: University of Chicago Press, 2013.

Evans, Brad. "Introduction: Rethinking the Disciplinary Confluence of Anthropology and Literary Studies." *Criticism* 49, no. 4 (August 22, 2008): 429–45.

Fabian, Johannes. *Time and the Other: How Anthropology Makes Its Object*. New York: Columbia University Press, 1983.

Farland, Maria. "Gertrude Stein's Brain Work." *American Literature* 76, no. 1 (2004): 117–48.

Fausto-Sterling, Anne. "Science Matters, Culture Matters." *Perspectives in Biology and Medicine* 46, no. 1 (2003): 109–24.

———. *Sex/Gender: Biology in a Social World*. New York: Routledge, 2012.

Fayad, Mona. "Aliens, Androgynes, and Anthropology: Le Guin's Critique of Representation in 'The Left Hand of Darkness.'" *Mosaic: An Interdisciplinary Critical Journal* 30, no. 3 (1997): 59–73.

Feldman, Evelyn, and Michael Barsanti. "Paying Attention: The Rosenbach Museum's

Marianne Moore Archive and the New York Moderns." *Journal of Modern Literature* 22, no. 1 (Autumn 1998): 7–30.

Felski, Rita. *The Gender of Modernity*. Cambridge, MA: Harvard University Press, 1995.

———. *The Limits of Critique*. Chicago: University of Chicago Press, 2015.

Ferguson, Roderick A. *The Reorder of Things: The University and Its Pedagogies of Minority Difference*. Minneapolis: University of Minnesota Press, 2012.

Filreis, Alan. *Counter-revolution of the Word: The Conservative Attack on Modern Poetry, 1945–1960*. Chapel Hill: University of North Carolina Press, 2008.

Flam, Jack D., and Miriam Deutch, eds. *Primitivism and Twentieth-Century Art: A Documentary History*. The Documents of Twentieth-Century Art. Berkeley: University of California Press, 2003.

Fleissner, Jennifer L. "Dictation Anxiety: The Stenographer's Stake in Dracula." *Nineteenth-Century Contexts* 22, no. 3 (January 1, 2000): 417–55. https://doi.org/10.1080/08905490008583519.

———. *Women, Compulsion, Modernity: The Moment of American Naturalism*. Chicago: University of Chicago, 2004.

Flint, Kate. *Flash! Photography, Writing, and Surprising Illumination*. New ed. New York: Oxford University Press, 2017.

———. "Surround, Background, and the Overlooked." *Victorian Studies* 57, no. 3 (2015): 449–61.

Foucault, Michel. *The History of Sexuality: An Introduction*. Translated by Robert Hurley. Vintage Books ed. Vol. 1. 3 vols. New York: Vintage Books, 1988.

———. *The Order of Things: An Archaeology of the Human Sciences*. New York: Vintage Books, 1973.

———. "Preface to Transgression." In *Language, Counter-memory, Practice: Selected Essays and Interviews*, translated by Donald F. Bouchard and Sherry Simon, 29–52. Ithaca, NY: Cornell University Press, 1977.

———. *"Society Must Be Defended": Lectures at the Collège de France, 1975–76*. 1st ed. New York: Picador, 2003.

Fraiman, Susan. *Cool Men and the Second Sex*. New York: Columbia University Press, 2003.

Frakes, Jonathan, dir. *Star Trek: First Contact*. Paramount, 1996.

François, Anne-Lise. *Open Secrets: The Literature of Uncounted Experience*. Meridian: Crossing Aesthetics. Stanford, CA: Stanford University Press, 2008.

Franklin, Seb. "The Contexts of Forms." *World Picture*, no. 11 (Summer 2016). http://www.worldpicturejournal.com/WP_11/Franklin_11.html.

Frege, Gottlob. *Begriffsschrift: A Formula Language, Modeled upon That of Arithmetic, for Pure Thought*. In *From Frege to Gödel: A Source Book in Mathematical Logic, 1879–1931*, edited by Jean Van Heijenoort, 1–82. Source Books in the History of the Sciences. Cambridge, MA: Harvard University Press, 1967.

Freud, Sigmund. *Introductory Lectures on Psycho-analysis*. New York: Norton, 1977.

———. "The 'Uncanny.'" In *An Infantile Neurosis and Other Works*, by Sigmund Freud, vol. XVII (1917–1919). The Standard Edition of the Complete Psychological Works of Sigmund Freud. London: Hogarth Press, 1955.

Fried, Michael. *Realism, Writing, Disfiguration: On Thomas Eakins and Stephen Crane*. Paperback ed. Chicago: University of Chicago Press, 1989.

Fuss, Diana. *Dying Modern: A Meditation on Elegy*. Durham, NC: Duke University Press, 2013.

Galison, Peter. *Image and Logic: A Material Culture of Microphysics*. Chicago: University of Chicago Press, 1997.

Gallagher, Catherine. "Formalism and Time." *MLQ: Modern Language Quarterly* 61, no. 1 (March 1, 2000): 229–51.

Galloway, Alexander R. *The Interface Effect*. Cambridge: Polity, 2012.

Galvin, Rachel. "Gertrude Stein, Pétain, and the Politics of Translation." *ELH* 83, no. 1 (2016): 259–92. https://doi.org/10.1353/elh.2016.0008.

———. *News of War: Civilian Poetry, 1936–1945*. Oxford: Oxford University Press, 2017.

Gannett, Henry. *Statistical Abstract of the World*. 1st ed. New York: J. Wiley & Sons, 1907.

———. *Statistical Atlas of the United States Based upon Results of the Eleventh Census*. Washington: Government Printing Office, 1898.

Gates, Barbara. *Kindred Nature: Victorian and Edwardian Women Embrace the Living World*. Chicago: University of Chicago Press, 1998.

Gates, Henry Louis. *The Signifying Monkey: A Theory of Afro-American Literary Criticism*. New York: Oxford University Press, 1988.

Genette, Gérard. "Figures." In *Figures of Literary Discourse*, translated by Alan Sheridan, 45–60. New York: Columbia University Press, 1982.

Ghamari-Tabrizi, Sharon. *The Worlds of Herman Kahn: The Intuitive Science of Thermonuclear War*. Cambridge, MA: Harvard University Press, 2005.

Gilbert, Sandra M. "Marianne Moore as Female Female Impersonator." In *Marianne Moore: The Art of a Modernist*, edited by Joseph Parisi, 27–46. Studies in Modern Literature, no. 109. Ann Arbor: UMI Research Press, 1990.

Gilman, Sander L. *Difference and Pathology: Stereotypes of Sexuality, Race, and Madness*. Ithaca, NY: Cornell University Press, 1985.

Gilmore, Ruth Wilson. *Golden Gulag: Prisons, Surplus, Crisis, and Opposition in Globalizing California*. Berkeley: University of California Press, 2007.

Ginzburg, Carlo. *Clues, Myths, and the Historical Method*. Translated by John Tedeschi and Anne C. Tedeschi. Baltimore: Johns Hopkins University Press, 1989.

Gladman, Renee, and giovanni singleton, eds. "Expanding the Repertoire: Continuity & Change in African-American Writing," special issue, *Tripwire: A Journal of Poetics* 5 (Fall 2001).

Goble, Mark. *Beautiful Circuits: Modernism and the Mediated Life*. New York: Columbia University Press, 2010.

Golding, Alan. "Experimental Modernisms." In *The Cambridge Companion to Modern American Poetry*, edited by Walter Kalaidjian, 37–49. Cambridge: Cambridge University Press, 2014.

Goldsby, Jacqueline Denise. *A Spectacular Secret: Lynching in American Life and Literature*. Chicago: University of Chicago Press, 2006.

Goldsmith, Kenneth. "A Response to Foulipo." *Drunken Boat*, no. 8 (2006). http://www.drunkenboat.com/db8/oulipo/feature-oulipo/essays/goldsmith/response.html.

Golinski, Jan. "'The Nicety of Experiment': Precision of Measurement and Precision of Reasoning in Late Eighteenth-Century Chemistry." In *The Values of Precision*, edited by M. Norton Wise, 72–91. Princeton, NJ: Princeton University Press, 1995.

Goncourt, Edmond de, and Jules de Goncourt. *Pages from the Goncourt Journal*. Translated by Robert Baldick. Oxford: Oxford University Press, 1962.

Gooding, David, T. J. Pinch, and Simon Schaffer, eds. *The Uses of Experiment: Studies in the Natural Sciences*. Cambridge: Cambridge University Press, 1989.

Gordin, Michael D. *The Pseudoscience Wars: Immanuel Velikovsky and the Birth of the Modern Fringe*. Chicago: University of Chicago Press, 2012.

Gordon, Deborah. "The Politics of Ethnographic Authority: Race and Writing in the Ethnography of Margaret Mead and Zora Neale Hurston." In *Modernist Anthropology: From Fieldwork to Text*, edited by Marc Manganaro, 146–62. Princeton, NJ: Princeton University Press, 1990.

Grant, Morag Josephine. "Pathways to Music Torture." *Transposition: Musique et Sciences Sociales*, no. 4 (July 15, 2014). https://doi.org/10.4000/transposition.494.

Green, David L. "*The Comedian as the Letter C*, Carlos, and *Contact*." *Twentieth Century Literature* 27, no. 3 (October 1, 1981): 262–71. https://doi.org/10.2307/441231.

Gregory, Elizabeth, ed. *The Critical Response to Marianne Moore*. Westport, CT: Praeger, 2003.

———. "'Still Leafing': Celebrity, Confession, Marianne Moore's 'The Camperdown Elm' and the Scandal of Age." *Journal of Modern Literature* 35, no. 3 (2012): 51–76.

Grier, David Alan. *When Computers Were Human*. Princeton, NJ: Princeton University Press, 2005.

Griffiths, Alison. *Wondrous Difference: Cinema, Anthropology & Turn-of-the-Century Visual Culture*. New York: Columbia University Press, 2002.

Grimstad, Paul. *Experience and Experimental Writing: Literary Pragmatism from Emerson to the Jameses*. Oxford: Oxford University Press, 2013.

Gunn, Thom. "Three Hard Women: H.D., Marianne Moore, and Mina Loy." In *Shelf Life: Essays, Memoirs and an Interview*, 33–52. London: Faber, 1994.

Gunning, Tom. "In Your Face: Physiognomy, Photography, and the Gnostic Mission of Early Film." *Modernism/Modernity* 4, no. 1 (1997): 1–29.

Hacking, Ian. *Representing and Intervening: Introductory Topics in the Philosophy of Natural Science*. Cambridge: Cambridge University Press, 1983.

Hale, Grace Elizabeth. *A Nation of Outsiders: How the White Middle Class Fell in Love with Rebellion in Postwar America*. Oxford: Oxford University Press, 2011.

Hales, Peter B. *Silver Cities: The Photography of American Urbanization, 1839–1915*. American Civilization. Philadelphia: Temple University Press, 1984.

Hall, Donald. "Marianne Moore, the Art of Poetry No. 4." *Paris Review*, Summer–Fall 1961. http://www.theparisreview.org/interviews/4637/the-art-of-poetry-no-4-marianne-moore.

Hannerz, Ulf. *Writing Future Worlds: An Anthropologist Explores Global Scenarios*. New York: Springer, 2016.

Haraway, Donna Jeanne. *Modest_Witness@Second_Millennium.FemaleMan_Meets_OncoMouse: Feminism and Technoscience*. New York: Routledge, 1997.

———. *Primate Visions: Gender, Race, and Nature in the World of Modern Science*. New York: Routledge, 1989.

Harding, Sandra G. *The Science Question in Feminism*. Ithaca, NY: Cornell University Press, 1986.

———. *Sciences from Below: Feminisms, Postcolonialities, and Modernities*. Durham, NC: Duke University Press, 2008.

Harney, Stefano, and Fred Moten. *The Undercommons: Fugitive Planning & Black Study*. New York: Minor Compositions, 2013.

Harrington, Anne. *Medicine, Mind, and the Double Brain: A Study in Nineteenth-Century Thought*. Princeton, NJ: Princeton University Press, 1987.

Harris, Kaplan. "Editing after Pound." *Paideuma* 40 (2013): 107–25.

Harvey, A. McGehee. "Creators of Clinical Medicine's Scientific Base: Franklin Paine Mall, Lewellys Franklin Barker, and Rufus C. Cole." *Johns Hopkins Medical Journal* 136, no. 4 (April 1975): 168–77.

———. "A New School of Anatomy: The Story of Franklin P. Mall, Florence R. Sabin, and John B. MacCallum." *Johns Hopkins Medical Journal* 136, no. 2 (February 1975): 83–94.

Hayek, F. A. "The Use of Knowledge in Society." *American Economic Review* 35, no. 4 (September 1, 1945): 519–30.

Hayles, N. Katherine. *My Mother Was a Computer: Digital Subjects and Literary Texts*. Chicago: University of Chicago Press, 2005.

Hegeman, Susan. *Patterns for America: Modernism and the Concept of Culture*. Princeton, NJ: Princeton University Press, 1999.

Heim, Stefania. "Race and the Poetic Avant-Garde." *Boston Review*, March 10, 2015. http://bostonreview.net/blog/boston-review-race-and-poetic-avant-garde.

Hejinian, Lyn. "Barbarism." In *The Language of Inquiry*, 318–36. Berkeley: University of California Press, 2000.

———. "En Face." *Boston Review*, March 10, 2015. http://bostonreview.net/poetry/lyn-hejinian-forum-response-race-avant-garde.

———. "Some Notes toward a Poetics." In *American Women Poets in the 21st Century: Where Lyric Meets Language*, edited by Claudia Rankine and Juliana Spahr, 235–41. Middletown, CT: Wesleyan University Press, 2013.

———. "Two Stein Talks." In *The Language of Inquiry*, 83–130. Berkeley: University of California Press, 2000.

Heller, Michael, ed. *Carl Rakosi: Man and Poet*. Orono, ME: National Poetry Foundation, 1993.

Helmreich, Stefan. "Power/Networks: A Rejoinder to Lansing." *Critique of Anthropology* 20, no. 3 (September 1, 2000): 319–27. https://doi.org/10.1177/0308275X0002000306.

Hewes, Fletcher W., and Henry Gannett. *Scribner's Statistical Atlas of the United States, Showing by Graphic Methods Their Present Condition and Their Political, Social and Industrial Development*. New York: C. Scribner's Sons, 1883.

Hicks, Marie. *Programmed Inequality: How Britain Discarded Women Technologists and Lost Its Edge in Computing*. Cambridge, MA: MIT Press, 2017.

Hinton, Laura, and Cynthia Hogue, eds. *We Who Love to Be Astonished: Experimental Women's Writing and Performance Poetics*. Tuscaloosa: University of Alabama Press, 2002.

HM Government. "Revised Prevent Duty Guidance: For England and Wales," 2015. https://assets.publishing.service.gov.uk/government/uploads/system/uploads/attachment_data/file/445977/3799_Revised_Prevent_Duty_Guidance__England_Wales_V2-Interactive.pdf.

Hoffman, Frederick L. *Race Traits and Tendencies of the American Negro*. Vol. 11. Publications of the American Economic Association. New York: Macmillan, 1896.

Holsinger, Bruce W. *Neomedievalism, Neoconservatism, and the War on Terror*. Paradigm 29. Chicago: Prickly Paradigm, 2007.

Hong, Cathy Park. "Delusions of Whiteness in the Avant-Garde." *Lana Turner*, no. 7 (2014): 248–53.

Horn, Nina, and Zeynep Tümer. "Menkes Disease and the Occipital Horn Syndrome." In *Connective Tissue and Its Heritable Disorders: Molecular, Genetic, and Medical Aspects*, edited by Peter M. Royce and Beat Steinmann, 651–85. New York: John Wiley & Sons, 2003.

Hotelling, Kirstin. "'The I of Each Is to the I of Each, a Kind of Fretful Speech Which Sets a Limit on Itself': Marianne Moore's Strategic Selfhood." *Modernism/Modernity* 5, no. 1 (1998): 75–96. https://doi.org/10.1353/mod.1998.0019.

Hunter, Matthew C. *Wicked Intelligence: Visual Art and the Science of Experiment in Restoration London*. Chicago: University of Chicago Press, 2013.

Hunter, Walt. "Lyric and Its Discontents." *Minnesota Review* 79, no. 1 (2012): 78–90.

Hutchison, David. "Education Secretary Nicky Morgan: 'Arts Subjects Limit Career Choices.'" *Stage*, November 11, 2014. https://www.thestage.co.uk/news/2014/education-secretary-nicky-morgan-arts-subjects-limit-career-choices/.

Huyssen, Andreas. *After the Great Divide: Modernism, Mass Culture, Postmodernism*. Bloomington: Indiana University Press, 1986.

Hymes, Dell. "Anthropology and Poetry." *Dialectical Anthropology* 11, no. 2 (June 1, 1986): 407–10. https://doi.org/10.1007/BF00245765.

Jackson, Noel. *Science and Sensation in Romantic Poetry*. Cambridge Studies in Romanticism 73. Cambridge: Cambridge University Press, 2008.

Jackson, Virginia Walker. *Dickinson's Misery: A Theory of Lyric Reading*. Princeton, NJ: Princeton University Press, 2005.

James, Robin. *Resilience & Melancholy: Pop Music, Feminism, Neoliberalism*. Alresford, UK: Zero Books, 2015.

Jameson, Fredric. *The Antinomies of Realism*. London: Verso, 2013.

———. *Archaeologies of the Future: The Desire Called Utopia and Other Science Fictions*. London: Verso, 2005.

———. *The Political Unconscious: Narrative as a Socially Symbolic Act*. London: Routledge, 2002.

Jarrell, Randall. "The Death of the Ball Turret Gunner." *Partisan Review* 12, no. 1 (Winter 1945): 60. Howard Gotlieb Archival Research Center, Boston University.

———. "Her Shield." In *Marianne Moore: A Collection of Critical Essays*, edited by Charles Tomlinson, 114–24. Twentieth Century Views. Englewood Cliffs, NJ: Prentice-Hall, 1969.

———. "Poetry in Peace and War." *Partisan Review* 12, no. 1 (Winter 1945): 120–26. Howard Gotlieb Archival Research Center, Boston University.

Jasanoff, Sheila, ed. *States of Knowledge: The Co-production of Science and Social Order*. London: Routledge, 2004.

Jay, Martin. "Modernism and the Specter of Psychologism." *Modernism/Modernity* 3, no. 2 (1996): 93–111.

Johnson, Barbara. "Apostrophe, Animation, and Abortion." *Diacritics* 16, no. 1 (April 1, 1986): 29–47. https://doi.org/10.2307/464649.

Johnson, Benjamin. "The Poetics of the Fall in Marianne Moore's 'The Jerboa.'" *Arizona Quarterly: A Journal of American Literature, Culture, and Theory* 63, no. 3 (2007): 61–89.

Jones, Bernard Edward. *Cassell's Cyclopaedia of Photography*. New York: Cassell, 1912.

Jordanova, L. J. *Nature Displayed: Gender, Science, and Medicine, 1760–1820: Essays*. London: Longman, 1999.

———. *Sexual Visions: Images of Gender in Science and Medicine between the Eighteenth and Twentieth Centuries*. New York: Harvester Wheatsheaf, 1989.

Kahan, Benjamin. *Celibacies: American Modernism and Sexual Life*. Durham, NC: Duke University Press, 2013.

Kane, Daniel. *"Do You Have a Band?": Poetry and Punk Rock in New York City*. New York: Columbia University Press, 2017.

Kaplan, Caren. "Precision Targets: GPS and the Militarization of U.S. Consumer Identity." *American Quarterly* 58, no. 3 (2006): 693–714. https://doi.org/10.1353/aq.2006.0061.

Kasson, John F. *Rudeness & Civility: Manners in Nineteenth-Century Urban America*. New York: Hill and Wang, 1990.

Kass-Simon, G., Patricia Farnes, and Deborah Nash, eds. *Women of Science: Righting the Record*. Bloomington: Indiana University Press, 1990.

Keep, Christopher. "The Cultural Work of the Type-Writer Girl." *Victorian Studies* 40, no. 3 (April 1, 1997): 401–26.

Keller, Evelyn Fox. "Gender and Science." In *Discovering Reality: Feminist Perspectives on Epistemology, Metaphysics, Methodology, and Philosophy of Science*, edited by Sandra Harding and Merrill B. Hintikka, 187–205. Dordrecht: Springer, 2003.

———. *The Mirage of a Space between Nature and Nurture*. Durham, NC: Duke University Press, 2010.

———. *Reflections on Gender and Science*. New Haven, CT: Yale University Press, 1985.

———. *Secrets of Life, Secrets of Death: Essays on Language, Gender, and Science*. New York: Routledge, 1992.

Keller, Evelyn Fox, and Helen E. Longino, eds. *Feminism and Science*. Oxford: Oxford University Press, 1996.

Kennicott, Philip. "President Obama Disses Culture with 'Art History Degree' Punch Line." *Washington Post*, January 30, 2014. http://www.washingtonpost.com/blogs/style-blog/wp/2014/01/30/president-obama-disses-culture-with-art-history-degree-punch-line/.

Kenny, Alexandra K., Thomas Killion, and Nancy Scheper-Hughes. "'Ishi's Brain, Ishi's Ashes': The Complex Issues of Repatriation; A Response to N. Scheper-Hughes, 17(1)." *Anthropology Today* 18, no. 2 (2002): 25–27.

Kittler, Friedrich A. *Discourse Networks 1800/1900*. Stanford, CA: Stanford University Press, 1990.

Knower, Henry McElderry. Editor's preface to *An Atlas of the Medulla and Midbrain*, by Florence Rena Sabin, edited by Henry McElderry Knower, 5–6. Baltimore: Friedenwald, 1901.

Kohlstedt, Sally Gregory. "Parlors, Primers, and Public Schooling: Education for Science in Nineteenth-Century America." *Isis* 81, no. 3 (September 1, 1990): 424–45.

Kolodny, Annette. *In Search of First Contact: The Vikings of Vinland, the Peoples of the Dawnland, and the Anglo-American Anxiety of Discovery*. Durham, NC: Duke University Press, 2012.

Koutstaal, Wilma. "Skirting the Abyss: A History of Experimental Explorations of Automatic Writing in Psychology." *Journal of the History of the Behavioral Sciences* 28 (1992): 5–27.

Kracauer, Siegfried. "The Mass Ornament." In *The Mass Ornament: Weimar Essays*, translated by Thomas Y. Levin, 75–86. Cambridge, MA: Harvard University Press, 1995.

———. "Das Ornament Der Masse." In *Das Ornament Der Masse: Essays*, 50–63. Frankfurt am Main: Suhrkamp, 1977.

Krauss, Rosalind E. *The Originality of the Avant-Garde and Other Modernist Myths*. Cambridge, MA: MIT Press, 1985.

Kreiner, Timothy. "The Politics of Language Writing and the Subject of History." *Post45*, January 10, 2019. http://post45.research.yale.edu/2019/01/the-politics-of-language-writing-and-the-subject-of-history/.

Kroeber, A[lfred] L[ouis]. *Anthropology: Race, Language, Culture, Psychology, Prehistory*. New ed. New York: Harcourt, Brace, 1948.

Lansing, J. Stephen. *Priests and Programmers: Technologies of Power in the Engineered Landscape of Bali*. Princeton, NJ: Princeton University Press, 1991.

Latour, Bruno. *Science in Action: How to Follow Scientists and Engineers through Society*. Cambridge, MA: Harvard University Press, 1987.

———. *We Have Never Been Modern*. Translated by Catherine Porter. Cambridge, MA: Harvard University Press, 1993.

Latour, Bruno, and Steve Woolgar. *Laboratory Life: The Construction of Scientific Facts*. Princeton, NJ: Princeton University Press, 1986.

Laughlin, James, ed. *Spearhead: 10 Years' Experimental Writing in America*. New York: New Directions, 1947.

Leavell, Linda. "'Frightening Disinterestedness': The Personal Circumstances of Marianne Moore's 'Marriage.'" *Journal of Modern Literature* 31, no. 1 (2007): 64–79.

———. *Holding On Upside Down: The Life and Work of Marianne Moore*. 1st ed. New York: Farrar, Straus and Giroux, 2013.

———. "Marianne Moore, the James Family, and the Politics of Celibacy." *Twentieth Century Literature* 49, no. 2 (July 1, 2003): 219–45. https://doi.org/10.2307/3176002.

Le Dœuff, Michèle. *The Sex of Knowing*. Translated by Lorraine Code and Kathryn Hamer. New York: Routledge, 2003.

Le Guin, Ursula K. "Indian Uncles." In *The Wave in the Mind: Talks and Essays on the Writer, the Reader, and the Imagination*, 10–19. Boston: Shambhala, 2012.

———. *The Left Hand of Darkness*. New York: Ace Books, 1969.

Leong, Michael. "Oulipo, Foulipo, Noulipo: The Gendered Politics of Literary Constraints." In *The Oulipo*, edited by G. N. Forester and M. J. Nicholls, 100–130. Singapore: Verbivoracious Press, 2017.

Levenson, Michael. "Novelty, Modernity, Adjacency." *New Literary History* 42, no. 4 (2011): 663–80. https://doi.org/10.1353/nlh.2011.0046.

Levine, George Lewis. *Darwin Loves You: Natural Selection and the Re-enchantment of the World*. Princeton, NJ: Princeton University Press, 2006.

——. *Dying to Know: Scientific Epistemology and Narrative in Victorian England*. Chicago: University of Chicago Press, 2002.

——, ed. *One Culture: Essays in Science and Literature*. Madison: University of Wisconsin Press, 1987.

——, ed. *Realism and Representation: Essays on the Problem of Realism in Relation to Science, Literature and Culture*. Madison: University of Wisconsin Press, 1993.

Levine, Lawrence W. *Highbrow/Lowbrow: The Emergence of Cultural Hierarchy in America*. The William E. Massey, Sr. Lectures in the History of American Civilization 1986. Cambridge, MA: Harvard University Press, 1988.

Levy, Ellen. *Criminal Ingenuity: Moore, Cornell, Ashbery, and the Struggle between the Arts*. Oxford: Oxford University Press, 2011.

Lilly, John Cunningham. *Man and Dolphin*. London: Victor Gollancz, 1962.

Limón, José E. "The Return of the Mexican Ballad: Américo Paredes and His Anthropological Text as Persuasive Political Performances." In *Creativity/Anthropology*, edited by Smadar Lavie, Kirin Narayan, and Renato Rosaldo. Ithaca, NY: Cornell University Press, 1993.

Litvak, Joseph. *Strange Gourmets: Sophistication, Theory, and the Novel*. Durham, NC: Duke University Press, 1997.

Liu, Lydia. *The Freudian Robot: Digital Media and the Future of the Unconscious*. Chicago: University of Chicago Press, 2010.

Love, Heather. "Truth and Consequences: On Paranoid Reading and Reparative Reading." *Criticism* 52, no. 2 (2010): 235-41. https://doi.org/10.1353/crt.2010.0022.

Lowe, Lisa. *The Intimacies of Four Continents*. Durham, NC: Duke University Press, 2015.

Lucas, Frederic A. *The Story of Museum Groups*. Guide Leaflet Series 53. 4th ed. New York: American Museum of Natural History, 1926.

Lucier, Paul. "The Professional and the Scientist in Nineteenth-Century America." *Isis* 100, no. 4 (December 1, 2009): 699-732. https://doi.org/10.1086/652016.

Luxemburg, Rosa. *The Crisis in the German Social-Democracy: The "Junius" Pamphlet [with a Portrait]*. New York: Socialist Publication Society, 1919.

Lye, Colleen. *America's Asia: Racial Form and American Literature, 1893-1945*. Princeton Paperbacks. Princeton, NJ: Princeton University Press, 2005.

Lyotard, Jean François. *The Postmodern Condition: A Report on Knowledge*. Minneapolis: University of Minnesota Press, 1984.

Macbeth, Danielle. *Frege's Logic*. Cambridge, MA: Harvard University Press, 2005.

MacKenzie, Donald A. *Inventing Accuracy: An Historical Sociology of Nuclear Missile Guidance*. Inside Technology. Cambridge, MA: MIT Press, 1990.

Mackey, Nathaniel. *Discrepant Engagement: Dissonance, Cross-Culturality, and Experimental Writing*. 1993. Reprint, Tuscaloosa: University of Alabama Press, 2000.

——. "Expanding the Repertoire," in "Expanding the Repertoire: Continuity & Change in African-American Writing," ed. Renee Gladman and giovanni singleton, special issue, *Tripwire: A Journal of Poetics* 5 (Fall 2001): 7–10.

———. *Whatsaid Serif*. San Francisco: City Lights Books, 1998.

Mak, Cliff. "On Falling Fastidiously: Marianne Moore's Slapstick Animals." *ELH* 83, no. 3 (September 8, 2016): 873–98. https://doi.org/10.1353/elh.2016.0033.

Malinowski, Bronislaw. *Argonauts of the Western Pacific: An Account of Native Enterprise and Adventure in the Archipelagoes of Melanesian New Guinea*. London: Routledge and Kegan Paul, 1966.

Manganaro, Marc. *Culture, 1922: The Emergence of a Concept*. Princeton, NJ: Princeton University Press, 2002.

———, ed. *Modernist Anthropology: From Fieldwork to Text*. Princeton, NJ: Princeton University Press, 1990.

Marcus, George E., and Michael M. J. Fischer. *Anthropology as Cultural Critique: An Experimental Moment in the Human Sciences*. 2nd ed. Chicago: University of Chicago Press, 1999.

Mariani, Paul L. *William Carlos Williams: A New World Naked*. New York: McGraw-Hill, 1981.

"Marianne Moore." *Wikipedia*, July 13, 2016. https://en.wikipedia.org/w/index.php?title=Marianne_Moore&oldid=729682587.

Marshall, Alan. *American Experimental Poetry and Democratic Thought*. New York: Oxford University Press, 2009.

Martin, Dawn Lundy. *Life in a Box Is a Pretty Life*. New York: Nightboat Books, 2015.

Martin, Emily. "The Egg and the Sperm: How Science Has Constructed a Romance Based on Stereotypical Male-Female Roles." *Signs* 16, no. 3 (1991): 485–501.

Martin, Wayne M. *Theories of Judgment: Psychology, Logic, Phenomenology*. Cambridge: Cambridge University Press, 2006.

Massey, H. S. W. "Leslie John Comrie, 1893–1950." *Obituary Notices of Fellows of the Royal Society* 8, no. 21 (1952): 97–107.

Mavor, Carol. *Reading Boyishly: Roland Barthes, J. M. Barrie, Jacques Henri Lartigue, Marcel Proust, and D. W. Winnicott*. Durham, NC: Duke University Press, 2007.

Mayr, Ernst. *The Growth of Biological Thought: Diversity, Evolution, and Inheritance*. Cambridge, MA: Harvard University Press, 1982.

Mbembe, Achille. "Necropolitics." *Public Culture* 15, no. 1 (December 21, 2003): 11–40. https://doi.org/10.1215/08992363-15-1-11.

McAlmon, Robert. "Contact and Genius." *Contact*, 1st ser., no. 4 (September 1921): 16–17.

———. "Modern Artiques." *Contact*, 1st ser., no. 2 (December 1920): n.p. [9–10].

McCabe, Susan. "Survival of the Queerly Fit: Darwin, Marianne Moore, and Elizabeth Bishop." *Twentieth Century Literature* 55, no. 4 (December 1, 2009): 547–71.

McCaffery, Steve. "The Death of the Subject: The Implications of Counter-Communication in Recent Language-Centered Writing." *Open Letter* 3, no. 7 (Summer 1977): 61–77.

McCoy, Alfred. *A Question of Torture: CIA Interrogation, from the Cold War to the War on Terror*. New York: Henry Holt, 2007.

McGann, Jerome J. "Contemporary Poetry, Alternate Routes." *Critical Inquiry* 13, no. 3 (April 1, 1987): 624–47.

———. *Towards a Literature of Knowledge*. Chicago: University of Chicago Press, 1989.

McGeough, Kevin M. "Victorian Archaeologies, Anthropologies and Adventures in the Final Frontier: Modes of Nineteenth-Century Scientific Exploration and Display in *Star Trek*." *Science Fiction Film and Television* 9, no. 2 (July 7, 2016): 229–52.

Melley, Timothy. *Empire of Conspiracy: The Culture of Paranoia in Postwar America*. Ithaca, NY: Cornell University Press, 2000.

Metzler Sawin, Mark. "Making *Contact!* William Carlos Williams' American Literary Aesthetic." *Umjetnost Riječi (The Art of Words: A Croatian/English Journal of Literary, Theatre and Film Studies*) 58, nos. 3/4 (December 2014): 331–54.

Meyer, Steven. *Irresistible Dictation: Gertrude Stein and the Correlations of Writing and Science*. Stanford, CA: Stanford University Press, 2001.

Middleton, Peter. *Physics Envy: American Poetry and Science in the Cold War and After*. Chicago: University of Chicago Press, 2015.

Miller, Cristanne. *Cultures of Modernism: Marianne Moore, Mina Loy, & Else Lasker-Schüler; Gender and Literary Community in New York and Berlin*. Ann Arbor: University of Michigan Press, 2005.

———. *Marianne Moore: Questions of Authority*. Cambridge, MA: Harvard University Press, 1995.

Miller, D. A. "Foutre! Bougre! Ecriture!" *Yale Journal of Criticism* 14, no. 2 (2001): 503–11. https://doi.org/10.1353/yale.2001.0030.

———. *Jane Austen, or The Secret of Style*. Princeton, NJ: Princeton University Press, 2003.

———. *The Novel and the Police*. Reprint ed. Berkeley: University of California Press, 1992.

Mitchell, Robert. *Experimental Life: Vitalism in Romantic Science and Literature*. Baltimore: Johns Hopkins University Press, 2013.

Mitchell, W. J. T. *What Do Pictures Want? The Lives and Loves of Images*. Chicago: University of Chicago Press, 2005.

Mizruchi, Susan. "Cataloging the Creatures of the Deep: 'Billy Budd, Sailor' and the Rise of Sociology." *Boundary* 2 17, no. 1 (April 1, 1990): 272–304. https://doi.org/10.2307/303225.

Monroe, Harriet. "A Symposium on Marianne Moore." *Poetry: A Magazine of Verse* 19, no. 4 (January 1922): 208–16.

Monteiro, George, ed. *Stephen Crane: The Contemporary Reviews*. American Critical Archives 17. Cambridge: Cambridge University Press, 2009.

Montessori, Maria. *The Montessori Method: Scientific Pedagogy as Applied to Child Education in the Children's Houses with Additions and Revisions by the Author*. Translated by Anne E. George. 2nd ed. New York: F. A. Stokes, 1912.

Moore, Marianne. *Becoming Marianne Moore: The Early Poems, 1907–1924*. Edited by Robin G. Schulze. Berkeley: University of California Press, 2002.

———. *Collected Poems*. New York: Macmillan, 1951.

———. *The Complete Poems of Marianne Moore*. New York: Penguin, 1982.

———. *The Complete Prose of Marianne Moore*. New York: Viking, 1986.

———. "Critics and Connoisseurs." *Others* 3, no. 1 (July 1916): 4–5.

———. "In the Days of Prismatic Color." *Lantern* 27 (Spring 1919): 35.

———. "Those Various Scalpels." *Lantern* 25 (Spring 1917): 50–51.

Moore, Marianne, and Donald Hall. "The Art of Poetry: Marianne Moore: An Interview with Donald Hall." In *Marianne Moore: A Collection of Critical Essays*, edited by Charles Tomlinson, 20–45. Twentieth Century Views. Englewood Cliffs, NJ: Prentice-Hall, 1969.

Morgan, Lynn M. "The Embryography of Alice B. Toklas." *Comparative Studies in Society and History* 50, no. 1 (January 2008): 304–25.

———. *Icons of Life: A Cultural History of Human Embryos*. Berkeley: University of California Press, 2009. https://www.jstor.org/stable/10.1525/j.ctt1ppxx8.8.

Morris, Aldon D. *The Scholar Denied: W. E. B. Du Bois and the Birth of Modern Sociology*. Oakland: University of California Press, 2015.

Moten, Fred. *In the Break: The Aesthetics of the Black Radical Tradition*. Minneapolis: University of Minnesota Press, 2003.

Motte, Warren F., ed. *Oulipo: A Primer of Potential Literature*. Lincoln: University of Nebraska Press, 1986.

Mullen, Harryette Romell. "Poetry and Identity." In *Telling It Slant: Avant-Garde Poetics of the 1990s*, edited by Mark Wallace and Steven Marks, 27–31. Tuscaloosa: University of Alabama Press, 2001.

———. "Untitled," in "Expanding the Repertoire: Continuity & Change in African-American Writing," ed. Renee Gladman and giovanni singleton, special issue, *Tripwire: A Journal of Poetics* 5 (Fall 2001): 11–14.

Murai, Shusuke. "Subsidies Used as Carrot to Prod National Universities to Streamline, Ditch Humanities." *Japan Times Online*, June 25, 2015. http://www.japantimes.co.jp/news/2015/06/25/national/subsidies-used-carrot-prod-national-universities-streamline-ditch-humanities/.

Murphy, [Claudette] Michelle. *The Economization of Life*. Durham, NC: Duke University Press, 2017.

Nakamura, Lisa. *Cybertypes: Race, Ethnicity, and Identity on the Internet*. New York: Routledge, 2002.

"NASA: Yes! We Are Involved!" *Afro American*, April 15, 1972, 16th Annual Career Planning edition.

National Poetry Foundation. "NFP Alumni." *National Poetry Foundation: Modern & Contemporary Poetry and Poetics at the University of Maine*. https://nationalpoetry foundation.wordpress.com/

Nelson, Alondra. "Introduction: Future Texts." *Social Text* 20, no. 2 (June 3, 2002): 1–15.

Nelson, Maggie. *The Argonauts*. London: Melville House, 2016.

Ngai, Sianne. *Ugly Feelings*. Cambridge, MA: Harvard University Press, 2005.

Nguyen, Mimi Thi. *The Gift of Freedom: War, Debt, and Other Refugee Passages*. Next Wave: New Directions in Women's Studies. Durham, NC: Duke University Press, 2012.

Nicholls, Peter. "Beyond *The Cantos*: Ezra Pound and Recent American Poetry." In *The Cambridge Companion to Ezra Pound*, edited by Ira B. Nadel, 139–60. Cambridge: Cambridge University Press, 1999.

———. "Difference Spreading: From Gertrude Stein to L=A=N=G=U=A=G=E Poetry." In *Contemporary Poetry Meets Modern Theory*, edited by Anthony Easthope and John O. Thompson, 116–27. New York: Harvester Wheatsheaf, 1991.

Nichols, Mike, dir. *The Day of the Dolphin*. Avco Embassy Pictures, 1973.

Nimoy, Leonard, dir. *Star Trek IV: The Voyage Home*. DVD. Paramount Home Entertainment, 2009.

Nixon, Rob. *Slow Violence and the Environmentalism of the Poor*. Cambridge, MA: Harvard University Press, 2011.

North, Michael. *The Dialect of Modernism: Race, Language, and Twentieth Century Literature*. New York: Oxford University Press, 1994.

———. *Novelty: A History of the New*. Chicago: University of Chicago Press, 2013.

Notley, Alice. *Dr. Williams' Heiresses*. Tuumba 28. Berkeley: Tuumba, 1980.

Oldenziel, Ruth. *Making Technology Masculine: Men, Women and Modern Machines in America, 1870–1945*. Amsterdam: Amsterdam University Press, 1999.

Olson, Charles. "Projective Verse." In *The New American Poetry, 1945–1960*, edited by Donald Merriam Allen, 386–97. Berkeley: University of California Press, 1999.

Oreskes, Naomi. "Objectivity or Heroism? On the Invisibility of Women in Science." *Osiris*, 2nd ser., 11 (January 1, 1996): 87–113.

Oreskes, Naomi, and Erik M. Conway. *Merchants of Doubt: How a Handful of Scientists Obscured the Truth on Issues from Tobacco Smoke to Global Warming*. New York: Bloomsbury Press, 2010.

Osworth, Ali. "You Need Help: What's The Deal With Scissoring?" *Autostraddle*, July 1, 2014. http://www.autostraddle.com/you-need-help-whats-the-deal-with-scissoring -242968/.

Otis, Laura. *Membranes: Metaphors of Invasion in Nineteenth-Century Literature, Science and Politics*. Baltimore: Johns Hopkins University Press, 2000.

"The Outing (*Seinfeld*)." In *Wikipedia*, July 30, 2016. https://en.wikipedia.org/w/index.php?title=The_Outing_(Seinfeld)&oldid=732232764.

Palmié, Stephan. *Wizards and Scientists: Explorations in Afro-Cuban Modernity and Tradition*. Durham, NC: Duke University Press, 2002.

Pandora, Katherine. "Popular Science in National and Transnational Perspective: Suggestions from the American Context." *Isis* 100, no. 2 (June 1, 2009): 346–58. https://doi.org/10.1086/599548.

Pandora, Katherine, and Karen A. Rader. "Science in the Everyday World." *Isis* 99, no. 2 (June 1, 2008): 350–64. https://doi.org/10.1086/588693.

Park, Katharine. *Secrets of Women: Gender, Generation, and the Origins of Human Dissection*. New York: Zone, 2006.

Parker, Andrew. *The Theorist's Mother*. Durham, NC: Duke University Press, 2012.

Patterson, Orlando. *Slavery and Social Death: A Comparative Study*. Cambridge, MA: Harvard University Press, 1982.

Pattullo, E. L. "About the Department: History of the Harvard Psychology Department." Department of Psychology, 2007. https://web.archive.org/web/20080407113011/http://www.isites.harvard.edu/icb/icb.do?keyword=k3007&pageid=icb.page19708&pageContentId=icb.pagecontent44003&view=view.do&viewParam_name=morehistory.html.

Paul, Catherine E. *Poetry in the Museums of Modernism: Yeats, Pound, Moore, Stein*. Ann Arbor: University of Michigan Press, 2002.

Paz, Octavio. *Alternating Current*. New York: Viking Press, 1973.

Peacock, Thomas Love. "The Four Ages of Poetry." In *Peacock's Four Ages of Poetry; Shelley's Defence of Poetry; Browning's Essay on Shelley*, edited by H. F. B. Brett-Smith, 3–19. Boston: Houghton Mifflin, 1921.

Pearson, Karl. *The Grammar of Science*. 2nd ed., rev. and enl. London: A. and C. Black, 1900.

Perelman, Bob. *The Marginalization of Poetry: Language Writing and Literary History*. Princeton, NJ: Princeton University Press, 1996.

———. "My Avant-Garde Card." *New Literary History* 41, no. 4 (2010): 875–94.

Perloff, Marjorie. "'Barbed-Wire Entanglements': The 'New American Poetry,' 1930–1932." *Modernism/Modernity* 2, no. 1 (January 1, 1995): 145–75. https://doi.org/10.1353/mod.1995.0009.

———. "Language Poetry and the Lyric Subject: Ron Silliman's Albany, Susan Howe's Buffalo." *Critical Inquiry* 25, no. 3 (April 1, 1999): 405–34.

———. *The Poetics of Indeterminacy: Rimbaud to Cage*. Princeton, NJ: Princeton University Press, 1981.

———. "Pound/Stevens: Whose Era?" *New Literary History* 13, no. 3 (April 1, 1982): 485–514. https://doi.org/10.2307/468795.

Phillips, Siobhan. "The Students of Marianne Moore." *Poetry Foundation*, March 14,

2017. https://www.poetryfoundation.org/articles/92768/the-students-of-marianne-moore.

Pickering, Andrew. *Constructing Quarks: A Sociological History of Particle Physics*. Chicago: University of Chicago Press, 1984.

——, ed. *Science as Practice and Culture*. Chicago: University of Chicago Press, 1992.

Pieper, Lindsay Parks. *Sex Testing: Gender Policing in Women's Sports*. Urbana: University of Illinois Press, 2016.

Poe, Edgar Allan. "The Man of the Crowd." In *Poe: Poetry, Tales, and Selected Essays*, 388–97. New York: Library of America, 1996.

Poovey, Mary. "Figures of Arithmetic, Figures of Speech: The Discourse of Statistics in the 1830s." In *Questions of Evidence: Proof, Practice, and Persuasion across the Disciplines*, edited by James Chandler, Arnold Ira Davidson, and Harry D. Harootunian, 401–21. Chicago: University of Chicago Press, 1994.

——. *A History of the Modern Fact: Problems of Knowledge in the Sciences of Wealth and Society*. Chicago: University of Chicago Press, 1998.

Porter, Theodore M. "How Science Became Technical." *Isis* 100, no. 2 (June 1, 2009): 292–309. https://doi.org/10.1086/599552.

——. *The Rise of Statistical Thinking, 1820–1900*. Princeton, NJ: Princeton University Press, 1986.

——. "Speaking Precision to Power: The Modern Political Role of Social Science." *Social Research: An International Quarterly* 73, no. 4 (2006): 1273–94.

Porzak, Simon. "Inverts and Invertebrates: Darwin, Proust, and Nature's Queer Heterosexuality." *Diacritics* 41, no. 4 (2013): 6–34. https://www.jstor.org/stable/43304250.

Posner, Miriam. "The Software That Shapes Workers' Lives." *New Yorker*, March 12, 2019. https://www.newyorker.com/science/elements/the-software-that-shapes-workers-lives.

Pound, Ezra. *ABC of Reading*. New York: New Directions, 2010.

——. *The Cantos of Ezra Pound*. New York: New Directions, 1993.

——. "Commission." *Poetry: A Magazine of Verse* 2, no. 1 (April 1913): 10–11.

——. "A Few Don'ts by an Imagiste." *Poetry: A Magazine of Verse* 1, no. 6 (March 1913): 200–206.

——. "How to Read." In *Literary Essays*, edited by T. S. Eliot, 15–40. Norfolk, CT: New Directions, 1954.

——. "I Gather the Limbs of Osiris (I–II)." *New Age* 10, no. 6 (December 7, 1911): 130–31.

——. "Marianne Moore and Mina Loy." In *The Critical Response to Marianne Moore*, edited by Elizabeth Gregory, 22–23. Critical Responses in Arts and Letters, no. 39. Westport, CT: Praeger, 2003.

——. "Marianne Moore and Mina Loy." *Little Review* 4 (March 1918): 56–58.

Pratt, Mary Louise. "Fieldwork in Common Places." In Clifford and Marcus, *Writing Culture*, 27–50.

Price, David H. *Cold War Anthropology: The CIA, the Pentagon, and the Growth of Dual-Use Anthropology*. Durham, NC: Duke University Press, 2016.

Price, Leah, and Pamela Thurschwell, eds. *Literary Secretaries/Secretarial Culture*. Aldershot: Ashgate, 2005.

Puff, Helmut. "Nature on Trial: Acts 'against Nature' in the Law Courts of Early Modern Germany and Switzerland." In *The Moral Authority of Nature*, edited by Lorraine Daston and Fernando Vidal, 232–53. Chicago: University of Chicago Press, 2010.

Ra, Sun. *Untitled*. Mp3. University of California, Berkeley, 1971. UbuWeb. https://ubusound.memoryoftheworld.org/ra_sun/Ra-Sun_Berkeley-Lecture_1971.mp3.

Raine, Anne. "Science, Nature Work, and the Kinaesthetic Body in Cather and Stein." *American Literature* 80, no. 4 (December 1, 2008): 799–830.

Rakosi, Carl. *The Collected Prose of Carl Rakosi*. Orono, ME: National Poetry Foundation, 1983.

Ramazani, Jahan, Richard Ellmann, and Robert O'Clair, eds. *The Norton Anthology of Modern and Contemporary Poetry*. 3rd ed. New York: W. W. Norton, 2003.

Rappaport, Roy Abraham. *Pigs for the Ancestors: Ritual in the Ecology of a New Guinea People*. New Haven, CT: Yale University Press, 1967.

Rasula, Jed. "Make It New." *Modernism/Modernity* 17, no. 4 (2010): 713–33. https://doi.org/10.1353/mod.2010.0043.

———. *Syncopations: The Stress of Innovation in Contemporary American Poetry*. Tuscaloosa: University of Alabama Press, 2004.

Rayner, Jonathan. *The Naval War Film: Genre, History, National Cinema*. Manchester: Manchester University Press, 2007.

Reed, Anthony. *Freedom Time: The Poetics and Politics of Black Experimental Writing*. Baltimore: Johns Hopkins University Press, 2014.

Reed, Ishmael. *Mumbo Jumbo*. New York: Scribner, 1996.

Retallack, Joan. *The Poethical Wager*. Berkeley: University of California Press, 2003.

Reynolds, Joshua. *The Literary Works of Sir Joshua Reynolds: . . . to Which Is Prefixed, a Memoir of the Author; with Remarks on His Professional Character, Illustrative of His Principles and Practice*. New and improved ed. Bohn's Standard Library. London: H. G. Bohn, 1852.

Riddell, Peter. "The Commissioner for Public Appointments Report on the Recruitment Campaign for the Office for Students." Commissioner for Public Appointments, HM Government, 2018. https://publicappointmentscommissioner.independent.gov.uk/wp-content/uploads/2018/02/Commissioner-for-Public-Appointments-Investigation-OFS-Final-.pdf.

Riis, Jacob. "Flashes from the Slums: Pictures Taken in Dark Places by the Lightning Process." *Sun* (New York). February 12, 1888, 10.

———. *How the Other Half Lives: Authoritative Text, Contexts, Criticism*. Edited by Hasia R. Diner. A Norton Critical Edition. New York: W. W. Norton, 2010.

Rockafellar, Nancy, and Orin Starn. "Ishi's Brain." *Current Anthropology* 40, no. 4 (1999): 413–15. https://doi.org/10.1086/200038.

Ross, Kristin. *Fast Cars, Clean Bodies: Decolonization and the Reordering of French Culture*. Cambridge, MA: MIT Press, 1995.

Rossiter, Margaret W. *Women Scientists in America: Struggles and Strategies to 1940*. Baltimore: Johns Hopkins University Press, 1982.

Rubin, Gayle. "The Traffic in Women: Notes on the 'Political Economy' of Sex." In *Toward an Anthropology of Women*, edited by Rayna Reiter, 157–209. New York: Monthly Review Press, 1977.

Rubin, Martin. *Showstoppers: Busby Berkeley and the Tradition of Spectacle*. New York: Columbia University Press, 1993.

Rudolph, John L. "Epistemology for the Masses: The Origins of 'The Scientific Method' in American Schools." *History of Education Quarterly* 45, no. 3 (October 1, 2005): 341–76.

Sabin, Florence Rena. *An Atlas of the Medulla and Midbrain*. Edited by Henry McElderry Knower. Baltimore: Friedenwald, 1901.

Saint-Amour, Paul K. *Tense Future: Modernism, Total War, Encyclopedic Form*. New York: Oxford University Press, 2015.

Saunders, Frances Stonor. *The Cultural Cold War: The CIA and the World of Arts and Letters*. New York: New Press, 2000.

Scarry, Elaine. *The Body in Pain: The Making and Unmaking of the World*. New York: Oxford University Press, 1985.

Scheper-Hughes, Nancy. "Ishi's Brain, Ishi's Ashes: Anthropology and Genocide." *Anthropology Today* 17, no. 1 (2001): 12–18.

Schiebinger, Londa L., ed. *Feminism and the Body*. Oxford, UK: Oxford University Press, 2000.

———. *The Mind Has No Sex? Women in the Origins of Modern Science*. Cambridge, MA: Harvard University Press, 1989.

———. *Nature's Body: Gender in the Making of Modern Science*. New Brunswick, NJ: Rutgers University Press, 2004.

Schoenberg, Bruce S. "Gertrude Stein's Neuroanatomic Investigations: Roses or Thorns?" *Southern Medical Journal* 81, no. 2 (1988): 250–58.

Schor, Naomi. *Reading in Detail: Aesthetics and the Feminine*. New York: Routledge, 2007.

Schuller, Kyla. *The Biopolitics of Feeling: Race, Sex, and Science in the Nineteenth Century*. Durham, NC: Duke University Press, 2018.

Schulze, Robin G. *The Degenerate Muse: American Nature, Modernist Poetry, and the Problem of Cultural Hygiene*. Modernist Literature & Culture. New York: Oxford University Press, 2013.

———. "How Not to Edit: The Case of Marianne Moore." *Textual Cultures: Texts, Contexts, Interpretation* 2, no. 1 (Spring 2007): 119–35.

———. "Marianne Moore's 'Imperious Ox, Imperial Dish' and the Poetry of the Natural World." *Twentieth Century Literature* 44, no. 1 (Spring 1998): 1–33.

Schuster, John A., and Graeme Watchirs. "Natural Philosophy, Experiment and Discourse: Beyond the Kuhn/Bachelard Problematic." In *Experimental Inquiries: Historical, Philosophical, and Social Studies of Experimentation in Science*, edited by H. E. LeGrand, 1–48. Dordrecht: Kluwer Academic, 1990.

Schuster, Joshua. "William Carlos Williams, *Spring and All*, and the Anthropological Imaginary." *Journal of Modern Literature* 30, no. 3 (2007): 116–32.

Schwartz, Vanessa R. *Spectacular Realities: Early Mass Culture in Fin-de-Siècle Paris*. Berkeley: University of California Press, 1998.

Schweik, Susan M. *A Gulf So Deeply Cut: American Women Poets and the Second World War*. Madison: University of Wisconsin Press, 1991.

Sedgwick, Eve Kosofsky. *Between Men: English Literature and Male Homosocial Desire*. Gender and Culture. New York: Columbia University Press, 1985.

———. *Epistemology of the Closet*. Berkeley: University of California Press, 1990.

———. "Paranoid Reading and Reparative Reading, or, You're So Paranoid, You Probably Think This Essay Is about You." In *Touching Feeling: Affect, Pedagogy, Performativity*, 123–51. Durham, NC: Duke University Press, 2003.

Seitler, Dana. *Atavistic Tendencies: The Culture of Science in American Modernity*. Minneapolis: University of Minnesota Press, 2008.

Sekula, Allan. "The Body and the Archive." *October* 39 (December 1, 1986): 3–64. https://doi.org/10.2307/778312.

Seldes, Gilbert. *The Seven Lively Arts*. New York: A. S. Barnes, 1962.

Selisker, Scott. *Human Programming: Brainwashing, Automatons, and American Unfreedom*. Minneapolis: University of Minnesota Press, 2016.

Seltzer, Mark. *Bodies and Machines*. New York: Routledge, 1992.

———. *The Official World*. Durham, NC: Duke University Press, 2016.

Senior, W. A. "Cultural Anthropology and Rituals of Exchange in Ursula K. Le Guin's *Earthsea*." *Mosaic: A Journal for the Interdisciplinary Study of Literature* 29, no. 4 (December 1996): 101–13.

Serpell, Namwali. "The Zambian 'Afronaut' Who Wanted to Join the Space Race." *New Yorker*, March 11, 2017. https://www.newyorker.com/culture/culture-desk/the-zambian-afronaut-who-wanted-to-join-the-space-race.

Setina, Emily. "Marianne Moore's Postwar Fables and the Politics of Indirection." *PMLA* 131, no. 5 (October 2016): 1256–73.

———. "'Mountains Being a Language with Me': Marianne Moore, Marsden Hartley, and Modernist Revision." *Modernism/Modernity* 22, no. 1 (2015): 153–82.

Shakespeare, William. *Othello*. In *The Complete Pelican Shakespeare*, edited by Stephen Orgel and A. R. Braunmuller, 1392–444. 2nd rev. ed. New York: Penguin, 2002.

Shapin, Steven. "The House of Experiment in Seventeenth-Century England." *Isis* 79, no. 3 (1988): 373–404.

———. "The Invisible Technician." *American Scientist* 77, no. 6 (1989): 554–63.

———. *The Scientific Life: A Moral History of a Late Modern Vocation*. Chicago: University of Chicago Press, 2008.

———. *The Scientific Revolution*. Chicago: University of Chicago Press, 1996.

Shapin, Steven, and Simon Schaffer. *Leviathan and the Air-Pump: Hobbes, Boyle, and the Experimental Life*. Princeton, NJ: Princeton University Press, 2011.

Sharpe, Christina Elizabeth. *In the Wake: On Blackness and Being*. Durham, NC: Duke University Press, 2016.

Shelton, Marie-Denise. "Primitive Self: Colonial Impulses in Michel Leiris's 'L'Afrique Fantôme.'" In *Prehistories of the Future: The Primitivist Project and the Culture of Modernism*, edited by Elazar Barkan and Ronald Bush, 326–38. Stanford, CA: Stanford University Press, 1995.

Sherry, Vincent B. *Ezra Pound, Wyndham Lewis, and Radical Modernism*. New York: Oxford University Press, 1992.

Shilliam, Robbie. "Ethiopianism, Englishness, Britishness: Struggles over Imperial Belonging." *Citizenship Studies* 20, no. 2 (February 17, 2016): 243–59. https://doi.org/10.1080/13621025.2015.1132572.

———. "'Ethiopia Shall Stretch Forth Her Hands unto God': Garveyism, Rastafari, and Antiquity." In *African Athena: New Agendas*, edited by Daniel Orrells, Gurminder K. Bhambra, and Tessa Roynon, 106–21. Classical Presences. Oxford: Oxford University Press, 2011.

Shockley, Evie. *Renegade Poetics: Black Aesthetics and Formal Innovation in African American Poetry*. Contemporary North American Poetry Series. Iowa City: University of Iowa Press, 2011.

Shteir, Ann B., and Bernard V. Lightman, eds. *Figuring It Out: Science, Gender, and Visual Culture*. Hanover, NH: Dartmouth College Press, 2006.

Shuttleworth, Sally. *The Mind of the Child: Child Development in Literature, Science, and Medicine, 1840–1900*. Oxford: Oxford University Press, 2010.

Sidney, Philip. *The Defense of Poesy*. Edited by Albert S. Cook. Boston: Athenaeum, 1890.

Siemens, Hermann W. *Race Hygiene and Heredity*. Translated by Lewellys F. Barker. New York: D. Appleton, 1924. https://catalog.hathitrust.org/Record/001492348.

Silliman, Ron, ed. *In the American Tree: Language, Realism, Poetry*. 2nd ed. Orono, ME: National Poetry Foundation, 2002.

———. *Ketjak*. In *The Age of Huts (Compleat)*, 1–101. Berkeley: University of California Press, 2007.

———. *The New Sentence*. New York: Roof Books, 1987.

———. "Poetry and the Politics of the Subject." *Socialist Review* 18, no. 3 (1988): 59–68.

———. *Tjanting*. Modern Classics. Applecross, WA: Salt, 2002.

———. "Untitled." *Silliman's Blog*, September 20, 2003. https://ronsilliman.blogspot.com/2003/09/death-of-wayan-limbak-at-age-of-106.html.

Silver, Curtis. "September 24, 1960: 1st Nuclear Carrier, USS *Enterprise* Launched." *Wired*, September 24, 2010. http://www.wired.com/2010/09/0924nuclear-aircraft-carrier-enterprise-launched/.

Sluga, Hans D. "Frege as a Rationalist." In *Studies on Frege*, edited by Matthias Schirn. Stuttgart-Bad Cannstatt: Frommann-Holzboog, 1976.

———. *Gottlob Frege*. London: Routledge and Kegan Paul, 1980.

Small, A[lbion] W. "The Era of Sociology." *American Journal of Sociology* 1, no. 1 (July 1895): 1–15.

Snediker, Michael D. "*Pierre* and the Non-transparencies of Figuration." *ELH* 77, no. 1 (2010): 217–35.

Solomon, Samuel. "Offsetting Queer Literary Labor." *GLQ* 24, nos. 2/3 (2018): 239–66. https://doi.org/10.1215/10642684-4324801.

Solomons, Leon, and Gertrude Stein. "Normal Motor Automatism." *Psychological Review* 3, no. 5 (1896): 492–512.

Sorensen, Leif. *Ethnic Modernism and the Making of US Literary Multiculturalism*. New York: Palgrave Macmillan, 2016.

Spahr, Juliana. "How to Teach Writing." *Overland* 231 (Winter 2018). https://overland.org.au/previous-issues/issue-231/feature-juliana-spahr/.

———. *Everybody's Autonomy: Connective Reading and Collective Identity*. Tuscaloosa: University of Alabama Press, 2001.

Spahr, Juliana, and Stephanie Young. "Foulipo." *Drunken Boat* 8 (2006). http://www.drunkenboat.com/db8/.

Spivak, Gayatri Chakravorty. "Can the Subaltern Speak?" In *Can the Subaltern Speak? Reflections on the History of an Idea*, edited by Rosalind C. Morris, 21–78. New York: Columbia University Press, 2010. http://www.jstor.org/stable/10.7312/morr14384.

Stange, Maren. "Jacob Riis and Urban Visual Culture: The Lantern Slide Exhibition as Entertainment and Ideology." *Journal of Urban History* 15, no. 3 (May 1989): 274–303.

Starr, Frederick. "The Degeneracy of the American Negro." *Dial: A Semi-Monthly Journal of Literary Criticism, Discussion, and Information* 22, no. 253 (January 1, 1897): 17–18.

Stein, Gertrude. *The Autobiography of Alice B. Toklas*. New York: Random House, 1955.

———. "Cultivated Motor Automatism: A Study of Character in Its Relation to Attention." *Psychological Review* 5, no. 3 (May 1898): 295–306.

——. *Everybody's Autobiography*. New York: Random House, 1937.

——. *How Writing Is Written*. Edited by Robert Bartlett Haas. The Previously Uncollected Writings of Gertrude Stein, vol. 2. Los Angeles: Black Sparrow Press, 1974.

——. "To Lewellys Barker." Typescript, n.d. The Alan Mason Chesney Archives. The Johns Hopkins Medical Institutions, Baltimore.

——. *Writings, 1903–1932: Q.E.D., Three Lives, Portraits and Other Short Works, The Autobiography of Alice B. Toklas*. Edited by Catharine R. Stimpson and Harriet Scott Chessman. New York: Library of America, 1998.

——. *Writings, 1932–1946: Stanzas in Meditation, Lectures in America, The Geographical History of America, Ida, Brewsie and Willie, Other Works*. Edited by Catharine R. Stimpson and Harriet Scott Chessman. New York: Library of America, 1998.

Steinlight, Emily. *Populating the Novel: Literary Form and the Politics of Surplus Life*. Ithaca, NY: Cornell University Press, 2018.

Stephens, Paul. "What Do We Mean by 'Literary Experimentalism'? Notes toward a History of the Term." *Arizona Quarterly: A Journal of American Literature, Culture, and Theory* 68, no. 1 (2012): 143–73. https://doi.org/10.1353/arq.2012.0003.

Stevens, Wallace. *Opus Posthumous*. Edited by Milton J. Bates. Rev. ed. London: Faber, 1990.

——. "A Poet That Matters." In *The Critical Response to Marianne Moore*, edited by Elizabeth Gregory, 113–18. Westport, CT: Praeger, 2003.

Stimpson, Catharine R. "The Mind, the Body, and Gertrude Stein." *Critical Inquiry* 3, no. 3 (April 1, 1977): 489–506.

Stocking, George W. "The Ethnographic Sensibility of the 1920s and the Dualism of the Anthropological Tradition." In *The Ethnographer's Magic and Other Essays in the History of Anthropology*, 276–341. Madison: University of Wisconsin Press, 1992.

Stockton, Kathryn Bond. "Why the (Lesbian) Child Requires an Interval of Animal: The Family Dog as a Time Machine." In *The Queer Child, or Growing Sideways in the Twentieth Century*, 89–117. Durham, NC: Duke University Press, 2009.

Stratton, Julius A. "Harold Eugene Edgerton (April 6, 1903–January 4, 1990)." *Proceedings of the American Philosophical Society* 135, no. 3 (1991): 445–50.

Sundquist, Eric J. *To Wake the Nations: Race in the Making of American Literature*. Cambridge, MA: Belknap, 1993.

Sutherland, Keston. "A Response to Jasper Bernes, Joshua Clover and Juliana Spahr." *UK Poetry*, March 6, 2014.

Tanakh: A New Translation of the Holy Scriptures according to the Traditional Hebrew Text. 1st ed. Philadelphia: Jewish Publication Society, 1985.

Taussig, Michael T. *Defacement: Public Secrecy and the Labor of the Negative*. Stanford, CA: Stanford University Press, 1999.

——. *Mimesis and Alterity: A Particular History of the Senses*. New York: Routledge, 1993.

Terada, Rei. "After the Critique of Lyric." *PMLA* 123, no. 1 (January 2008): 195–200. https://doi.org/10.1632/pmla.2008.123.1.195.

Thurschwell, Pamela. *Literature, Technology, and Magical Thinking, 1880–1920*. Cambridge, UK and New York: Cambridge University Press, 2001.

———. "Supple Minds and Automatic Hands: Secretarial Agency in Early Twentieth-Century Literature." *Forum for Modern Language Studies* 37, no. 2 (April 1, 2001): 155–68. https://doi.org/10.1093/fmls/37.2.155.

Tiffany, Daniel. *Radio Corpse: Imagism and the Cryptaesthetic of Ezra Pound*. Cambridge, MA: Harvard University Press, 1995.

Torgovnick, Marianna. *Gone Primitive: Savage Intellects, Modern Lives*. Chicago: University of Chicago Press, 1990.

Trachtenberg, Alan. "Experiments in Another Country: Stephen Crane's City Sketches." In *American Realism: New Sketches*, edited by Eric J. Sundquist, 138–54. Baltimore: Johns Hopkins University Press, 1982.

Trotter, David. "Becoming Media: Modernist Writing, Hollywood Cinema, and the Scene of Female Toilette." Talk delivered at the University of Sussex Centre for Modernist Studies, April 16, 2015.

Turner, Fred. *From Counterculture to Cyberculture: Stewart Brand, the Whole Earth Network, and the Rise of Digital Utopianism*. Chicago: University of Chicago Press, 2006.

Underwood, Ted. "Why Literary Time Is Measured in Minutes." *ELH* 85, no. 2 (June 6, 2018): 341–65. https://doi.org/10.1353/elh.2018.0013.

Viegener, Matias. "Experimental Writing: Negation or Potentiality?" In *The Noulipian Analects*, edited by Christine Wertheim and Matias Viegener, 70–74. Los Angeles: Les Figues, 2007.

Vilkko, Risto. "The Reception of Frege's *Begriffsschrift*." *Historia Mathematica* 25 (1988): 412–22.

Villiers de L'Isle-Adam, Auguste. *L'Ève future*. Paris: Charpentier, 1909. https://archive.org/details/lvefutureoovilluoft.

Virilio, Paul. *War and Cinema: The Logistics of Perception*. London: Verso, 1989.

Walker, Alice. "Looking for Zora." In *In Search of Our Mothers' Gardens: Womanist Prose*, 93–116. New ed. London: Women's Press, 2000.

Wallis, Roy, ed. *On the Margins of Science: The Social Construction of Rejected Knowledge*. Keele, UK: University of Keele Press, 1979.

———. "Science and Pseudo-science." *Social Science Information* 24, no. 3 (September 1, 1985): 585–601. https://doi.org/10.1177/053901885024003009.

Walters, Suzanna Danuta. "From Here to Queer: Radical Feminism, Postmodernism, and the Lesbian Menace (or, Why Can't a Woman Be More Like a Fag?)." *Signs* 21, no. 4 (1996): 830–69.

———. "You Say Nature, I Say Nurture . . . Let's Call the Whole Thing Off." In *The Tolerance Trap: How God, Genes, and Good Intentions Are Sabotaging Gay Equality*,

115–42. New York: New York University Press, 2014. http://www.jstor.org/stable/j.ctt9qg0c3.9.

Wang, Dorothy. *Thinking Its Presence: Form, Race, and Subjectivity in Contemporary Asian American Poetry*. Stanford, CA: Stanford University Press, 2013.

Wang, Jackie. *Carceral Capitalism*. South Pasadena, CA: Semiotext(e), 2018.

Warner, Michael. *Publics and Counterpublics*. New York: Zone, 2005.

———. "Value, Agency, and Stephen Crane's 'The Monster.'" *Nineteenth-Century Fiction* 40, no. 1 (June 1, 1985): 76–93. https://doi.org/10.2307/3044837.

Watten, Barrett. *The Constructivist Moment: From Material Text to Cultural Poetics*. Middletown, CT: Wesleyan University Press, 2003.

———. "Presentism and Periodization in Language Writing, Conceptual Art, and Conceptual Writing." *Journal of Narrative Theory* 41, no. 1 (2011): 125–61.

———. "The Turn to Language and the 1960s." *Critical Inquiry* 29, no. 1 (September 1, 2002): 139–83. https://doi.org/10.1086/368001.

Watten, Barrett, Ted Pearson, Rae Armantrout, Steve Benson, Kit Robinson, Tom Mandel, Ron Silliman, Carla Harryman, Lyn Hejinian, and Bob Perelman. *The Grand Piano: An Experiment in Collective Autobiography: San Francisco, 1975–1980*. Vol. 2. 10 vols. Detroit: Mode A, 2007.

Weigel, Sigrid. "The Flash of Knowledge and the Temporality of Images: Walter Benjamin's Image-Based Epistemology and Its Preconditions in Visual Arts and Media History." Translated by Chadwick Truscott Smith and Christine Kutschbach. *Critical Inquiry* 41, no. 2 (January 1, 2015): 344–66. https://doi.org/10.1086/679079.

Weinstein, Cindy. "How Many Others Are There in the Other Half? Jacob Riis and the Tenement Population." *Nineteenth-Century Contexts* 24, no. 2 (2002): 195–216. https://doi.org/10.1080/08905490220000017869.

White, Eric. "In the American Grain: *Contact* (1920–3, 1932) and *Pagany: A Native Quarterly* (1930–3)." In *The Oxford Critical and Cultural History of Modernist Magazines*, edited by Peter Brooker and Andrew Thacker, vol. 2: *North America, 1894–1960*, 249–70. Oxford: Oxford University Press, 2012.

———. *Transatlantic Avant-Gardes: Little Magazines and Localist Modernism*. Edinburgh Studies in Transatlantic Literatures. Edinburgh: Edinburgh University Press, 2013.

White, Gillian C. *Lyric Shame: The "Lyric" Subject of Contemporary American Poetry*. Cambridge, MA: Harvard University Press, 2014.

———. "Poetics of Contingency." *Textual Practice* 32, no. 3 (March 16, 2018): 529–50. https://doi.org/10.1080/0950236X.2018.1442399.

Whitworth, Michael H. *Einstein's Wake: Relativity, Metaphor, and Modernist Literature*. Oxford: Oxford University Press, 2001.

Wilder, Craig Steven. *Ebony & Ivy: Race, Slavery, and the Troubled History of America's Universities*. New York: Bloomsbury Press, 2013.

Will, Barbara. *Gertrude Stein, Modernism, and the Problem of "Genius."* Edinburgh: Edinburgh University Press, 2000.

Williams, Oscar, ed. *The War Poets: An Anthology of the War Poetry of the Twentieth Century*. New York: John Day, 1945.

Williams, William Carlos. "Further Announcement." *Contact*, 1st ser., no. 1 (December 1920): 10.

———. *In the American Grain*. New York: New Directions, 2009.

———. "Issued." *Contact*, 1st ser., no. 1 (December 1920): 1.

———. "Marianne Moore." In *Imaginations*, 310–20. New York: New Directions, 1970.

———. "Note: The American Language and the New Poetry, So Called." TS. New Haven, CT, 1931. YCAL MSS 116 Box 30 Folder 891. Beinecke Library.

———. *Paterson*. Edited by Christopher J. MacGowan. New Directions Paperbook 806. Rev. ed. New York: New Directions, 1995.

———. "Spring and All." In *Imaginations*, 83–151. New York: New Directions, 1970.

———. *Spring and All*. New York: New Directions, 2011.

Willis, Elizabeth. "Lyric Dissent." *Boundary* 36, no. 3 (September 1, 2009): 229–34. https://doi.org/10.1215/01903659-2009-032.

Willis, Patricia C. "The Road to Paradise: First Notes on Marianne Moore's 'An Octopus.'" *Twentieth Century Literature* 30, nos. 2/3 (1984): 242–66. https://doi.org/10.2307/441116.

Willis, Patricia C., and Marianne Moore. *Marianne Moore: Vision into Verse*. Philadelphia: Rosenbach Museum & Library, 1987.

Wilson, Edmund. "The Theatre." *Dial* 74, no. 4 (April 1923): 420–22.

Wilson, Sarah. "Black Folk by the Numbers: Quantification in Du Bois." *American Literary History* 28, no. 1 (January 1, 2016): 27–45. https://doi.org/10.1093/alh/ajv062.

Winks, Robin W. *Cloak & Gown: Scholars in the Secret War, 1939–1961*. New York: Morrow, 1987.

Winters, Yvor. "Primitivism and Decadence: A Study of American Experimental Poetry." In *In Defense of Reason*, 16–150. London: Routledge & Kegan Paul, 1960.

Wise, M. Norton, ed. *The Values of Precision*. Princeton, NJ: Princeton University Press, 1995.

Wittgenstein, Ludwig. *Philosophical Investigations*. Translated by G. E. M. Anscombe. 3rd ed. Malden, MA: Blackwell, 1997.

Wolfe, Audra J. *Competing with the Soviets: Science, Technology, and the State in Cold War America*. Baltimore: Johns Hopkins University Press, 2013.

———. *Freedom's Laboratory: The Cold War Struggle for the Soul of Science*. Baltimore: Johns Hopkins University Press, 2018.

Wordsworth, William, and Samuel Taylor Coleridge. *Wordsworth and Coleridge: Lyrical Ballads*. Edited by R. L. Brett and Alun R. Jones. London: Routledge, 2005.

Worthington, Arthur M. *The Splash of a Drop*. London: Society for Promoting Christian Knowledge, 1895.

Wynter, Sylvia. "Unsettling the Coloniality of Being/Power/Truth/Freedom: Towards the Human, after Man, Its Overrepresentation—an Argument." *CR: The New Centennial Review* 3, no. 3 (2003): 257–337. https://doi.org/10.1353/ncr.2004.0015.

Yeo, Richard R. "Scientific Method and the Rhetoric of Science in Britain, 1830–1917." In *The Politics and Rhetoric of Scientific Method: Historical Studies*, edited by John Andrew Schuster and Richard R. Yeo, 259–97. Dordrecht: Reidel-Kluwer, 1986.

Yu, Timothy. *Race and the Avant-Garde: Experimental and Asian American Poetry since 1965*. Stanford, CA: Stanford University Press, 2009.

Zambreno, Kate. "What Is Experimental Literature? Five Questions: Kate Zambreno. Interview by Christopher Higgs." March 14, 2011. http://htmlgiant.com/random/what-is-experimental-literature-five-questions-kate-zambreno/.

Zola, Emile. *Nana*. Edited by Colette Becker. Paris: Garnier, 1994.

———. *Le roman expérimental*. Paris: Flammarion, 2006.

Index